EVANGELICAL INFLUENCES

Profiles of Figures and Movements
Rooted in the Reformation

J. I. PACKER

Evangelical Influences: Profiles of Key Figures and Movements Rooted in the Reformation

Hendrickson Publishers Marketing, LLC
P.O. Box 3473
Peabody, Massachusetts 01961-3473

ISBN 978-1-61970-156-4

First published in 1999 by Paternoster Press as *Honouring the People of God*.

Paternoster Press is an imprint of Authentic Media, 52 Presley Way, Crownhill, Milton Keynes, MK8 0ES, UK. www.authenticmedia.com

Scripture quotations marked NIV are taken from the Holy Bible, New International Version®, NIV®. Copyright © 1973, 1978, 1984, 2011 by Biblica, Inc.™ Used by permission of Zondervan. All rights reserved worldwide. www.zondervan.com The "NIV" and "New International Version" are trademarks registered in the United States Patent and Trademark Office by Biblica, Inc.™

Scripture quotations marked RSV are taken from the Revised Standard Version of the Bible, copyright © 1946, 1952, 1971 by the Division of Christian Education of the National Council of the Churches of Christ in the USA. Used by permission. All rights reserved.

Scripture quotations maked RV are taken from the Revised Version of 1885. Also known as the English Revised Version.

Please note that any italics in biblical quotations are the author's.

Printed in the United States of America

First Printing — April 2014

Library of Congress Cataloging-in-Publication Data

A catalog record for this book is available from the Library of Congress

Hendrickson Publishers Marketing, LLC ISBN 978-1-61970-156-4

EVANGELICAL INFLUENCES

Titles by
J. I. Packer
published by Hendrickson Publishers

Engaging the Written Word of God

Revelations of the Cross

Seeing God in the Dark

Evangelical Influences

Contents

Foreword   vii

Biographies

1. Martin Luther   3
2. John Calvin and Reformed Europe   13
3. Richard Baxter: A Man for All Ministries   23
4. The Spirit with the Word: The Reformational Revivalism
   of George Whitefield   39
5. D. Martyn Lloyd-Jones: A Kind of Puritan   57
6. David Martyn Lloyd-Jones   73
7. Francis Schaeffer: No Little Person   83

Christian History and Theology

8. Luther against Erasmus   93
9. 'Sola Scriptura' in History and Today   109
10. Calvin the Theologian   125
11. John Calvin and the Inerrancy of Holy Scripture   145
12. Predestination in Christian History   173
13. Justification in Protestant Theology   187
14. Thomas Cranmer's Catholic Theology   201
15. Richard Baxter on Heaven, Hope, and Holiness   225
16. Arminianisms   237
17. British Theology in the First Half of the Twentieth Century   259
18. The Theological Challenge to Evangelicalism Today   275
Notes   285

Foreword

When Martin Luther wrote the Preface to the first collected edition of his many and various writings, he went to town explaining in detail that theology, which should always be based on the Scriptures, should be done according to the pattern modelled in Psalm 119. There, Luther declared, we see that three forms of activity and experience make the theologian. The first is prayer for light and understanding. The second is reflective thought (*meditatio*), meaning sustained study of the substance, thrust, and flow of the biblical text. The third is standing firm under pressure of various kinds (external opposition, inward conflict, and whatever else Satan can muster): pressures, that is, to abandon, suppress, recant, or otherwise decide not to live by, the truth God has shown from his Word. Luther expounded his point as one who knew what he was talking about, and his affirmation that sustained prayer, thought, and fidelity to truth, whatever the cost, become the path along which theological wisdom is found is surely one of the profoundest utterances that the Christian world has yet heard.

In introducing this mass of fugitive pieces I would only say that behind each of them lies a conscious attempt over more than forty years to hew to Luther's line, in hope that by adhering to his theological wisdom I might arrive at substantive wisdom in and through the grace of our Lord Jesus Christ. How far I have attained my goal is something that readers must judge for themselves. In retrospect, writing this material does not seem to have been time wasted, and it is my prayer that no one who explores it will feel that their time has been wasted either.

I thank Jim Lyster, Isobel Stevenson, Tony Graham, and the rest of the staff at Paternoster for all their hard work in putting this collection together.

BIOGRAPHIES

CHAPTER 1

Martin Luther

I

Luther was the Father of the Reformation in the same sense in which George Stephenson was the Father of Railways—that is, he pioneered the whole subsequent development. Without Luther, nationalist revolts against the papacy and Empire would still have taken place; absolutism and capitalism would still have reshaped community life; the principle that the civil power determines the form of religion in its own territory (*cuius regio, eius religio,* the basic principle of the Religious Peace of Augsburg, 1555) would still have been established in Western Europe; the Renaissance would still have run its course, secularizing culture and challenging all forms of authoritarianism; but the gospel would not have been recovered, nor would Christian faith and life have been renewed, nor would there have been any evangelical leaven to work in the upsurging life of the new European national states. There would have been no Bucer, Tyndale, Cranmer, or Calvin, for all these were disciples of Luther. Apart from Luther, the historical Reformation is as unintelligible as *Hamlet* would be without the Prince.

Luther put forward the idea that whenever God means to move decisively in his church, he raises up a wonder-man (*Wundermann*), a hero (*vir heroicus*), a great individual leader, to be his instrument. Certainly this principle was exemplified in Luther himself. By 1521, he had caught the imagination of all Europe. He was idolized as a crusader of superhuman stature, the champion of Germany, of freedom, and of truth. A Holbein cartoon of 1522 pictures him as 'the German Hercules.' In the same year, Spalatin compared him with Elijah, and the description stuck: a Saxon medallion calls him 'Elijah of the last time' (*Elias ultimi saeculi*), and Melanchthon broke the news of his passing to the Wittenberg students by adapting 2 Kings 2:12, 'Alas, gone is the horseman and the chariots of Israel.' What manner of man was this, we ask, to have called forth such estimates of himself?

The first thing to say is that he was a remarkable man by nature. Though a commoner (his father ran a copper mine), with a racy, homely style of speech and what we now call the common touch, he was no boorish countryman, as is sometimes supposed. He was in fact a gifted don, a brilliant scholar, a tremendous worker, and a magnetic teacher. In 1505, having crammed a six-year course into four years, he headed the list in the M.A. examination at Erfurt. In 1512, at the age of twenty-nine he became a Doctor of Theology and Professor of Biblical Studies at Wittenberg. He was a star lecturer from his first term to his death.

A man of great personal force—his eyes, they said, looked right through you—and also of great charm and vivacity, he would have won affection and made his mark as a leader in any context. Also, he was a man temperamentally made for battle, at his strongest in debate and polemics, as his reforming career showed.

Once he had grasped the truth of sovereign grace that was locked up in the biblical phrase 'the righteousness of God'—an event probably belonging to 1513, when he was thirty and preparing his first lectures on the Psalms—he became an evangelical volcano. In the University, he challenged 'Aristotle' (semi-Pelagian legalistic scholasticism) in the name of 'Augustine' (biblically controlled reasoning about sin, grace, and faith in Christ). On a wider stage, he challenged the theory of indulgences in 1517, with his Ninety-five Theses, and in 1519, at the Leipzig Disputation with John Eck, he allowed his opponent to bring out the fact that he was really challenging the whole basis of papal jurisdiction.

In 1520, he defied the Pope by publicly burning the Bull which excommunicated him, and adding the Canon Law to the bonfire; a gesture which he followed up by becoming a pamphleteer and issuing his three great Reformation manifestos—*The Babylonish Captivity of the Church*, *To the Christian Nobility of the German Nation*, and *The Liberty of a Christian Man*. In 1521, having stood firm before the Holy Roman Emperor at Worms, he was put under the Imperial ban. But Frederick the Wise and, later, other princes kept him safe, and he continued till his death in 1546 teaching at Wittenberg and writing for the furtherance of reformation in the German kingdoms. It has been estimated that for many years he produced on an average a tract a fortnight. His complete works fill ninety-four volumes of about 750 pages each in the standard Weimar edition. He wrote almost twice as much as Calvin!

Naturally, so titanic a figure has been variously estimated. Four centuries of Germans have seen him primarily as a patriot. Thomas Carlyle saw him as the archetypal 'free man,' defying tradition and convention to follow his inner vision—a proto-liberal, in fact! But Luther saw himself simply as a theologian and a pastor, a preacher and teacher of the Word of God. He never thought of himself even as a reformer; the Reformation, he insisted, was not his work, but the work of God through his Word in the first instance and then, under God, of the German princes obeying God's Word. His own part had merely been to let the Word loose.

Thus, his approach to reformation appears as wholly theological and theocentric. Reformation in its essence was to him not a human achievement, any more than salvation was, but God's own work of restoring his church from a state of ruin to one of life and health through the power of his Word.

The phrase 'the Word of God,' or 'the Word' simply, is a key-phrase in Luther's thought. It meant to him, not just the Scriptures formally regarded as inspired (though of course he assumed their inspiration, as all churchmen did in his day), but something wider—namely, the message and content of the Scriptures, that is, the gospel concerning the Lord Jesus Christ, which is the sum and substance of what God has to say to man. Often, indeed, Luther applies the phrase 'the Word of God' to Christ himself, and when he uses it of biblical teaching, the thought of the living Lord whom the written Word sets forth is never far from his mind. Only by exploring Luther's understanding of 'the Word of God' can we fully grasp his approach to reformation; to this task, therefore, we now turn.

II

The theology which Luther reached through study, prayer, and inner conflict between 1512 and 1517, and which from then on he taught virtually without change, had three overall characteristics. It was *exegetical,* being propounded by the method of letting individual texts talk; it was *evangelical,* being a sustained assertion of the gospel of God's grace to sinners; and it was *polemical,* firing in turn at Roman superstition, radical Protestant 'enthusiasm,' and the folly and futility of the ways of this proud and sinful world. It represented essentially a rediscovery of the living God, Father, Son, and Holy Spirit.

The title of P. S. Watson's introduction to Luther's thought, *Let God Be God!* well focuses its ruling motivation. Luther asserts God's active sovereignty in providence and grace with tremendous vigour. All created things, he says, are God's 'masks' (*larvae Dei*)—that is, behind all that happens with such seeming haphazardness in this world of sight and sense is the hidden face, the guiding hand, the ruling mind, of its Maker. And in *The Bondage of the Will,* Luther's broadside against Erasmus, he speaks of the truth of man's absolute enslavement by nature to sin and Satan, and his consequent absolute dependence on sovereign divine grace for salvation, as the 'hinge' on which the whole theological conflict of the Reformation really turned.

Luther's constant aim was to inculcate the biblical knowledge of God, and to this end he constantly rang the changes on the following five staple themes:

1. The Authority of the Biblical Word of God

Luther affirmed this against the practice of appealing to unwritten traditions, papal pronouncements, canon law, and the trivial sophistries of allegorical exegesis—all of which appeals, so he maintained, have the effect of gagging the Scriptures, so that their true voice cannot be heard. His account of the Scriptures was essentially as follows.

The Bible is a clear, straightforward book, for 'the Holy Ghost is the plainest writer and speaker in heaven and earth.' It should therefore be understood in its 'literal, ordinary, natural sense,' letting one text and phrase throw light on another. (It was by this means, as it seems, that Luther's evangelical enlightenment took place: the words 'deliver me in thy righteousness' in Psalms 31:1 and 71:2 suggested to him that 'the righteousness of God' in Romans 1:17 also signified an outgoing, not of vindicatory justice, but of saving mercy.) Thus 'literally' understood, Scripture proved to contain a double communication from God: a disclosure of *law*, to induce self-knowledge and self-despair, and a proclamation of *promises*, and of Christ as the sum and substance of these promises, to be the object of faith and hope.

From this standpoint the Scriptures, and those of the New Testament in particular, appear as 'the swaddling-clothes in which Christ is wrapped.' Romans is the key to the Bible,

> the true masterpiece of the New Testament, the purest gospel of all . . . We find in this epistle in the most abundant fashion that which a Christian ought to know, viz. what are Law, Gospel, Sin, Punishment, Grace, Faith, Righteousness, Christ, God, Good Works Love, Hope, the Cross . . . It seems as if Paul wanted briefly to summarize in this epistle the whole of Christian evangelical teaching, and to provide an introduction to the whole Old Testament.

This evangelical teaching is the true rule of Christian faith: we must ask that the Holy Spirit will enable us to grasp it by showing us its application to ourselves, and that we may be enabled to cleave to it amid the distractions and errors whereby Satan seeks to wean us from it.

2. *The Greatness of Sin*

Luther affirmed this against current scholastic teaching about natural ability and the perfection (i.e., sinlessness) of a Christian's good deeds. It was on this teaching that the contemporary doctrine of merit, a blatant assertion of salvation by works and effort, was based. Luther in effect addressed its expositors in the accents of Anselm—'you have not yet considered the weightiness of sin (*quanti ponderis sit peccatum*).' Claiming Augustine as his forerunner, Luther stressed the total inability of the natural man, and the guilt of the Christian, even at his best, because all his service of God is stained by sin. Like Augustine, Luther made much of Romans 7:14–25, as proving the latter point. Romans, the key book of the Bible, as we saw, was written, so Luther strikingly tells us, to pull down, and pluck up, and destroy, all 'the wisdom and righteousness of the flesh, however great it may be . . . and to implant, establish, and magnify sin'; for it is not till this job is done, and self-righteousness finally abolished, that we can grasp the dimensions of the divine mercy. We cannot know the greatness of grace, says Luther, till we have learned the greatness of sin.

3. The Graciousness of Christ

Against the background of the popular picture of Jesus as a stern and dreadful judge, whom sinful men dare not approach directly at all, Luther stressed the point that the incarnation, lowly manhood, and patient suffering of the Son of God all prove that his attitude towards us is really one of overflowing love. The thought of Jesus' voluntary identification of himself with us in our helplessness and misery and, on the cross, in our deepest spiritual darkness and distress (*anfechtung*), and of his continuing sympathy with others who are tempted, was basic to Luther's teaching on the life of faith. Also, Luther challenged all forms of the doctrine of salvation by works, whether by personal merit or by the purchase of indulgences or by the offering of the mass as a propitiatory sacrifice, by appeal to the sufficiency of Christ's atoning death as a ground of full salvation for 'everyone that believeth.'

Luther was the first theologian to give prominence to the thought that the satisfaction to God for sin which, as Anselm had established, Christ rendered on our behalf on the cross, was penal and substitutionary in its nature. Anselm had thought of satisfaction as an alternative to the inflicting of the due penalty, a compensatory act of homage which 'made up' for the damage God had suffered through our sins.

'Damages,' indeed, is the precise modern equivalent for Anselm's conception of the atonement. But Luther saw that in Scripture satisfaction to God means satisfaction of the penal claims of divine law—that is, punishment vicariously borne. The following extract from the sixteenth-century translation of Luther's comment on Galatians 3:13 shows how vividly he set forth this thought:

> The doctrine of the gospel ... speaketh nothing of our works, or of the works of the law, but of the inestimable mercy and love of God towards most wretched and miserable sinners; to wit, that our most merciful Father ... sent his only Son into the world, and laid upon him all the sins of all men, saying, Be thou Peter, that denier; Paul, that persecutor, blasphemer, and cruel oppressor; that sinner which did eat the apple in Paradise; that thief which hanged upon the cross and briefly, be thou the person which hath committed the sins of all men; see therefore that thou pay and satisfy for them. Now cometh the law, and saith: I find him a sinner, one that hath taken upon him the sins of all men, and I see no sins but in him: therefore let him die upon the cross; and so it setteth upon him, and killeth him. By this means the whole world is purged ... God would see nothing else in the whole world, if it did believe, but a mere cleansing and righteousness.

This led Luther to display atonement and justification as the two complementary stages of St. Paul's 'great exchange' as set forth in 2 Corinthians 5:21:

> Learn to know Christ and him crucified; learn to sing unto him, and say, Lord Jesus, thou art my righteousness, I am thy sin. Thou hast taken upon thee what was mine, and hast set upon me what was thine. Thou hast become what thou wast not, that I might become what I was not.

Luther's answer, therefore, to ideas of salvation by works and priestly mediation was to set forth the promise of full acceptance—the imputing of righteousness and the non-imputing of sin, together with the bestowal of sonship to God and liberty from the law—for all who rest their faith directly upon Jesus Christ and his atoning blood.

This was the 'theology of the cross,' the saving knowledge of God received through the gospel, which Luther opposed to the futile 'theology of glory,' the conventional attempts of scholastic theologians to know God by abstract speculative logic. To know God, said Luther, is to know the grace of Christ, and this knowledge comes only through humbly contemplating Calvary.

4. The Vitality of Faith

Luther challenged the current assumption that faith is essentially credence (*fides*), and as such a meritorious work, by insisting that faith is essentially trust (*fiducia*), and that, so far from being meritorious, it is trust in Christ on the basis of a clear recognition that one has no merit at all, but that all merit, first to last, is found in him alone. Faith is thus an empty hand stretched out to receive Christ, grasping him and holding him fast. 'Faith taketh hold of Christ, and hath him present, and holdeth him enclosed, as the ring doth the precious stone.' Faith is God's gift, given as part of his gracious work of 'calling' (effectual calling, as later generations would say). Faith, thus supernaturally given, is a vital principle, resilient and active, triumphant in conflict and endlessly energetic:

> When faith is of the kind that God awakens and creates in the heart then a man trusts in Christ. He is then so securely founded on Christ that he can hurl defiance at sin, death, hell, the devil, and all God's enemies. He fears no ill, however hard and cruel it may prove to be . . .

> Right faith is a thing wrought by the Holy Ghost in us, which changeth us, turneth us into a new nature . . . Faith is a lively thing, mighty in working, valiant and strong; so that it is impossible that he who is endued therewith should not work always good works without ceasing . . . for such is his nature.

5. The Spiritual Nature of the Church

Luther repudiated the conventional equation of the Church with the Roman system. Indeed, before his excommunication in 1520, he had accepted the idea, which had appeared before among medieval radicals, that the papacy was Antichrist, and he constantly insisted that according to the New Testament the church was not to be thought of in the first instance as a system or organization at all. Luther held that the church is essentially, as the creed says, a communion, that is, a fellowship of saints (*communio sanctorum*), 'the lambs who hear the shepherd's voice,' as he put it in the Schmalkald Articles.

Though the church has a visible aspect, namely a corporate life of worship and service, it is essentially invisible, for the relationship of faith in Christ is not the sort of fact that we can see. Only the Lord knows them that are his. One can belong to a congregation (*Gemeinde*) and yet be outside the church as God knows it; equally, one can be expelled from organized congregations (as Luther was when the Pope excommunicated him) and still belong to the church. The visible life by which the presence of the church is recognized has two leading features: the ministry of the Word and sacraments, and the exercise of the priesthood of all believers, which to Luther meant mutual service at all levels on the basis of recognized mutual responsibility.

It is sometimes thought that Luther made nothing of discipline as a mark of the church but this is not so. In two works, published in 1539 and 1540 respectively, he included discipline among the seven marks of the church visible: preaching; baptism; the Lord's Supper; 'the keys of Christian discipline and forgiveness'; an ordained ministry; public worship; and 'suffering, the possession of the holy Cross.'

We have now surveyed the five themes which made up the central content of 'the Word' as Luther understood it. It was in this field that all Luther's main concerns lay. It was here, rather than in his somewhat unreflective and stubborn speculations about, for instance, baptismal regeneration through infant faith (against the Anabaptists), or the physical reception of Christ in non-transubstantiated bread and wine at the Lord's Supper (against Rome and Zwingli), that he made his abiding contribution to theology. Here, then, we have 'the Word' which under God, so Luther held, must reform the church.

III

Luther's connection with the ecclesiastical reorganization of Germany was purely an advisory one: he was regularly the person whom the princes consulted first when reordering religion in their kingdoms. Luther's own bent was pastoral and academic rather than administrative, and in any case his advice was not always taken, so that it is no wonder that the Lutheran reformation, by contrast with, say, Calvin's work at Geneva, appears as a series of rather ramshackle improvisations.

Luther's advice was concerned with, on the one hand, removing hindrances to congregations becoming true fellowships of saints (such hindrances as priestcraft, superstition, the mass, and an anti-evangelical hierarchy), and, on the other hand, instituting the appropriate means to godliness and spiritual growth (such things as regular preaching and teaching, scriptural administration of the sacraments, and evangelical forms of worship, together with the provision of sound pastors).

It is clear that it never occurred to him to question the centuries-old pattern of local churches in each kingdom forming an administrative unit (the *Landeskirche*), nor the propriety of appealing to the princes to take the work of reform into their own hands when Rome declined to do it from the centre. (This was the burden of Luther's *To the Christian Nobility of the German Nation*: he based his appeal first on the princes' position as supreme magistrates and second on the principle of the priesthood of all believers, which obliges rulers to serve the interests of their fellow-Christians in every way they can.)

There was, however, one question of principle to which Luther gave careful thought: that is, the propriety of retaining ceremonies and forms (vestments, images, etc.) which Scripture did not prescribe, but which had become traditional in use during the previous centuries. In his anti-iconoclastic sermons in Wittenberg in 1522, and often afterwards, Luther argued that the church was at liberty to retain these 'things indifferent' (*adiaphora*), and should be chary of abolishing them, lest weak consciences be injured. His thesis here was that the New Testament, unlike the Old Testament, does not dictate a church order, but leaves churches free to determine the outward circumstances of their worship and corporate life in whatever way seems most convenient and edifying. Unlike the Anglican reformers, however, who proceeded on the same principle, Luther held no brief for an imposed uniformity of liturgy or ceremonies. 'I am, I confess,' he wrote in 1545,

> disinclined to all ceremonies, even necessary ones, and I am the enemy of those which are not necessary ... Ceremonies so easily grow into laws, and laws, once established, speedily become snares of the conscience. Ultimately pure doctrine is obscured and overthrown, and people strive more for ceremonies than for mortification of the flesh ...

Some of the reforming princes imposed more uniformity in their kingdoms than Luther could approve of.

The German church reforms began after the Diet of Speyer in 1526, at which the princes resolved that until a general council or national assembly was called to deal with religious abuses each of them would 'so live, govern, and behave, as he hopes and trusts to answer for it to God and the emperor.' This was understood to mean that each prince who desired reformation in his territory was free to get on with the job. Saxony led the way, followed by Brandenburg, Hesse, and other lesser kingdoms. The effect of these reforms was to produce a series of state churches managed by the princes, in the ordering of which neither the clergy nor the laity had any effective voice.

Luther recoiled from the idea of congregational autonomy, which had at first attracted him, after the Peasants' Revolt of 1525, and when Philip of Hesse later proposed to give the people of Hesse some rights in ordering their churches, Luther advised against it. In the light of this, Luther's sharp distinction between the spheres of civil and ecclesiastical authority, and his insistence that, just as church rulers must not, like the popes, grasp after civil power (the power of the Word), so civil governors must not intrude into the exercise of church power (the power of the sword), comes to look somewhat hollow.

The procedure in Saxony, worked out over a period of fifteen years, may be summarized as follows. (1) 'Visitors'—several sets of them, in the event—reported on conditions to the Elector. (2) Recusant bishops were replaced, first by individual visitors on a temporary basis, then by 'superintendents' ('bishops'), who were administrators directly responsible to the Elector. (Luther later ordained at least one prince, George of Anhalt, to be his own superintendent-bishop.) (3) Endowments were diverted to the Elector, to be disbursed by him directly. (4) One of Luther's two revisions of the mass replaced the Roman rite. (5) Ordination, administered always after 1535 by members of the Wittenberg theology faculty, was by use of non-priestly forms. (6) In 1542, a consistory court was set up at Wittenberg, staffed by two law dons and two theology dons from the University, all nominated by the Elector. Similar patterns were followed in other states.

Shortage of competent clergy was a universal problem. German rural ministers were alarmingly ignorant—some did not know the Lord's Prayer or the Commandments—and in many cases were immoral as well. In one area the clergy brewed beer all week and spent sermon-time on Sunday teaching their congregations how to go and do likewise!

To meet this situation, Luther wrote two catechisms and several books of *Postils* (expository sermonettes for public reading by clergy who could not write sermons of their own). 'Emergency preachers' (untrained laymen of some little competence) were ordained for a few years, but it was recognized that the only long-term solution was to train a new ministry from scratch, which Luther and his colleagues at Wittenberg set themselves to do.

IV

Luther was no statesman, and the ecclesiastical reorganizations that took place under his general guidance were hardly models of what reformation should be. The principle of the church governing itself under Christ had to wait for Calvin before it was given substance. Yet there are lessons of great value that Luther can teach us. Among them are the following:

1. The necessity of reformation when the church's outward form and life contradict the gospel, whether doctrinally or practically.
2. The nature of reformation as spiritual renewal, wrought from within by the Word of God.

3. The pastoral purpose that must govern church reorganization. Good church order is not an end in itself, but must be thought of as a means to the good of souls by inducing fellowship, edification, and holiness.

4. The primacy of preaching and teaching the Word as the means to reformation. All Luther's emphasis was laid on teaching, by catechisms, sermons, books, and schools. This emphasis on Christian instruction was itself epoch-making.

5. Piecemeal improvement is better than none: and it is better to carry out innovations in a slow and piecemeal fashion than to outstrip weak consciences and make them stumble.

6. Patience is needed by those who seek reformation: having set ourselves to teach the Word, we must wait for it to do its own God-appointed work. Only God can build up Zion, and he is not always in such a hurry as we are.

CHAPTER 2

John Calvin and Reformed Europe

Place in History

Calvin's signet shows a heart held by a huge hand and bears the motto *prompte et sincere in opere Dei* (with readiness and whole-heartedness in God's work). So Calvin wished to be; so in fact he was. Proud, prejudiced, and self-willed, as he afterwards acknowledged, young John had originally planned a life of quiet scholarship, but a 'sudden conversion' (his phrase) at or soon after age twenty led him to want God's will rather than his own and to accept God's call when it eventually came.

As a result, he spent most of his adult life exiled from his native France, serving God in Geneva, Switzerland, with maximum public exposure as preacher and teacher of the Bible, pastor, reformer, theologian, and universal Christian counsellor, selflessly seeking God's honour and glory in church and community. And hereby he became the most influential man in the world in the sense that his ideas made more history than did those of anyone else alive in his day and for at least a hundred years after. The epoch from the middle of the sixteenth century to the beginning of the age of Sir Isaac Newton, towards the end of the century following, was in truth the age of Calvin. No other description covers the facts.

To see this, think of the great men and movements of those days. Think of the shaping of the churches of England and Scotland after 1550. Think of Bishop John Jewel and John Knox. Think of the Puritans in England, the heroes of the 'second Reformation,' and the Covenanters in Scotland, the Huguenots in France, the Pilgrim Fathers in New England, the 'Beggars' in Holland. Think of the revolt of the Netherlands, the English Civil War, and the Continental wars of religion. Think of William the Silent, Gaspard de Coligny, Oliver Cromwell, John Owen, John Milton, and Richard Baxter. Think too of the great ideals for which men fought.

Think of the ideal of the Christian commonwealth, in which the national church and the civil government stand independent of each other, yet recognize each other's divine authority and support each other within their own spheres. Think of the ideals of toleration, of representative democracy, of establishing the rights and liberties of subjects, of constitutionalizing monarchy. Think of the ideal, dear to all the Puritans, of a universal Christian culture, in which the secular is

seen as sacred, and arts, crafts, sciences, and industries all develop freely, harmo-
niously, and on a moral base, to the glory of God the Creator.

The Survival of Protestantism

The inspiration of these movements, men, and quests flowed directly from
Calvin. Without him, pure Protestantism might not have survived beyond the
middle of the seventeenth century, for it is simple truth that the only Protestants
who would stand and fight, to the last ditch if necessary, against Roman and
Erastian pressures, were the Calvinists. In all the great confrontations before the
Age of Reason set in, it was Calvinism—Calvin's ideas, that is, in some shape or
form—that set the agendas and called the shots.

In fact, Calvin's influence extended further. If we look at more recent history
and think of men like Jonathan Edwards, David Brainerd, George Whitefield, Sir
Isaac Newton, William Wilberforce, Lord Shaftesbury, C. H. Spurgeon, William
Carey, Robert Moffat, John Paton, James Chalmers, Robert Murray McCheyne,
Abraham Kuyper, and Martyn Lloyd-Jones, we see at once that the evangelical
movement that began with revival in the eighteenth century and overflowed into
social, political, missionary, and church structural expression in the nineteenth
could not have been what it was without John Calvin, for all those leaders, plus
a host of others who stood with them, were Calvinists in their basic creed. We
may fairly say, indeed, that it is not possible to understand our own religious
and cultural heritage today without knowing something about Calvin, since his
shadow hangs over so much of it.

Calvin the Man

What kind of man was he? Not the ogre of legend! Calvin the egoistical fanatic, hard and humourless, the doctrinaire misanthrope, the cruel dictator with
his arbitrary, uncaring, devilish God is a figure of fancy, not of fact. The real Calvin
was very different.

He was a sallow, sharp-featured, black-haired, slightly-built Frenchman, with
big brown eyes that sparkled or glared according to his mood. To avoid attacks
of migraine he ate little (one meal a day), and as he aged and his health ebbed he
grew bent, gaunt, and emaciated. He was never physically strong, and by the age
of thirty he had broken his health. In the closing years of his life (he died at fifty-
four), he was constantly ill with indigestion, headaches, gallstones, hemorrhoids,
gout, and fever, all superimposed upon chronic asthma and probably pulmonary
tuberculosis. Yet John Calvin spent himself unstintingly to the last in the service
of God and men.

He would not sleep more than four hours a night, and even when ill he kept four secretaries going with his French and Latin dictation, getting through an amount of work that was not far from miraculous. Daily sermons and lectures, the production of commentaries on most of the Bible, a steady flow of theological treatises, a massive correspondence, not to mention constant counselling, labour in Geneva's consistory court, and entertaining endless visitors — how did he manage it all? It is easier to ask the question than to answer it.

Though bad health made Calvin's temper increasingly short, as he himself apologetically acknowledged more than once, he was never sour. His free use of satire as a weapon in argument expressed a sense of the ugliness of untruth rather than of the worthlessness of any who embraced it. In himself he was neither malicious nor morbid, and as he loved books and beauty, so he loved people. His choleric, excitable sensitivity made him ardent and intense in friendship no less than in controversy and pastoral address. His rhetoric was simultaneously passionate and rational, cool-headed and warm-hearted, and showed him resolute and steady even when he felt timid and hurt. He wrote to his former colleague Viret, when his wife died, 'I subdue my grief as well as I can, but you know how tender, or rather soft, my mind is. Had not strong self-control been given me I could not have borne up so long.' Such feelings were frequent in Calvin's life.

Calvin's Will

Spiritually, he was honest and humble, innocent of self-pity, and with no illusions about himself. In his will, made on his deathbed, he voiced his faith as follows:

> I give thanks to God who had mercy on me . . . He delivered me out of the deep darkness of idolatry in which I was plunged, that he might bring me into the light of his gospel . . . I have no other defense or refuge for salvation than his free adoption, on which alone my salvation depends. With all my soul I embrace the mercy that he has exercised towards me through Jesus Christ, atoning for my sins with the merits of his death and passion, that in this way he might satisfy for all my offences and faults and blot them from his remembrance. I testify also and declare that I earnestly beg him to be pleased so to wash and purify me in the blood that my Sovereign Redeemer has shed for the sins of mankind, that under his shadow I may be able to stand at the judgment-seat . . .
>
> I also testify and declare that in all the battles and disputations in which I have been engaged with the enemies of the gospel, I have used no falsehood, no wicked and sophistical devices, but have acted straightforwardly and sincerely in defending the truth. Yet, alas, my ardour and zeal (if indeed worthy of the name) have been so slack and languid that I confess I have failed countless times to execute my office properly, and had not he, of his boundless goodness, assisted me . . . those mental

powers that the Lord gave me would at his judgment-seat prove me more and more guilty of sin and sloth.

> For these reasons I testify and declare that I trust to no other security for my salvation than this alone, that as God is the Father of mercy, so he will show himself such a Father to me, who acknowledge myself to be a miserable sinner.

To Geneva's elders at the same time he said:

> I have had much infirmity that you have had to bear, and the sum total of all that I have done has been worth nothing. Evil men will catch at this word, but I still say that all I have done has been worth nothing, and I am a pitiable creature. Yet I can say that I desired your good, and that my faults have always displeased me, and the root of the fear of God was in my heart.

Plainly, the stereotype of Calvin as a haughty, scornful, ruthless, self-righteous, power-loving autocrat needs some adjusting.

Sudden Conversion

Born at Noyon, Picardy, on July 10, 1509, John Calvin was religiously inclined from an early age, and his father, Gerard, a diocesan legal official, sent him to Paris University to take an arts degree in preparation for the priesthood. By John's graduation, Gerard had however changed the plan, and he directed his son to Orleans University for legal studies. Then came John's 'sudden conversion' from papist prejudice to Protestant conviction, and this brought with it a spiritual quickening that made legal studies seem tame and dull by comparison with Scripture and theology. Soon Calvin was preaching, teaching, and pastoring informally among his peers, though his wish to enjoy the life of a leisured, learned, quiet-living Protestant Erasmus remained—'literary ease, with something of a free and honourable station,' as he wrote later. In 1532 he produced a commentary on the *De Clementia* of Seneca, a Stoic philosopher believed at that time to have had Christian sympathies, hoping that this would establish him as a humanist scholar. But God had a different goal in view.

The year 1534 saw French Protestants posting placards in major towns attacking the mass. Official persecution then threatened, and Calvin moved to Basel, where in March 1536 the first edition of his *Institutes* appeared. In the manner of that pre-blurb age, its title page was fulsome, not to say grandiloquent. Translated from the Latin, it reads:

> *Basic Instruction [Institution] in the Christian Religion comprising almost the whole sum of godliness and all that needs to be known in the doctrine of salvation. A newly published work very well worth reading by all who aspire to godliness [pietah]. The preface is to the most Christian King of France, offering to him this book as a confession of faith by the author, Jean Calvin of Noyon.*

Calvin's preface was a fine apologia for Protestant faith, and the six catechetical chapters into which his 516 small-format pages were divided (on the law, the creed, the Lord's Prayer, the dominical sacraments, false sacraments, and Christian liberty) were brilliantly written. The work was an immediate success, and so it was as a distinguished young Protestant author that Calvin arrived in Geneva in August, five months later.

Called to Geneva

He was there by accident, as it seemed. He was heading for Strasbourg by a roundabout route, forced on him by a local war. But someone recognized him and took him to meet Guillaume Farel, one of the Protestant pastors who had struggled there since Geneva went nominally Protestant a decade before.

Farel, a red-headed fire-eater, was on this occasion (says Beza, Calvin's first biographer) 'obviously inspired with a kind of heroic spirit.' He told Calvin that he must stay and help, and when Calvin pleaded other plans he threatened him with a curse.

> You are following only your own wishes, and I tell you, in the name of God Almighty, that if you do not help us in this work of the Lord, the Lord will punish you for seeking your own interests rather than his.

Terrified, convicted, and ashamed, Calvin stayed and continued his Geneva ministry without a break, apart from three years of banishment between 1538 and 1541, till his death in 1564.

Calvin's goal in Geneva was a teaching, nurturing church, coterminous with the body politic, honouring God by orthodox praise and obedient holiness. There should be daily gatherings for psalm singing and expository preaching, monthly administration of the Lord's Supper (Calvin wanted this weekly but could never secure it), and an autonomous ecclesiastical court for censuring and, if necessary, excommunicating delinquent members.

Calvin was not a magistrate (he was not even a citizen until 1559), but as a preacher he told the magistrates long and often that Scripture made it their duty to back the church in all of this. He fought to a standstill their contrary craving to control the church, reinforced though this was by the anti-Calvin stance of several influential families in Geneva's high society who ominously called themselves Libertines and saw the Reformer as an upstart French whippersnapper who had grown too big for his boots.

Battle began when Calvin defied a state directive about eucharistic liturgy in 1538, an act that led to his three-year banishment, and hostilities continued after his recall until the Libertines, having gone too far by fomenting an armed riot against French immigrants, fled the city in 1555. Thereafter Calvin's church order, and with it his position as the Grand Old Man of Geneva and the Reformed world, went unchallenged.

Calvin's Geneva

Modern writers tend to depict the Genevan theocracy as a kind of gulag or concentration camp, with the officers of the consistory court doing duty as a malevolent KGB. But it was not so. Granted, the principle of treating heresy, blasphemy, and immorality as civil crimes meant a closer confining of the liberties of the subject than is found in the modern secular state. Yet those who were prepared to respect biblical orthodoxy, observe Christian standards of public decency, and attend church regularly found Calvin's regime admirable. The six thousand Protestant refugees who flocked there in Calvin's time from England, Scotland, and France thought Geneva exemplary—'the most perfect school of Christ since the apostles,' said John Knox—and they made it their model for reforming action when they went back home.

The anti-Trinitarian campaigner Servetus was burned at Geneva in 1553, and this is often seen as a blot on Calvin's reputation. But weigh these facts: (1) The belief that denial of the Trinity and/or Incarnation should be viewed as a capital crime in a Christian state was part of Calvin's and Geneva's medieval inheritance; Calvin did not invent it. (2) Anti-Trinitarian heretics were burned in other places beside Geneva in Calvin's time, and indeed later—two in England, for instance, as late as 1612. (3) The Roman Inquisition had already set a price on Servetus' head. (4) The decision to burn Servetus as a heretic was taken not by Calvin personally but by Geneva's Little Council of twenty-five, acting on unanimous advice from the pastors of several neighbouring Reformed churches whom they had consulted. (5) Calvin, whose role in Servetus' trial had been that of expert witness managing the prosecution, wanted Servetus not to die but to recant, and spent hours with him during and after the trial seeking to change his views. (6) When Servetus was sentenced to be burned alive, Calvin asked for beheading as a less painful alternative, but his request was denied. (7) The chief Reformers outside Geneva, including Bucer and the gentle Melanchthon, fully approved the execution.

The burning should thus be seen as the fault of a culture and an age rather than of one particular child of that culture and age. Calvin, for the record, showed more pastoral concern for Servetus than anyone else connected with the episode. As regards the rights and wrongs of what was done, the root question concerns the propriety of political paternalism in Christianity (that is, whether the Christian state, as distinct from the Christian church, should outlaw heresy or tolerate it), and it was Calvin's insistence that God alone is Lord of the conscience that was to begin displacing the medieval by the modern mind-set on this question soon after Servetus' death.

Calvin's Theology

The amount of misrepresentation to which Calvin's theology has been subjected is enough to prove his doctrine of total depravity several times over. How we hate those who squelch our pride by demolishing our self-righteousness and exalting God's sovereign grace!

Calvin is still widely regarded as a misanthrope who projected his dislike of the human race into a theology whose main point was that most people are irretrievably damned—even though the *Institutes* is in fact centrally concerned with grace, and with Christ the Saviour! It is still thought that predestinarian speculation is the main mark of his teaching, though in fact he never made any assertion about predestination or anything else for which he did not offer scriptural proof. His doctrine of sin as total depravity is still taken to mean that we are all by nature as bad as we could be, despite his explicit teaching that common grace, working through conscience, law, environment, and civil government, constantly restrains the full outworking of corruption and moves even the ungodly to social and cultural enterprises of abiding worth. These are just *three* of the thickets of distortion through which we must hack our way if we are to reach a true estimate of Calvin as a teacher about God.

He was, in fact, the finest exegete, the greatest systematic theologian, and the profoundest religious thinker that the Reformation produced. Bible-centred in his teaching, God-centred in his living, and Christ-centred in his faith, he integrated the confessional emphases of Reformation thought—by faith *alone*, by Scripture *alone*, by grace *alone*, by Christ *alone*, for God's glory *alone*—with supreme clarity and strength. He was ruled by two convictions that are written on every regenerate heart and expressed in every act of real prayer and real worship: God is all and man is nothing, and praise is due to God for everything good. Both convictions permeated his life, right up to his final direction that his tomb be unmarked and there be no speeches at his burial, lest he become the focus of praise instead of his God. Both convictions permeate his theology too.

Calvin was a *biblical* theologian—not a speculator, but an echoer of the Word of God. The *Institutes* itself, in which the consistent teaching of the sixty-six canonical books is topically spelled out, was written, as Calvin's preface to the second edition makes plain, to be a general preparation for Bible study, orienting the reader to the divine wisdom that all Scripture, when properly exegeted, is found to set forth, and specifically paving the way to Calvin's own commentaries, which took the *Institutes* as read. Nothing is affirmed in the *Institutes* for which scriptural support is not offered.

Also, Calvin was a *systematic* theologian—not a taker of haphazard soundings, but an integrator of earlier gains. He was a second-generation Reformer, labouring to confirm and conserve what those who preceded him—Luther, Zwingli, Melanchthon, Bucer, and their colleagues—had set forth. He stood consciously on their shoulders, as he did on the shoulders of the early Fathers, and theologized as a mainstream spokesman for the true universal church (as distinct from the papal system, which for him was something else).

The final (1559) version of the *Institutes*, in four books, eighty chapters, and more than a thousand pages in translation, combines in itself the qualities of catechetical handbook, theological textbook, Protestant apologia, Reformation manifesto, hammer of heresies, and guide to Christian practice. It is a systematic masterpiece, one that has carved out a permanent niche for itself among the greatest Christian books. The work is worth describing in some detail.

The Knowledge of God

The theme that Calvin develops to bind his material together is a biblical theme that unites in itself all Christian doctrine, experience, and behaviour—namely, *knowledge of God* (*cognitio Dei*). As a treatise on knowledge of God, the *Institutes* deals both with knowing God (which is religion) and with what is known about God (which is theology). Both theology and religion are to be learned and taught from God's own teaching (*doctrina*), that is, from Holy Scripture.

To the question, What does it mean to know God? Calvin's answer is: it means acknowledging him as he has revealed himself in Scripture and through Christ, worshipping him and giving him thanks, humbling oneself before him as a stupid sinner and learning from his Word, loving the Father and the Son for their love in adoption and redemption, trusting the promises of pardon and glory that God has given in Christ, living in obedience to God's law, and seeking to honour God in all human relationships and all commerce with created things.

To the question, Whence comes knowledge of God, thus conceived? Calvin's answer is: from the Holy Spirit, speaking in and through the written Word and uniting us to the risen Christ for new life.

To the question, On what intellectual basis does this practical knowledge of God and communion with God rest? the *Institutes* replies by expounding in its four books (1) the revealed truth about God the Creator and our need to know it; (2) the revealed truth about Christ the Mediator and our need of him; (3) the revealed truth about the grace of Christ and the salvation it brings us through the Spirit; (4) the revealed truth about the means of grace that are given us in the church and what is involved in using them.

Topically, Calvin follows in this the sequence of the Apostles' Creed—'I believe in (1) God . . . almighty, maker of heaven and earth; (2) and in Jesus Christ . . . ; (3) I believe in the Holy Ghost; (4) the holy catholic church . . .'

Felicities of formulation occur constantly. 'Oh, what a good book Calvin's *Institutes* is!' cried the Reformer's younger contemporary, the classical scholar Julius Scaliger. 'Oh, what a great man!' Scaliger was right, on both counts. Reading the *Institutes* shows why Melanchthon used to refer to Calvin simply as 'the theologian.' Well may we concur.

Calvinism in Europe

Most of the two-thirds of Germany that embraced the Reformation, along with Scandinavia and England, followed the Lutheran ecclesiastical pattern whereby the head of state becomes head of the church. But France, Scotland, northern Switzerland, the Netherlands, Hungary, Poland, and parts of Germany (Friesland, Hesse, the Palatinate) embraced Calvin's model, which keeps civil and churchly authority-structures distinct.

Churches of the first group, apart from the Church of England, identified with the theological heritage of Luther and/or Melanchthon, highlighting justification by faith as the essential gospel, maintaining a consubstantiationist view of the Lord's Supper, and allowing, if not endorsing, the Melanchthonian drift into a synergistic doctrine of grace.

The Calvinist churches however—'Reformed' (capital 'R') as they now called themselves—upheld the teaching of the *Institutes*; they set justification in a God-centred, sanctification-oriented, covenantal frame, they detached Christ's eucharistic presence from the elements, and they maintained an activist, crusading ethical stance, drawn from Calvin's 'third use' of the law as a family code, guiding and spurring Christians in the service of their heavenly Father. They all, including the Elizabethan Church of England, went along more or less with Beza's Aristotelian recasting of Calvin's soteriology in a supralapsarian mould, and they all shared in the Synod of Dort's condemnation of Arminianism in 1619. Confessional and catechetical statements of high quality, notably the Heidelberg Catechism (1563), the Second Helvetic Confession (1566), and the Westminster Confession and Catechisms (1646–48), plus constant battles everywhere for the crown rights of Christ the royal Redeemer in his church, show to what extent the *Institutes* became an international source of homogenous theological conviction. The Pilgrim Fathers brought Calvinism to America, and today English-speaking Calvinism of the classical type (as distinct from Barth's reconstructed and arguably distorted version) has its main strength in the United States.

The bodies of four centuries of Calvinists lie mouldering in the grave, but Calvinism goes marching on.

CHAPTER 3

Richard Baxter: A Man for All Ministries

I

The seventy-six years of Richard Baxter's life spanned an era in English history that was tragic, heroic, and pathetic by turns to an extraordinary degree. It was a time of revolution and counter-revolution in church and state; of brutal religious persecution; of fierce controversy in print about almost everything; of disruptive socio-economic shifts which nobody at the time understood; of widespread bad health, growing towns innocent of hygiene, and nightmarishly primitive medicine; in short, it was a time of hardship for just about everyone. And at the head of the list of factors that led to the tragedies, the heroisms, and the miseries, stood rival understandings of Christianity. That is a sad thing to have to say, but it is true.

Had you been a Christian of consistent principles, whatever they were, living through those seventy-six years, you too would have had a rough ride. If you had been a Roman Catholic, you would have been an object of general distaste in the community all the time, constantly suspected of being a political subversive. Had you been a High Anglican, wedded to the Prayer Book, the ministry of bishops, and the royal supremacy in church and state, you would have watched your side lose the Civil War in the 1640s, you would have wept over the (to you) traitorous act of executing the king for treason against his people, you would have seen Prayer Book and episcopacy at one stage outlawed by Parliament, and if you had been a clergyman you would have lost your living for the best part of twenty years before the Restoration (1660).

And if, like Baxter, you had been a Puritan, practising and propagating the religion of St. Augustine on the basis of the theology of John Calvin, you would have had to endure the Arminianizing of Anglican leadership for two decades before the Civil War, the ejecting of almost two thousand Puritan-type clergy from English parishes at the Restoration, the consequent Anglican slide away from the gospel, and the great persecution of Protestant non-conformists that put tens of thousands in jail for not using the Prayer Book in their worship of God during the quarter-century before toleration came in 1689. Whatever your principles, you would have experienced much unhappiness during those years.

A moment ago I called Richard Baxter a Puritan; and since that word still carries prejudicial overtones for many, as it did throughout Baxter's own life, I had better say at once that my reason for using it is simply that it was as a Puritan that Baxter saw himself. Noting in 1680 that two of his opponents in print had called him (in Latin) a dyed-in-the-wool Puritan and one who oozed the whole of Puritanism from every pore, he responded by commenting: 'Alas I am not so good and happy.' Though he was, as we would say, ecumenically oriented, sympathetically alert to all the main Christian traditions and happy to learn from them all, he constantly equated the Puritan ideal with Christianity—'mere Christianity' to use his own phrase, which C. S. Lewis later borrowed from him—and all his writings display him as the classic mainstream Puritan that he ever sought to be.

What, then, was Puritanism? Matthew Sylvester, the not-too-competent editor of Baxter's posthumous narrative of his life and times (published as *Reliquiae Baxterianae*, 800 folio pages, 1696) notes in his preface that in matters of history, as in everything else, Baxter had

> an Eagle's Eye, an honest Heart, a thoughtful Soul, a searching and considerate [i.e., reflective] Spirit, and a concerned frame of Mind to let the present and succeeding Generations duly know the real and true state and issues [of things].[1]

What description of Puritanism then, would Baxter have acknowledged as fair and true? The question is not too hard to answer.

Puritanism, as Baxter understood it and as modern scholarship, correcting centuries of caricature, now depicts it, was a total view of Christianity, Bible-based, church-centred, God-honouring, literate, orthodox, pastoral, and Reformational, that saw personal, domestic, professional, political, churchly, and economic existence as aspects of a single whole, and that called on everybody to order every department and every relationship of their life according to the Word of God, so that all would be sanctified and become 'holiness to the Lord.' Puritanism's spearhead activity was pastoral evangelism and nurture through preaching, catechizing, and counselling (which Puritans themselves called casuistry), and Puritan teaching harped constantly on the themes of self-knowledge, self-humbling, and repentance; faith in, and love for, Jesus Christ the Saviour; the necessity of regeneration, and of sanctification (holy living, by God's power) as proof of it; the need for conscientious conformity to all God's law, and for a disciplined use of the means of grace; and the blessedness of the assurance and joy from the Holy Spirit that all faithful believers under ordinary circumstances may know. Puritans saw themselves as God's pilgrims, travelling home; God's warriors, battling against the world, the flesh, and the devil; and God's servants, under orders to do all the good they could as they went along. This was the Christianity with which Baxter identified, and of which he was a shining example throughout the vicissitudes of his own long life.

II

Let us get a little closer to Baxter. Here are the key personal facts. Summarized in *Who's Who* fashion, with a few intrusions as we move through them, they are as follows:

'Baxter, Richard, gentleman' (for his father owned a small estate); 'born 12 November, 1615, at Rowton, Salop; educated at Donnington Free School, Wroxeter, and privately' (Baxter never went to a university); 'ordained deacon by Bishop of Worcester, 1638; curate of Bridgnorth, 1639–40; lecturer'—that is, salaried preacher—'of Kidderminster, 1641–42; chaplain with the Parliamentary army, 1642–47; vicar of Kidderminster, 1647–61'—a ministry during which he just about converted the whole town—'at Savoy Conference, 1661' (this was the abortive consultation between Puritan and Anglican leaders for the improving of the Prayer Book for the restored Church of England); 'lived privately in or near London, 1662–91; married Margaret Charlton (1636–81), 1662; imprisoned for one week in Clerkenwell jail, 1669, for 21 months in Southwark jail, 1685–86; died 8 December, 1691; author of *The Saints' Everlasting Rest* (1650)'—an all-time devotional classic on how thoughts of God and heaven can renew the heart for service here below, a volume of 800 pages that sold an edition a year for the first decade of its life: '*The Reformed Pastor* (1656)'—another all-time classic, admonishing, motivating, and instructing the clergy; '*A Call to the Unconverted* (1658)'—the first evangelistic pocket-book in English, which in its year of publication sold 20,000 copies, and brought an unending stream of readers to faith during Baxter's lifetime; '*A Christian Directory* (1673)'—a unique million-word compendium of Puritan teaching about Christian life and conduct; 'and over 130 other books; special interests, pastoral care, Christian unity; hobbies, medicine, science, history.' Such was the man the tercentenary of whose death we are now commemorating.

Is it important for later generations to remember Baxter? In 1875 in Kidderminster they thought it was, and a fine statue of him preaching was erected in the town centre, with the following inscription:

BETWEEN THE YEARS 1641 AND 1660
THIS TOWN WAS THE SCENE OF THE LABOURS OF
RICHARD BAXTER
RENOWNED EQUALLY FOR HIS CHRISTIAN LEARNING
AND PASTORAL FIDELITY.
IN A STORMY AND DIVIDED AGE
HE ADVOCATED UNITY AND COMPREHENSION
POINTING THE WAY TO THE EVERLASTING REST.
CHURCHMEN AND NONCONFORMISTS
UNITED TO RAISE THE MEMORIAL, A.D. 1875.

The phrases used show what it was about Baxter that was thought worth remembering in 1875. 'Christian learning,' for instance, points to the fact that he was in fact an omnivorous polymath, always studying, reading quickly and remembering well what he had read, and consistently thoughtful and discerning in the opinions he expressed on what the books set before him. Once he complained that the loss of time for study due to his many illnesses (for he was a sick man all his life) was the greatest burden he had to bear; anyone, however, who observes his mastery of biblical material and of the entire Christian tradition, and of the dozens of positions that he controverts, will marvel at the amount of studying that he actually accomplished.

He was in fact the most voluminous English theologian of all time, and in addition to the approximately four million words of pastoral, apologetic, devotional, and homiletic writing that are reprinted in his *Practical Works*, he produced about six million more on aspects of the doctrine of grace and salvation, church unity and non-conformity, the sacraments, Roman Catholicism, antinomianism, millenarianism, Quakerism, politics and history, not to mention a systematic theology in Latin; and in all of these writings, whether or not one finally agrees with Baxter's positions, one finds oneself confronted with the mature judgement of a clear, sharp, well-stocked, wise mind, as distinguished for intellectual integrity as for spiritual alertness. I do not think Baxter was always right, but I see him, as did the memorialists of 1875, as one of the most impressive of Christian thinkers, and I urge that there is just as much reason to honour him as such today as there was at that time.

Then, again, the 1875 inscription celebrates Baxter's constant pleas, uttered both *viva voce* and in print over more than forty years, for 'unity and comprehension.' In his own day, Baxter's pleading on these topics went unheeded, partly because of the sharpness of the rhetoric in which much of it was couched, but mainly because it was an age in which party spirit and dog-eat-dog wrangling were taken as proper signs of Christian seriousness. By 1875, however, the basic right-mindedness of what Baxter was saying had become apparent, and it ought to be even more apparent today.

Baxter's call to unity depended on distinguishing tolerable from intolerable differences among professing Christians and churches. On the basis of this distinction, his plea was, first, that love, peace, and communion should be maximized on the basis that in reality all Christian essentials are already held by those who accept the Apostles' Creed, the Ten Commandments, and the Lord's Prayer, as fixing the shape of their Christianity; and, second, that all would henceforth observe the maxim, unity in necessary things, liberty in non-necessary things, and charity in all things. Thus (so he argued) the unity Christians already have in Christ will find its appropriate expression. Almost nobody listened to him.

Baxter's call for comprehension depended on his view of the Church of England as being what its first Reformers saw it as—namely, a federation of congregations standing for 'mere Christianity,' that is, a Christianity defined in terms of the essentials and no more, and committed together to the task of evangelizing and discipling the English. Here, his plea was for a relaxation of the restored Anglican uniformity of 1662 that would allow Presbyterian, Independent, and Baptist groups a place within the federation, for the furtherance of the common calling. His reasoning was noble and cogent in itself, and more than timely during those years in which all non-conformists (120,000 or so, according to one estimate) faced fines and imprisonment if they were caught worshipping in company in their own way. But as before, his pleas achieved nothing.

Baxter's pitch was queered by Anglican hatred and suspicion of non-conformists as being all revolutionaries at heart, by the prevalence among Anglicans of High Church theology which saw non-Episcopal churches as no churches and their ministers as no ministers, and by non-conformist bitterness and contempt for the persecuting Church of England, and unwillingness ever to associate with it again, so that in the event his argumentation was ignored throughout his lifetime. But we can see why in 1875, before hurricanes of unbelief laid waste great sections of both the Free Church and the Anglican worlds and permanently changed the shape of the comprehension issue, the memorialists wished to celebrate the witness Baxter had borne.

And what, now, of ourselves? Are Baxter's theological attainments, and pastoral strengths, and arguments for unity and comprehension, and testimonies to the supreme importance of fixing one's hopes on the saints' everlasting rest, worth our remembrance today? I maintain not only that they are worth remembering in themselves as inspiring examples of vision, vitality, and wisdom in Christ, but that Baxter has more to say, and to give, to those who remember him today than ever was the case with the men and women of 1875, just because we have drifted further from that vision, vitality, and wisdom than they had. The title of this lecture is 'A Man for All Ministries.' I propose to spend the rest of my time looking more closely at Baxter the man and at the serving roles that he fulfilled, and my suggestion at each point will be that we today need to learn from him in the way that small, superficial, shallow people always need to learn from the giants. To this agenda I now turn.

III

Often described as seraphic, because of the way that his rhetoric soars when he is dilating on the grace of God and the blessings of the gospel, Baxter appears throughout his ministry as the very epitome of single-minded ardour in seeking the glory of God through the salvation of souls and the sanctification of the church. To contemplate the independence, integrity, and zeal with which the public Baxter fulfilled his ministry is fascinating and inspiring; but even more fascinating and inspiring, to my mind at any rate, is contemplation of the private Baxter, the man behind the ministry, who in an elaborate self-analysis, written it seems about 1665, when he was fifty, and published posthumously as part of his *Reliquiae,* opens his heart about the changes he sees in himself since his younger years in Christian service.

In general, what he delineates is a progress from raw zeal to ripe simplicity, and from a passionate narrowness that was somewhat self-absorbed and majored in minors to a calm concentration on God and the big things, with a profound capacity to see those big things steadily and whole. I subjoin some extracts from this gem of humble, honest witness to the transforming work of God in a human life so that you may get the flavour of Baxter directly, and judge for yourself whether I exaggerate in what I have just said.[2]

> I have perceived that nothing so much hindereth the reception of the truth as urging it on men with too harsh importunity, and falling too heavily on their errors.

> In my youth I was quickly past my fundamentals and was running up into a multitude of controversies . . . But the elder I grew the smaller the stress I laid upon those controversies and curiosities (though still my intellect abhorreth confusion) . . . And now it is the fundamental doctrines of the Catechism which I highliest value and daily think of, and find most useful to myself and others.

> The Creed, the Lord's Prayer and the Ten Commandments do find me now the most acceptable and plentiful matter for all my meditations. They are to me as my daily bread and drink . . . I value all things according to their use and ends, and I find in the daily practice and experience of my soul that the knowledge of God and Christ, and the Holy Spirit, and the truth of Scripture, and the life to come, and of a holy life, is of more use to me than all the most curious speculations . . . That is the best doctrine and study which maketh men better and tendeth to make them happy.

> Heretofore I placed much of my religion in tenderness of heart, and grieving for sin, and penitential tears . . . but my conscience now looketh at love and delight in God, and praising him, as the top of all my religious duties.

> My judgment is much more for frequent and serious meditation on the heavenly blessedness than it was heretofore in my younger days . . . now I had rather read, hear or meditate on God and heaven than on any other subject . . . I was once wont to meditate on my own heart . . . poring either on my sins or wants, or examining my sincerity; but now, though I am greatly convinced of the need of heart-acquaintance . . . I see more need of a higher work, and that I should look often upon Christ, and God, and heaven, [rather] than upon my own heart.

> I now see more good and more evil in all men than heretofore I did . . . I less admire gifts of utterance and bare profession of religion than I once did . . . I once thought that almost all that could pray movingly and fluently, and talk well of religion, had

been saints. But experience hath opened to me what odious crimes may consist with high profession.

I was wont to look but little further than England in my prayers, as not considering the state of the rest of the world . . . But now, as I better understand the case of the world and the method of the Lord's Prayer . . . no part of my prayers are so deeply serious as that for the conversion of the infidel and ungodly world.

He goes on to express admiration for the missionary pioneer John Eliot, 'the apostle of the Indians in New England,' whose work he helped to support financially, and to voice the wish that all two thousand Puritan clergy ejected in 1662 could have become overseas missionaries.

I am deeplier afflicted for the disagreements of Christians than I was when I was a younger Christian. Except the case of the infidel world, nothing is so sad and grievous to my thoughts as the case of the divided churches. And therefore I am more deeply sensible of the sinfulness of those prelates and pastors of the churches who are the principal cause of these divisions. The contentions between the Greek Church and the Roman, the Papists and the Protestants, the Lutherans and the Calvinists, have woefully hindered the kingdom of Christ.

Though my works were never such as could be any temptation to me to dream of obliging God by proper merit in commutative justice, yet one of the most ready, constant, undoubted evidences of my . . . interest in his covenant is the consciousness of my living as devoted to him. And I the easilier believe the pardon of my failings through my Redeemer while I know that I serve no other master, and that I know no other end, or trade, or business, but that I am imployed [sic] in his work, and make it the business of my life, and live to him in the world, notwithstanding my infirmities. And this bent and business of my life, with my longing desires after perfection in the knowledge and belief and love of God, and in a holy and heavenly mind and life, are the two standing, constant, discernible evidences which most put me out of doubt of my sincerity. [He means, of his being truly regenerate and born again.]

And though I before told of the change of my judgment against provoking writings, I have had more will than skill since to avoid such. I must mention it by way of penitent confession, that I am too much inclined to such words in controversial writings which are too keen, and apt to provoke the person whom I write against . . . And therefore I repent of it, and wish all over-sharp passages were expunged from my writings, and desire forgiveness of God and man.

It is surely apparent that these are the words of a great and holy man, naturally gifted and supernaturally sanctified beyond most; humble, patient, realistic, and frank to a very unusual degree. The quiet peace and joy that shine through these almost clinical observations on himself are truly impressive; here is an endlessly

active man whose soul is at rest in God all the time as he labours in prayer Godward and in persuasion manward. And the poise of his spirit is the more impressive when we recall that of all the great Puritan sufferers—and the Puritans as a
body were great sufferers—none had a heavier load of pain and provocation to
endure than did he.

He suffered throughout his adult life from a multitude of bodily ailments (a
tubercular cough; frequent nosebleeds and bleeding from his finger-ends; migraine headaches; inflamed eyes; all kinds of digestive disorders; kidney stones
and gallstones; and more), so that from the age of twenty-one he was, as he says,
'seldom an hour free from pain,' and expected death constantly through the next
fifty-five years of partial disablement before his release finally came. Then, after
1662, he suffered a great deal of hatred and harassment because he was a promi-
nent non-conformist leader: this led to arrests for preaching, two spells in prison,
the distraining (confiscation) of his goods to pay fines, including on one occasion
the very bed on which he was lying sick, and finally a trial, if it can be called that,
before the appalling Judge Jeffreys, Lord Chief Justice of England (answerable
therefore to no one) and James II's human whip for flaying rebels. This was the
lowest point of public degradation that Baxter was ever reduced to, and it is worth
pausing to get a glimpse of it.[3]

The charge was sedition: a ridiculous, trumped-up accusation based on expository words in his *Paraphrase of the New Testament* about the Pharisees and
Jewish authorities, into which was read an attack on England's rulers in church
and state. (Baxter later commented that by the same logic he could have been
indicted for uttering the words, 'Deliver us from evil,' in the Lord's Prayer.) Jeffreys would not let Baxter and his six legal representatives say anything coherent
at any stage, and the disputed passages in the *Paraphrase* were never discussed;
Jeffreys simply ranted on against the seventy-year-old Puritan veteran as (these
are the words of an eye-witness) 'a conceited, stubborn, fanatical dog, that did
not conform when he might have been preferred [that is, been a bishop: Baxter
was offered the see of Hereford at the Restoration]; hang him! This one old fellow hath cast more reproach upon the constitution and excellent discipline of
our Church than will be wiped out this hundred years ... by God! he deserves
to be whipped through the city.' When Jeffreys had finished haranguing the jury,
Baxter said: 'Does your lordship think any jury will pretend to pass a verdict on
me upon such a trial?' 'I'll warrant you, Mr. Baxter,' replied Jeffreys; 'don't you
trouble yourself about that.' And the jury promptly found him guilty without
retiring. The result for Baxter was eighteen months in jail.

It should be added, however, that after Baxter was dead at seventy-six, and
Jeffreys had drunk himself into the grave at the age of forty, and it was known that
Matthew Sylvester was to be Baxter's biographer, Tillotson, the Archbishop of
Canterbury, wrote Sylvester a letter of encouragement containing the following
sentences about the trial:

Nothing more honorable than when the Rev. Baxter stood at bay, berogued [slandered], abused, despised; and never more great than then. Draw this well . . . This is the noblest part of his life, and not that he might have been a bishop. The Apostle (2 Corinthians 11) when he would glory, mentions his labours and strifes and bonds and imprisonments; his troubles, weariness, dangers, reproaches; not his riches and coaches and advantages. God lead us into this spirit and free us from the worldly one which we are apt to run into.[4]

One can only say Amen to that.

IV

We have seen something of Baxter the man; let us now look at some of the ministering roles he fulfilled. First, I focus on Baxter as an evangelistic and pastoral communicator—preacher, teacher, and writer.

The best curtain-raiser for this section is Baxter's own account of the fruitfulness of his Kidderminster ministry. He found the town's two thousand adults 'an ignorant, rude, and revelling people, for the most part . . . they had hardly ever had any lively serious preaching among them.' Soon, however, things began to happen. Wrote Baxter:

> When I first entered upon my Labours in the Ministry I took special notice of everyone that was humbled, reformed or converted; but when I had laboured long, it pleased God that the Converts were so many, that I could not afford time for such particular Observations . . . Families and considerable Numbers at once . . . came in and grew up I scarce knew how.
>
> The Congregation was usually full, so that we were fain to build five Galleries after my coming thither . . . [The Church would have held about a thousand without the galleries.] Our private Meetings [small groups, as we would nowadays call them] were also full. On the Lord's Days [which had been sports days before Baxter arrived] there was no disorder to be seen in the streets, but you might hear an hundred families singing Psalms and repeating Sermons, as you passed through the Streets. In a word, when I came thither first, there was about one Family in a Street that worshipped God and called on His Name, and when I came away there were some streets where there was not past one Family in the side of a Street that did not so; and that did not by professing serious Godliness, give us hopes of their sincerity . . . When I set upon Personal Conference and Catechising them, there were very few families in all the Town that refused to come . . . [Baxter asked them to call on him at his home, since his bad health constantly disabled him from visiting their homes.] And few families went from me without some tears, or seemingly serious promises of a Godly Life.[5]

What was the secret of Baxter's success (so far, at least, as this can be analysed in terms of means to ends)? He notes, as significant factors in the situation, that his people had not been gospel-hardened; that he had good helpers, both assistant clergy and members of the flock; that his converts' holy living was winsome while the town's black sheep made sin appear most repulsive; that Kidderminster was free of rival congregations and sectarian bickerings; that most of the families were at home most of the time, working as weavers, so that they had 'time enough to read or talk of holy Things . . . as they stand in their Loom they can set a Book before them or edify one another';[6] also, it was helpful (Baxter continues) that he fulfilled a long ministry; that he practised church discipline; that, being un-married, he could concentrate on serving his people; that he gave out Bibles and books (he received every fifteenth copy of each of his own books in lieu of royalties for free distribution); that he gave money to the needy; and that he ful-filled for a time the role of amateur physician—effectively, it seems, and without charge—until he could persuade a qualified doctor to move to the town. He held that all these factors helped the gospel forward, and no doubt he was right. But the key element in his success, humanly speaking, was undoubtedly the clarity, force, and skill with which he communicated the gospel itself.

The content of Baxter's gospel was not in any way distinctive. It was the historic Puritan, evangelical, New Testament message of ruin, redemption, and regeneration. Baxter called for conversion from the life of thoughtless self-centredness and sin to Jesus Christ, the crucified Saviour and risen Lord, and he spelled out in great detail what this must mean in terms of repentance, faith, and new obedience. He saw the unconverted as on the road to hell, and as spiritually asleep in the sense of not recognizing their danger, so he set himself both in the pulpit and in his annual personal conversation ('catechising,' as he called it) with each family of the parish, to wake them up and persuade them to thoroughgoing Christian commitment before it was too late. What he said, and how he said it, may be learned from his classic writings on conversion, among them: *A Treatise of Conversion, Directions and Persuasions to a Sound Conversion,* and *A Call to the Unconverted* (full title, *A Call to the Unconverted to Turn and Live, and Accept of Mercy while Mercy may be Had, as ever they would find Mercy in the Day of their Extremity: from the Living God*). All these were originally sermons preached in series to Baxter's Kidderminster congregation.

We should not suppose that conversion was Baxter's only theme in his Kidderminster ministry. He himself tells us that he ranged much wider:

> The thing which I daily opened to them, and with the greatest importunity laboured to imprint upon their minds, was the great Fundamental Principles of Christianity contained in their Baptismal Covenant, even a right knowledge, and belief of, and sub-jection and love to, God the Father, the Son, and the Holy Ghost; and Love to all Men, and Concord with the Church and one another: I did so daily inculcate the Knowledge of God our Creator, Redeemer, and Sanctifier, and Love and Obedience to God, and Unity with the Church Catholic, and Love to Men, and Hope of Life Eternal, that these were the matter of their daily Cogitations and Discourses, and indeed their Religion.[7]

But Baxter was an evangelist, and he constantly led his hearers back to the life-and-death question: 'Will you, or will you not, turn and live?' 'Will you now take seriously the things you say you believe about sin, and Christ, and heaven, and hell?'

Here is a sample of Baxter's evangelistic rhetoric as he applies a message on Hebrews 11:1, 'Faith is the substance of things hoped for, the evidence of things not seen.' He has made the point that faith treats as real the realities of which Scripture speaks: God, Christ, Satan; the final judgement, heaven, and hell. He has pressed the question:

> Are you in good earnest, when you say, you believe in a heaven and hell? And do you think, and speak, and pray, and live, as those that do indeed believe it? . . . Deal truly . . . if you would know where you must live for ever, know how, and for what, and upon what it is that you live here.

He has invited his hearers to think what difference it would make to them if they could actually see, with their physical eyes, Christ, their own forthcoming death, judgement day, with Satan accusing, and the condition of those already experiencing heaven and hell. Now he pins the congregation to the wall.[8]

> Answer these following questions, upon the foregoing suppositions.
>
> 1. If you saw but what you say you do believe, would you not be convinced that the most pleasant, gainful sin is worse than madness? And would you not spit at the very name of it?
>
> 2. What would you think of the most serious, holy life, if you had seen the things you say you do believe? Would you ever again reproach it as preciseness [a long-standing contemptuous label for the Puritan lifestyle], or count it more ado than needs, and think your time were better spent in playing than in praying; in drinking, and sports, and filthy lusts, than in the holy services of the Lord?
>
> 3. If you saw but what you say you do believe, would you ever again be offended with the ministers of Christ for the plainest reproofs, and closest exhortations, and strictest precepts and discipline . . . ? Then you would understand what moved ministers to be so importunate with you for conversion; and whether trifling or serious preaching was the best.
>
> 4. . . . I durst then ask the worst that heareth me, Dare you now be drunk, or gluttonous, or worldly? Dare you be voluptuous, proud, or fornicators any more? Dare you go home, and make a jest at piety, and neglect your souls, as you have done? . . .
>
> 5. And oh how such a sight would advance the Redeemer, and his grace, and promises, and word, and ordinances in your esteem! It would quicken your desires, and make you fly to Christ for life, as a drowning man to that which may support him. How sweetly then would you relish the name, the word, the ways of Christ, which now seem dry and common things!

That is vintage Baxter, arousing the complacent. It remains only to add that he was preaching before King Charles II, England's merry monarch, and his merry court, and that the sermon was in fact published by royal command, though not, it seems, heeded by the royal conscience. The quality that the 1875 inscription calls 'pastoral fidelity' made Baxter willing to say 'boo' to any goose, even a royal one. That was the kind of preacher he was.

The second sphere of Baxter's ministry at which we glance is the field of ecclesiastical statesmanship, where Baxter, the advocate of a comprehensive national church, as we saw, was in constant action after 1662 negotiating for agreement with the Independents and a rapprochement with the Church of England, and writing documents and publishing books to that end. Not much need be said about this, because it was an area in which he did not shine at all. His provocative manner in discussion and debate totally thwarted his unitive purpose. His schoolmasterly strictures upon the cherished beliefs of others only made enemies.

As the sermon just quoted would suggest, he was too blunt and oracular in style to be a bridge-builder. The position from which he reached out in all these discussions, however, was a non-sectarian, noble one, which when applying for a licence to preach under the royal Indulgence of 1672 he formulated as follows:[9]

> My religion is merely Christian; but as rejecting the Papal Monarchy and its attendant evils, I am a Protestant.
>
> The rule of my faith and doctrine is the law of God in Nature and Scripture.
>
> The Church which I am a member of is the Universality of Christians, in conjunction with all particular churches of Christians in England or elsewhere in the world whose communion according to my capacity I desire.

Sometimes he called this position 'Catholicism against all sects.' In his day it was thought eccentric; in ours, it might appear as prophetic, marking the path whereby the exclusiveness of denominationalism comes to be transcended. It was never correct to call Baxter a Presbyterian, as was often done, nor after 1662 could one call him an Anglican; he was a 'mere non-conformist' in relation to the Anglican settlement, and that, denominationally speaking, was all. In an ecumenical age it is worth reflecting on the significance of Baxter's non-denominational stance.

A further sphere of ministry in which Baxter moved was the delineating of Christian social justice, and here he shows great skill in reforming medieval formulae and bringing them up to date for seventeenth-century Protestant use. Part IV of the *Christian Directory*, comprising about two hundred thousand words, deals in detail with rulers and subjects, lawyers, physicians, schoolmasters, soldiers, murder and suicide, scandal, theft, contracts, borrowing, buying and selling, the charging of interest (i.e., usury), wages, landlords and tenants, and lawsuits. Baxter distils our practical guidance for serving and pleasing God in all these relationships, by managing them as expressions of neighbour-love and cooperative service, and avoiding any form of callous or careless exploitation.

One must not try, he says, 'to get another's goods or labour for less than it is worth,' nor must one make profit out of the customer's ignorance or necessity:

'it is a false rule of them that think a commodity is worth so much as anyone will give' for it. 'To wish to buy cheap and sell dear is common (as St. Augustine observes), but it is a common vice.'[10] And landlords must not squeeze rents so that tenants cannot live decently or have leisure to care for their souls. This point Baxter made again, later, in a separate tract, *The Poor Husbandman's Advocate to Rich Racking Landlords,* which he finished only six weeks before his death (it was his last writing), and which did not in fact see the light of day till this century.[11]

I wish that time allowed me to explore the idyll of Baxter's marriage, a nineteen-year partnership with a brilliant woman, twenty-one years younger than himself, whom he memorialized in an account of her life written 'under the power of melting Grief' a few weeks after her death in 1681. The account was well and lovingly edited by J. T. Wilkinson in 1928 under the title *Richard Baxter and Margaret Charlton: A Puritan Love-Story;* it was recently reprinted under my name, with the title *A Grief Sanctified.*

> When we were married, [writes Baxter] her sadness and melancholy vanished: counsel did something to it, and contentment something; and being taken up with our household affairs did somewhat. And we lived in inviolated love and mutual complacency sensible of the benefit of mutual help.

Baxter's account of his wife's ministry to him has in it many such hints of his ministry as a husband to her, and it is evident that in this he did well, although he writes of himself, with that devastating perfectionist honesty that we saw in him before:

> My dear wife did look for more good in me than she found, especially lately in my weakness and decay. We are all like pictures that must not be looked on too near. They that come near us find more faults and badness in us than others at a distance know.[12]

Well maybe so; yet if one picks up all the hints in the narrative, Baxter's marital ministry appears as something to be very much admired, and in days like ours to be viewed as something of a model. But that theme cannot be explored now.[13]

V

It was usual to end Puritan funeral sermons with a reference to the dead person's final hours: for it was an age in which people died at home, in company, without pain-killing drugs, and often in full consciousness to the very end, and it was taken for granted that their dying behaviour and their last words, spoken from the edge of eternity, would have special significance for those whom they left behind.

This is not a funeral sermon, but a celebratory speech; nonetheless it is, I think, fitting to end it in this Puritan way. So let it be said that on the day before he died, as on every day of his life it seems for the previous forty and more years, Baxter was meditating on heaven, focusing on the description of the heavenly Jerusalem in Hebrews 12:22–24, a passage which, so he told two of his visitors, 'deserves a thousand thousand thoughts'; and that he told those same visitors, 'I have peace; I have peace'; and that he brushed aside praise for his books with words of almost arrogant humility, 'I was a pen in God's hand; what praise is due to a pen?'; and that his last words, spoken through pain, to Matthew Sylvester, whose pastoral assistant he had been for the previous four years, were 'Oh I thank him, I thank him. The Lord teach you to die.' And let it further be said that Sylvester himself, preaching Baxter's memorial sermon on Elisha's words, 'Where is the Lord God of Elijah?', was constrained to end by looking ahead to resurrection day (which, of course, for God's people will be reunion day also) and to ask aloud:

> What must I do to meet with our Elijah and his God in peace? Must not my eye be inward, upward, forward, backward, round about? Must I not endeavour to know my errand, warrant, difficulties, duties and encouragements? Must I not . . . tell what I believe? . . . practice what I preach? And promote the Christian interest with all wisdom, diligence, and faithfulness; as my predecessor did before me?[14]

Baxter's brand of spiritual straightforwardness in the service of the triune God regularly affects Christians as it affected Sylvester; it makes one seek to be energetic and businesslike in one's discipleship and service, just as he was, and gives one a conscience about aimlessness, and casualness, and spiritual drift. For this reason alone it is good for us to remember Baxter, and I have counted it a privilege to be able to introduce you to him in this all too sketchy way. From my own acquaintance with him, which now goes back more than fifty years, I say to you all—clergy, lay folk, young Christians, senior Christians—get to know Baxter, and stay with Baxter. He will always do you good.

For Further Reading

Baxter's *Practical Works,* in four vast volumes, are periodically available by mail order from Soli Deo Gloria, 213 West Vincent, Ligonier, PA 15658, USA (1990–91). Volume 1 contains *A Christian Directory;* volume 2, Baxter's treatises on conversion; volume 3, *The Saints' Everlasting Rest* and other writings on discipleship and fellowship with God; volume 4 includes *The Reformed Pastor.*

The Reformed Pastor is in print separately, with an introduction by J. I. Packer (Edinburgh: Banner of Truth, 1974).

The Autobiography of Richard Baxter, ed. J. M. Lloyd Thomas (1925) and re-edited by N. H. Keeble (London: J. M. Dent, Everyman's Library, 1974), is a drastic abridgement of *Reliquiae Baxterianae* (1696), concentrating on Baxter himself. N. H. Keeble and Geoffrey F. Nuttall, *Calendar of the Correspondence of Richard Baxter* (2 vols.; Oxford: Clarendon Press, 1991), is a monument of detailed and illuminating research.

The standard *Lives of Baxter* by F. J. Powicke (2 vols., 1924, 1927) and G. F. Nuttall (1965) are unhappily out of print, as is *Richard Baxter and Margaret Charlton: A Puritan Love-Story* (*A Breviate The Life of Margaret Baxter, by Richard Baxter*), ed. J. T. Wilkinson (London: George Allen and Unwin,1928). The *Breviate*, edited and introduced by J. I. Packer, is now available again as *A Grief Sanctified* (Ann Arbor: Servant Books, and Leicester: Crossway, 1998).

Martin, Hugh, *Puritanism and Richard Baxter* (London: SCM Press, 1954), and N. H. Keeble, *Richard Baxter: Puritan Man of Letters* (Oxford: Clarendon Press, 1982), are good general introductions.

See also J. I. Packer, *A Quest for Godliness: The Puritan Vision of the Christian Life* (Wheaton: Crossway Books, 1990) = *Among God's Giants* (Eastbourne: Kingsway, 1990).

CHAPTER 4

The Spirit with the Word: The Reformational Revivalism of George Whitefield

I

If you ask an English Christian today who was the central figure of the mid-eighteenth-century revival, he or she will probably name John Wesley, the ex-Oxford don who for half a century led the network of societies which after his death became the Methodist Church, and whose Journal remains a classic of inspirational literature.[1] If you ask a modern American Christian to identify the central figure in New England's Great Awakening (1739–42), he or she is likely to point to Jonathan Edwards, still, perhaps, America's greatest theologian, whose *Narrative of a Surprising Work of God in the Conversion of Many Hundred Souls in Northampton and the Neighbouring Towns and Villages* (1735) became the model for all subsequent revival histories, and whose theology of the matter, set out in a series of masterful treatises published after the Awakening had subsided,[2] has commanded virtually unanimous evangelical assent from that day to this. But if these two questions had been put in Edwards's and Wesley's own lifetime to anyone with the least knowledge of either movement, it is as certain as anything can be that the same name would have been given in reply to both, and it would not have been either of theirs; it would have been the name of George Whitefield, the 'Grand Itinerant,' whose preaching sparked off and sustained revival religion of the Puritan type—reflective, assured, joyful, powerful, life-transforming—in tens of thousands of lives on both sides of the Atlantic for more than thirty years, from the time of his ordination in 1736 to his death in 1770.

Preaching the grace of God in Christ was Whitefield's life, both metaphorically and literally. He kept a record of over eighteen thousand formal preaching occasions, and if the informal 'exhorting' (his term) which he regularly did in private homes be added in it is probably true to say that he preached twice that number of times. Three stated sermons a day was common; four was not unknown; and the 'exhorting' was done on top of that. 'Who would think it possible,' wrote Henry Venn, vicar of Huddersfield, who knew Whitefield well, that a person . . . should speak in the compass of a single week (and that for years) in general forty hours, and in very many, sixty, and that to thousands; and after this labour, instead of taking any rest, should be offering up prayers and intercessions, with hymns and spiritual songs, as his manner was, in every house to which he was invited.[3]

Whitefield squandered himself unstintingly, and it is no wonder that in 1765, when he [Whitefield] was fifty-one, John Wesley, eleven years his senior, should have noted after a breakfast meeting with him: 'Mr. Whitefield . . . seemed to be an old, old man, being fairly worn out in his Master's service.'[4] The wonder is, rather, that Whitefield was able to maintain his non-stop preaching routine for nearly five more years, constantly testifying that the preaching which exhausted his body energized his heart.

To the last, a visit from Whitefield to any location was a major event, and he drew much larger crowds on his tours than did any other revival spokesman. Often over ten thousand, sometimes more than twenty thousand, attended his open-air orations, and all heard his huge voice distinctly, even in the two-hour message he gave at Exeter, New Hampshire, the afternoon before the cardiac asthma attack that ended his life. It has been estimated that during his ministry he preached to combined audiences of over ten million, and that four-fifths of America's colonists, from Georgia to New Hampshire, heard him at least once— something that could be said of no other person. About eight years of his life were spent in America, where he died in the middle of his seventh tour; otherwise, apart from two months in Bermuda in 1748, the British Isles were his stamping-ground, and he criss-crossed them again and again as a messenger of the gospel of Christ. Cried John Wesley in his memorial sermon for Whitefield, which he preached in both the London centres (Moorfields Tabernacle and Tottenham Court Chapel) that had been put up as stations for Whitefield's ministry:

Have we read or heard of any person since the Apostles, who testified the gospel of the grace of God . . . through so large a part of the habitable world? Have we read or heard of any person who called so many thousands, so many myriads, of sinners to repentance? Above all, have we read or heard of any who has been a blessed instrument in his [God's] hand of bringing so many sinners from 'darkness to light, and from the power of Satan unto God'?[5]

The expected answer, of course, was no; and the same answer would have had to be given through the next two centuries, right up to the glory days of electronically boosted Billy Graham.

In Whitefield's own lifetime he had celebrity status as a preaching phenomenon, and was recognized as the pioneer of all the distinctives that marked the revival in Britain: use of the name 'Methodist';[6] evangelistic preaching in the open air as well as in churches, and on planned tours as well as in response to direct invitations; forming local Methodist societies and lining up lay circuit riders to provide them with regular evangelical instruction and exhortation;[7] publishing news of the ongoing revival in a weekly paper;[8] and printing his journals, a personal record of his life and ministry, as he did between 1737 and 1741. It is usual to credit Wesley with these procedural innovations, but in fact at each point Wesley did no more than follow the younger man's example.[9] Today, however, Whitefield's pastoral pioneering, like so much else about him, is largely forgotten; which is, to say the least, an injustice and a pity.

When I became a Christian in 1944, Whitefield's role in the evangelical life of his day was unknown to those who nurtured me. But I knew his name, for I had attended his old school, the Crypt School, Gloucester,[10] and had seen him represented in a school pageant (not very accurately, as I later learned) hammering sabbath-breakers. Three months after my conversion, lying in bed with bronchitis, I read both volumes of Luke Tyerman's 1876 biography, and the career of the great Gloucestrian made a tremendous impression on me, securing him pride of place in my private heroes' gallery. I subsequently found that Whitefield had made a similar impact on C. H. Spurgeon, the nineteenth-century's greatest pastoral evangelist,[11] and on Martyn Lloyd-Jones, Spurgeon's nearest twentieth-century counterpart.[12] Interest in Whitefield has grown in recent years, as witness the publishing of the first collected edition of his journals,[13] the facsimile reprint of his letters up to 1742 from the edition of 1771,[14] the big and painstaking 'filiopietistic' life of Whitefield by Arnold Dallimore, *George Whitefield: The Life and Times of the Great Evangelist of the Eighteenth-Century Revival*,[15] John Pollock's vivid and racy *George Whitefield and the Great Awakening*,[16] and Harry S. Stout's not-so-filiopietistic but shrewd biography, *The Divine Dramatist: George Whitefield and the Rise of Modern Evangelicalism*,[17] plus most recently the spring 1993 number of the widely circulated journal of popular scholarship, *Christian History*.[18] Perhaps the recognition of greatness and significance that is Whitefield's due is coming to him at last. In any case, however, I am confident that my honoured friend James Atkinson, who is himself as much a preacher of the gospel as he is a historical scholar and theologian, will have some interest in the attempt of this essay to determine Whitefield's place in the Reformation succession for which he cares so deeply.

II

With his Oxford education, natural ease of manner, and slight West-country twang, which made him seem attractively human (his resonant speech was always somewhat nasal, and he pronounced 'Christ' as 'Chroist' all his life), Whitefield, having been ordained at twenty-one in 1736, shot quickly into prominence as a Bible-preaching pastoral evangelist on the grand scale. At a time when other Anglican clergy were writing and reading flat sermons of a mildly moralistic and apologetic sort, Whitefield preached extempore about heaven and hell, sin and salvation, the dying love of Christ, and the new birth, clothing his simple expository outlines with glowing dramatic conscience-challenging rhetoric, and reinforcing his vocal alternations of soothing and punching with a great deal of body movement and gesture, thereby adding much energy to the things he was saying. At a time when other Anglican clergy were watching their churches empty, Whitefield went out to preach in the open air, loved the experience, and saw vast crowds gather to hear him and many come to faith through his messages. To put his extraordinary ministry in perspective, we need to note that he was, first, a born orator; secondly, a natural actor; thirdly, an English Protestant pietist; fourthly, an Anglican Calvinist of the older Puritan type; fifthly, a disciplined, somewhat ascetic clergyman of inflexible single-mindedness and integrity, childlike in humility and passionately devoted to his Lord; sixthly, a transparently friendly, forthcoming, care-giving man, as far from standoffishness as could be, to whose spontaneous goodwill was added the evangelist's gift of making all the members of the crowd feel they were being addressed personally in what he said;[19] and seventhly, a Christian of catholic and ecumenical spirit whose vision of continuous revival throughout the English-speaking world led him to renounce all forms of institutional leadership and control so that he might be entirely at the service of all. Each of these points calls for separate comment.

First, on Whitefield as an orator, the most insightful remarks come from a transcribed address by one who was himself a notable pulpit orator, and thus knew what he was talking about, Martyn Lloyd-Jones. I quote him at some length.

> A man is born an orator. You cannot make orators. You are either an orator or you are not. And this man was a born orator. He could not help it . . . and like all orators, he was characterized by the great freedom and appropriateness of his gestures. The pedantic John Wesley was not an orator, and he sometimes tended to be a bit critical of George Whitefield in this respect. I remember reading in Wesley's journal of how once they both happened to be in Dublin at the same time and how John Wesley went to listen to Whitefield. In his account of the service, Wesley refers to his gestures, and says that it seemed to him that Whitefield was a little bit too much like a Frenchman in a box. He means that Whitefield tended to speak with his hands as much as with his lips and mouth. But that is oratory. One of the greatest orators of all time was Demosthenes. Somebody asked Demosthenes one day, 'What is the first great rule of oratory?' And Demosthenes answered, 'The first great rule of oratory is—action; and the second great rule of oratory is—action; and the third great rule of oratory is—action' . . . We are living in evil days; we know nothing about oratory. George Whitefield was a born orator. Have you heard what David Garrick is reported to have said? David Garrick was the leading actor in London in those times and whenever he had an opportunity he always went to listen to Whitefield. He was not so much interested in the gospel as in the speaking and the gestures . . . Garrick is reported to have said that he would give a hundred guineas if he could only say 'Oh!' as George Whitefield said it.[20]

Second, Whitefield was an actor—'a born actor,' in Lloyd-Jones's phrase[21]—who, as his contemporaries sometimes observed, might have been equal or superior to Garrick had he gone on the stage. As a boy, he had excelled in school theatricals, where evidently he had mastered the actor's two arts, expression and projection. Stout underlines the significance of this actor's training. Acting manuals of Whitefield's day, he tells us, pinpointed

> ten dramatic passions to which appropriate actions and facial expressions were attached: joy, grief, fear, anger, pity, scorn, hatred, jealousy, wonder, and love. With these ten tools the actor could play any part, for they encompassed the sum and substance of the human condition. Of Whitefield's great contemporary David Garrick it was said that he could entertain guests by 'throwing his features into the representation of Love, Hatred, Terror, Pity, Jealousy, Desire and Joy in so rapid and striking a manner [as to] astound the whole country.' In place of thinking man the manuals substituted impassioned man.[22]

All this Whitefield absorbed in his youth, and as a result his public style was that of 'an actor-preacher, as opposed to a scholar-preacher.'[23]

As a born actor, now trained to wear his heart on his face and to pour it into his voice, Whitefield's instinct was for performance.[24] He lived to evangelize and nurture, and 'his private life shrank into a small and relatively insignificant interlude between the big performances.'[25] Stout, with others, speaks of Whitefield's 'shameless' self-promotion,[26] but the adjective does not fit ('uninhibited' might do): no pride, self-aggrandizement or exploitation of others entered into what he did at any stage of his career to publicize his preaching of the gospel. As God's anointed barnstormer, he simply advertised coining performances, looking to God to cause each congregation to pull out of him fresh dramatic creativity in communicating the material he knew so well. It is in these terms that we should understand his statement, in a letter of 1750: 'The more we do, the more we may do; every act strengthens the habit; the best preparation for preaching on Sunday is to preach every day of the week.'[27] We need to remember that for an actor every performance is, among other things, a rehearsal for the next one.

Third, Whitefield was a pietist, that is, one who saw practical personal devotion to the Father and the Son through the Spirit as always the Christian's top priority. Mark Noll types pietism in terms of

> (1) its experiential character—pietists are people of the heart for whom Christian living is the fundamental concern; (2) its biblical focus—pietists . . . take standards and goals from the pages of Scripture; (3) its perfectionist bent—pietists are serious about holy living and expend every effort to follow God's law, spread the gospel, and provide aid for the needy; (4) its reforming interest—pietists usually oppose what they regard as coldness and sterility in established church forms and practices.[28]

The pietism of Whitefield's day grew out of the devotional revival that broke surface in both Protestantism and Roman Catholicism in the seventeenth century, partly as a reaction against the hard-shell controversialist, imperialist, and formalist mind-sets that the Reformation conflicts had left behind, partly as a renewed perception of biblical Christianity in its own terms. In Protestant England, this seventeenth-century movement was channelled mainly through Puritanism, where justification by faith and regeneration and assurance through the Holy Spirit were set in a clear and classic Augustinian frame of sovereign grace. The High Church devotional development, fed more by the Greek Fathers, was at first less influential, just as it was doctrinally less clear. But it was High Church pietists who developed the religious societies (midweek gatherings for devotional exercises) in Restoration times, and it was as a participant in one of these, John Wesley's 'Holy Club,' whose members were called 'Methodists' because of their methodical rule of life, that Whitefield first realized his need of the characteristic pietist experience, namely, the new birth.

Through a long and painful conversion process Whitefield finally found the new birth that he sought—assurance of sins forgiven and Christ's love set upon him, newness of heart, and an overflow of joy in God. One of his first acts then was to buy and devour Matthew Henry's commentary, a brilliant pietistic exposition of Scripture that draws on a century of Puritan theology, Bible study, and homiletics. This classic became his lifelong companion,[29] and, reinforced by subsequent association with America's latter-day Puritans, Jonathan Edwards and the Tennents, it established his pietism in the Puritan mould. Thereafter all the marks of pietism as Noll profiles it—devotional ardour, Bible-centredness, holiness with evangelism and philanthropy, hostility to cold and formal religion—became marks of Whitefield's life and ministry. His printed sermons and pastoral letters, the latter numbering over 1,400, show that he concentrated throughout his ministry on the basics of personal religion—new birth, faith, repentance, righteousness and good works, praise of God and love to Christ. No breath of scandal ever touched his personal life; the lures of sex, shekels and empire building never enmeshed him. The pietism of his outlook was given credibility by the piety of his life.

Fourth, he was an Anglican Calvinist of the Puritan type. He embraced the sovereign-grace teaching of the Thirty-nine Articles with regard to personal salvation (see especially Articles 9–13 and 17), affirmed the developed federal theology of the seventeenth century, and insisted that sovereign-grace teaching, with its rejection of salvation by self-effort in all its forms, bears directly on the purity or otherwise of the believer's devotion. Two extracts from his letters show this.

This ... is my comfort, 'Jesus Christ, the same yesterday, today, and for ever.' He saw me from all eternity; He gave me being; He called me in time; He has freely justified me through faith in His blood; He has in part sanctified me by His Spirit; He will preserve me underneath His everlasting arms till time shall be no more. Oh the blessedness of these evangelical truths! These are indeed Gospel; they are glad tidings of great joy to all that have ears to hear. These bring the creature out of himself. These make him hang upon the promise, and cause his obedience to flow from a principle of love.

The doctrines of our election, and free justification in Christ Jesus are daily more and more pressed upon my heart. They fill my soul with a holy fire and afford me great confidence in God my Saviour.[30]

Whitefield constantly maintained these doctrines and the spirituality of dependent gratitude that flowed from them, declaring: 'I embrace the Calvinistic scheme, not because Calvin, but Jesus Christ has taught it to me,'[31] and insisting that Anglicanism's historic formularies and best theologians were on his side at this point.

Whitefield's identification with the Puritan type of theology, both in and outside the Church of England, is apparent from his 'Recommendatory Preface' to the 1767 reprint of the works of the Baptist John Bunyan, which contained the following sentences:

Ministers never write or preach so well as when under the cross: the spirit of CHRIST and of glory then rests upon them.

It was this, no doubt, that made the Puritans of the last century such burning and shining lights. When cast out by the black *Bartholomew-act* [the 1662 Act of Uniformity, which triggered 2000 ejections from the ministry of the Church of England] . . . they in an especial manner preached and wrote as men having authority. Though dead, by their writings they yet speak: a peculiar unction attends them to this very hour; and for these thirty years past I have remarked, that the more true and vital religion hath revived either at home or abroad, the more the good old puritanical writings, or the authors of a like stamp who lived and died in the communion of the church *of England,* have been called for.[32]

When in 1829 selections from Whitefield's works were published under the title *The Revived Puritan,* the phrase was uncannily apt.[33] That, precisely, is what Whitefield was.

Fifth and *sixth,* Whitefield displayed qualities of Christian character that added credibility to his public ministrations. He was no hypocrite, nor did those closest to him find great flaws and weaknesses in him. They found him, rather, to be a person of real genuineness, integrity, humility, poise and charm, affable and courteous in all company, with a genius for friendships, great practical wisdom, simple tastes, and much joy in living for God. To illustrate this properly would require virtually a retelling of his life story, which is not possible here,[34] but a few facts may be mentioned.

In 1738 Whitefield committed himself to fund Bethesda, Georgia's orphan house which he himself had founded. He carried this responsibility for the rest of his life, and nearly ruined himself in the process of discharging it.

In 1739 he and Benjamin Franklin became friends, though neither then nor thereafter did Franklin embrace his message of salvation from sin through new birth. But Franklin wrote of him in 1747: 'He is a good man and I love him,'[35] and after his death: 'I knew him intimately upwards of 30 years. His Integrity, Disinterestedness and indefatigable Zeal in prosecuting every good Work, I have never seen equalled, I shall never see excelled.'[36]

In 1739 Whitefield also became friends with Howell Harris, the dynamic Welsh exhorter, and the friendship was lifelong, despite a period during which Harris's behavioural aberrations strained it to its limit.[37] In 1743 Whitefield was chosen as moderator for life of the Calvinistic Methodist Association of Wales, a body founded to regulate the evangelical religious societies that Harris and others had formed throughout the country, and Harris's praise for Whitefield's handling of his role was unstinting.[38]

In 1748, aged thirty-three, having reviewed the journals he published[39] at twenty-three, he wrote in a letter:

> Alas! alas! In how many things have I judged and acted wrong . . . I frequently wrote and spoke in my own spirit, when I thought I was writing and speaking by the assistance of the Spirit of God . . . I have likewise too much made inward impressions my rule of acting, and too soon and too explicitly published what had been better kept in longer, or told after my death. By these things I have given some wrong touches to God's ark, and hurt the blessed cause I would defend, and also stirred up needless opposition. This has humbled me much . . . bless him [God] for ripening my judgment a little more, for giving me to see and confess, and I hope in some degree to correct and amend, some of my mistakes.[40]

Whitefield in maturity was able to see and eliminate the imprudences of his youthful zeal: they did not recur during the last twenty-two years of his life.

Finally, Whitefield distinguished himself as 'the peace-maker' (John Fletcher's description)[41] between John Wesley and himself, bending over backwards to heal the breach after Wesley and he had diverged in print over the meaning of predestination and 'free grace' (1740–41). Wesley's imperious single-mindedness and donnish didacticism, plus his eleven-year seniority to Whitefield and his fixed habit of treating Whitefield as his pupil and protégé, as he does most unbeautifully throughout his printed journals, made him a difficult man for Whitefield to get back on terms with; but he managed it, at the cost of renouncing all his leadership roles in England and Wales in 1748 and operating thereafter from time to time as one of Wesley's assistants.[42] It was a triumph of humility on the part of the public celebrity who at the close of his life was signing his letters 'Less than the least of all, George Whitefield.'[43]

The *seventh* key fact about Whitefield, his passion for Christian unity as part of his vision of sustained spiritual vitality undergirding and transforming community life both sides of the Atlantic, is sufficiently illustrated by the foregoing paragraph, and need not be further displayed here.

III

We learn Whitefield's theology from his tracts and letters, and also from his seventy-five printed sermons.[44] These vary in style and provenance. They are all based on biblical texts, expounded, however sketchily, in context, but forty-six of them were printed before Whitefield was twenty-five, and some were written out after being preached rather than before, and some were transcribed *viva voce* from Whitefield's lips as he orated and put in print sometimes with and sometimes without his approval. Such material needs to be handled with care, but theologically it is all homogeneous, and in no way innovative. We have already noted that, like all England's evangelical clergy then and since, Whitefield insisted that the religion he modelled and taught was a straightforward application of Anglican doctrine as defined in the Articles, the Homilies and the Prayer Book. We have seen that he took his interpretations of Scripture mainly if not entirely from the 'unparalleled,' 'incomparable'[45] Matthew Henry. His developed understanding of justification by faith only through the imputed righteousness of Christ, and of the federal plan of salvation that five-point Calvinism spells out, came to him from Puritan and Scottish sources.[46] But the things he took from the Reformed tradition came out in his own way, cast into meditations and messages that called for present response, and that located every such response, or refusal of it, as part of the drama which the Puritans had already mapped with great skill, namely the personal drama of the soul's ongoing journey to heaven or to hell. 'Dramatize! Dramatize!' urged Henry James; plots and characters of novels should be full of 'felt life.' Whitefield's instinct for drama led him to preach sermon after sermon that dramatized the issues of eternity, and summoned his hearers to seek, in his phrase, a 'felt Christ.' We can sum up the substance of Whitefield's sermons in a series of imperatives, as follows.

First, Face God. People live thoughtlessly, drifting through their days, never thinking of eternity. But God the Creator, our lawgiver and holy judge, who made us for himself and holds us in his hands every moment has revealed in Scripture that a day of judgement is coming when he will either welcome us into heaven's eternal joy or banish us for ever to hell's misery. So—*wake up! and reckon, here and now, with God!* Whitefield repeatedly shed tears of agonized compassion as he preached about the ruinous, suicidal, self-hating folly of those who would not do this.

Secondly, Know Yourself. We mortals all see in ourselves, and in our children, and in all our fellow-humans, self-centred, self-pleasing, worldly minded, really vicious dispositions. These bespeak the universal corruption of nature called original sin. G. K. Chesterton called original sin the one Christian doctrine that admits of demonstrative proof, and that was how Whitefield presented it. From Genesis 3 and Romans 5 he analysed it in the standard Reformed way: the sin of Adam, our progenitor and covenant head, was imputed to us, his posterity, in the

sense that we all now share the penal deprivations that his sin incurred for himself
bodily decay and mortality, plus a morally twisted disposition that makes faith,
love, and obedience Godward a natural impossibility, just as it flaws all the godliness of those whose hearts God supernaturally renews. The doctrine of original
sin thus answers the question. Why am I no better than I am? It does not excuse
us by letting us shift the blame for our perversities onto Adam; it just confirms to
us that we are all naturally lost, spiritually impotent and helpless, without hope of
commending ourselves to God by anything we do. This is the bad news that we
must accept and internalize before we can appreciate the good news of salvation.

Thirdly, See Jesus. Whitefield's preaching, like his personal faith, centred upon
the person of 'the dear Jesus,' the once-crucified, now glorified God-man, the
gift of the Father's love and the embodiment of divine mercy. From Scripture
Whitefield would set forth with rhapsodic rhetoric and arms-lifted, foot-stamping
passion the incarnation, Jesus' friendship with sinners, his pity for the needy, his
agonizing death for our sins, his bodily resurrection and ascension, his present
heavenly reign and coming return to judgement, and then he would go to town,
as we would say, on the invitations to faith, promises of justification, preservation
and glorification, and guarantees of his own fidelity that comprise Jesus' present
word to the world. It was said of Charles Finney that in his evangelistic preaching
he rode sinners down with a cavalry charge; Whitefield's way, however, was to
sweep them off their feet with an overflow of compassionate affection, model-
ling his Master's goodwill towards the lost. Thus by word and action Whitefield
enabled his hearers mentally and spiritually to see Jesus, with constantly over-
whelming effect.

Fourthly, Understand Justification. Following the Restoration many Anglican
minds, recoiling from all things Calvinistic, took up with a moralistic, indeed
legalistic, recasting of justification by faith. Faith ceased to be thought of as self-
despairing trust in the person, work, promises, and love of Jesus Christ the Mediator, and became, in the words of the influential Bishop Bull, 'virtually the whole
of evangelical obedience'—in other words, a moral life of good works lived in
hope of acceptance for it at the last day, despite its actual shortcomings. The
significance of the cross in the process of salvation was that, in Jeremy Taylor's
grotesque phrase, Christ has 'brought down the market'—that is, made it possible
to secure final salvation through a devotion that is far from flawless. The bottom-
line effect of Christ's death was thus to rehabilitate self-righteousness. Works are
the way to heaven, after all.[47]

This was in essence the theology of John Wesley during his Holy Club period,
as it was of conventional Anglicanism all through Whitefield's life. It produced a
religion of aspiration, perspiration, and, in sensitive souls, periodic desperation.
Whitefield came to see it as blasphemous impiety, the religion of the natural man
masquerading as Christianity, and he laboured constantly to wean people away
from it. So he denounced self-righteousness, insisted that nothing we do is free

from sin, and called on his hearers to come to Christ as guilty, helpless, hell-deserving offenders, and find righteousness and life in him.

Put your trust in Jesus Christ, said Whitefield, over and over again, and present justification (pardon and acceptance, both lasting for ever) will be yours—not because of what you are or have done, but because Christ's righteousness wrought out by his active and passive obedience, his law-keeping and sin-bearing, is now imputed to you. The Holy Spirit will help you to believe if you are willing to believe and show your willingness by asking to be helped to do so, and the Spirit will witness to your justification and God's fatherly love for you once a true change of heart has taken place. Keep seeking through prayer to turn fully to Christ till you know you have been enabled to do just that, so that the gift of righteousness is now yours, and then you will worship and obey your God and Saviour out of unending gratitude for being saved.

I quote at length the peroration of one of Whitefield's sermons, to give the flavour of this:

> Are any of you depending upon a righteousness of your own? Do any of you here think to save yourselves by your own doings? I say to you . . . your righteousness shall perish with you. Poor miserable creatures! What is there in your tears? What in your prayers? What in your performances, to appease the wrath of an angry God? Away from the trees of the garden; come, ye guilty wretches, come as poor, lost, undone, and wretched creatures, and accept of a better righteousness than your own. As I said before, so I tell you again, the righteousness of Jesus Christ is an everlasting righteousness; it is wrought out for the very chief of sinners. Ho, every one that thirsteth, let him come and drink of this water of life freely. Are any of you wounded by sin? Do any of you feel you have no righteousness of your own? Are any of you perishing for hunger? Are any of you afraid you will perish for ever? Come, dear souls, in all your rags; come, thou poor man; come, thou poor distressed woman; you, who think God will never forgive you, and that your sins are too great to be forgiven; come, thou doubting creature, who art afraid thou wilt never get comfort; arise, take comfort, the Lord Jesus Christ, the Lord of life, the Lord of glory, calls for thee . . . O let not one poor soul stand at a distance from the Saviour . . . O come, come! Now, since it is brought into the world by Christ, so, in the name, in the strength, and by the assistance of the great God, I bring it now to the pulpit; I now offer this righteousness, this free, this imputed, this everlasting righteousness, to all poor sinners who will accept of it . . . Think, I pray you, therefore, on these things; go home, go home, go home, pray over the text, and say, 'Lord God, thou hast brought an everlasting righteousness into the world by the Lord Jesus Christ; by the blessed Spirit bring it into my heart!' then, die when ye will, ye are safe; if it be tomorrow, ye shall be immediately translated into the presence of the everlasting God; that will be sweet! Happy they who have got this robe on; happy they that can say, 'My God hath loved me, and I shall be loved by him with an everlasting love!' That every one of you may be able to say so, may God grant, for the sake of Jesus Christ, the dear Redeemer; to whom be glory for ever . . . Amen.[48]

Fifthly, Welcome the Spirit. When Whitefield burst on the Anglican scene, very little was being said about the Holy Spirit, and it was commonly affirmed that the Spirit's activity in Christians' lives was something of which they would not be conscious. At the cost of being accused over and over of 'enthusiasm' (meaning, the fanaticism that thinks it receives direct revelations from God), Whitefield ridiculed this idea, and insisted that the Holy Spirit's presence in human lives would always be consciously felt, because of the change in experience that the Spirit would bring about. This change, which the Bible calls regeneration, new birth, new creation, sanctification, transition from death to life, and Christ being formed in us, and which expresses itself in a sense of one's sin, leading to self-despair, leading one out of oneself to look to Christ and trust him alone for salvation, as was described above, is wrought only by the Holy Spirit; therefore we should desire, seek, and be ready for the Spirit's ministry in our lives, bringing about and continually deepening the change itself. In a sermon on conversion, Whitefield expounds the matter as follows:

> They that are truly converted to Jesus, and are justified by faith in the Son of God, will take care to evidence their conversion, not only by the having grace implanted in their hearts, but by that grace diffusing itself through every faculty of the soul, and making a universal change in the whole man . . . The author of this conversion is the Holy Ghost . . . nothing short of the influence of the Spirit of the living God can effect this change in our hearts . . . and though there is and will be a contest between these two opposites, flesh and spirit, yet if we are truly converted, the spirit will get the ascendency . . . God grant we may all thus prove that we are converted. This conversion, however it begins at home, will soon walk abroad; as the Virgin Mary was soon found out to be with child, so it will be soon found out whether Christ is formed in the heart. There will be new principles, new ways, new company, new works; there will be a thorough change in the heart and life . . . first we are in bondage, afterwards we receive the Spirit of adoption to long and thirst for God, because he has been pleased to let us know that he will take us to heaven. Conversion means a being turned from hell to heaven . . . the heart once touched with the magnet of divine love, ever after turns to the pole . . .
>
> What say you to this change, my dear souls? Is it not godlike, is it not divine, is it not heaven brought down to the soul? Have you felt it, have you experienced it?[49]

It will be observed that this teaching on conversion has an essentially Augustinian structure: God in grace gives us the faith and love that he requires of us. John Wesley focused on this Augustinianism, with which he claimed to identify, when he declared, in his memorial sermon for Whitefield:

> His fundamental point was, 'Give God all the glory of whatever is good in man'; and, 'In the business of salvation, set Christ as high and man as low as possible.' With this point he and his friends at Oxford, the original Methodists, so called, set out. Their grand principle was: There is *no power* (by nature) and *no merit* in man. They insisted, all power to think, speak, or act aright, is in and from the Spirit of Christ.[50]

Working with this perspective. Whitefield followed the Puritans in presenting the conversion process in a two-sided way, as Augustinians typically do. When speaking psychologically and evangelistically, he depicted the realizing of one's sin and need, the praying and seeking to which this must lead, and the decision-making that faith and repentance involve, as a person's own acts, which we must ask for the Holy Spirit's help to perform. When speaking theologically and doxologically, however, he interpreted the entire process as one which the Holy Spirit works from first to last, in which each of our steps Godward is taken only because the Holy Spirit is moving us forward by his secret action within us. God's irresistible prevenient grace (meaning, the Holy Spirit's work that dissolves resistance away) overcomes our natural inability, as slaves of sin, to turn ourselves to God: that is how we come to be born again and converted.

This, then, was the theological frame within which Whitefield admonished: 'See that you receive the Holy Ghost, before you go hence [i.e., die]: for otherwise, how can you escape the damnation of hell?'[51] Without the Holy Spirit there is no transformation through new birth: without this there is no salvation for anyone, and, though God has his own sovereign ways of breaking into people's lives, only those who seek the Spirit's influence, and open themselves deliberately to it can expect to undergo it in a converting way.

The key principles of Whitefield's gospel message are now before us. On these themes his printed sermons ring endless changes, with remarkable rhetorical freshness and pungency, the impact of which, so we are told, was much intensified by his pulpit manner. 'The Lord gave him a manner of preaching, which was peculiarly his own,' wrote John Newton.

> His familiar address, the power of his action, his marvellous talent in fixing the attention even of the most careless, I need not describe to those who have heard him, and to those who have not, the attempt would be in vain. Other ministers could, perhaps, preach the Gospel as clearly, and in general say the same things, but . . . no man living could say them in his way.[52]

All the evidence suggests that this was fair comment. Unmatched in his day for applying Reformed teaching about conversion and the converted life to the conscience, Whitefield was entirely free of doctrinal novelties. All he ever preached about, or desired to preach about, was personal salvation and godliness, and for that Puritan orthodoxy served him supremely well.

IV

Revivals—that is, animatings and deepenings of the awareness of God, of the sense of sin, of the knowledge of Christ, and of the evangelical responses of faith, repentance, righteousness, prayer, and praise—have from time to time

characterized the inner life of Protestant communities ever since the Reformation.[53] The revival pattern of fresh outpourings of the Holy Spirit to reverse spiritual decline has recurred many times. The human lightning-rods through whose
ministrations the power of God strikes in revival are naturally called revivalists,
and the ministrations themselves are denominated revivalism. The tide of this
essay speaks of Whitefield's 'Reformational Revivalism.' We are now in a position
to scrutinize this phrase, to justify the description, and to form an opinion about
Whitefield's place in the history of Christian springtimes down the centuries.

But was Whitefield a revivalist? Here a distinction must be drawn, for the
word 'revivalist' has a contemporary meaning that both dilutes the significance
that it has when applied to Whitefield and distracts the attention from what
Whitefield was actually doing—or perhaps we should say, was being used to
do. Revivalism nowadays is a name for an American institutional development
among conservative churches that directly reflects the populism, love of novelty
and entertainment, fascination with technique, and consumerist orientation that
have characterized America during the past two centuries. In terms of spiritual
significance, this kind of revivalism has lost most of its links with revivals in the
sense that Jonathan Edwards and George Whitefield and the Wesley brothers
gave to that word. Revivalism in modern America means mounting what Charles
Finney called 'protracted meetings,' that is, a linked series of gatherings with a
centrally evangelistic purpose, at which, in addition to forceful preaching that
calls for decision and action, there is a programmed back-up of music (solos,
choir items, and congregational songs, often with some twist of novelty), plus testimonies with an arresting human interest, plus ordinarily a modicum of hayseed
humour from the emcee and the preacher, so that the entertainment dimension
remains strong throughout. The purpose of the meetings is to renew Christian
vision and commitment, and in particular to bring about on-the-spot entries into
the reality of the new birth. By confronting people with one or two larger-than-
life celebrities to admire and enjoy, and by grafting onto the vestigial remains of
a church service something comparable to variety entertainment, these meetings
are designed to stir up, warm up, and open up the audience in the early stages so
that they will be readier for decisive commitments later on. Such is modern revivalism, and today's revivalists are those who regularly minister within this kind
of framework, whether in churches and meeting halls or on radio and television.
Professor Stout sees Whitefield as their distant but direct progenitor, and so tends
to describe Whitefield's ministry in a way that assimilates it to the modern development. But the differences between what Whitefield did and what revivalists
nowadays do are at least as important as the similarities, and we shall misconceive
Whitefield if we do not see this.

There is a watershed dividing the propagation of Christianity by Whitefield
and his peers in the eighteenth-century awakening from the revivalism that has
just been described. This parting of the ways is not always well plotted on our

theological graphs. It does not concern the substance of our presentation of Jesus Christ as Saviour of sinners; nor does it relate to how we emphasize the importance of feeling and facing our need of him; nor does it touch the pietistic presupposition that our relationship with God is the most important issue for everyone; nor does it occur over the priority or otherwise of evangelism, for Whitefield went on record saying: 'God lets me see more and more, that I must evangelize';[54] nor does it have anything to do with the personal styles of different evangelists (Whitefield the dramatic actor, Wesley the paternalist martinet, Finney the prosecuting attorney, Billy Graham the giant-size man in the street, and so on). On all these matters the two sorts of revivalism see eye to eye at the level of principle, and are in full harmony with each other. The cleavage is over a single question: whether we approve of Whitefield and the other eighteenth-century leaders sending people away from the preaching to pray for a change of heart through new birth, and to keep praying and using the means of grace till they know they have been given what they sought, or whether with Finney and most moderns we opt for the so-called 'invitation method', 'drawing in the net' by calling for an immediate full-scale cognitive and volitional commitment to Christ in faith and repentance. The assumption that immediate conversion is within everyone's present power has far-reaching implications (it is semi-Pelagian at least, perhaps Pelagian), and the effect of making it is inevitably manipulative, for it turns the applicatory part of the sermon into a tussle of wills between preacher and people and radically obscures the sovereignty of the Holy Spirit in the bestowing of spiritual life.[55]

I spoke of Whitefield's revivalism as 'Reformational' to make clear that on this issue he was in solidarity with more than two centuries of Reformed thought—not to mention Luther's theology as it was before Lutherans adjusted it[56]—and that he could not have countenanced the pragmatic anthropocentrism sponsored by Finney. Finney and his modern revivalist followers require people to find God; Whitefield, and those who have stood in the Whitefieldian succession, as did Spurgeon and Lloyd-Jones, required them to seek God. There is a difference.

Was Whitefield, then, in full accord with the Reformation and Puritan heritage to which he laid claim? In broad terms, the answer is yes; but on the surface, some differences appear.

We must certainly grant that no one with an itinerant ministry on Whitefield's pattern, and no one with comparable powers of rhetoric and projection, had ornamented British Christianity during the previous two centuries. Reformers like John Bradford, and Puritans like Richard Baxter and John Bunyan, excelled in evangelistic applications of gospel truth, but none of them could hold a candle to the torrential outpourings of compassionate persuasion that flowed from Whitefield's lips and heart every time he preached.

We must grant too that only in a culture where interest in playwriting, playgoing, and playacting had blossomed, as it did in England in the early eighteenth century, could a sanctified barnstormer like Whitefield emerge. Whitefield, like the Puritans before him, opposed actual theatres as centres of vice,[57] but whereas the Puritans had been negative about acting too, with a negativism ranging from mild to furious, Whitefield, as we have seen, was deploying his actor's expertise in the pulpit all the time, and his dramatic way of conceiving life and its relationships, including the Christian's faith-relationship with 'the dear Jesus,' went beyond anything that had been known in earlier times.

And finally, we should grant that by his regular preaching outside churchly contexts Whitefield, though himself an Anglican clergyman who took his office seriously and who saw himself as serving all the churches all the time, did in fact unwittingly encourage an individualistic piety of what we would call a parachurch type, a piety that gave its prime loyalty to transdenominational endeavours, that became impatient and restless in face of the relatively fixed forms of institutional church life, and that conceived evangelism as typically an extra-ecclesiastical activity. To foment tension between discipleship and churchmanship was the last thing Whitefield wanted to do, but involuntarily he did it. By contrast, the Puritans on both sides of the Atlantic, and Protestants generally before White-field's time, were consistently churchly in outlook, and were always careful to set personal religion in a communal, ecclesiastical frame. Whitefield's own preach-ing about the fellowship aspect of discipleship seems not to have gone further, however, than to urge faithful participation in the life of the religious societies.[58] Thus in effect, as Mark Noll observes, 'Whitefield helped shift the theological emphasis in preaching. Up to the early 1700s, British Protestants preached on God's plans *for the church*. From the mid-1700s, however, evangelicals empha-sized God's plans *for the individual*.'[59] So it has been among evangelicals ever since.

All these are significant moves beyond, or away from, the Puritan model, and should not be played down.

Basically, however, the assertion that Whitefield's mind and method as a re-vivalist were Reformational still stands. For, in the first place, the doctrinal soli-darity is real and obvious. Whitefield's evangelistic message centred, as we saw, on what was central in the theology of the Reformers and Puritans, namely human fallenness and inability for spiritual good; the sufficiency, glory, and accessibility of Jesus Christ; the law demonstrating the reality of our sin to our consciences, and the gospel promises leading us out of all forms of self-sufficiency and self-reliance to trust Christ alone for salvation; and finally, the sovereignty of the Holy Spirit, and of God through the Holy Spirit, in bringing sinners into newness of life. Regeneration, or new birth, had not been a central focus of thought for the Reformers, but pastoral Puritanism had developed the doctrine to the full dimen-sions that Whitefield's preaching gave it, and here, supremely, solidarity is seen. Then, in the second place, Puritanism in its pastoral aspect was essentially a move-ment of revival, as I have tried to show elsewhere;[60] and Whitefield's ministry was a true ministry of pastoral revival, blessed by God to the quickening of saints and the conversion of sinners in a most outstanding way. The Great Awakening of 1740, the Cambuslang revival of 1742 (the 'Cam'slang Wark,' as Scottish locals called it), the Cheltenham visitation of 1757,[61] and many other exalted episodes that were put on record, bear ample witness to this.

The conclusions to which I believe this survey leads can be stated thus: (1) Whitefield was in essence very much a Reformational revivalist. (2) Though not everything he said and did was totally wise, and though there were weaknesses as well as strengths in his pattern of working, yet his pietistic priorities, according to which being alive to God is what most matters, were magnificently right. (3) The overall quality of his ministry, as he sought to embody the compassion of Christ in pointing and directing lost souls to faith in Christ, was beyond praise. (4) A good dose of Whitefieldian revivalism, should God raise up a preacher capable of imparting it, would do today's churches more good than anything I can imagine. 'I speak to sensible people; judge for yourselves what I say' (1 Cor. 10:15 NIV).

CHAPTER 5

D. Martyn Lloyd-Jones: A Kind of Puritan

'Sometimes he's a kind of a Puritan.' So, for quite wrong reasons, said Shakespeare's Maria of the bad-humoured buffoon Malvolio. So, for better reasons, did many say of David Martyn Lloyd-Jones. The verdict was a true one, but it lies open to misunderstanding.

What does it mean to call a person a Puritan? Maria's view has been common from Shakespeare's day to our own: namely, that Puritanism is a matter essentially of temperament and personal disposition, a habit of taking oneself too seriously and playing the role of a natural-born sourpuss and killjoy. Such was Macaulay's notion when he told the world that the Puritans hated bear-baiting not because it gave pain to the bear but because it gave pleasure to the spectators, and such was Mencken's idea when he defined a Puritan as a person who fears that somewhere, somehow, someone may be happy. A variant of this view, often found among Roman Catholics, sees Manichean convictions as shaping this sourpuss spirit, as witness the following lines:

> The Puritan through life's sweet garden goes
> And plucks the thorn, and throws away the rose;
> He thinks to please, by this peculiar whim,
> The God who framed and fashioned it for him.

The stereotypes are familiar, but the belief that they catch the essence of Puritanism is nonsense.

Would individuals who felt and behaved according to the stereotypes have been found among the Puritans of history—that is, among the Calvinistic Protestants who sought to reshape or replace the Church of England between the 1560s, when the label 'Puritan' was coined, and the 1660s, when the would-be reformers had finally to admit defeat? No doubt there were some such persons among them, just as there have been in similar movements since. Any group of Christians with high moral standards is likely to attract hangers-on of this kind, from whom the unfriendly world is likely then to form its image of the group in question. But it must be said with emphasis that no Puritan teacher ever approved the ethos of censorious gloom or supposed that pleasure excludes piety and vice versa. Rather, with Calvin, the teachers condemned these attitudes, as showing ingratitude to a kind and generous Creator. And here Dr Lloyd-Jones was right with them. Posturing asceticism was to him childish immaturity, if not indeed superstitious folly. In this he was as purely Puritan, in the historically valid sense of that word, as a man could be. The Puritan pastors of history always insisted that healthy piety would ordinarily be cheerful and full of joy. 'There is no mirth like the mirth of believers,' wrote Richard Baxter. Though grimmish-looking in public and never in his prime smiling for the camera, 'the Doctor' was himself a supremely cheerful, affable, humorous man, and the reality of God's gift of joy, both joy in created things and the joy of salvation, was one of the constant emphases of his ministry.

Authentically Puritan traits do not, then, always coincide with what Puritanism is popularly thought to be; sometimes, as in the present case, they contradict the stereotype directly. Of other elements in the stereotype—pharisaism, philistinism, fanaticism, for instance—the same is true. So I had better lay it down at once in black and white that what this essay will explore is not how far Dr Lloyd-Jones fitted the popular stereotype of a Puritan, but how far he matched up to the historical reality. As I shall show, he knew what real historic Puritanism had been and heartily identified with most of it. Granted, he often said that he was more an eighteenth- than a seventeenth-century man; by this he meant that evangelism and revival ministry in the style and with the theology of George Whitefield and Jonathan Edwards was his supreme ideal for the church and his supreme goal for himself. But his references to Puritan writers when preaching, his constant advice to budding and burned-out pastors to read them, his own reading of them (Owen's and Baxter's works were among his wedding presents!), his chairing the annual Puritan and Reformed Studies Conference (later, with changed personnel, the Westminster Conference) from 1950 to 1979, his backing of the Puritan reprint programme of the Banner of Truth Trust, and his support for the ministry of the Evangelical Library, which majors in books by and about the Puritans, all show how he valued the seventeenth-century material. In an address on 'Puritanism and Its Origins' in 1971 he declared that since 1925 'a true and living interest in the Puritans and their works has gripped me, and I am free to confess that my whole ministry has been governed by this.'[1] The dependence was always in fact clear and obvious.

My own first meeting with the Doctor took place when Raymond Johnston and I, both still students, went to his vestry to float before his eyes our vision of an annual Puritan Studies Conference and to seek his help in making it a reality. I was struck at the time by the air of suppressed excitement with which he welcomed the idea, as well as by his extreme forthcomingness: not only would he host us at Westminster Chapel, but he would be permanent chairman, and get the ladies of the church to produce free lunches and teas! Thereafter he treated the two days of the conference as an unbreakable engagement, and when one year I could only be present for one day he was very cross and accused me of getting my priorities wrong! Years down the line, when the conference had grown from the twenty who met in 1950 to two hundred and more, he told me that he had seen the interest that Raymond and I showed in publicizing Puritan standards of faith and devotion as one of a series of signs that God was starting to revive his work in Britain, and therefore he had given it all the backing he could. Certainly, when he and I met in his vestry over tea at each conference to plan the next one he had always given the matter advance thought and was full of suggestions about both themes and speakers. Every one of the many anniversaries that the conference celebrated was his proposal. At no stage did his interest flag, and the historical acumen which his opinions and conference contributions reflected was always of a very high order.

Like the Anglican J. C. Ryle (whom he much admired) and the Catholic Hilaire Belloc (about whom he would have felt differently) he had a flair for bringing history to life at a popular level, and he was in himself living proof that, as Belloc once said, 'history adds to a man, giving him, as it were, a great memory of things—like a human memory, but stretched over a longer space than one human life.' The truth is that, though a formidably independent thinker, the Doctor was emotionally a traditionalist, very conscious of his heritage (Welsh, Free Church, and Reformed), very fascinated by it and very respectful towards it. Within that heritage the Puritans of history held a place of honour, as we now see.

At the conference itself, year by year, his contribution was far more significant than that of anyone else. As chairman of each of the first five two-hour sessions, he would elicit, control, and sum up a discussion lasting up to an hour after the paper had been read. Watching him with his head down as the paper-reader spoke you might have thought him near to sleep, but the discussion showed that he had been very much awake! His remarkable memory enabled him, though he took no notes, to remember with exactness all that the speaker had said, and with the lighting mental energy that always marked him he had weighed its implications and decided what he thought about it before ever the general debate began. The overall agenda was to explore the wealth of the Puritan heritage, plus other elements of Reformed history and historical theology, so as to see what guidance this legacy affords for Christian faith, life, and ministry today. As he himself put it, in his last Westminster Conference address, 'one of the chief reasons for our interest in these 17th-century men . . . is that our world is strangely similar to theirs. I, for one, am interested in them mainly for that reason, that we may learn from them, as they battled with the same problems and difficulties which confront us. That is the main purpose of this conference.'[2]

Most of the conferees were ministers (minus wives: Dr Lloyd-Jones disliked the presence of women at what were to him professional meetings, and made no secret of the fact), and accordingly most of the discussion questions which he posed or, more often, drew from the floor were double-barrelled and ministry-related, thus: was there truth and wisdom in what had been presented? and if so, how should we act on it today? The Doctor's mastery of discussion as a teaching tool has often been remarked on, and his skill in handling these particular discussions, keeping them on the point, bringing out the logic of speakers' suggestions, demanding biblical assessment of and backing for all views expressed, feeding in relevant facts that seemed not to be generally known, and finally pulling out of the air, as it seemed (actually, out of the depths of a well-stocked mind), clarifying and encouraging comments to conclude, was to me at least a source of constant admiration.

Also, from 1959 to 1978 he gave the closing conference address. A partial list of his titles shows the wide range and practical thrust of his historical interests. 'Revival: an historical and theological survey' (1959). 'Puritan Perplexities: some lessons from 1640–1662' (1962). 'John Owen on Schism' (1963). 'John Calvin and George Whitefield' (1964). ' "Ecclesiola in Ecclesia" ' (1965: in a series entitled *Approaches to Reformation of the Church*). 'Henry Jacob and the First Congregational Church' (1966). 'Sandemanianism' (1967). 'William Williams and Welsh Calvinistic Methodism' (1968). 'Can We Learn from [Reformation and Puritan] History?' (1969). 'Puritanism and Its Origins' (1971). 'John Knox—the Founder of Puritanism' (1972). 'Living the Christian Life: new developments in the 18th and 19th century teaching' (1974). 'The French Revolution and After' (1975: in a series entitled *The Christian and the State in Revolutionary Times*). 'Preaching' (1977: in a series entitled *Anglican and Puritan Thinking*). 'John Bunyan: Church Union' (1978). These transcribed addresses, which if reprinted together would make a fascinating book, reveal easy mastery of relevant facts; vivid empathy with historical figures; shrewd discernment of people's motives, purposes, achievements, failures, blind spots, and follies; and great insight in judging how particular events furthered or frustrated the cause of God and truth. Sometimes, to be sure, the deliberately popular, non-technical, simple-man style of presentation borders on the slapdash; sometimes the generalizations are broader and more categorical than the evidence cited can bear; sometimes complex issues are oversimplified. Overall, however, Dr Lloyd-Jones's evident purpose of providing passionate wisdom and vision for spiritual edifying through mental stimulus and challenge was masterfully fulfilled each time, so that the closing address was regularly the high spot of the conference. When folk who were there think back to these gatherings, they will remember the Doctor's contribution before that of anyone else.

I undertook to consider how far Dr Lloyd-Jones was himself in line with the Puritanism that he celebrated so vigorously. I must now say some general things to pave the way to that.

He was, to start with, Welsh: which meant that he had a Welshman's view of Englishmen. He saw them—perhaps I had better say, us—as having a genius for compromise and for maintaining inert institutions, but as chronically hazy on matters of principle and hardly ever able to see anything in black and white. He perceived the Church of England as an expression of this spirit, and the Puritans as an exception—from his standpoint, a glorious exception—to it. Regarding me as a latter-day Puritan (which I took as I was meant to do, as a compliment), he once told me that I was not a real Anglican, and predicted with some distress that my fellow-Anglicans would not accept me. Though not a typical Welshman, since he was unsentimental, nor a typical Welsh preacher, since he spoke and thought like a barrister and put no imaginative flights into his sermons, his Welsh-ness—geniality, courtesy, sensitivity, warmth, magnetic vitality—remained pure and potent, and it was as a Welshman contemplating Englishmen that he viewed the Puritans and the battles they fought.

Then, he was a physician by natural inclination and training, and as a physician he brought both to Christians and their problems in the present, and also to his study of Christians and their problems in the past, a rigorously diagnostic habit of mind. Starting from a clear view of what constituted theological and spiritual wholeness, he analysed everything and everyone systematically, as a matter of habit, to detect first of all what was disordered and then also what was lacking; for he recognized that what is not seen, or not said, can be as significant a sign of spiritual or theological ill-health as any actual sin or error. He was, in fact, a brilliant diagnostician both spiritually and theologically, just as he had been medically in his Bart's Hospital and Harley Street days. (Yet he was not always a good judge of men, being too confident that right belief and zeal would make up for deficiencies in intelligence and character. Sheer kindness, too, could blind him to a supporter's limitations.) One thing that delighted him about the Puritan writers was that they, too, in their character as physicians of the soul (their own phrase to describe themselves), were thorough in diagnostic analysis within the frame of their profound understanding of what, according to Scripture, consti-tutes theological and spiritual well-being, and of the damage that one-sidedness, imbalance, and tunnel vision can do to one's Christian life. His appreciation of the Puritans was a case of deep calling to deep in this regard.

Furthermore, he was a biblical, rational, practical, pastoral theologian of outstanding gifts and acumen. He once spoke of a person we knew as having 'a naturally theological mind': well, we are told that it takes one to know one, and if I am any judge that is exactly what must be said about him. Though he never attended a theological college and was to all intents and purposes self-taught, he read constantly, thought deeply, and during the years that I knew him could keep his conservative Reformed end up in any company—indeed, could dominate any theological discussion in which he was involved. I saw him do that as a member of the portentously named Group on Differing Biblical Presuppositions which met periodically at the British Council of Churches; I also saw him tie a Cambridge don in knots because of the looseness of the latter's biblicism. His formidable power in this regard was the fruit of habitually thinking issues out thoroughly. I am told he was a slow reader, but nonetheless he regularly went for the big books on each topic, whether he expected to agree with them or not. I remember him singing to me the praises of *The Vision of God,* a highly technical treatise on the theology of spiritual life and discipline by the Anglo-Catholic Kenneth E. Kirk; and one lunch-time in the late 1960s, when separatism was much in his thoughts, I found him carrying back to Sion College library W. H. C. Frend's heavy tome, *The Donatist Church.* No 'smatterbooks' for him! From this standpoint too, deep called to deep when he turned to the Puritans. The thorough theological discipline that marked all their thinking gave him much pleasure and their great length and painstaking exhaustiveness, which lesser mortals nowadays find so exhausting, put them right up his alley.

Again, there was a prophetic quality about his ministry which during the years when I knew him isolated him from the religious establishments and the mainstream religious cultures of both England and Wales. He had his admirers, of course, clerical as well as lay, but while woolly sentimentalism in Welsh chapels and anti-intellectualism among English Evangelicals and unbelief of the Bible and its gospel both sides of the border were coming under his lash, his peers in official Christianity treated him as scarcely more than an extremely able freak. Being themselves consciously and complacently 'progressive,' they saw him as a throwback to a type of ministry that as a general pattern had long since ceased to be viable. They could not deny his ability but they could not approve or take seriously what he was doing. Swimming against the stream, standing for unpopular truth, criticizing conventional complacency, exposing folly in both the world and the church, prodding people to think about things they had no wish to think about, displaying the bankruptcy of modernity and recalling its proud exponents to the old paths, has never been a prescription for popularity in the corridors of power, and it was not so in the Doctor's case.

He was, to be sure, strong enough to cope with the isolation, and it was in fact given him in the post-war years to see the quality of evangelical teaching in England and Wales change for the better through his own weaving back into it the binding thread of Reformed theology—a thread which had snapped after Spurgeon was defeated in the Downgrade controversy, and Keswick teaching swamped Anglican Calvinism, and liberalism and the social gospel captured the pulpits of Wales. Ultimately responsible for his ministry having this happy impact was Douglas Johnson, first General Secretary of the Inter-Varsity Fellowship, who both drew the Doctor into student work, where he could shape the outlook of the rising generation of evangelical leaders, and also persuaded him to found his influential ministers' fraternal, the Westminster Fellowship, which in effect made him bishop to literally hundreds of clergy in all denominations.

Yet deep-level isolation from most of his ecclesiastical peers was a permanent part of the Doctor's experience, and this, I think, gave him a special sense of affinity with the Puritans, who were the odd men out in relation to the Anglican establishment in the century after the Reformation. As we shall see in a moment, he viewed them as classic instances of Christian determination to stop at nothing, and to refuse no form of unpopularity and rejection, in order to get God's church into fully scriptural shape; and his own mind-set, natural as well as spiritual (for I suspect it would have been Lloyd-Jones *contra mundum* as a matter of mental habit, even if he had never become a Christian), was powerfully reinforced by the Puritan example.

The final point needing to be noted at this stage is that he was a dyed-in-the-wool Reformed churchman—not, that is, an institutionalist (which is what the word tends to mean when used of Anglicans), but one who saw that in Scripture the church is central to both the fulfilling of God's purposes and the furthering of his praise, and one for whom therefore the state of the church was always a matter of prime concern. Overall, it is not too much to say that his preaching, first to last, started from, revolved round, and homed upon just two areas: one, the state of the church, for which his final remedy was Holy Ghost revival through a return to the old paths of faith and practice; the other, the state of the world, for which his final remedy was the biblical gospel of the three R's—ruin, redemption, regeneration—set forth in the Holy Spirit's power. He described himself as primarily an evangelist, but in fact the condition of the church weighed upon him as heavily as did that of the lost. He did not think that any Anglican, not even a Puritan Anglican, was or could be as seriously concerned about the church as he was himself, and during the 1960s he occasionally put the boot into me on that point. His ecclesiology had developed over the years: ordained a Presbyterian and officially one to his dying day, he became in polity 'a convinced Independent' (his phrase to me), and ceased to baptize covenant children, though retaining affusion as his mode of baptizing adults. This combination of tenets and procedures was unusual if not unique. But he would never make polity an issue; he urged, rather, that evangelical churches should accept without question each other's varieties of organization and usage provided these did not directly contradict Scripture, and concentrate together on the common quest for doctrinal purity, spiritual profundity, and missionary vitality, under the guidance and authority of God's written Word. It was thus, to his mind, that true Christian unity would be shown and the church's real health promoted.

At first, therefore, he left on one side the question of denominations. But over the years he came to think that since there was little hope of the main Protestant churches in England and Wales accepting biblical reform of faith and life and seeking spiritual revival together, since too their links with the World Council of Churches were compromising their future (for the Doctor never doubted that a single super-church based on doctrinal horse-trading lay at the end of the WCC road), the wisest course was for evangelical ministers and congregations to withdraw from these bodies and form a new 'non-denominational' association of old-fashioned Independent type. He once told me that he had privately believed that something of this kind would have to happen ever since J. Gresham

Machen was put out of the ministry of the Presbyterian Church of the USA in 1936, and thus became a living proof of how resistant to biblical authority and reform mainline churches can be. In the 1960s, following the commemoration of the 1662 ejectment of two thousand Puritan clergy, the Doctor began to publicize his view, and to call on his denominationally involved peers within evangelicalism to separate. His gestures evoked strong feelings both ways. At a large gathering of the non-separatist Evangelical Alliance in London in 1966, believing that he had been briefed to do this and giving his opportunist instincts full rein, he pulled out all the stops in making this plea, and John Stott rose from the chair to argue against him. That night my phone rang in Oxford, and a woman's voice greeted me with the words: 'Jim—is John Stott mad?' Next day one who had been at the meeting told me that my friend Martyn Lloyd-Jones had gone off his rocker, and how glad he was that John Stott acted as he did. How did the Doctor put his case? Essentially, his argument was three-pronged: that separation was prudent in the light of the unattractive ecumenical rapprochements into which mainline denominations were being drawn; that separation was an effective and glorious, even necessary, way of manifesting evangelical unity, which it was really schismatic not to take; and that separation was a present duty since evangelicals were guilty by association of all the evils currently found in their own denominations. No matter how vigorously one opposed these evils and sought to change them, one was ruinously compromised by them: only by withdrawal could one's integrity be recovered. Understandably, some of this failed to convince, and while acknowledging their freedom to withdraw if it seemed right, most of England's evangelical ministers in doctrinally mixed church bodies concluded that God was calling them to stay where they were and go on fighting there. The way that in the last fifteen years of his life Dr Lloyd-Jones highlighted this issue, and the pressure he put on Anglicans in particular over it, led to individual estrangements, from which the present writer was not exempt; it disrupted evangelical community (for those who backed the Doctor and saw themselves as separated felt that they would themselves be compromised should they collaborate with unseparated brethren); and it diminished the Doctor's overall influence in England, which was at least a pity and perhaps a tragedy. To his own understanding, however, he was doing no more (and no less) than maintaining in a necessary present-day form something biblical and Puritan—namely, the holy zeal that repudiates half measures, and the holy impatience which, when things are out of joint in the church, insists on 'reformation without tarrying' so that God may be glorified. For this spirit was to him the real heart of Puritanism, as we shall now see.

In the addresses 'Puritanism and Its Origins' and 'John Knox—the Founder of Puritanism' his notion of its essence is made very clear. He rejects what he calls 'the Anglican view' of Puritanism as 'essentially pastoral theology' according to Greenham, Rogers, and Perkins, and of Puritans as clergy who while pursuing this interest stayed in the Church of England even though reforms they sought were not forthcoming. He rightly observes that this view deals only with how the word 'Puritan' was used historically, not with the human reality to which it was applied.[3] With M. M. Knappen he sees Puritanism as a mentality that first appeared as early as William Tyndale, one that starts with independent Bible study and insists on applying the fruits of that study to the reordering of church life; a spirit that demands 'reformation without tarrying' and that will challenge the magistrate's control of the church and break with the ecclesiastical establishment whenever necessary in order to secure that reformation. Application of biblical truth was and always will be central in Puritanism:

> There is no such thing, it seems to me, as a theoretical or academic Puritan. There are people who are interested in Puritanism as an idea; but they are traitors to Puritanism unless they apply its teachings; for application is always the characteristic of the true Puritan.[4]

And the church as such was and remains the prime object of this application; the Puritan study of piety and pastoral care was, as a matter of history, 'subsidiary to the desire for true reform of the church. Indeed, the underlying argument is that only a truly Reformed church . . . guarantees the possibility of that full flowering of the truly religious type of life.'[5] In sum, then:

> The Puritan is primarily concerned about a pure church, a truly Reformed church. Men may like aspects of the Puritan teaching, their great emphasis on the doctrine of grace, and their emphasis on pastoral theology; but however much a man may admire these aspects of Puritanism, if his first concern is not for a pure church, a gathering of saints, he surely has no right to call himself a Puritan . . . if we fail to put the doctrine of the church in a central position we are departing from the true Puritan attitude, the Puritan outlook, the Puritan spirit, and the Puritan understanding.[6]

Is this delineation of the Puritan mentality right? Basically, yes, though two qualifying comments are perhaps in order. The first is that the Puritans of history were reformed medievals, who inherited the medieval sense of the wholeness of life and the involvement of the individual with the group—a perception that we, with our compartmental and individualistic way of thinking about life, can easily overlook and ignore. For the Puritans, as for that marvellously modern man John Calvin who preceded them, the church's confession, order, discipline, and worship; the Christian's personal godliness and uprightness; and the justice and moderation (balance) that should mark every aspect of socio-politico-economic life in the human community; all formed parts of a single great whole that required comprehensive attention from those who would please God, however much present circumstances might require them to concentrate on one or another of these matters in a way that would make it seem for the moment to be their one exclusive interest. It is therefore really a false question to ask which of these concerns is regularly and characteristically subordinated to which—in other words, which

under ordinary circumstances has priority in their thinking. Everything in individual life and in church and community life was linked in the Puritan mind with
everything else, and it all had to be 'holiness to the Lord.' Each item in their range
of concerns was thus co-ordinate with all the rest. That, I think, is the truest way
to focus what historic Puritanism was about.

The second comment is that we must not minimize the variety of views
within Puritanism on specific questions of policy. The Puritans did not differ
much in their ultimate goals, nor in their theological principles, nor in their sense
of the urgency of action against scandalous things, nor in their judgement that the
honour of God and the welfare of Christians were always directly bound up with
the current state of the church; but they frequently differed among themselves as
to when and in what form action to remedy abuses and reinforce righteousness
could best be taken. It would thus be misleading to generalize about them as if at
each stage one group and one line of action have more right to be called Puritan
than another—Presbyterian national-churchmen opposing toleration, for instance, rather than Independent gathered-churchmen supporting it, or vice versa.

There were many matters on which men with an equal right to be called
Puritans—good, active, devoted, consistent Puritans, who prayed and longed in-
cessantly for a church that was in all respects biblically pure—took different lines,
and we must avoid generalizations that suggest that those who took the one were
more authentically Puritan than those who took the other. As Dr Lloyd-Jones
himself once noted, 'until about 1640 you had that kind of original Puritan who
was essentially Anglican, and who was non-Separatist of course; then you had the
Presbyterian type of Puritan, also non-Separatist; then right at the other extreme
you had the Separatists quite plain and clear and open'—to which groupings were
then added the Independents, who practised 'occasional conformity' with the
Church of England and 'have been rightly called semi-Separatists.'[7]

Yet he, with historians generally, was surely right when he viewed these as
divisions within a body of people whose common outlook on basics made it
proper to call them all Puritans, whether they were so called in their own day or
not. That is my own my point exactly. No doubt on occasion it was tempting to
Dr Lloyd-Jones and his admirers to think of their own preferred options within
the Puritan spectrum as 'really' Puritan in a way that other options were not. But
such temptations have to be resisted, at least by those for whom history is more
than a resource for propaganda. Concerning the separation campaign, in which
the Doctor's commitment to Puritan ideals of church purity found its final expression, a question may be asked about his apparent lack of realism. It was observed
that, while speaking forcefully in public about the issue of principle, he never gave
substance to his vision by producing, or getting others to produce, a blueprint
for the new para-denomination (the 'non-denominational' denomination) that
he had in view. He seemed at one time to look to a small anti-ecumenical body,
the British Evangelical Council, to provide the necessary structural network, but

no serious planning seems ever to have been done. Why was this? I once asked him whether he was not really saying that we should all join the Fellowship of Independent Evangelical Churches; he replied that that would not do, but did not say why not, nor what the alternative was, save that something new was called for.

Though he disliked organizing and always had in mind that the more highly organized a venture was, the less spiritual was it likely to be, he was a competent enough manager and must have seen that some organizing would be needed to effect any new grouping. I have wondered, I confess, whether he was not more interested in making the gesture of calling for separation, with the accompanying criticism of evangelical Anglicans, Baptists in the Baptist Union ('in it to win it'), and the world ecumenical movement, than he was in seeing the gesture succeed; whether, anticipating rejection as Isaiah and Jeremiah were told to anticipate rejection, his main purpose was not, rather, to leave a testimony the significance of which, though ignored in his own day, might be seen afterwards. He once observed to me with reference, as I recall, to the fall of David Lloyd-George, whose political acumen he had once admired, that you cannot be a leader if you do not have followers, and he was certainly shrewd enough to foresee that, humanly speaking, he could not expect many followers on this particular issue. Probably the truest thing to say about his campaign of words without plans is that he was testing the waters, looking to see if the Holy Spirit would use what he said to evoke major support and a widespread desire for action, and he would not risk prejudicing his own prophetic role in the process by any appearance of wanting to be a denominational boss. And who will blame him for that?

Though Dr Lloyd-Jones and I did not wholly agree about church polity and policy, we were together in thinking that the Puritan spirit is in essence New Testament Christianity and as such something with which we ought to identify today. What, now, was most notably Puritan about his own ministry? Over and above matters already mentioned, I single out the following items.

First, his concept of theology as a rational, practical study corresponded perfectly to William Perkins's definition of it as 'the science of living blessedly for ever' and his view of the Bible as the source of theology (i.e., as God's revealed truth), and of the system of thought that the Bible yields, was in entire accord with that classic of Puritan theology, the Westminster Confession.

Second, his practice of preaching was altogether Puritan in its philosophy, method, and substance, even though it was entirely twentieth century in its style and verbal form. Doctrine, reason, and 'use'—taking truths from texts, confirming them by other Scripture passages plus rational reflection, and then applying them—was the regular pattern. As declaration to us of God's work, preaching was praise; as instruction in God's ways with us, preaching was food; in both respects, it was the climax of public worship, and was to be honoured as such. Christ and gospel grace, set forth with relevance to present human need and perplexity, must be central always, albeit in the large frame of the whole counsel of God. In the application (of which, for the Doctor, the introduction was really part) one must speak to the times and seek to get inside one's hearers, speaking directly to their anxieties and their guilt before God. A simple, serious, plain-talking idiom, without frivolous illustrations, purple passages, or flights of fancy, suits this purpose best. (The phrase 'noble negligence,' first used of Richard Baxter's writings, fits Dr Lloyd-Jones's transcribed sermons and lectures admirably; persuasive man-to-man clarity, speech that was 'familiar' in the Puritan sense of that word, was what he was always after, and no attempt at verbal elegance was ever made.) Unction from God, giving liberty and forthrightness, empathy and energy, passion and compassion, and enabling one to get inside people, was to be sought on each occasion for the act of preaching so that, in Baxter's words, the preacher might always be said to have

> ... preached as one that ne'er should preach again,
> And as a dying man to dying men.

Continuous systematic wide-swinging exposition of chapters and whole books of Scripture, with as many sermons on each text as it was felt to warrant as part of the larger design, was a fruitful way to preach. Sermons might reasonably be up to an hour long at any time. All this was as Puritan as could be.

Third, the Doctor conceived Christian experience in Puritan terms. His understanding hinged on two principles: first, the primacy of the mind in man, as guide to his will and judge of his feelings; second, the indirectness of the work of the Holy Spirit, who teaches and moves us by first making us actively learn and then rousing us to move ourselves. When the Spirit is at work, illuminating and imparting, he stirs mind and feelings together to an affective awareness of divine realities; God, Christ, grace, pardon, adoption, new creation, and the rest. Christianity is therefore, to use the Puritan word, 'experimental' (we would say, experiential) in its very essence, and the idea that the best Christianity is that into which least emotion enters is a shallow and absurd middle-class English reaction against strong feelings of any sort. Such an idea merits both ridicule, since it is silly, and tears, since it quenches the Spirit.

Conversion was individual response to the crucified, risen, and enthroned Christ who ever and to all says 'Come to me.' Coming to Christ involves repentance (leaving sin, and making Christ one's Master) as well as faith (admitting sin and inability, and taking Christ as one's Saviour). Preachers should constantly point their hearers to Christ and celebrate the peace, joy, change of heart, and new resources for living that those who come to him will find. Conventional twentieth-century evangelism, to the Doctor's mind, had three great weaknesses: its manipulative emotionalism, displacing intellectual persuasion, was a kind of brainwashing that encouraged false conversions; the standard form of appeal ('now I give you an opportunity to respond ... I want you to get up out of your seat and come forward . . .'), in which the preacher acts as if he were the Holy Spirit, has the same unhappy tendency; and the constant failure to insist on radical and thorough repentance in conversion sentences true converts to shallow and stunted growth thereafter. Perceiving these weaknesses led him to say on occasion that certain evangelists were not preaching the gospel at all, and to stand apart from modern institutionalized evangelism on principle, so that the difference between its standards and his would not be obscured.

In teaching holiness, the life of obedience to Christ whereby one abides in him, Dr Lloyd-Jones saw quietist passivity as a kind of modern demon possessing evangelical minds and needing explicit exorcism. Slogans like 'let go and let God,' 'stop trying and start trusting,' seemed to him from this standpoint so misleading as to be scandalous. The formulae of holiness are 'do this,' 'don't do that again,' 'pray first, then act,' and wisdom is to guide always in the application of biblical principles. Determination and effort are needed for the practice of holy living, since opposition from indwelling sin is multiform and constant, as Galatians 5:15–17 shows. The Doctor parted from the Puritans in declining to read Romans 7:14–25 as testimony to this conflict between the spirit (the regenerate self) and the flesh (indwelling sin); he argued, unconvincingly in my view, that this passage delineates the final stage of pre-regenerate life. But he was entirely with the Puritans in stressing the lifelong reality of the spirit-flesh conflict and the folly of any perfectionist claims to have got beyond it.

Spiritual depression, a condition distinct from though often linked with the clinical depression that physicians and psychiatrists treat, was a problem to which the Doctor devoted attention. The condition has at its heart unbelief of God's gracious promises. The remedy for it is to learn to fight the feelings that unbelief begets by keeping one's spiritual eyes on God's faithfulness to his promises as he disciplines his children, and by talking to oneself in the style of Psalm 42 about the certainty that some day one will be praising God for turning one's sorrow into joy.

Assurance of God's everlasting love and of heaven to come was to him the supreme blessing in his life, and the supreme form of assurance, which all Christians should seek, was the direct witness of God's Spirit with our spirit that we are children and heirs of God. Equating this witness, of which Romans 8:15–17 speaks, with the seal of the Spirit (Ephesians 1:13; 4:30; cf. 2 Corinthians 1:22), with baptism with the Spirit (John 1:33), and with receiving the Spirit in some passages of Acts, the Doctor always spoke of it as a particular occasional experience, and illustrated it from a wide range of testimonies to intense and transforming moments of assurance that saints from Pascal to Edwards to Moody, with Puritans like John Flavel among them, had put on record. He had himself enjoyed one such experience while reading a book on heaven, as he told me in a private conversation thirty years ago in which he tried out on me the line of exposition summarized above. He lectured at the first Puritan Conference on this theme, commending the Puritan doctrine of direct assurance as a neglected truth that we needed to recover and in elaborate treatments (all now in print) of the Romans, Ephesians, and John texts he gave it high exposure during the second half of his London ministry. While some Puritans understood Romans 8:16 and Ephesians 1:13 as he did, others took the Spirit's witness to refer to a constant quality of experience rather than to one single moment of experience, and understood the seal of Ephesians 1:13 to be the gift of the Spirit upon believing rather than a work of the Spirit some time after believing; and the case for the latter view against the former seems conclusive. But it was characteristic of all Puritans to seek, and urge others to seek, the clearest experiential assurance of our adoption that God will give, in whatever form it comes, and in reviving and highlighting this emphasis the Doctor once again endorsed the Puritan perspective and revealed his Puritan roots.

Finally, the Puritans, with Christians of every age till this century, viewed dying well as the crown upon a godly life. Dr Lloyd-Jones often stressed in his preaching the need to be ready for death, and he told a colleague towards the close of his life that he saw it as the final work of his ministry to make a good end. Thus he maintained the Puritan view of things to the last.

Only at one point did he go beyond seventeenth-century Puritan teaching on Christian experience: namely, in his embrace of Jonathan Edwards's belief that cyclical revival is God's main and regular way of extending his kingdom. Revival, on this view, is an outpouring of the Holy Spirit on the church which deepens Christian experience enormously. God, however, is sovereign in determining when the outpouring shall occur; Christians may and should pray and prepare for it, but they cannot precipitate it. God works to his own timetable. Now, there is nothing of this in the Puritans. Though they all recognized that the Reformation was, among other things, a revival of true religion, and though men like John Howe had vivid expectations of quickening for Christians when the Spirit was poured out to herald the latter-day glory, the Puritans did not at any stage interpret their own ministry and the history of their own times in terms of the cyclical vision, whereby a day of small things leads on to days of great things for individual congregations and the wider community around. Dr Lloyd-Jones did, however, think in these terms, and it was a source of sadness to him that he never saw revival in England, at Westminster Chapel, as in real measure he had seen it in his South Wales pastorate in 1929–31. How his belief about the sovereignty of God in revival related to the certainty he seemed to show that an alliance of separated churches would have unique spiritual vitality and power, much beyond anything that had preceded its formation, was something that to my knowledge he never explained, and I think that real inconsistency was present here; for certainly the Edwardsean doctrine of revival was in his heart all along. But the greatest men can fall into wishful thinking.

Sometimes 'a kind of Puritan'? Yes, most of the time in fact. Spurgeon in his own day was called the last of the Puritans, but the title surely passed to the

Doctor while he was alive, and maybe still belongs to him. Yet, please God, it will not be his for ever. For part of his legacy to the world was men—pastors, young and middle-aged, for whom his Puritanism was an inspiration and he himself, as Americans would say, a role-model. No doubt there have been among his admirers immaturities, imprudences, unspiritual apings, and downright failures, and the years of separatist drumbeating since 1962 do appear in retrospect as something of a scorched-earth era in English evangelical life, when much that was of value was destroyed. But the Puritan type of godliness is still New Testament Christianity at its noblest and most thoroughgoing, and the God of the Puritans is not dead, and it will be right for us to look to God to raise up, perhaps from the ranks of those whom the Doctor inspired in his lifetime, perhaps from a younger age group, persons who will be clear-sighted enough to discern what Puritan principles of preaching, praying, and living require as the twenty-first century approaches, and who with that will be big enough, intellectually and spiritually, to carry the mighty torch of Puritan ministry that the Doctor has passed to us.

In one sense, of course, it has to be said of the greatest Puritans, Owen, Baxter, Goodwin, Sibbes, Perkins, and Howe, and of their greatest followers over three centuries, Edwards, Spurgeon, Ryle, and now Dr Lloyd-Jones, that we shall not see their like again; each great man is unique. In another sense, however, we may hope and should pray that tomorrow's church will be blessed with many like them in stature, principles, wisdom, gifts, and godliness, and so in every generation until the Lord comes. Men who faithfully maintain the essence of the Christianity that the Doctor stood for are the memorial that he himself would have desired. May such a memorial be forthcoming; for there is nothing today that the church needs more.

CHAPTER 6

David Martyn Lloyd-Jones

David Martyn Lloyd-Jones, 'the Doctor' as he was called in public by all who knew him (even his wife!), resigned in 1968 after thirty years as pastor of London's Westminster Chapel. He died on St. David's Day, March 1, 1981. He was the greatest man I have ever known, and I am sure that there is more of him under my skin than there is of any other of my human teachers. I do not mean that I ever thought of myself as his pupil, nor did he ever see himself as my instructor; what I gained from him came by spiritual osmosis, if the work of the Holy Spirit can be so described. When we met and worked together, as we did fairly regularly for over twenty years, we were colleagues, senior and junior, linked in a brotherhood of endeavour that for the most part overrode a quarter of a century's difference in our ages.

It was a shared concern that first brought us together: I, who did not know him, went with a friend who did in order to ask if he as a Puritan-lover would host and chair a conference that we hoped to mount on Puritan theology. He did so, and the conference became an annual event. Other shared concerns—explaining evangelicalism to the British Council of Churches; the now-defunct *Evangelical Magazine*; Reformed fellowships and preaching meetings; the quest for revival— these kept us together from 1949 to 1970. For me it was an incalculably enriching relationship. To be wholly forthcoming, genial, warm-hearted, confidential, sympathetic, and supportive to ministerial colleagues of all ages was part of the Doctor's greatness. It was, I think, a combined expression of his Presbyterian clericalism, based on the parity of all clergy, plus his feeling as a physician for the common dignity of all who have charge of others' welfare, plus the expansive informality of the Welsh family head. It was an attitude that left countless ministers feeling like a million dollars—significant in their calling, purposeful about it, and invigorated for it. The Doctor's magnetic blend of clarity, certainty, common sense, and confidence in God made him a marvellous encourager as well as a great moulder of minds. He was a pastor of pastors *par excellence*. He would have hated to be called a bishop, but no one ever fulfilled towards clergy a more truly episcopal ministry. I know that much of my vision today is what it is because he was what he was, and his influence has no doubt gone deeper than I can trace.

To be sure, we did not always see eye to eye. Over questions of churchly responsibility we were never on the same wavelength, and this led eventually to a parting of the ways. Ironically, what made our head-on collision possible was the convictions we had in common, which for many years had bound us together and distinguished us from many if not most of England's evangelicals.

What these convictions added up to was a consuming concern for the church as a product and expression of the gospel. We both saw the centrality of the church in God's plan of grace. Both of us believed in the crucial importance of the local congregation as the place of God's presence, the agent of his purposes, and the instrument of his praise. We both sought the church's spiritual unity, internal and external—that is, oneness of evangelical faith and life, appearing in a unanimous Bible-based confession and a challenging Spirit-wrought sanctity. Both of us sought the church's purity—the elimination of false doctrine, unworthy worship, and lax living. We both backed interdenominational evangelical activities, not as an ideal form of Christian unity, but as a regrettable necessity due to the inaction of the churches themselves, which made it certain that if parachurch bodies did not do this or that job it would never get done at all. Had these convictions not been so central to both our identities, we should not have clashed as we did.

The possibility of an explosion was there from the start. I was English and Anglican and the Doctor was a Welsh chapel-man to his fingertips. He had little respect for Englishness, or for Anglicanism as a heritage or Anglicans as a tribe. (He saw the English as pragmatists, lacking principle, and Anglicans as formalists, lacking theology. When he told me that I was not a true Anglican he meant it as a compliment.) His world was that of seventeenth-century Puritans, eighteenth-century evangelicals, and nineteenth-century Welsh Calvinists. It was a world of bare chapel walls and extended extempore prayer; of preachers as prophets and community leaders; of spiritual conversions, conflicts, griefs and joys touching the deep heart's core; of the quest for power in preaching as God's ordinary means of enlivening his people; and of separation to start new assemblies if truth was being throttled in the old ones. In all of this the Doctor was a precise counterpart of the Baptist, C. H. Spurgeon, who himself fulfilled an awesome ministry of Puritan evangelical type in London nearly a century earlier. The only difference was that Spurgeon learned his non-conformity not in Wales but in East Anglia. I never heard the Doctor described as Spurgeon *redivivus*, but the description would have fitted. Like Spurgeon, he thought Anglicanism discredited and hopeless. To look for genuine, widespread evangelical renewal in the Church of England seemed to him 'midsummer madness' (his phrase), and he was sure that in doing this I was wasting my time. 'They won't accept you,' he used to tell me, and it was plain that he hoped eventually to see me leave the Anglican fold.

Denominationalism finally became the break-point. Officially a minister of the Presbyterian Church of Wales, the Doctor had become a convinced

Independent, viewing each congregation as a wholly self-determining unit under Christ, in the Spirit, and before God. In the 1960s he began to voice a vision of a new fellowship of evangelical clergy and congregations in England that would have no links with 'doctrinally mixed' denominations, that is, the Church of England, the English Methodist Church, and the English Baptist Union. To winkle evangelicals out of these bodies he invoked the principle of secondary separation, maintaining that evangelicals not only were free to leave such denominations but must do so, for they were guilty by association of all the errors of those from whom they did not cut themselves off ecclesiastically. Opposing and repudiating those errors, so he urged, does not clear one of guilt unless one actually withdraws. Because my public actions showed that I disagreed with all this and remained a reforming Anglican despite it, our work together ceased in 1970.

The Doctor believed that his summons to separation was a call for evangelical unity as such, and that he was not a denominationalist in any sense. In continuing to combat error, commend truth, and strengthen evangelical ministry as best I could in the Church of England, he thought I was showing myself a denominationalist and obstructing evangelical unity, besides being caught in a hopelessly compromised position. By contrast, I believed that the claims of evangelical unity do not require ecclesiastical separation where the faith is not actually being denied and renewal remains possible; that the action for which the Doctor called would be, in effect, the founding of a new, loose-knit, professedly undenominational denomination; and that he, rather than I, was the denominationalist for insisting that evangelicals must all belong to this new grouping and no other. His claim that this was what the times and the truth required did not convince me. Was either of us right? History will judge, and to history I remit the matter.

Born and reared in South Wales, he was fourteen in 1914 when his family moved to London. He entered the medical school of St Bartholomew's Hospital at the early age of sixteen, graduated brilliantly in 1921, and soon became chief clinical assistant to his former teacher, the Royal Physician, Sir Thomas (later, Lord) Horder, an outstanding diagnostician whose analytical habit of mind reinforced his own. But he soon found that medical practice did not satisfy him, since it centred on the body while the deepest problems are in the soul. Having found his own way to an assurance of God's pardoning mercy towards him, he became sure that God was calling him to preach the gospel to others. By 'gospel' he meant the old-fashioned, Bible-based, life-transforming message of radical sin in every human heart and radical salvation through faith in Christ alone—a definite message quite distinct from the indefinite hints and euphoric vaguenesses that to his mind had usurped the gospel's place in most British pulpits. In 1927, having decided that seminary training was not for him, he became lay pastor of the Forward Movement Mission Church of the Presbyterian (Calvinistic Methodist) Church of Wales in Sandfields, Aberavon, not far from Swansea. On his first Sunday as pastor he called for spiritual reality in terms so characteristic of his subsequent ministry that it is worth quoting his words at length.

> Young men and women, my one great attempt here at Aberavon, as long as God gives me strength to do so, will be to try to prove to you not merely that Christianity is reasonable, but that ultimately, faced as we all are at some time or other with the stupendous fact of life and death, nothing else is reasonable. That is, as I see it, the challenge of the gospel of Christ to the modern world. My thesis will ever be, that, face to face with the deeper questions of life and death, all our knowledge and our culture will fail us, and that our only hope of peace is to be found in the crucified Christ ... My request is this: that we all be honest with one another in our conversation and discussions ... Do let us be honest with one another and never profess to believe more than is actually true to our experience. Let us always, with the help of the Holy Spirit, testify to our belief, in full, but never a word more ... I do not know what your experience is, my friends, but as for myself, I shall feel much more ashamed to all eternity for the occasions on which I said I believed in Christ when in fact I did not, than for the occasions when I said honestly that I could not truthfully say that I did believe. If the church of Christ on earth could but get rid of the parasites who only believe that they ought to believe in Christ, she would, I am certain, count once more in the world as she did in her early days, and as she has always done during times of spiritual awakening. I ask you therefore tonight, and shall go on asking you and myself, the same question: Do you know what you know about the gospel? Do you question yourself about your belief and make sure of yourself?[1]

'Prove'—'reasonable'—'modern world'—'honest'—'the crucified Christ'—'the help of the Holy Spirit'—'experience'—'spiritual awakening'—'question yourself'— these were keynote terms and phrases in the Doctor's preaching, first to last. He started as he meant to go on, and as he did in fact go on, seeing himself as an evangelist first and foremost and seeking constantly the conversion and quickening of folk in the churches who thought they were Christians already.

Though the Sandfields ministry was directed to working-class people, the intellectual challenge was always at its forefront. Social activities were scrapped, and with intense seriousness the Doctor gave himself to preaching and teaching the Word of God. Soon he was ordained; the congregation grew, many conversions occurred, the church was admired as a model, and its minister was the best-known preacher in Wales.

In 1938 the Doctor moved to London's Congregational cathedral, Westminster Chapel, as colleague to the veteran G. Campbell Morgan. There, after Morgan's retirement in 1943, he was sole pastor for a quarter of a century, preaching morning and evening every Sunday save for his annual vacations in July and August. As in Wales, he lived at full stretch. Guest preaching during the first part of the week and pastoral counselling by appointment were regular parts of his life. On each Friday night he taught publicly at the Chapel, for fifteen years or so by discussion, then by doctrinal lectures, and for the last twelve years by exposition of Paul's Letter to the Romans. At both Sunday services, and on the Friday nights when Romans was explored, attendance was regularly nearer two thousand than one. In addition to his steady converting and nurturing ministry there, he exercised much influence on English evangelicalism as a whole.

He did a great deal to guide, stabilize, and deepen the evangelical student work of the young Inter-Varsity Fellowship of Evangelical Unions (IVF). At first he hesitated to touch IVF, for he was Welsh, middle-class, church-oriented, and intellectually and theologically alert, whereas IVF was a loose interdenominational grouping that had grown out of children's and teenagers' ministry and was characterized by what the Doctor saw as brainless English upper-class pietism. But in partnership with another ex-medical man, the quiet genius Douglas Johnson, he fulfilled a leadership role in IVF for twenty years, and did more than anyone to give the movement its present temper of intellectual concern, confidence, and competence.

In due course the International Fellowship of Evangelical Students (IFES) was formed, an umbrella organization uniting student-led movements of IVF-type all round the world. The Doctor drew up its basis, defined its platform, chaired its meetings for the first twelve years, and continued in association with it, first as president and then as vice-president, to the end of his life. In this, too, he was closely linked with the self-effacing Johnson, whose behind-the-scenes activity was a major factor in bringing IFES to birth.

Throughout his London years, the Doctor was also host and chairman of the Westminster Ministers' Fraternal (the Westminster Fellowship, as it was called), which met monthly at the Chapel for a day of discussion and mutual encouragement. Originally an idea of Johnson's, the Fraternal grew to a membership of four hundred in the early 1960s. Through his masterful leadership of it, the Doctor focused its vision and shaped the ideals of many evangelical clergy in all denominations.

He campaigned steadily for the study of older evangelical literature, particularly the Puritans, Jonathan Edwards, and eighteenth- and nineteenth-century biography, from which he had himself profited enormously. Also, he gave much support to the Banner of Truth Trust, a publishing house specializing in reprints which was formed and financed from within his congregation. It can safely be said that the current widespread appreciation in Britain of older evangelical literature owes more to him than to anyone.

What a fascinating human being he was! Slightly built, with a great domed cranium, head thrust forward, a fighter's chin and a grim line to his mouth, he radiated resolution, determination, and an unwillingness to wait for ever. A very strong man, you would say, and you would be right. You can sense this from any photograph of him, for he never smiled into the camera. There was a touch of the old-fashioned about him: he wore linen collars, three-piece suits, and boots in public, spoke on occasion of crossing-sweepers and washerwomen, and led worship as worship was led a hundred years before his time. In the pulpit he was a lion, fierce on matters of principle, austere in his gravity, able in his prime both to growl and to roar as his argument required. Informally, however, he was a delightfully relaxed person, superb company, twinkling and witty to the last degree. His wit was as astringent as it was quick and could leave you feeling you had been licked by a cow. His answer to the question, posed in a ministers' meeting, 'Why are there so few men in our churches?' was: 'Because there are so many old women in our pulpits!' (Americans, please note: that was no reference to female preachers! In Britain an 'old woman' is any dithery man with a gripe.) In 1952 he complained to me of the presence at the Puritan conference of two young ladies from his congregation. 'They're only here for the men!' said he. 'Well, Doctor,' I replied, 'as a matter of fact I'm going to marry one of them.' (I had proposed and been accepted the night before.) I thought that would throw him but it didn't at all. Quick as a flash came the answer, 'Well, you see I was right about one of them; now what about the other?' There's repartee for you! He did not suffer fools gladly and had a hundred ways of deflating pomposity. Honest, diffident people, however, found in him a warmth and friendliness that amazed them.

For he was a saint, a holy man of God: a naturally proud person whom God made humble; a naturally quick-tempered person to whom God taught patience; a naturally contentious person to whom God gave restraint and wisdom; a natural egoist, conscious of his own great ability, whom God set free from self-seeking to serve the servants of God. In his natural blend of intelligence with arrogance, quickness with dogmatism, and geniality with egocentricity, he was like two other small men who also wanted to see things changed, and spent their mature years changing them.

The first, John Wesley, another great leader and encourager just as shrewd and determined as the Doctor though less well focused theologically, shaped a new, passionate style of piety for over a hundred thousand Englishmen in his own lifetime. The second, Richard Wagner, not a Christian, but a magnetic, emotional, commanding personality, charming, ingenious, well aware of his own powers, and very articulate (though muddily; not like the Doctor!), changed the course of Western music. The Doctor might not have appreciated either of these comparisons, but I think they are both accurate. It is fascinating to observe what sort of goodness it is that each good man exhibits, and to try to see where it has come from. The Doctor was an intellectual like John Calvin, and like him said little about his inward experiences with God, but as with Calvin the moral effects of grace in his life were plain to see. His goodness, like Calvin's had been distilled out of the raw material of a temperament inclined to pride, sharpness, and passion. Under the power of gospel truth, those inclinations had been largely mortified and replaced by habits of humility, goodwill, and self-control. In public discussion he could be severe to the point of crushing, but always with transparent patience and good humour. I think he had a temper, but I never saw him lose it, though I saw stupid people 'take him on' in discussion and provoke him in a manner almost beyond belief. His self-control was marvellous: only the grace of God suffices to explain it.

Beyond all question, the Doctor was brilliant: he had a mind like a razor, an almost infallible memory, staggering speed of thought, and total clarity and ease of speech, no matter what the subject or how new the notions he was voicing. His thinking always seemed to be far ahead of yours; he could run rings round anyone in debate and it was hard not to treat him as an infallible oracle. However, a clever man only becomes a great one if two further qualities are added to his brilliance, namely, nobility of purpose and some real personal force in pursuing it. The Doctor manifested both these further qualities in an outstanding way. He was essentially a preacher, and as a preacher primarily an evangelist. Some might question this since most of his twenty books (edited sermons, every one of them) have a nurturing thrust, and the quickening of Christians and churches was certainly the main burden of his final years of ministry. Also, his was supremely what Spurgeon called an 'all round' ministry, in practice as rich pastorally as it was evangelistically. But no one who ever heard him preach the gospel from the Gospels and show how it speaks to the aches and follies and nightmares of the modern heart will doubt that this was where his own focus was, and where as a communicator he was at his finest. He was bold enough to believe that because inspired preaching changes individuals it can change the church and thereby change the world, and the noble purpose of furthering such change was the whole of his life's agenda. As for force in pursuing his goal, the personal electricity of his pulpit communication was unique. All his energy went into his preaching: not only animal energy, of which he had a good deal, but also the God-given liveliness and authority that in past eras was called *unction*. He effectively proclaimed the greatness of God, and of Christ, and of the soul, and of eternity, and supremely of saving grace—the everlasting gospel, old yet ever new, familiar yet endlessly wonderful.

Unction is the anointing of God's Holy Spirit upon the preacher in and for his act of opening up God's written Word. George Whitefield, who was in his own day the undisputed front-man of the evangelical awakening on both sides of the Atlantic, and whom the Doctor confessedly took as a role-model, once in conversation gave a printer *carte blanche* to transcribe and publish his sermons provided that he printed 'the thunder and the lightning too'—but who could do that? In some way there was in the Doctor's preaching thunder and lightning that no tape or transcription ever did or could capture—power, I mean, to mediate a realization of God's presence (for when Whitefield spoke of thunder and lightning he was talking biblically, not histrionically, and so am I). Nearly forty years on, it still seems to me that all I have ever known about preaching was given me in the winter of 1948–49, when I worshipped at Westminster Chapel with some regularity. Through the thunder and lightning, I felt and saw as never before the glory of Christ and of his gospel as modern man's only lifeline and learned by experience why historic Protestantism looks on preaching as the supreme means of grace and of communion with God. Preaching, thus viewed and valued, was the centre of the Doctor's life: into it he poured himself unstintingly; for it he pleaded untiringly. Rightly, he believed that preachers are born rather than made, and that preaching is caught more than it is taught, and that the best way to vindicate preaching is to preach. And preach he did, almost greedily, till the very end of his life—'this our short, uncertain life and earthly pilgrimage,' as by constant repetition in his benedictions he had taught Christians to call it. I mentioned thunder and lightning: that could give a wrong impression. Pulpit dramatics and rhetorical rhapsodies the Doctor despised and never indulged in; his concern was always with the flow of thought, and the emotion he expressed as he talked was simply the outward sign of passionate thinking. The style is the man, 'the physiognomy of the mind,' as Schopenhauer rather portentously said, and this was supremely true of the Doctor. He never put on any sort of act, but talked in exactly the same way from the pulpit, the lecture-desk, or the armchair, treating all without exception as fellow-enquirers after truth, who might or might not be behaving in character at just that moment. Always he spoke as a debater making a case (the Welsh are great debaters); as a physician making a diagnosis; as a theologian blessed with what he once recognized in another as a 'naturally theological mind,' thinking things out from Scripture in terms of God; and as a man who loved history and its characters and had thought his way into the minds and motives, the insights and the follies, of very many of them.

He had read widely, thought deeply, and observed a great deal of human life with a clear and clinical eye, and as he was endlessly interested in his fellow-men, so he was a fascinating well of wisdom whenever he talked. When he preached, he usually eschewed the humour which bubbled out of him so naturally at other times and concentrated on serious, down-to-earth, educational exposition. He planned and paced his discourses (three-quarters of an hour or more) with evident care, never letting the argument move too fast for the ordinary listener and sometimes, in fact, working so hard in his first few minutes to engage his hearers' minds that he had difficulty getting the argument under way at all. But his preaching always took the form of an argument, biblical, evangelical, doctrinal and spiritual, starting most usually with the foolishness of human self-sufficiency, as expressed in some commonly held opinions and policies, moving to what may be called the Isaianic inversion whereby man who thinks himself great is shown to be small and God whom he treats as small is shown to be great, and always closing within sight of Christ—his cross and his grace. In his prime, when he came to the Isaianic inversion and the awesome and magnificent thing that he had to declare at that point about our glorious, self-vindicating God, the Doctor would let loose the thunder and lightning with a spiritual impact that was simply stunning. I have never known anyone whose speech communicated such a sense of the reality of God as did the Doctor in those occasional moments of emphasis and doxology. Most of the time, however, it was clear, steady analysis, reflection, correction, and instruction, based on simple thoughts culled from the text, set out in good order with the minimum of extraneous illustration or decoration. He knew that God's way to the heart is through the mind (he often insisted that the first thing the gospel does to a man is to make him think), and he preached in a way designed to help people think and thereby grasp truth—and in the process be grasped by it, and so be grasped by the God whose truth it is.

A Welshman who inspired Englishmen, as David Lloyd-George once did on the political front; an eighteenth-century man (so he called himself) with his finger firmly on mid-twentieth century pulses; a preacher who could make 'the old, old story of Jesus and his love' sound so momentously new that you felt you had never heard it before; a magisterial pastor and theologian whose only degrees were his medical qualifications; an erudite intellectual who always talked the language of the common man; a 'Bible Calvinist' (as distinct from a 'system Calvinist': his phrase again) whose teaching all evangelicals could and did applaud; an evangelical who resolutely stood apart from the evangelical establish-ment, challenging its shallowness and short-sightedness constantly; a spiritual giant, just over five feet tall; throwback and prophet; loner and communicator; a compound of combative geniality, wisdom, and vision, plus a few endearing quirks—the Doctor was completely his own man, and quite unique.

On February 6, 1977, the fiftieth anniversary of the start of his ministry at Sandfields, the Doctor returned and preached. He announced as his text 1 Corin-thians 2:2, 'For I determined not to know any thing among you, save Jesus Christ, and him crucified' (KJV). His sermon, printed in the *Evangelical Magazine of Wales* in April 1981, the first issue following his death, began as follows:

> I have a number of reasons for calling your attention tonight to this particular state-ment. One of them—and I think you will forgive me for it—is that it was actually the text I preached on, on the first Sunday night I ever visited this Church . . .
>
> I call attention to it not merely for that reason, but rather because it is still my determination, it is still what I am endeavouring, as God helps me, to do. I preached on this text then—I have no idea what I said in detail, I have not got the notes—but I did so because it was an expression of my whole attitude towards life. It was what I felt was the commission that had been given to me. And I call attention to it again because it is still the same, and because I am profoundly convinced that this is what should control our every endeavour as Christian people and as members of the Christian Church at this present time.

There followed a very clear exposition of salvation through the atoning death of Jesus Christ, and then from the seventy-seven-year-old preacher came the application:

Men and women, is Jesus Christ and him crucified everything to you? This is the question. It is a personal matter. Is he central? Does he come before anything and everything? Do you pin your faith in him and in him alone? Nothing else works. He works! I stand here because I can testify to the same thing. 'E'er since, by faith, I saw the stream Thy flowing wounds supply, Redeeming love has been my theme, And shall be till I die.' [William Cowper] 'God forbid that I should glory, save in the cross of our Lord Jesus Christ, by whom the world is crucified unto me, and I (crucified) unto the world' (Gal 6:14).

My dear friends, in the midst of life we are in death. This is not theory; this is personal, this is practical. How are you living? Are you happy? Are you satisfied? How do you face the future? Are you alarmed? Terrified? How do you face death? You have got to die . . . What will you have when that end comes? You will have nothing, unless you have Jesus Christ and him crucified. Do you know him? Have you believed in him? Do you see that he alone can avail you in life, in death, and to all eternity? If not, make certain tonight. Fall at his feet. He will receive you, and he will make you a new man or a new woman. He will give you a new life. He will wash you. He will cleanse you. He will renovate you. He will regenerate you and you will become a saint, and you will follow after that glorious company of saints that have left this very place and are now basking in the sunshine of his face in the glory everlasting. Make certain of it, ere it be too late!

Four years later, on the feast day of Wales's patron saint, the preacher himself was taken home. He died of cancer. He lies buried in the cemetery of the Phillips family, from which his wife came, in Newcastle Emlyn, near the farm which had belonged to his mother's people. The words 'For I determined not to know any thing among you, save Jesus Christ, and him crucified' are inscribed on his gravestone. Nothing more appropriate could be imagined.

'When nature removes a great man,' said Emerson, 'people explore the horizon for a successor, but none comes and none will. His class is extinguished with him.' That is the case here. There is no one remotely resembling the Doctor around today, and we are the poorer as a result. To have known him was a supreme privilege, for which I shall always be thankful. His last message to his family, scribbled shakily on a notepad just before he died, when his voice had already gone, was: 'Don't pray for healing; don't try to hold me back from the glory,' and for me those last words, 'the glory,' point with precision to the significance that under God he had in my life. He embodied and expressed 'the glory'—the glory of God, of Christ, of grace, of the gospel, of the Christian ministry, of humanness according to the new creation—more richly than any man I have ever known. No man can give another a greater gift than a vision of such glory as this. I am for ever in his debt.

CHAPTER 7

Francis Schaeffer: No Little Person

He was physically small, with a bulging forehead, furrowed brow, and goatee beard. Alpine knee-breeches housed his American legs, his head sank into his shoulders, and his face bore a look of bright abstraction. Nothing special there, you would think; a serious, resolute man, no doubt, maybe a bit eccentric, but hardly unique on that account. When he spoke, his English though clear was not elegant, and his voice had no special charm; British ears found it harsh, and if stirred he would screech from the podium in a way that was hard to enjoy. Nevertheless, what he said was arresting, however he might look or sound while saying it. It had firmness, arguing vision; gentleness, arguing strength; simple clarity, arguing mental mastery; and compassion, arguing an honest and good heart. There was no guile in it, no party narrowness, no manipulation, only the passionate persuasiveness of the prophet who hurries in to share with others what he himself sees.

I knew him slightly, and admired him tremendously. I remember him as a great man, and wish I could have spent more time in his company. Yet anyone who reads his books ends up knowing him pretty well, and that at least I have done.

Francis Schaeffer was an important evangelical: that is, an evangelical of importance to evangelicals, as well as to others. He saw himself, so he tells us, as an evangelist. He has been accused (I think, unjustly) of trying to be a pioneer theoretician in philosophy and apologetics. He has been applauded (again, I think, unjustly) for trying to foster a Christian renewal of the fine arts, as if a program in aesthetics was the heart of his work. But his concern under God, it seems to me, was for people as people rather than for procedures or products. Therefore I think it is truest to call him a prophet-pastor, a well-informed Bible-based visionary who by the light of his vision sought out and shepherded the Lord's sheep.

In that role he had influence. Under God, he changed people. Among evangelicals he became an opinion-maker, a consciousness-raiser, and a conscience-stirrer, particularly regarding abortion on demand, for which the *Roe v. Wade* decision laid the foundation in 1973. More than three million copies of his twenty-two books have been sold, and his complete works in five volumes, first published in 1982, have gone through five printings in three years. L'Abri (French for 'the shelter'), the international study centre that he founded in Switzerland, has replicated itself in England, France, Sweden, the Netherlands, and the United States, and L'Abri seminars and conferences, plus the showing of L'Abri films made by his son Franky, have become a regular part of today's Christian scene. Schaeffer himself spoke frequently to prestigious gatherings in prestigious places, and was noticed outside evangelical circles as an evangelical leader. What gave Schaeffer his importance among evangelicals? The brief answer is that he embodied to an outstanding degree qualities of which mid-twentieth-century English-speaking evangelicalism was very short, and so brought a measure of depth to themes on which that era of English-speaking evangelicalism was very shallow. He was not original in any far-reaching sense; he was a conservative Presbyterian who professed what was in essence the old Princeton system of theology, with some garnishings of detail from Gordon Clark and Cornelius Van Til, and he had no fault to find with any part of this doctrinal heritage.

But Schaeffer was felt to be original because he did seven things (at least) that other evangelicals, by and large, were not doing.

First, with his flair for didactic communication he coined some new and pointed ways of expressing old thoughts (the 'true truth' of revelation, the 'man-nishness' of human beings, the 'upper story' and 'lower story' of the divided Western mind, etc.).

Second, with his gift of empathy he listened to and dialogued with the modern secular world as it expressed itself in literature and art, which most evangelicals were too cocooned in their own subculture to do.

Third, he threw light on the things that today's secularists take for granted by tracing them, however sketchily, to their source in the history of thought, a task for which few evangelicals outside the seminaries had the skill.

Fourth, he cherished a vivid sense of the ongoing historical process of which we are all part, and offered shrewd analysis of the *Megatrends–Future Shock* type concerning the likely effect of current Christian and secular developments.

Fifth, he felt, focused, and dwelt on the dignity and tragedy of sinful human beings rather than their grossness and nastiness.

Sixth, he linked the passion for orthodoxy with a life of love to others as the necessary expression of gospel truth, and censured the all-too-common unlovingness of front-line fighters for that truth, including the Presbyterian separatists with whom in the thirties he had thrown in his lot.

Seventh, he celebrated the wholeness of created reality under God and stressed that the Christian life must be a corresponding whole—that is, a life in which truth, goodness, and beauty are valued together and sought with equal zeal. Having these emphases institutionally incarnated at L'Abri, his ministry understandably attracted attention. For it was intrinsically masterful, and it was also badly needed.

Evangelicalism (by which I mean the position of all Protestants, of whatever stripe, who combine belief in the divine truth and authority of Holy Scripture with the Reformational-Puritan-Pietist understanding of justification by faith and the new birth) reached the mid-twentieth century in a somewhat battered condition. Liberal bureaucrats and boards in most major denominations and older educational institutions had given evangelicals a bad beating, leaving them sore and suspicious, anti-intellectual and defensive, backward-looking and culturally negative, enmeshed in ideological isolationism with regard to the world of thought, and lacking all vision for the future of the church save the defiant hope that a faithful remnant would survive somewhere. Evangelism, nurture, and evangelical church life were set in a distinctly old-fashioned mould.

Evangelicals as a body seemed to their peers to be superficial, sentimental, and sometimes smug, certainly strong-minded but often shallow, apathetic on social issues, pharisaic on personal morality, philistine towards the arts, and apt to regard religion as one compartment of life rather than as a way of living it all. Young people were conditioned to believe that only overseas missionary service and full-time pastoral ministry were fully worthwhile vocations; the value of other employments was merely that the money you made could be used to support missions and churches. Beyond this, let the world go by! Separation, understood as uninterested detachment, was the only proper Christian stance in relation to it.

The upshot of all this, not surprisingly, was that young people were rebelling, congregations were aging, and despite some impressive evangelistic efforts, evangelical credibility was diminishing overall. The crude conversionist folk-religion of America, especially of its Bible Belt, and the simplistic Moodyesque pietism of England, seemed to have had their day. As a significant force in the community, evangelicalism, so it seemed, was finished.

The funeral orations that some meditated and others actually delivered proved, however, to be premature. Into this degenerate situation God sent renewers of evangelicalism, men like Martyn Lloyd-Jones and John Stott in Britain, Carl Henry and Harold Ockenga in the United States, and with them, operating from his Swiss base, Francis Schaeffer.

Schaeffer was a reading, listening, thinking man who lived in the present, learned from the past, and looked to the future, and who had an unusual gift for communicating ideas at a non-technical level. His communicative style was not that of the cautious academic who labours for a complete coverage that never exaggerates or gets proportions wrong. It was rather that of the crusading cartoonist whose simple sketches leave behind photographic rectitude and embrace a measure of the grotesque in order to ram home a judgement. Academics censured Schaeffer for communicating this way, but his informal cartoonist's style was apt enough for what he was trying to do.

His complete works are subtitled 'A Christian World-View,' and the title of each separate volume is A Christian View of some great reality—(1) Philosophy and Culture; (2) the Bible as Truth; (3) Spirituality; (4) the Church; (5) the

West. All of them offer genetic and homiletic analyses of the relativism, irrationalism, fragmentation, and incipient nihilism of our culture and community today,
with an equally comprehensive recall to the absolutes of God's revealed truth
as the only road to rationality. In these volumes Schaeffer the prophet-pastor is
preaching to the post-Christian Protestant West, diagnosing its deep existential
questions, detecting its drift from its former credal moorings, and delineating
the desert lands into which today's trends have led us; after which he points up
in each area the true way back—belief of the biblical system, commitment to the
biblical Christ, and the hallowing of all relationships and life activities by the
light of the value-pattern revealed in creation and reinforced by redemption. It is
all compassionate, well-informed, popularly phrased pastoral evangelism, with a
remarkably wide range and a very probing thrust.

Determining the shape of this one-man literary mission to the Western world
was a set of perceptions which it may be helpful to list at this point.

First, Schaeffer vividly perceived the wholeness of created reality, of human
life, of each person's thinking, and of God's revealed truth. He had a mind for
first principles, for systems and for totalities, and he would never discuss issues
in isolation or let a viewpoint go till he had explored and tested its implications
as a total account of reality and life. He saw fundamental analysis of this kind as
clarifying, for, as he often pointed out, there are not many basic world-views, and
we all need to realize how much our haphazard, surface-level thoughts are actually
taking for granted. Exposure of presuppositions was thus central to Schaeffer's
method of encounter with all opinions on any subject, and he always presented
Christianity in terms of its own presuppositions and in theologically systematic
form as the revealed good news of our rational and holy Creator becoming our
gracious and merciful redeemer within the space-time continuum of this world's
history and life.

Second, Schaeffer perceived the primacy of reason in each individual's
makeup and hence the potency of ideas in the human mind. He saw that, as it
has been put, ideas have legs so that how we think determines what we are. So the
first task in evangelism, in the modern West or anywhere else, is to persuade the
other person that he ought to embrace the Christian view of reality; and the first
step in doing this would be to convince him of the non-viability of all other views,
including whatever form of non-Christianity is implicit in his own thinking up to
this point. This is to treat him, not as an intellectual in the socio-cultural sense (he
might or might not be that), but as the human being that he undoubtedly is. To
address his mind in this way is to show respect for him as a human being, made
for truth because he is made in God's image.

At this point Schaeffer's enterprise was in direct continuity with the lesson in basic theism that was Paul's first move in his attempt to evangelize the
Athenian Areopagites, before they howled him down (Acts 17:22–34). For only
when a theistic frame of reference has been established can words like *sin, guilt,*

redemption, faith, repentance, creativity, and *love* bear their authentic Christian meaning. One must begin at the beginning.

Third, Schaeffer perceived the Western mind as adrift on a trackless sea of relativism and irrationalism just because the notion of truth as involving exclusion of untruth, and of value as involving exclusion of dysvalue had perished in both sophisticated and popular thinking. Into its place had crept the idea of ongoing synthesis, the idea, that is, that anything may eventually prove to be an aspect of anything else to which at present it seems to be opposed, so that infinite openness to everything, with negation of nothing and no value judgements, is the only appropriate way for anyone to go.

Now, as a result most mainstream Westerners, religious and irreligious alike, whether intellectual, anti-intellectual, or merely conventional, were held more or less firmly in the grip of this category-less 'pan-everythingism' (as Schaeffer called it), from which they need to be rescued. To make people realize how this viewpoint has victimized them across the board, and thus to free them from it, Schaeffer regularly introduced all topics by a genetic historical analysis showing how Western thought about it had reached its current state of delirium. The aim of these analyses was to re-establish the notion that there is an absolute antithesis between truth and error, good and evil, beauty and the obscenely ugly, and so to refurnish our ravaged and pillaged minds in a way that makes significant thinking about life, death, personhood, and God possible for us once more.

It is a fact that many younger thinkers and artists, whose 'mannishness' (instinctual craving for the absolutes of personal reality, rationality, significance, and love) was in outraged agony at fashions in their professional fields that were tyrannizing them to destruction, have found in Schaeffer's analyses a lifeline to sanity without which they literally could not have gone on living. This fact should be borne in mind when academic criticisms of these non-academic genetic 'cartoons' are brought forward. Whether or not the cartoons satisfy the fastidious, they have in case after case spoken to the condition of real people in real trouble, and thus done the pastoral job that they were created to do. What more, one wonders, should one ask?

Fourth, Schaeffer perceived the importance of identifying in all apologetic and evangelistic discussion, and all teaching on what being a Christian involves, that which he called the antithesis and the point of tension. The antithesis is between truth and untruth, right and wrong, good and evil, the meaningful and the meaningless, Christian and non-Christian value systems, secular relativism and Christian absolutism; the point of tension is between clashing elements in incoherent world-views and between the logical implications of non-Christian ontologies on the one hand and the demands of our inalienable 'mannishness' on the other. He made it his business on every topic he handled to cover the 'either/or' choices that have to be made (and, whether consciously or not, actually are made) at the level of first principles and to show that the biblical-Christian options for personal and community life are the only ones that are consistently rational and satisfyingly human. In this way he sought to remake disordered and disorderly minds with regard both to ontological options facing the individual and to ethical options facing the contemporary West.

To him, as must now be evident, these two fields for persuasion ran into each other and belonged together, both historically (because, as he saw it, the West of today grew out of the Christian West as shaped by the Reformation, and the America of today grew out of Christian America as defined by the Constitution) and also theologically (because biblical truths and values derive from a single whole, a transcript of the declared thoughts of the infinite-personal triune God).

Schaeffer's fiercest polemics were accordingly launched against professed Christians who seemed to him to have lost sight of the true antithesis between what God tells us in the Bible and the false alternatives developed by fanciedly autonomous man in the folly of his fallenness. He berated, for instance, liberal and neo-orthodox Protestants who, as he saw it, took faith out of the realm of 'true truth' into that of blind mysticism and reduced 'Christ' to a vacuous 'connotation word.' He was sharply critical of non-inerrantist students of Scripture who, as he thought, claimed to believe biblically while evading part of the Bible's witness to space-time realities, thus in principle disjoining the 'upper story' of faith from the 'lower story' of fact just as ruinously as the liberals and neo-orthodox did. He assailed evangelicals who in his view compromised truth by declining to apply and obey it in a radical way, but instead accommodated themselves to craven unfaithfulness on the ecclesiastical front and to the cruel and callous lifestyle of the secular world.

Settling for peace at any price was never to Schaeffer's mind a Christian way to go. The prophet-pastor could find in himself much compassion for victims of modern madness who had never encountered anything else, but little for those who, having been shown the light, dehumanized themselves to a degree by backing off from it into mental or moral semi-darkness. In his attempts to stir Christians to stand in particular for the sanctity of human life, and to pray and fight appropriately against the abortion industry, this became very plain. The brokenhearted scorn that marked his manner on these occasions made one think of Jeremiah: which statement (let my reader note) I mean as a compliment. For Schaeffer the most tragic—because the most anti-human—thing in life was willful refusal by a human being to face the antithesis, or rather the series of antitheses, with which God in Holy Scripture confronts us, and in this perception I think he was right.

Fifth, Schaeffer perceived the need to live truth as well as think it, and to demonstrate to the world through the transformed lifestyle of believing groups that—as he himself put it in the foreword to his wife Edith's narrative *L'Abri*—'the Personal-Infinite God is *really there* in our generation.' Hence the emergence of the parent L'Abri in Huémoz, Switzerland, and of the satellite L'Abris around the Western world. Each L'Abri is study centre, rescue mission, extended family, clinic, spiritual convalescent home, monastery, and local church rolled into one: a milieu where visitors learn to be both Christian and human through being part of a community that trusts God the Creator and worships him through Christ the Redeemer.

Ordinarily truth and love must combine for effective evangelism and nurture. The testimony of twenty years is that in the world of L'Abri they do, and lives have been transformed as a result. Schaeffer's varied books, as preaching on paper, show him as one who always remembered that the proof of the pudding is in the eating and that Christians living with God are the final proof of Christian truth about God. Here too his sense of wholeness and his refusal to separate what God has joined were in full evidence. Christian credibility, he saw, requires that truth be not merely defended, but practiced, not just debated, but done. The knowledge that God's truth was being done at L'Abri sustained his boldness as he called for that same truth to be done elsewhere.

Schaeffer has been criticized as a grandiose guru, but the criticism is inept. It assumes a degree of egoism and calculation that was simply not there. Schaeffer was no more, just as he was no less, than a sensitive man of God who sought to minister the everlasting gospel to twentieth-century people, showing what it means in our time to believe it, to think it through, and to live it out. There was no grand strategy in his ministry; everything developed in a relatively haphazard way as needs, applications, and insights became clear one after another. The needs of bemused young people in the 1950s and 1960s produced L'Abri and the first books; the needs of drifting America in the 1970s and 1980s produced the seminars recalling to spiritual roots and the later books and films.

Edith Schaeffer indicated this developing, responsive quality of her husband's ministry in 1968 as she answered the question 'Where did your husband get all this?' God, she affirmed, brought a variety of people to L'Abri not just for their own sakes but also

as a training-ground and as a means of developing, in the arena of live conversation, that which Fran is giving in his apologetic today. Rather than studying volumes in an ivory tower separated from life, and developing a theory separated from the thinking and struggling of men, Fran has been talking for thirteen years now to men and women in the very midst of their struggles. He has talked to existentialists, logical positivists, Hindus, Buddhists, liberal Protestants, liberal Roman Catholics, Reformed Jews and atheistic Jews, Muslims, members of occult cults, and people of a wide variety of religions and philosophies, as well as atheists of a variety of types. He has talked to brilliant professors, brilliant students, and brilliant drop-outs! He has talked to beatniks, hippies, drug addicts, homosexuals, and psychologically disturbed people. He has talked to Africans, Indians, Chinese, Koreans, Japanese, South Americans, people from the islands of the sea, from Australia and New Zealand and from all the European countries as well as from America and Canada. He has

talked to people of many different political colours. He has talked to doctors, lawyers, scientists, artists, writers, engineers, research men in many fields, philosophers,
businessmen, newspapermen and actors, famous people and peasants. He has talked
to both generations!

In it all God has been giving him an education which it is not possible for many
people to have. The answers have been given, not out of academic research (although
he does volumes of reading constantly to keep up) but out of this arena of live conversation. He answers real questions with carefully thought out answers which are
the real answers. He gets excited himself as he comes to me often saying, 'It really
is the answer, Edith; it fits, it really fits. It really is truth, and because it is true it
fits what is really there.' The excitement is genuine. This is what I mean when I say
that God has given him an education in addition to unfolding a work in these past
thirteen years.[1]

What long-term significance has Schaeffer for the Christian cause? Neither this
foreword nor the book that it introduces can answer that question; it is far too
soon to tell. Schaeffer's basic books still sell and are presumably being read. He left
a team of trained helpers who now run the various L'Abris and who publish on
their own account within what might be called Schaefferian Christian-humanist
parameters. His son Franky, a self-styled activist agitator, carries the torch, rather
raucously it must be said, for a Schaefferian socio-cultural shift in the United
States; what will come of that remains to be seen.

Perhaps the clique for whom 'Schaeffer says' has long been the last word in
human wisdom will disperse; or perhaps its members will now labour to build the
prophet's tomb, embalming into hallowed irrelevance thoughts that were once
responses to the desperations of our time. We wait to see. The law of human fame
will no doubt treat Schaeffer as it has treated others, eclipsing him temporarily
now that he is dead and only allowing us to see his real stature ten or twenty years
down the road; and probably then some of the things he said will seem more
significant than others. My guess is that his verbal and visual cartoons, simplistic
but brilliant as they appear to me to be, will outlive everything else, but I may
be wrong. I am sure, however, that I shall not be at all wrong when I hail Francis
Schaeffer, the little Presbyterian pastor who saw so much more of what he was
looking at and agonized over it so much more tenderly than the rest of us do, as
one of the truly great Christians of my time.

CHRISTIAN HISTORY AND THEOLOGY

CHAPTER 8

Luther against Erasmus

I

On September 6, 1524, Desiderius Erasmus, the foremost literary man of his day, sat in his study writing a letter to a distinguished friend and patron, Henry VIII, King of England.[1] In the course of his letter came the words: 'The die is cast. The little book on free-will has seen the light of day.'[2]

He was referring to his *Diatribe seu collatio de libero arbitrio* ('Discussion or Conference Concerning Free Will'), which had been published at Basel five days earlier. He wrote more truly than he knew. The die was now cast indeed. A Rubicon had been crossed, and one of the great storms of history was about to break.

Why had Erasmus written—at a single sitting, we are told—this 'little book on free-will'? Because he had become convinced that the only way of keeping the friends on whose generosity and protection his career depended was publicly to dissociate himself from that stormy petrel, Martin Luther, whose revolutionary views and fiery manner of expressing them in print were setting all Christendom by the ears. Thereby hangs a tale, which we must briefly tell.

Born at Rotterdam in 1466, the illegitimate son of a priest and a doctor's daughter, Erasmus had become Europe's leading classical scholar before Luther's public career began. The position he had gained was that of what we would now call a literary lion. There was an open door for him into all the cultured circles which the Renaissance had brought into being, and he could command a welcome as an honoured guest in any university. Aspirants after scholarly distinction scraped his acquaintance and took their cue from him. His words and attitudes had wide influence, and his support was an asset to any cause.

Though primarily a philologist, classicist, and satirist, rather than a theologian, Erasmus was not wholly secular in his interests. In 1516 he brought out his pioneer critical edition of the Greek New Testament, and since 1502, when he wrote *Enchiridion militis Christiani* ('The Christian Soldier's Handbook'), he had not sought to conceal his concern that abuses in the church should be removed. His ideal of reformation, however, was neither as thoroughgoing nor as evangelical as that which Luther later maintained.

In face of obscurantism, superstition, corruption, and moral laxity, Erasmus pleaded for a return to the 'Christian philosophy' (*philosophic Christiana*) of the New Testament. But by this he meant New Testament ethics rather than New Testament doctrine. For Erasmus did not regard questions of theological truth as having ultimate importance for the Christian. His attitude was that as long as one tries to be good and says one's prayers, keeping humble and admitting one's faults and weaknesses, being loyal as a churchman and law-abiding as a citizen, one need not bother one's head about matters of doctrine.

Theological debates could safely be left to the theologians; they did not concern the ordinary Christian one way or the other. What Erasmus sought, then, was a reformation, not of doctrine, but simply of manners. And he believed that the classical studies which he loved had an important part to play in bringing about such a reformation.

His ideal was to unite 'good letters' (the classics) with 'sacred letters' (the Bible), for the furthering of a moral culture and a cultured morality. Hence, on principle as well as from inclination, he was always a man of peace, for he knew that humanistic studies could not prosper in conditions of social or ecclesiastical instability. Anything disruptive or revolutionary was anathema to Erasmus, and his instinct was to keep clear of such things if he possibly could.

In 1517 Dr Martin Luther, aged thirty-four, Professor of Biblical Studies at Wittenberg University, was suddenly catapulted into prominence by broadcasting throughout Germany in broadsheet form his Ninety-five Theses against the current theology of indulgences. When Luther followed this up with a shower of inflammatory pamphlets assaulting accepted ideas on a whole series of topics relating to the doctrine and life of grace, Erasmus' feelings were mixed. He did not see the point of Luther's protests, nor did he like their ferocious polemical style; yet he sympathized with many of Luther's grievances against current evils, and was not prepared to join the chorus of those who cried out against him. For some years, therefore, when asked for his views on Luther, Erasmus contented himself with observing that Luther's motives were transparently honest and his intentions undoubtedly good, which was more than could be said of some of the latter's opponents.

So in 1520 we find him, when quizzed by Luther's patron and protector, Frederick the Wise, making his famous remark: 'Luther has committed a great sin; he has hit the monks in their belly and the Pope in his crown!' ('What a wonderful little man,' Frederick grumbled afterwards; 'you never know where you are with him.') Erasmus would not pronounce against Luther, but at the same time he had no intention of getting involved in the storm Luther was raising.

But the situation soon reached a point where Erasmus felt he could no longer stand aloof. In 1520 the Pope excommunicated Luther for heresy. In the same year Luther denounced the papal claim to supremacy, burned the Pope's bull of excommunication, attacked the established sacramental and hierarchical system

(*The Babylonian Captivity of the Church*), and called on the estates of the Holy Roman Empire to summon a council and reform the German church at once (*Address to the German Nobility*). Erasmus' unwillingness to condemn Luther, coupled with his own known wish for reform, had already brought him under suspicion of being a crypto-Lutheran. For a time he had been content merely to joke about the accusation that, as he once put it, he had laid the egg which Luther hatched, and he must have thought it very funny to be suspected, as in 1521 he was, of being the real author both of Luther's *The Babylonian Captivity* and of Henry VIII's *Assertion of the Seven Sacraments,* written in reply to it. But things were getting beyond a joke.

Erasmus had powerful enemies, and with Luther in utter disgrace, it was becoming increasingly important for the master of 'good letters' that nobody should be able to take him for a Lutheran in disguise. In 1520 he had been offered a bishopric if he would write against Luther, and he had refused; but in 1523 he decided, reluctantly as we may believe, that he would have to take this step after all. Rupp calls his decision to oppose Luther in print Erasmus' 'greatest act of appeasement.'[3]

Having made his decision, Erasmus faced the problem of finding a suitable topic on which to write. In 1520 Luther had published a counterblast to his ex-communication entitled *Assertion of All of the Articles of Dr. Martin Luther Condemned by the Bishop of Rome Leo X.* The thirty-sixth of these reaffirmed articles described free will as a mere fiction. This paradoxical thesis seemed to Erasmus to provide an ideal theme for his purpose. The defense of free will accordingly became the subject of his *Diatribe.*

II

Inspection shows that Erasmus' book is intended to make three points: one about Luther, one about Erasmus, and one about the topic announced in its title.

1. Regarding Luther, Erasmus seeks to make his readers feel that a certain unbalance and, as we should say, crankiness marks him. The prefatory section of the book (the substance of which, writes Erasmus, 'appears more important than the disputes on paper')[4] is a long reflection on the fact that on an issue that is obscure and in practice unimportant, at a point where Holy Scripture is unclear and no good purpose can be served by controversy, Luther has taken up an extreme and eccentric position, in which he has the weight of ecclesiastical opinion against him and is now arguing it in a way that cannot but seem arrogant, opinionated, and pastorally irresponsible. Erasmus insinuates that Luther is, to say the least, conceited and lacking in a sense of proportion.

2. Regarding himself, Erasmus is at pains to appear, by contrast to Luther, reasonable, tolerant, peace-loving, and humble. He dwells on his distaste for

'assertions' and polemics. He assures us that on many aspects of the free-will question he keeps an open mind and is ready to learn from those better instructed. His book, he explains, is merely a discussion of the problem, not a determination of it; all he is doing is tentatively to submit his present views for the judgement of others. He invites his readers to applaud his moderation, just as he invites them to censure Luther's apparent extremism and arrogance.

3. Regarding free will, Erasmus is concerned to say, mildly but firmly, that it is undoubtedly real in the sense that, as most churchmen have always believed, fallen man still retains power to 'apply himself to or turn from that which leads unto eternal salvation.'[5] Erasmus thinks of God as, first, the lawgiver, laying down the terms on which salvation may be had, and second, the helper, strengthening those who choose to follow after salvation so that they actually fulfil the pre-scribed conditions and attain that which they desire.

He illustrates his view of free will and grace by the analogy of a father and a baby boy who cannot quite walk. The father sets before the child an apple some-where beyond its reach. The child stretches for the apple but cannot touch it, nor, unaided, can he walk towards it; however, the father lifts him to his feet and holds him up. Thus supported, he is now able to toddle over to where the apple is.

> Thus the child comes, led by the father, to the apple, which the father places willingly into his hand, like a reward for his walking.
> The child could not have raised itself without the father's help; would not have seen the apple without the father's showing; would not have stepped forward with-out the father's helping his weak little steps; would not have reached the apple with-out the father's placing it into his hand. What can the child claim for himself? Yet he did do something . . .
> Let us assume it is the same with God.[6]

Erasmus here shows himself to be firmly anchored in the 'semi-Pelagian' legalism of the Middle Ages, according to which one's will to do good works merits divine help for the doing of them. On this view, the decisive factor in salvation is man's meritorious choices. Erasmus assumes without question, first, that the gospel is the nature of law—'do this, and live'—and, second, that all men can will the will of God, even though they lack power to perform it. It is this scheme that is in his mind when he writes of the sentiments of those who attribute a little to the freedom of the will, the most, however, to grace.[7] Erasmus thinks of the bringing of man to glory as a joint enterprise in which, though God does the lion's share, the issue depends ultimately on our own acts of will.

Strangely enough, Erasmus had no idea that there was any deep cleavage between Luther and himself over this scheme. In 1523 he had written to Zwingli: 'I think I have taught almost everything that Luther teaches, only I have not done it so fiercely and have abstained from certain riddles and paradoxes.'[8] He did not see that Luther's teaching about divine grace abolishes 'semi-Pelagian' legalism altogether. Luther's blunt statement at the end of his reply, 'God has not yet willed nor granted that you should be equal to the subject of our present debate,'[9] was no more than the truth.

Yet for all that, Erasmus lives triumphantly on. Thousands on the fringes of our churches, and many who are much nearer the centre than that, still think Erasmus' thoughts and speak with Erasmus' accents. Such people manifest, first, an attitude of doctrinal indifferentism.

> Oh, [they say] what matters is not what a man believes but what he is and does. Leave theology to the theologians, and let us plain men get on with the business of living. It's the way you live that counts.

With this they manifest a spirit of soteriological optimism.

> Do your best, [they say,] and God will certainly smile on you and help you and accept you. He is good and kind and will never reject anyone who lives a decent, honest life. God is merciful, so salvation presents no problem, and there is no need to worry about it. Why some people get troubled about their salvation we cannot understand—unless it just means that they are morbid or psychologically odd.

But doctrinal indifferentism linked with soteriological optimism—unconcern about 'the redemption that is in Christ Jesus,' plus confidence in the goodness of natural man—is the essence of the standpoint of Erasmus. The truth seems to be that there is more of the Erasmian outlook in our English churches at the present time than there is of any other sort of thinking. The issue over which Luther and Erasmus clashed thus remains a live one, and the battle which Luther fought against the Erasmian version of the religion of the natural man still needs fighting today.

III

How did Luther react to Erasmus' essay? In the words of Margaret Mann Phillips, he 'met the graceful little book with a bomb.'[10] In December 1525 he published a full-scale reply, four times the length of Erasmus' 'little book' under the uncompromising title *De servo arbitrio* ('Of the Slave Will'). This reply was described by B. B. Warfield as 'in a true sense, the manifesto of the Reformation.'[11] Professor Gordon Rupp has quoted with approval a contemporary description of it as 'the finest and most powerful Soli Deo Gloria to be sung in the whole period of the Reformation.'[12] Luther himself afterwards declared that of all his published works it alone, along with his little catechism for children, deserved to survive, for it alone was 'right' (*justum*).[13] It is undoubtedly the greatest piece of sustained theological writing that he ever did, and it stands for all time as the clearest, indeed, the classical elucidation of what the Reformation conflict was all about.

A word must be said at the outset concerning the tone and temper of Luther's frequent personal references to Erasmus. To Erasmus himself they seemed needlessly bitter and gratuitously offensive, and many since have agreed with him. But it must be remembered that the main point of the *Diatribe* had been a personal one—that Luther had shown himself inconsiderate and irresponsible in making the denial of free will an issue, and that by contrast Erasmus' strictures upon him for taking this line were the acme of Christian sobriety and good sense. For a full answer, therefore, Luther was bound to show why the denial of free will was of such capital importance as to require the emphasis he gave it, and this meant that he had to controvert not merely Erasmus' arguments but also Erasmus' assumption that the question itself was unimportant. Luther believed that every Christian knows from personal experience that this issue is crucial: how, then, could the great and learned Erasmus not know it? Luther felt fully entitled in the circumstances to raise the question—which is all that his personal references are really doing—whether Erasmus himself is not a stranger to grace, for, says Luther grimly, he certainly thinks and writes like one.

Or, rather (since Luther's treatise was cast in the form of an open letter to Erasmus), '*you* think and write like one!' This was certainly straight speaking, but it was not prompted by either vainglory or contempt. Instead, Luther's attitude to Erasmus was one of undisguised pastoral concern. 'Who knows,' he wrote, 'but that God may even condescend to visit you, most excellent Erasmus, by me, his poor weak vessel, and I may come to you by this book in a happy hour and gain a beloved brother. From my heart I beseech the Father of mercies through Christ our Lord that it may be so.'[14] There is no reason to suspect Luther of insincerity here.

Luther's regular way in controversy, like that of most sixteenth-century writers, was to meet his opponents on their own ground, to accept their statement of the issues in dispute and to make his rejoinders in the form of critical comments on what they had said, paragraph by paragraph. Such a method is thorough but tortuous, and the reader of *De servo arbitrio* often finds it hard to see the wood for the trees. In Philip S. Watson's judgement, Luther's 'real intentions are not a little obscured because he adheres so closely to Erasmus's statement of the issue.'[15] Accordingly, instead of following Luther's own order of exposition, we shall now arrange his main contentions in the way which will bring out most clearly their basic thrust.

Two points serve to define Luther's approach to the debate, as contrasted with that of Erasmus.

1. The Crucial Nature of the Free-Will Question

Luther thanks Erasmus for giving him his first opportunity to treat fully the matter which had been his own main concern all along.

You alone ... have attacked the real thing, that is, the essential issue. You have not worried me with those extraneous issues about the Papacy, purgatory, indulgences, and such like—trifles, rather than issues—in respect of which almost all to date have sought my blood ... you, and you alone, have seen the hinge on which all turns, and aimed for the vital spot [literally, 'taken me by the throat']. For that I heartily thank you; for it is more gratifying to me to deal with this issue.[16]

The question whether or not man has free will, in Erasmus' sense of the term, was to Luther the hinge of the whole Reformation debate. Why did he regard it so? Because, to him, what he and his opponents were really arguing about was whether the Christian message tells man how, with God's help, he may save himself, or whether Christianity declares that it is God in Christ who saves, and God alone. Luther's fundamental purpose as theologian and churchman was to explicate and establish the second view against the medieval habit of taking the first for granted.

All his reforming activity sprang from this concern. And the reason he saw the free will question as 'the hinge on which all turns' was that the assertion of free will, in Erasmus' sense, is basic to the first position, whereas the denial of it undercuts at a stroke every form of the gospel of self-salvation and shuts us up to the second view, making us spiritual realists by forcing us to recognize that unless God freely works our whole salvation, we cannot be saved at all.

Luther's exposition of his thesis that we are saved by grace alone has two parts. The first and better-known part is his insistence that we are justified not on the ground of any merit of our own (for we have none) but through God's own gift of righteousness, freely bestowed on us in virtue of the obedience and sacrifice of Christ and received through faith alone. The second part, often underemphasized today, is his equally vigorous insistence that our very faith depends not on any natural ability to trust God (again, we have none) but on God's calling; that is, his supernatural work by the Spirit of creating in us a response to the word of the gospel. God in grace gives not only righteousness but also faith to receive it. First to last, salvation is of the Lord. The importance of the doctrine of the enslaved will is that it clears the road for this account of salvation by grace, by establishing the inability of sinners to supply either works or faith from their own natural resources.

Erasmus had dismissed the free-will debate as 'idle' and 'superfluous' from the standpoint of piety. It will be in the interest of Christian practice, he had said, if a ban is placed on it. Luther castigates him for this. If, says Luther, the 'common sense' assumption of human ability goes unchallenged, nobody will ever attain to the practice of true piety at all.

For if I am ignorant of the nature, extent, and limits of what I can and must do with reference to God, I shall be equally ignorant and uncertain of the nature, extent, and limits of what God can and will do in me—though God, in fact, works all in all ... Now, if I am ignorant of God's works and power, I am ignorant of God himself, and if I do not know God, I cannot worship, praise, give thanks, or serve him, for I do not know how much I should attribute to myself and how much to him. We need, therefore, to have in mind a clear-cut distinction between God's power and ours, and God's work and ours, if we would live a godly life.[17]

The man who never learns to reject the false assumption that he has free will, and who in consequence is never weaned away from the self-confident, self-reliant religion to which this assumption gives rise, will never know Christ, or worship God in truth. 'If we know nothing of these things,' declares Luther roundly, 'we shall know nothing whatsoever of Christianity.'[18]

2. The Necessity of Dogmatism in a Christian

Erasmus had expressed distaste for the positive, definite, categorical way in which Luther held his views and had abjured any such attitude on his own part. 'So great is my dislike of assertions that I prefer the views of the Sceptics wherever the inviolable authority of Scripture and the decision of the Church permit.'[19] Luther finds this shocking.

To take no pleasure in assertions is not the mark of a Christian heart; indeed, one must delight in assertions to be a Christian at all . . . Away, now, with Sceptics . . . let us have men who will assert . . . Take away assertions, and you take away Christianity . . . What Christian can endure the idea that we should deprecate assertions? That would be denying all religion and piety in one breath.[20]

Why is Luther so insistent here? Because of what he believes about Holy Scripture and the Holy Spirit. Holy Scripture, he maintains, is not the obscure book that late medieval theology made it out to be, but a book that is in itself perfectly clear, provided only that one acknowledges the Christ of Scripture as the key to Scripture and reads everything in the light of his work. It is true that the natural man is unable to perceive the biblical message to be divine truth, but this is not because the message is unclear; it is because his mind is darkened and blinded through sin. (Luther maintains the blindness of the *mind* as well as the bondage of the *will*.) The Holy Spirit, however, is given to cure this blindness and to write on our hearts, as truth from God, the biblical proclamation of Christ.

The truth is that nobody who has not the Spirit of God sees a jot of what is in the Scriptures. All men have their hearts darkened, so that, even when they can discuss and quote all that is in Scripture, they do not understand or really know any of it. They do not believe in God, nor do they believe that they are God's creatures, nor anything else . . . The Spirit is needed for the understanding of all Scripture and every part of Scripture.[21]

'Believe' and 'understand' here are words which point to a God-given, experimental, 'existential' conviction of divine truth—the kind of conviction which, to Luther's mind, Erasmus patently lacked. So he writes: 'Leave us free to make assertions, and to find in assertions our satisfaction and delight; and you may applaud your Sceptics and Academics—till Christ calls you too! The Holy Spirit is no Sceptic, and the things he has written in our hearts are not doubts or opinions, but assertions—surer and more certain than sense and life itself.'[22]

This being so, Luther insists, Christianity is necessarily confessional. To confess Christ and the truth about him is the heart of the Christian calling and the basic activity of every person into whose life the Spirit of God has come. 'The Holy Spirit is given to Christians from heaven in order that he may glorify Christ and in them confess him even unto death.'[23]

Christianity is thus by its very nature an assertive, dogmatic faith. Luther knows, of course, that the world and the church are often bedevilled by a dogmatism which springs from nothing higher than pig-headedness, obscurantism, and sheer superstition, but he disclaims all intention of defending dogmatism of that sort. His point is not that it is never desirable to have an open mind, but simply that on the central issues of the gospel—the person, place, and work of Jesus Christ, the *sola gratia,* and the way of salvation—an open mind, so far from being a true expression of Christian humility and self-distrust, is sub-Christian and indeed anti-Christian, for it argues ignorance, both theological and experimental, of the work of the Holy Spirit. The question Luther would press on anyone who, like Erasmus, extolled an undogmatic temper in Christian theology would be this: 'Do you believe in the Holy Ghost?'

IV

From what has been said so far, we have seen that the thesis of *De servo arbitrio* is one which Luther regards as essential to the gospel and one about which he expects every Spirit-taught man to be clearly and strongly convinced. What, now, is this thesis? In a sentence, it is that fallen man is by nature the helpless slave of sin and Satan, so that when he is saved, his salvation is the work of God alone. Luther once described Paul's aim in Romans as being to magnify sin, in order that he might magnify grace. This was precisely Luther's own aim when he wrote against Erasmus. The full explication of this thesis requires us to consider three topics.

1. Man's Will

In discussing the human will, both Erasmus and Luther were encumbered by the theological and philosophical vocabulary which they inherited. The traditional term 'will' (*arbitrium,* 'power of decision') could be used in both psychological and metaphysical contexts, and these two spheres of discourse were not clearly differentiated in Luther's day. Also, the very use of the word tended to encourage the conception of a man's will as something distinct from him and in a sense external to him, in the way that his hand, foot, or finger, or his faculties of sight and hearing are. This, of course, is a mistake; 'will' does not denote a particular part of man, but the word has to be understood as a logical abstraction denoting man himself, viewed as a conative, active, and morally responsible being.

The will is the self, regarded from a particular point of view. Thus the question of whether the will is free is, and always was, really the question of whether we, as men, are free in the decisions we make. Erasmus' mind is patently confused about this; Luther, however, shows himself clearly aware of the bondage of the will, and throughout his treatise we find him skilfully manipulating the traditional vocabulary of free will in order to make it express the biblical truth that the natural man in all his decisions shows himself to be enslaved to the powers of evil, sin, and Satan until grace sets him free to serve God.

Free will, says Luther, is something that exists, not simply when an agent has power to make a personal choice as distinct from being compelled to act willy-nilly, but when the agent has power in himself to choose all the various alternatives which the situation presents to him. If, however, he has not (as we say) 'got it in him' to choose one or more of them, then to that extent free will is lacking to him. Thus we may truly say that man has free will in relation to 'things below him'—that is, the created order, which man was made to rule—because he really has 'got it in him' to choose at each point any of the whole gamut of physical possibilities. 'Man should realise that in regard to his money and possessions he has a right to use them, to do or to leave undone, according to his own "free will."' [24]

According to Luther, then, we all have genuine free will in regard to whether or not we have marmalade, honey, or jam for breakfast, whom we marry, what career we take up, whether we spend our money on a car or not, and, if so, what car we buy, and all decisions of that order. Also, says Luther, we all have genuine free will in relation to civil righteousness and the outward keeping of the moral law.

Luther has no wish to deny that we have 'got it in us' to keep the rule of the road, or to pay our income tax, or to tell the truth. But Erasmus had defined free will as power to 'apply to, or turn from, that which leads to eternal salvation.' That means, as Luther expands the definition,

> a power of the human will which can of itself will and not will the word and work of God, by which it is to be led to those things that exceed its grasp and comprehension. If it can will and not will . . . it can in measure keep the law and believe the gospel. [25]

And it is here, Luther insists, in relation to 'things above him'—God, and the Word of God—that fallen man lacks free will, and the free will that he fancies he has is a non-entity. For the truth about him is that deliberately, spontaneously, heartily, voluntarily, he always chooses the way of non-compliance and non-conformity when the full demands of the law confront him. Thus he shows himself to be what Scripture declares him to be—the slave of sin.

Erasmus had invoked God's repeated summons to us in the Scriptures to choose the path of obedience and life as proof that we all have power to make such a choice; if we lacked this power, said Erasmus, the summons would be completely pointless. Not at all, replies Luther; the summons is issued in order to make us discover in experience that we lack power to respond to it, and so to make us realize our inability to save ourselves. Satan would hide this inability from us by deceiving us about ourselves; but God sends his law to undeceive us, and so to prepare us to receive his grace.

> The Scripture sets before us a man who is not only bound, wretched, captive, sick and dead, but who, through the operation of Satan his lord, adds to his other miseries that of blindness, so that he believes himself to be free, happy, possessed of liberty and ability, whole and alive. Satan knows that if men knew their own misery he could keep no man in his kingdom; God could not fail at once to pity and succour wretchedness that knew itself and cried to him, for God is proclaimed with mighty praise throughout the Scripture as being near to the broken-hearted . . . Hence, the work of Satan is to hold men so that they do not recognize their wretchedness, but presume they can do everything that is stated. But the work of Moses the lawgiver is the opposite of this—namely, through the law to lay open to man his own wretchedness, so that, by thus breaking him down, and confounding him in his self-knowledge, he may make him ready for grace, and send him to Christ to be saved.[26]

The law of God, with its daunting standards and its inexorable sanctions, works in our consciences, on the one hand, a sense of our need of righteousness and, on the other hand, an awareness of our lack of it and our consequent exposure to God's wrath and condemnation. The doctrine of the will's slavery to sin deepens this latter awareness and extends it into a realization that not only do we lack righteousness now, but we have no ability, try as we will, to achieve righteousness in the future.

The prisoners have no strength to break their bonds, for the bonds are in truth part of themselves. A man sins because he is a sinner by nature, and is not free for righteousness. This is what slavery to sin means. The knowledge that there is no such thing in man as free will in Erasmus' sense—power, that is, to please God, to gain merit, and so to secure divine help for salvation—thus completes the work of the Law and drives men into the self-despair of conscious impotence which is the necessary preparation for grace. Writes Luther:

> God has surely promised his grace to the humbled: that is, to those who mourn over and despair of themselves. But a man cannot be thoroughly humbled till he realises that his salvation is utterly beyond his own powers, counsels, efforts, will and works, and depends absolutely on the will, counsel, pleasure and work of Another—God alone.
>
> As long as he is persuaded that he can make even the smallest contribution to his salvation, he remains self-confident and does not utterly despair of himself, and

so is not humbled before God; but plans out for himself (or at least hopes and longs for) a position, an occasion, a work, which shall bring him final salvation. But he who is out of doubt that his destiny depends entirely on the will of God despairs entirely of himself, chooses nothing for himself, but waits for God to work in him; and such a man is very near to grace for his salvation.[27]

2. God's Rule

Part of Erasmus' trouble, says Luther, is that his thoughts of God are 'too human.' He thinks of God as merely a spectator of man's actions, just as we are spectators of each other's actions. But in fact God is far more than this. Not only is he an observer of men's actions; he is in a real sense the doer of them.

God works in all. The common-sense idea that in human action God is more or less passive, so that man stands over against God as an independent agent, is an illusion. Erasmus' conception of free will as a power in the exercise of which God plays no part is unbiblical, untheological, and untrue. The truth is that God is always active everywhere, energizing each created thing to act according to its nature. This is true of Satan no less than of men, and of unregenerate men no less than of the regenerate. Luther states the matter thus:

> Now, Satan and man, being fallen and abandoned by God, cannot will good (that is, things that please God, or that God wills), but are ever turned in the direction of their own desires, so that they cannot but seek their own . . . Since God moves and works all in all, he moves and works of necessity even in Satan and the ungodly. But he works according to what they are, and what he finds them to be: which means, since they are evil and perverted themselves, that when they are impelled to action by the movement of divine omnipotence they do only that which is perverted and evil. It is like man riding a horse with only three, or two, good feet; his riding corresponds with what the horse is, which means that the horse goes badly.
>
> Here you see that when God works in and by evil men, evil deeds result; yet God, though he does evil by means of evil men, cannot act evilly himself, for he is good, and cannot do evil; but he uses evil instruments . . . The fault which accounts for evil being done when God moves to action lies in these instruments, which God does not allow to be idle. In the same way a carpenter would cut badly with a saw-toothed axe. Hence it is that the ungodly man cannot but err and sin always, because under the impulse of divine power he is not allowed to be idle, but wills, desires and acts according to his nature.[28]

It is in the light of this that we should understand Luther's image, borrowed from Augustine, whereby he expresses the thought that every man is actively dominated either by God or by the devil.

> Man's will, [Luther writes] is like a beast standing between two riders. If God rides, it wills and goes where God wills . . . If Satan rides, it wills and goes where Satan

wills. Nor may it choose to which rider it will run . . . but the riders themselves fight to decide who shall have and hold it.[29]

There is no implication here of an ultimate dualism; on the contrary, Luther is emphatic that the God with whom Satan fights as an enemy himself works in Satan according to Satan's nature. Satan is God's tool as well as his foe, and when it is his pleasure to translate a man from Satan's kingdom to that of his Son, Satan cannot prevent his doing so. In this connection, Luther makes much of Christ's picture of the strong man's goods being despoiled by the stronger man. No element of contingency or uncertainty attaches to the outcome of God's conflict with Satan; God reigns, and at every point his will is done. Luther expresses this thought elsewhere by affirming that God is the one Being whose will is, in a completely unqualified sense, free, inasmuch as his purposes cannot in principle be thwarted.

The deeds of Satan and of all men who oppose God, his truth, his Christ, and his people (Luther instances Pharaoh, Shimei, and Judas as examples) are done spontaneously, voluntarily, and without constraint (*coactio*). Nonetheless, they are in a sense necessitated. The necessity is not absolute, as Luther is careful to point out in *WA* 43, pp. 457–63. The Lutheran symbolical books (Formula of Concord SD II 44) appeal explicitly to this passage. This is so, first, because of the nature and character of the agent and, second, because of the purposive decision of God. Behind the self-determination of character, the fact that one does what one does because one is what one is (in this case, a slave to sin), lies in the predetermining resolve of the Creator, who works all things according to the counsel of his will. God resolves either to change the sinner's nature and character, so that he trusts Christ for righteousness, loves God's law, and serves God gladly, or else not to change him, but simply to allow him to run his course according to his present natural impulses, so that he brings upon himself just judgement.

3. God's Grace

What has been said so far has already indicated the richness of Luther's concept of grace. By grace he means, quite simply and comprehensively, the loving action of a sovereign Creator saving guilty sinners who cannot lift a finger to save themselves. Grace appears not only in God's free gift of righteousness, a gift bestowed in virtue of the merit and atoning death of Christ, but also in God's regenerative work, whereby the Holy Spirit brings us to faith, renews our heart, and so makes new individuals of us. Rebirth sets us free from sin's dominion so that henceforth we serve God, not only outwardly, but from our hearts, which we could never do before.

> When God works in us, the will is changed under the sweet influence of the Spirit of God . . . [I]t cannot be mastered or prevailed upon even by the gates of hell; but it goes on willing, desiring and loving good, just as once it willed, desired and loved evil.[30]

Grace both justifies and sanctifies. Nor is this all. God's acts of grace towards men in time flow from his election of them to salvation from all eternity, and this election of grace is God's guarantee not merely of present acceptance but of final glory also. God's purpose of grace will stand, and those whom he has chosen and called and justified will be preserved until the day when they are glorified, according to his promise. Such, according to Luther, is the grace of God.

Erasmus' scheme, by contrast, made final salvation altogether uncertain of attainment, because it was made contingent on our success in performing a series of acts of free will independently of God. What a comfort, says Luther, to know that this scheme is a falsehood, that free will in Erasmus' sense does not exist, and that God has taken the question of our salvation into his own omnipotent hands! Luther writes:

> I frankly confess that, for myself, even, if it could be, I should not want free-will to be given me, nor anything to be left in my own hands to enable me to endeavour after salvation; not merely because in face of so many dangers, and adversities, and assaults of devils, I could not stand my ground and hold fast my 'free-will' ... but because, even were there no dangers, adversities, or devils, I should still be forced to labour with no guarantee of success ... But now that God has taken my salvation out of the control of my own will, and put it under the control of his, and promised to save me, not according to my working or running, but according to his own grace and mercy, I have the comfortable certainty that he is faithful and will not lie to me, and that he is also great and powerful, so that no devils or opposition can break him or pluck me from him. 'No one,' he says, 'shall pluck them out of my hand, because my Father which gave them me is greater than all' (John 10:28–29 AUTHOR TRANS.).
>
> Furthermore, I have the comfortable certainty that I please God, not by reason of the merit of my works, but by reason of his merciful favour promised to me; so that, if I work too little, or badly, he does not impute it to me, but with fatherly compassion pardons me and makes me better. This is the glorying of all the saints in their God.[31]

It is obvious that Luther's evangelical doctrine of grace, based as it is on a flat rejection of the common-sense Pelagian, or 'semi-Pelagian' view of man as an independent agent and of God as a mere spectator of man's doings, raises for the speculative mind the acutest problems of theodicy, for it makes God's will the deciding factor in salvation and damnation alike. Luther himself felt these problems acutely.

> Doubtless it gives the greatest possible offence to common sense or natural reason, that God, who is proclaimed as being full of mercy and goodness, and so on, should of his own mere will abandon, harden and damn men ... It seems an iniquitous, cruel, intolerable thought to think of God; and it is this that has been a stumbling block to so many great men down the ages. And who would not stumble at it? I have stumbled at it myself more than once, down to the deepest pit of despair, so that I wished I had never been made a man. (That was before I knew how health-giving that despair was, and how close to grace.)[32]

How are we to cope with such 'intolerable' thoughts when they assail us? They turn God into a tyrannical monster and throw our souls into panic and expose them to the severest temptation (*Anfechtung*); how can we stop them? Luther has two pieces of advice for us. The first is to leave alone all speculation and enquiry into God's hidden purposes and confine our attention to what he has revealed and affirmed in his Word. Luther makes this point by developing the distinction between 'God revealed' (*Deus revelatus*) and 'God hidden' (*Deus absconditus*).

> Wherever God hides himself, and wills to be unknown to us, there we have no concern ... God in his own nature and majesty is to be left alone ... We have to do with him as clothed and displayed in his Word ... God does many things which he does not show us in his Word, and he wills many things which he does not in his Word show us that he wills ... We must keep in view his Word and leave alone his inscrutable will; for it is by his Word, and not by his inscrutable will, that we must be guided.[33]

What this means in practice is that we must listen to, and deal with, God as he speaks to us in Christ and not attempt to approach or contemplate him apart from Christ. 'We may not debate the secret will of Divine Majesty ... But let man occupy himself with God Incarnate, that is, with Jesus crucified ...'[34] In Christ, says Luther, God comes seeking the salvation of all and offering life and righteousness to all. It is for us who hear the Word of God in Christ to be humble and teachable before it, to receive and believe it as God's message to us, and to trust Christ on the basis of it, however unable we may be to square it with what we think we know of God's hidden purposes. And then we are to let God's gracious promises fill our minds and gladden our hearts and keep at bay dark thoughts arising from forbidden guesswork about the will of 'God hidden.' To know that God's promises in Christ stand sure should be enough for us.

Luther's second piece of advice to us, following on the first, is to remember that theodicy is ultimately a matter of eschatology—that is, that we cannot fully understand God's purposes, in the nature of the case, till we see them in the light of glory, when they have all been worked out to the full. When tempted to deny God's justice on the ground that he hardens and damns some men according to his own will, we should meet the temptation by reminding ourselves that here we live by faith, but one day faith will pass into sight; and when that happens, we shall know the reasons for all God's doings which baffled us here below and shall certainly discover that any appearance which may have been given of injustice, or of amoral arbitrariness, or of division and incoherence in the will of God, was entirely illusory. Luther writes:

> By the light of grace, it is inexplicable how God can damn him who by his own strength can do nothing but sin and become guilty. Both the light of nature and the light of grace here insist that the fault lies not in the wretchedness of man, but in the

injustice of God . . . But the light of glory insists otherwise, and will one day reveal God . . . as a God whose justice is most righteous and evident—provided only that in the meanwhile we *believe* it, as we are instructed and encouraged to do.[35]

God knows what he is doing, and we may be sure, even though we cannot at present see, that the Judge of all the earth is doing, and will do, right.

V

The book ends with an appeal to Erasmus to acknowledge that he was wrong and to receive Luther's elucidation of the biblical doctrine of grace as divine truth. This, Luther implies, would be Erasmus' salvation. But Erasmus did not respond as Luther hoped. With his tremendous resources of theological power and polemical rhetoric, Luther had belaboured Erasmus harder, perhaps, than he realized.

Erasmus was bitterly offended and wrote a two-volume reply to Luther, *Hyperaspistes* (which we might render as 'Protector,' or 'Defender'), in which he assaults the Wittenberg theologian as a destroyer of all civil, religious, and cultural order. He did not appear to have seen the theological and religious point of Luther's thesis about sin and grace, and Luther did not trouble to answer him again. There was no reconciliation; Erasmus continued in acid contempt for Luther, and Luther 'wrote off' Erasmus as an enemy of God because he was an enemy of grace.

The personal side of the exchange, then, was not happy. Yet the exchange itself was supremely worthwhile. It achieved something of the highest importance. It established once and for all that the Reformation conflict was not primarily about obscurantist superstitions and ecclesiastical abuses, matters over which humanists like Erasmus and theologians like Luther might under certain circumstances have made common cause; but that it was essentially concerned with the substance of the gospel and the significance of grace, matters over which Luther opposed the humanists, with their moralistic, Platonistic réchauffés of Pelagianism, no less directly than he opposed the papacy, with its grandiose claims to disburse merit and grace. To have this made clear, once and for all, was real gain.

CHAPTER 9

'Sola Scriptura' in History and Today

'*Sola Scriptura*'—by Scripture *only*—is a Reformation slogan which stands for the Reformers' total view of how the Bible should function as an authority in the conscience of the individual and in the church's corporate life. This view is more complex than the slogan might suggest, and a major part of this survey will be spent elucidating it. Then we shall attempt a bird's-eye view of how the Reformers' principle has fared since their day, and we shall end by reflecting on some of the factors involved in maintaining it in ours. Our own belief that the Reformers' view was and is essentially right will not be disguised, and our hope is that the evidence to be passed in review will go some small way towards justifying it.

The Meaning of '*Sola Scriptura*'

To the Reformers, the principle of bowing to the authority of Scripture was basic in all that they did and taught. Melanchthon called *sola Scriptura* the formal principle of the Reformation, *sola fide* being its material principle.

In articulating the principle of *sola Scriptura,* as in so much else, Luther was the pioneer. Many have traced how, from the positive declaration that to hear or read the Scripture is nothing else than to hear God[1]—a conviction common to the whole Christian church from the earliest times—Luther was led to set the authority of 'the infallible Word of God' (*verbum Dei infallibile*)[2] over that of popes, councils, church fathers, and tradition in all its forms, until on April 18, 1521, at Worms, when called on by Johann von Eck, Official General of the Archbishop of Trier, to renounce his alleged errors, he spoke these tremendous words:

> Unless I am convinced by testimonies of Scripture or evident reason (*ratione evidente*)—for I believe neither the Pope nor Councils alone, since it is established that they have often erred and contradicted themselves—I am the prisoner of the Scriptures cited by me, and my conscience has been taken captive by the Word of God; I neither can nor will recant anything, since it is neither safe nor right to act against conscience. God help me. Amen.[3]

What Luther thus voiced at Worms shows the essential motivation and concern, theological and religious, of the entire Reformation movement: namely, that the Word of God alone must rule, and no Christian man dare do other than allow it to enthrone itself in his conscience and heart.

Luther's reference to 'evident reason' as a source of conviction does not cut across the principle of Scripture *only*, for 'reason' here means precisely 'logical inference from biblical principles.' Luther rejected the idea that fallen man's rational reflection could be a source of religious truth apart from the Bible, and when he envisaged reason trying to pronounce on divine things independently of Scripture he called it 'the devil's whore.' This is his distinction between the *magisterial* use of reason, which he condemns as a damnable expression of human pride, and the *ministerial* use of it, which he treats as right and necessary.[4] None of the Reformers were irrationalists! But all of them, with Luther, insisted that it is by Scripture only that God and his grace may be known and our souls fed. For Luther, '*Sola Scriptura* was not only the battle-cry of the crusade,' writes Arthur Skevington Wood; 'it was the pole star of his own heart and mind.'[5] All that Luther was and did he owed to the Bible. The same could be said of all the Reformers, who in this as in other matters were a remarkably homogeneous body of men.[6]

What was new here? Not the idea that the Bible, being God-given, speaks with God's authority—that was common ground to both the Reformers and their opponents, and was indeed at that time an unquestioned Christian commonplace, like the doctrine of the Trinity. Nor was there anything new in the Reformers' insistence that Bible reading is a sweet and nourishing activity for Christian people. What was new was the belief, borne in upon the Reformers by their own experience of Bible study, that Scripture can and does interpret itself to the faithful from within—Scripture is its own interpreter, *Scriptura sui ipsius interpres*, as Luther put it[7]—so that not only does it not need popes or councils to tell us, as from God, what it means; it can actually challenge papal and conciliar pronouncements, convince them of being ungodly and untrue, and require the faithful to part company with them.

From the second century on, Christians had assumed that the traditions and teachers of the church, guided by the Holy Spirit, were faithful to the biblical message, and that it was safe to equate church doctrine with Bible truth. The Reformers tested this assumption by the self-interpreting Scripture which they found they had and discovered that the assumption was mostly justified in the case of the Fathers (save that apart from Augustine none of them seemed to be quite clear enough on the principle of salvation by grace and not even Augustine had fully grasped imputed righteousness).[8] In relation, however, to the pronouncements of medieval popes and councils and the teaching of the 'sophists' (scholastic theologians), the assumption was beyond all hope and rescue. It was no part of the Reformers' case to affirm that there was no value at all in the church's tradition of witness and theology; their point was simply that church tradition, which offered itself as exposition and application of Bible teaching,[9] should be tested by the Scriptures which it sought to subserve in order to check that it had not run off the track. This was part of the meaning of 'only' in the slogan 'by Scripture *only*'; as Scripture was the only *source* from which sinners might gain true knowledge of God and godliness, so Scripture was the only *judge* of what the church had in each age ventured to say in her Lord's name.[10]

It would be wrong to view Reformation theology as the projection into words of an experience, but equally it would be wrong to forget that it was born out of a tremendous renewal of Christian experience. The Reformation was a spiritual revival, if any movement in Christendom ever was; and at its heart was a renewed awareness both of what Scripture says about God and also that what Scripture says, God says. Luther's own *Türmerlebnis* ('discovery in the tower') in 1514 illustrates this: God there taught him the meaning of the divine righteousness in Romans 1:17 and how the just, i.e., justified man lives by faith, so that, in Luther's own words, 'I felt just as though I had been born again, and believed I had entered Paradise through wide-opened doors.'[11] It was with this experience, as Dr Skevington Wood says with perfect justice, 'that the Protestant Reformation really started.'[12] But the presupposition of the experience was that what Scripture says has divine authority, and had Luther not vividly felt that, his insight into Paul's meaning in Romans 1:17 would have had for him no more than historical interest—as indeed is the case with many moderns who agree that Luther's exegesis of Paul is right but have no sense of its being God's message to them. In truth, the root and matrix of the Reformation experience of God was the conviction that what Scripture declares is God's authentic message to us who hear and read it.

In affirming Holy Scripture to be the only source of true knowledge of God, and the only judge of the truth or otherwise of Christians' beliefs, the Reformers set their faces against any trust in natural theology. They based their distrust of it on a denial, not of God's general revelation, in the manner of Karl Barth, but of fallen man's ability to apprehend general revelation correctly. Quite apart from the fact that general revelation, as described by Paul in Romans 1:18–23, 32; 2:12–16 (the passages on which the Reformers based their view), tells of God only as Creator, Lawgiver, and Judge, and not as Redeemer of sinners, fallen man's proud intellect (so the Reformers held) always distorts what comes through to him from general revelation by his own self-willed speculation or self-induced obtuseness. Facing the non-biblical scholastic theology of the Roman Church and the fantastic idolatries of the pagan world, the Reformers argued constantly that those who do not in humility and self-distrust allow the Bible to teach men its message about God and grace will never have their false notions of God corrected, nor see the light of saving truth, but will walk in darkness for ever; only those who become pupils of Scripture will find the true God and eternal life.

Theologically, and religiously too, this point is bound up with another: namely, the clear understanding of the ministry of the Holy Spirit which blossomed at the

Reformation in a way that was quite without precedent since the apostles Paul
and John laid down their pens. Warfield held that the most appropriate of all
possible titles for Calvin was 'the theologian of the Holy Spirit,' and it is certainly
true that in the pages of the *Institutes* we find, briefly but powerfully expressed, a
fully worked-out account of the dispensation of the Spirit in bringing us through
the Scriptures the knowledge and life of God in Christ—an account which historically proved epoch-making.[13] Yet the fact is that all Calvin's points about the
Spirit's work with the Word were made by Luther before him,[14] and can be amply
paralleled from other Reformation divines. As we said before, these theologians
were an uncommonly homogeneous body of men, and the extent to which they
are at one on central issues is most striking. Theologically, the Reformers' grasp
of the nature and power of the Spirit's ministry sprang straight from the Scriptures, which as scholarly Renaissance men they read, not to allegorize in terms
of inherited ideas as medieval preachers had done, but to enter into the thinking
of the authors; and, reading them thus, they learned from God's penmen of the
Spirit's covenanted work in Christians and in the church. Subjectively, however,
what determined the emphasis which they gave to the Spirit's ministry was the
fact that, reading the Scriptures not just as scholars but as Christians, conscious
of the darkness of their own minds and praying for light, they had enjoyed in
answer to their prayers a deep personal experience of the Spirit's inner witness
to the authenticity of Scripture as God's Word, and of the Spirit's power to use
what was written as a source of instruction, hope, and strength.

Calvin makes this clearer than anyone in some magnificent sentences declaring that this conviction is the universal outcome of the Spirit's inner witness to
Scripture—that is, his bestowal of spiritual sight so that we perceive in Scripture
the divine light that shines forth from it. Calvin writes:

> Let it therefore remain a fixed point, that those whom the Holy Spirit has inwardly
> taught rest firmly upon Scripture, and that Scripture is indeed self-authenticated, nor
> is it right that it be subjected to proof and arguments; but that it attains the certainty
> in our eyes that it merits by the witness of the Spirit. Even if it wins reverence for itself
> by its own majestic quality (*majestate*), it only affects us seriously when sealed on
> our hearts by the Spirit. Enlightened by his power, we do not believe that Scripture
> is from God on our own judgement or that of others; but, rising above human judge-
> ment, we declare it utterly certain (just as if we saw God's own divinity there) that by
> men's ministry it has flowed to us from God's own mouth . . . we are fully conscious
> that we hold the unconquerable truth . . . we feel the unmistakable power of the
> divine majesty living and breathing there . . . Such, then, is the conviction that does
> not require reasons; such the knowledge with which the best reason agrees—that
> is, in which the mind knows surer and steadier repose than in any reasons; such is
> the awareness (*sensus*) which cannot be born save by heavenly revelation. I *speak
> only of what each believer experiences in himself,* save that my words fall far short of a
> just account of it.[15]

Again:

> The power which is peculiar to Scripture appears from the fact that no human writings, however skilfully polished, are able so to affect us at all. Read Demosthenes or Cicero; read Plato, Aristotle, or any of that crowd; they will wonderfully allure, delight, move and thrill you; but betake yourself from them to read the sacred book, and willy-nilly it will so affect you, move your heart and fix itself in your very marrow that compared with the force of that realisation (*sensus*) the impression made by the orators and philosophers will just about vanish away. So it is easy to see that the Holy Scriptures, which so far surpass in their effect all the gifts and graces of human endeavour, *breathe out something divine.*[16]

Therefore Calvin can confidently oppose to the claim of the Anabaptist 'enthusiasts' that their private revelations were Spirit-given, the common awareness of Christians that it is through the Word, and as confirmer of the Word, that the Spirit of God is truly known.

> The Lord has so bound together our certainty concerning his word and his Spirit that firm reverence for the Word possesses our minds when the Spirit shines to make us behold God's face there, and we in turn embrace the Spirit with no fear of being deceived when we recognise him in his own image, that is, in the Word ... God ... sent down the Spirit by whose power he has delivered the Word to complete his work by effective confirmation of the word ... as the children of God ... see themselves bereft of all the light of truth without the Spirit of God, so they are aware that the Word is the instrument by which the Lord bestows on believers the illumination of his Spirit. They know no other Spirit than him who dwelt and spoke in the apostles, *him by whose oracles they are repeatedly recalled to the hearing of the Word.*[17]

It is apparent that an overwhelmingly vivid awareness of Scripture as God's Word to us was central to the Reformation experience, or none of these paragraphs could ever have been written; and it is apparent also that to the extent that this awareness is absent the Reformers' understanding of what *sola Scriptura* means cannot be sustained.

The Reformers' whole understanding of Christianity, then, depended on the principle of *sola Scriptura*: that is, the view that Scripture, as the *only* Word of God in this world, is the *only* guide for conscience and the church, the *only* source of true knowledge of God and grace, and the *only* qualified judge of the church's testimony and teaching, past and present. This view rests upon a further series of principles, several of which have been hinted at already, but which may now conveniently be presented in order, thus:

(1) God's people need instruction from God, as a teacher informing and educating his pupils, because their minds are blind and ignorant through sin, and it is beyond their power to work out any true knowledge of God for themselves.

(2) God intends to enlighten and teach us, and so bring us to faith and knowledge of himself in Christ, by the Spirit through the Scriptures. That is why the Scriptures exist, that is what they are for, and that is how their character as a *canon* should be understood. 'Canon' means a rule or a measuring-rod: the Reformers' concept was that the function of a measuring-rod for faith and life is through God's appointment fulfilled by this unique composite *textbook*, of which he himself is both author and interpreter.

(3) The Scriptures were so directly produced ('spoken' or 'dictated') by the Holy Spirit that there is no room for doubt that whatever they teach, God himself teaches.

(4) As would be expected of documents that were written, not to mystify, but to be understood, the Scriptures are essentially clear in their meaning and do not need an authoritative human voice to speak for them as if they were intrinsically obscure. In any case, no such authoritative voice is available: the infallibility which the medievals claimed for the church does not exist.

(5) Scripture teaching is sufficient for our guidance in all matters of faith and life, and there is no need, just as there is no possibility, of supplementing the Bible from any other source of revelation.[18]

(6) Through the inner witness of the Spirit, Christians recognize that the Scriptures 'breathe out something divine' and come with God's own authority to all who hear or read them. The church is 'a witness and a keeper of Holy Writ.'[19] but it is not in the last analysis the church's testimony as such which gives certainty concerning either the nature of Scripture or the extent of the canon. The church's certainty about the canon rests finally, after all has been said that can be said about the history and pedigree of the separate books, on the Spirit-given awareness that they bear divine witness to Christ, and God himself speaks to us what they say.

(7) As the Spirit who inspired these books attests them to us as the Word from God, so he enables us to understand them in their true theological sense, as a complex unity of witness to our Lord and Saviour Jesus Christ, who in one way or another is the *scopus* (end in view, goal, object or aim) of them all.

(8) The biblical message which is God's teaching stands over the church and over individual Christians, God's pupils, at all times, to judge, correct and amplify their understanding of, and witness to, God's works and ways. To differ from the Bible is to differ from God, and so to be wretchedly wrong.

(9) The people of God must wait on the ministry of his Word by those whom he has qualified for this task. This is the way the church must feed its faith and nourish its life. Where the Word is not faithfully preached and taught, spiritual darkness and death always and necessarily supervene.

On three issues involved in the above account something further needs to be said to make the Reformers' view quite clear in face of modern discussions.

1. The Authority of Scripture

Authority is a relational and hierarchical concept with a wide range of applications. It needs to be said explicitly that when the Reformers ascribe authority to Scripture they are not just thinking of a relative human authority which the biblical writers might be held to have by virtue of their religious experience or expertise, or of the fact that their witness to God's acts of revelation and redemption in history is near to being first-hand and is in any case of better quality than any other available to us. Many today construe biblical authority in these terms, but such a view falls far short of the Reformers' meaning.

They were concerned to ascribe to the Scriptures an absolute divine authority, springing from the fact that God gave them and now says to us what they say. The inspiration of the prophets, whose human utterances were also and equally oracles of God, were to the Reformers the model of all biblical inspiration, while the universal and permanent application of statute law (a principle exhibited in Scripture in the abiding authority of the God-given Mosaic law over Israel) was the model for their belief that Scripture as a whole is God's instruction and guide for all his people in every age. Because God is God, his authority is ultimate and final; and because all Scripture is divinely inspired, final divine authority, in the sense of an absolute claim on our credence and our obedience, attaches to all that it has to say.

James Barr draws a useful distinction between 'hard' and 'soft' concepts of authority, as follows:

> A 'hard' idea would mean that the authority of the Bible was (i) antecedent to its interpretation and (ii) general in its application. The reader or user of the Bible would be expected to *expect* that biblical passages would be authoritative and therefore illuminating; ... and this expectation would be firm *before* the interpretation was carried out, and not therefore be a decision based afterwards upon the results of the interpretation. A 'soft' idea of authority would suggest that authority was (i) posterior to interpretation and (ii) limited accordingly to the passages where an authoritative effect had in fact been found.[20]

While most modern Protestants espouse a 'soft' view of biblical authority, that of the Reformers was as 'hard' as could be.

2. The Clarity of Scripture

The Reformers have sometimes been suspected of holding that Spirit-taught Bible students would find no difficulties in Scripture, nor would they need to bring to Scripture technical knowledge of a linguistic, cultural, and historical sort in order to find out its meaning. Whatever currency these ideas may have had in later pietistic circles, they were no part of the Reformers' view.

This appears from their own exegetical practice, which made the fullest use possible in their day of all these technical resources; it appears too from their demand for a learned ministry, which was based on their conviction that preaching and teaching require a high degree of disciplined scholarship; and their own statements show that they fully recognized that the Bible contains passages whose meanings are elusive. But when Erasmus spoke largely and loosely about the obscurity of Scripture, Luther replied as follows:

> I certainly grant that many *passages* in the Scriptures are obscure and hard to elucidate, but that is due, not to the exalted nature of their subject, but to our own linguistic and grammatical ignorance; and it does not in any way prevent us knowing all the *contents* of Scripture. For what solemn truth can the Scriptures still be concealing, now that the seals are broken, the stone rolled away from the door of the tomb, and that greatest of all mysteries brought to light—that Christ, God's Son, became man, that God is Three in One, that Christ suffered for us, and will reign for ever? And are not these things known, and sung in our streets? Take Christ from the Scriptures—and what more will you find in them? You see then, that the entire content of the Scriptures has now been brought to light, even though some passages which contain unknown words remain obscure.[21]

And he went on to say that if anyone finds the Bible wholly obscure the fault is not in the Bible, but in him—he is spiritually blind, and cannot discern Christ, and he needs the help of the Holy Spirit to make him see.

Calvin, too, believed that the substance of the biblical message was clear, and the fact that he never saw cause to change his mind on any point of doctrine throughout almost thirty years of theological writing of itself lends confirmation to his belief; yet, as T. H. L. Parker notes, he was not 'authoritarian in exegesis. Very frequently he will leave the precise meaning of a word, clause, or even sentence undecided . . . he will sometimes change his mind on the exegesis of a passage.'[22] Like Luther, Calvin insisted that the essential message was plain, but allowed that the meanings of some passages were uncertain. (And he said he did not understand the book of the Revelation at all!)

There are circles today in which it is fashionable to highlight the remoteness of the biblical world from ours and the problematical nature of the composition and background of the biblical books, and on this basis to ask whether it can be wise or fruitful to expect ordinary Christians to be benefited, as distinct from perplexed, by personal Bible reading. Thus, for instance, D. E. Nineham writes: 'It is perhaps a pity that the proposed new Anglican catechism appears to regard the private reading of the Bible as mandatory for every literate member of the Church. Is that realistic . . .?'[23] This is a return to Erasmus, and the Reformers' comment on it would certainly be the same as Luther's to Erasmus: namely, that if you have eyes for Christ as the *scopus* of Scripture, according to its own testimony to itself, you will find that, just as the grace of the biblical Christ is relevant to you, so the essence of the biblical witness to him is clear to you. Millions of Bible-readers in the world today will testify that this indeed is so.

3. The Unity of Scripture

A further contemporary fashion is to dwell on the contrasts of style and vocabulary found within the Bible, and on this basis to deny that there is any such thing as 'the biblical theology' at all. The suggestion is that what we have, rather, in the Bible as a whole, and in the New Testament particularly, is a series of distinct theologies balancing each other, to which we do violence if we try to integrate them into one. Gospel harmonies, for instance, are misguided endeavours; we best grasp the witness of the Gospels to Jesus Christ not by combining them, as the church has been doing since Tatian, but by noting the differences between them. Similarly, the theologies of Luke-Acts, Paul, Hebrews, and the Johannine writings should be separated out and kept distinct, so that each can be appreciated in its divergence from the others.

James Barr acts as sounding-board for this approach when, describing the current flow of opinion about the Bible, he writes:

> There is less confidence in the idea that the Bible must be read 'as a whole.' There are those who feel, on the contrary, that the diversity and disagreement found within the Bible is a more sure characteristic of its nature and a more promising clue to its meaning... If the emphasis on the Bible 'as a whole' grew up in reaction against the purely analytic interests of scholars, so in turn the strivings after synthesis in post-war exegesis ended up by seeming like old-fashioned harmonization and made people turn again with relief to analysis as a fresher approach. Once again, therefore, we find that people are giving different values to different parts of the Bible.[24]

The Reformers would have seen this approach as abusing a half-truth, a monumental case of getting hold of the wrong end of the stick. Calvin, who came to the Bible as a gifted linguist and literary man, shows himself every whit as sensitive as modern scholars are to the verbal and stylistic differences between one author and another, and he was not alone in this. But what the Reformers found was that when the Bible is allowed to interpret itself from within, on the basis that 'the mind of the Spirit is understood when the text of the document is understood,'[25] then as the various parts of each individual book join up together by internal thematic links, so do the various books with each other to form a single coherent body of teaching. The verbal and conceptual resources of the different writers vary, but the theology which they teach is one.

The Reformers took Scripture 'literally' in the sense that they abandoned the arbitrariness of allegorizing, treated the historical character of the documents seriously, and concentrated on discovering what the human writer had in mind and why he was concerned to say it. Handling the Bible so, they found in it unity of doctrine, in a way that medieval exegesis never had. Their expository method as theologians both reflected and confirmed their discovery: they built up their accounts of each matter inductively, by adducing successive Scriptures bearing on each theme.

This was what Warfield meant when he said that Calvin's theological method

> was persistently, rigorously, some may even say exaggeratedly, *a posteriori*. All *a priori* reasoning here he not only eschewed but vigorously repelled. His instrument of research was not logical amplification but exegetical investigation.[26]

What was true of Calvin was true of Luther before him, and of all the Reformation masters.

To Calvin, the grace of Christ the Mediator, and the history of the covenant of grace which Christ mediated through successive dispensations, are the two overarching and complementary themes which run through all the Bible and hold it together.[27] Luther also has this insight, though the key to the unity of Scripture of which he makes most is the apparent antithesis of law and gospel: God, says Luther, first drives us out of ourselves through the law his ('strange work') so that he may draw us as needy sinners to the Christ of the gospel promise, of whom the Old Testament said much and the New Testament is full to overflowing.[28] Both Luther and Calvin laboured to present Bible teaching as a coherent corpus of instruction from God the Holy Spirit about God and ourselves—the redeeming work in history of the God who made us, and the godliness to which knowledge of this should give rise in all human lives.[29]

It is surely clear that the Reformation tradition of exegesis, with its unitive, evangelical, Christocentric thrust and its unqualified acceptance as from God of all that Scripture is found to teach, prompts uncomfortable questions about its modern counterpart which stresses differences within the Bible, real or alleged, as the clue to understanding it. Did the Reformers succeed in showing that beneath the surface diversity of the documents lies a deep unity of evangelical teaching? If so, how can we regard a type of exegesis which does not show this as other than a failure? If unity is inescapable when exegesis is adequate, failure to find unity shows only that exegesis has been inadequate. But in that case the movement of thought described by Professor Barr must be judged, not an advance, but a regression. We may and must allow that if a unitive exegesis cannot be made convincing the Bible falls apart and the principle of *sola Scriptura* is exploded. But with that we must also insist that if a unitive exegesis can be vindicated, then the viability of the principle is established and its challenge becomes inescapable.

'Sola Scriptura' in Christian History

In the older Lutheran and Reformed churches of Western Europe and the British Isles, in conservative Presbyterian, Congregational, Baptist, and Methodist circles, and now in the fast-growing Pentecostal churches, *sola Scriptura* has been enthroned as the architectural and critical principle of all sound theology. On the history of this principle over more than four centuries we make the following comments.

1. The Extent of Unanimity among Its Adherents Has Been Remarkable

If one reviews the historic Lutheran, Reformed, Anglican, Congregational, and Baptist confessions, or compares, for example, Calvin's *Institutes* with the systematic theologies of F. Pieper the Lutheran, Charles Hodge and Louis Berkhof the Presbyterians, E. A. Litton and W. H. Griffith Thomas the Anglicans, W. B. Pope the Methodist, and A. H. Strong the Baptist, or if one examines the preaching and spirituality of churches which actively upheld *sola Scriptura* as a principle for determining faith and action, what impresses is the oneness of overall outlook and the width of the area over which substantially identical positions were taught. Whether those involved felt close to each other as they sparred over points of specific disagreement, or defended their denominations against criticism from fellow-biblicists, is perhaps doubtful; but what is not doubtful is that those who historically have held to *sola Scriptura,* recognizing no *magisterium* save that of the Bible itself, have been at one on all essentials and on most details too, in a very striking way. If evidence tending to confirm the clarity of Scripture is called for, this fact will surely qualify.

2. The Matters on Which Adherents of This Principle Have Differed Have Been Secondary

To the traditional Roman Catholic complaint that Protestant biblicism produces endless divisions in the church, the appropriate reply is twofold: firstly, the really deep divisions have been caused not by those who maintained *sola Scriptura,* but by those, Roman Catholic and Protestant alike, who rejected it; second, when adherents of *sola Scriptura* have split from each other the cause has been sin rather than Protestant biblicism, for in convictional terms the issues in debate have not been of the first magnitude. Leaving aside the deep unorthodoxies of sects like Mormons and Jehovah's Witnesses—and their hostility to the Christian tradition and distrust of ordinary canons of biblical scholarship obliges one to put them in a class by themselves—one finds that the main theological issues that have divided Protestants who hold to *sola Scriptura* have been these: (1) how to understand God's sovereignty in salvation—the issue between Calvinists on the one hand and Arminians and Lutherans on the other; (2) how to understand the presence of Christ in the Lord's Supper—the issue between Lutherans and other Protestants; (3) how far, if at all, Scripture legislates in the realm of church order—the issue between Flacians and 'adiaphorists' in Lutheranism, and between the Puritans, Cartwright, and Travers, on the one hand, and Whitgift and Hooker, on the other, in Elizabethan England; (4) how the churches should be related to the state—the issue in debates about establishment throughout the world since the sixteenth century; (5) whether believers' children may properly be baptized in infancy or not—the issue between Baptist and all other Protestant churches; (6) what circumstances will surround the Lord's return—the issue between postmillennialists, premillennialists, and amillennialists.

Other issues debated within Protestantism—anthropological, Christological, soteriological—have involved abandoning the Reformers' view of biblical inspiration, and thus defecting from *sola Scriptura* in its original sense, so we leave these questions out of account. (That lowered views of Scripture produce endless division within the churches is a fact too well known to need comment here, and we forbear to dwell on it.)

What are we to say to these six matters of debate? First, that whatever divisions they may have occasioned in the past it is very arguable that, being in reality secondary questions, they need not, and ideally would not, have this effect. Second, that it is also very arguable that in each of these cases unexamined assumptions brought to the task of exegesis, rather than any obscurities arising from it, were really at the root of the cleavage. The trouble was that presuppositions were read into Scripture rather than read out of it, as follows:

(1) The first debate seems to have sprung from the assumption made by some that if man's free agency and responsibility were to be affirmed as Scripture affirms them, then God's absolute control of human action which Scripture also affirms must be denied.

(2) The second debate seems to have arisen because there were exegetical questions about our Lord's words of institution at the Last Supper which the Swiss Reformers raised and Luther would not face.

(3) The third debate reflected a taking for granted by some that apostolic acts in ordering church life have normative force for later generations, whether or not anything to this effect is said in the text, and equally that practices in the church which lack direct biblical sanction by precept or precedent are prohibited.

(4, 5) The fourth and fifth debates reflected the presupposition that Scripture must legislate on the issues in question, even though no biblical author addresses himself to either.

(6) The sixth debate reflects an unexamined difference of assumptions as to what constitutes 'literal' exegesis of prophetic Scriptures. It is a confusion to blame the principle of *sola Scriptura* for conflicts which sprang from insufficient circumspection in exegesis.

3. To Limit God's Sovereignty Is to Undermine 'Sola Scriptura'

This is not simply because the Bible views God's sovereignty as unlimited, though it does: it is because any such limitation strikes at the truth of inspiration.

If God is not in absolute control of free human acts generally, then he was not in absolute control of the writings done by the biblical authors, and it cannot in that case be fully true that 'the mind of the Spirit is understood when the text of the document is understood.'

It was inevitable that Arminian and Deist theology, which both take God's governing hand away from man's self-determined actions, should have produced lowered views of inspiration and a style of exegesis which convicted the inspired authors of making mistakes. Kant was being no more than a good Deist, with his own epistemological trimmings, when he denied that God can send us verbal messages. The unwillingness of the neo-orthodox Barth, Bultmann, and their followers, to equate the normative Word of God with what the Bible says, and their preference for identifying the Word with what the biblical writers are thought to have meant despite what they said, or with Christ beyond the Bible rather than the Bible itself, or with a subjective psychic event rather than the objective truth that causes it, shows that they too do not wish to be lumbered with the historic doctrine of inspiration, and that in turn points to the fact that they too have an inadequate grasp of God's sovereignty over all his world. (This is an inadequacy which Barth's view of history and Bultmann's view of nature have in fact long made plain:[30] it has undoubtedly been the fundamental weakness in the theologies of both men.) The *sola Scriptura* which Protestants of this kind may profess in refusing to turn for knowledge of God to any extra-biblical source (e.g., the Roman Catholic *magisterium*) has to be differentiated from the *sola Scriptura* of the Reformers, whose essential point was that the teaching of the Bible is to be received as instruction from God without any qualification at all. The Reformation principle of *sola Scriptura* presupposes the Reformation view of God, and cannot be maintained apart from it.

Maintaining '*Sola Scriptura*' Today

What has been said suggests three concluding points.

1. The Necessity of Upholding '*Sola Scriptura*'

It is inescapable that, as this principle determines one's whole account of Christianity, so one cannot abandon it without one's whole view of Christianity changing, more or less, at fundamental level. This is so whether the abandonment takes the form of giving up belief in absolute divine sovereignty and plenary biblical inspiration, or of accepting the Roman claim that a charisma of interpretive infallibility attaches to popes, councils, and their dogmas. For this reason the latest stage in the general ecumenical discussion of Holy Scripture (in which, of course, Roman Catholic scholars take their share) must be judged intensely depressing.

Accomplished biblical scholars like D. E. Nineham, Christopher Evans, and James Barr[31] reject all concepts of a revealed Word of God or a *Heilsgeschichte* that is normative for faith.

The era when ecumenical Bible study was shaped by the concerns of Barth and Cullmann has ended. Barr notes in contemporary theological thought

> a shift in the locus of authority, or indeed an abandonment of the concept of authority altogether. The older theology seems to us today to have suffered from an authority neurosis; in all diversities there was an attempt to proceed from an agreed authority centre, defined and known in advance, which would serve as criterion in doubtful questions . . . Today we are content to have criteria which are less clear, to leave the nature of authority to emerge at the end of the theological process rather than to be there in defined form at the beginning.[32]

This is as sad as it is clear. Barr is opting for a theological programme which sees Christianity as an historical phenomenon of which biblical and theological study is one continuing aspect, and he views the theological task humanistically as a venture in analytical description and free construction. On his programme, what authority the end-product has will presumably be decided by estimating its coherence as an historical analysis on the one hand and its vitality as a stimulus to discussion on the other; and the question of its *truth*, in the sense of whether it squares with God's view of things or not, will never be raised. Thus the 'authority neurosis' of older Protestant theology, and the 'really pathological' concern of fundamentalists and others to learn from Scripture how to discriminate between orthodoxy and heresy, i.e., true and false belief,[33] will be transcended and left behind.

It is not unknown for intelligent persons of neurotic and pathological opinions to diagnose the views of others as being neurotic and pathological, and the question arises whether that is not happening here; but, intriguing as that question is, we cannot pursue it now. Our only present point is that current theological developments, as illustrated by the views of Barr, confirm beyond all doubt what our earlier analysis indicated—namely, that those who wish to affirm any concept of *Heilsgeschichte* (particularly a divinely interpreted *Heilsgeschichte*), or any concept of a revealed Word of God (particularly one that is identical with the Bible) must do so on the basis of the Reformation principle of *sola Scriptura*, or they will not be able to do it at all.

2. The Importance of Vindicating a Unitive Theological Exegesis of Scripture

In the passage quoted above, Barr continues by predicating his approach on the existence in the Bible of

> a multiplicity of theologies. The older theological principle, if I do not misjudge it, did not think in this way: rather, it set forth a criterion of authority which would, it

was implied, generate the 'right' theology . . . There was a strict line between the one authority and the one true theology.[34]

Again we may be grateful to Professor Barr for his clarity; this is exactly correct, and the Reformers' principle of *sola Scriptura* will only appear viable or credible if it can be shown that a unitive biblical exegesis which plots the 'strict line' to true theology is actually plausible. Is this, in the present state of studies, an impossible task?

Certainly current exegesis, which has theological pluralism in its presuppositions and method, has such pluralism in abundance in its conclusions; but we do well to remember this has not always been the way of scientific biblical study. On the dust jacket of the most recent volumes of the latter-day Scottish translation of Calvin's New Testament commentaries to come into my hands, the three which contain his Harmony of the Synoptic Gospels, it says:

> These are the classic commentaries of the Reformation which laid the basis for all later scholarly exegesis of the Bible and which are proving as 'modern' as ever in their honest careful handling of the text, and in the relevance of their exposition to our deep religious and human needs. The interpretation . . . makes the Bible live and speak not only to the preacher and the scholar but to the common man concerned to understand the Word of God.

Yet the exegesis of Calvin, who over a quarter of a century expounded almost all the Bible in his own distinctive and distinguished way, was unitive through and through, as indeed that of Protestant commentaries generally was till fairly recent times.

Could it be that the dust jacket is right, and that Calvin's theological exegesis points a way which is still open to us today, if we will take it? If so, we must face the fact that many of our contemporaries are sure that Calvin's road is not open, and the contrary can only be established in face of their scepticism when theological exegesis of Scripture which is both contemporary and unitive is actually produced. Here, perhaps, is the major task for evangelical scholarship in the next generation.

General apologetics for biblical theism and the formal principle of *sola Scriptura* may keep the invading waters at bay, but only theological work which makes credible to modern doubters the inner unity of the message of the two Testaments and the sixty-six canonical books will turn the tide. In this twentieth century, the most sustained quest for exegesis of the kind described has been that of Karl Barth: and if we think that his venture was not wholly a success, it behoves us not to dismiss his objective, but to take the task in hand ourselves and try to do better. No general return to *sola Scriptura* can be expected today or tomorrow till the inner unity, consistency, and coherence of the Bible message has been demonstrated to the Christian world afresh.

3. *The Cruciality of Divine Sovereignty in the Case for* 'Sola Scriptura'

The customary apologetic for biblical authority operates on too narrow a front. As we have seen, faith in the God of Reformation theology is the necessary presupposition of faith in Scripture as 'God's Word written,'[35] and without this faith *sola Scriptura* as the God-taught principle of authority more or less loses its meaning. Only as we acknowledge the sovereign power and wisdom of the God who guided and controlled the writers of his infallible Word, and who now wills to guide and control our fallible minds and hearts through that Word, will the phrase *Sola Scriptura* carry its full significance for us. We may wish to defend against criticism our inherited evangelical habit, learned from Calvin's *Institutes*, and the Westminster Confession, of dealing with the Bible, as the principle of true theological knowledge, prior to any other subject in the body of divinity; but we must never lose sight of the fact that our doctrine of God is decisive for our concept of Scripture, and that in our controversy with a great deal of modern theology it is here, rather than in relation to the phenomena of Scripture, that the decisive battle must be joined.[36]

CHAPTER 10

Calvin the Theologian

'The Theologian' was the affectionate and admiring phrase by which Philip Melanchthon, Professor of Greek at Wittenberg University and leader of the German Reformation after Luther's death, regularly referred to his twelve-years-younger contemporary, the senior pastor in the Swiss city of Geneva. 'Minister of the Word of God' was the only title to which John Calvin himself laid claim. Yet he would have agreed that in this capacity he could not help being a theologian of some sort. For to him the word 'theologian' denoted, not just a member of the church's academic elite, but anyone who ventured to make statements about God.

Calvin's Calvinism

What sort of theologian was Calvin? Not the sort that he is often thought to have been. It is depressing to observe how, despite all the disciplined Calvin-research of the past century, the old hostile misrepresentations persist. Thus, many still think that the main mark of Calvin's theology, so far as it was distinctive, was audacity of speculative logic, especially regarding predestination; though in fact, as has often been shown, all his teaching was conscientiously biblical, and on predestination in particular he declined to go a hair's breadth beyond what he understood Scripture actually to say.

Many still take his doctrine of sin (later called 'total depravity') to mean, not just that no man is at any point as good as he should be, but that every man is at every point as bad as he can be—though Calvin explicitly taught that a kindly providence (later called 'common grace') operated through conscience, law, custom, and example to restrain the full outworking of inborn perversity and to move even ungodly men to ethical and cultural achievements of abiding worth. Many still equate Calvin's faith in divine sovereignty with physical or metaphysical determinism (with which it had nothing to do), and on the moral level with fatalism—though Calvin always stressed that man is responsible to God for his choices, and that God's will is done by means of intelligent, calculated action on man's part, and that God's ordering of our circumstances is for ethical ends, to wean us from sin and to train us in faith, patience, and love.

In recent years, Calvinism has been seriously construed as a psychopathic phenomenon, a projection of sublimated cruelty, or disgust at human life, or an inferiority complex, or some other neurotic disorder resulting in a malevolent 'anti-gospel' whose main point is that God is fierce, and most people are irremediably damned. Many who would not go so far still think of Calvinism as inimical to evangelism and as narrowing the bounds of God's mercy—though Calvin held that in the gospel Christ is offered to all, and spent his whole working life seeking to spread the gospel throughout Europe by praying, writing, advising, and training leaders. Many still see Calvin as a theological iconoclast who swept aside the post-apostolic Christian heritage as so much useless lumber—though the Anabaptists, who actually were iconoclasts of this kind, had no sterner foe than John Calvin, nor in the Reformation era did the Fathers have a more diligent student. The popular idea of him is still of a chilly, arrogant intellectualist—though in fact no Reformation leader was more consistently practical in his teaching, or more humble and adoring in his thoughts of God. Yet all serious Calvin-scholars now know that the Calvin of legend—the slobbering ogre, the egoistical fanatic, the doctrinaire misanthrope, the inhuman dictator with a devilish God—is a figure of fancy, not of fact.[1] The real Calvin was not like that, nor was his theology the monstrous and misshapen thing that the legendary image would suggest.

Not that all ever accepted this image, or that Calvin ever lacked partisans. In each century from his day to ours, self-styled 'Calvinists' have claimed him as their patron. But it would not always be safe to judge his theology by theirs. The 'five points of Calvinism' formulated at the Synod of Dort—total depravity, unconditional election, particular redemption, irresistible grace (better, effectual calling), and the preservation of the saints—do indeed proclaim the sovereignty of grace in a way Calvin would have endorsed. Four of these 'points' he insisted on himself, and there is little doubt that the Dort formula of particular redemption states what he would have said had he faced the developed Arminian thesis.[2] But other 'Calvinistic' developments have involved a certain shift from Calvin's view of things. Examples are the divine-right Presbyterianism of Beza, Gillespie, and the Westminster Confession; the Puritan treatment of assurance as the main problem of religion; and the scholastic custom of setting the gospel promise in the context of the double decree, rather than, as in Calvin's definitive (1559) *Institutio* and Paul's Epistle to the Romans, vice versa.

Whether these developments be seen as the perfecting of Calvinism or the distorting of it, at all events they should not be read back into Calvin himself, any more than the 'Christomonism' of Karl Barth should be, or the 'hyper-Calvinism' classically voiced in old Mr. Ryland's shout from the chair when William Carey mooted a missionary society—'Sit down, young man; when God pleases to convert the heathen he will do it without your aid or mine.' (Calvin, who himself sent out, to an island off Brazil, the first Protestant foreign missionaries in history, would not have approved of that!) If we would know Calvin the theologian, we must do more than study the 'Calvinists'; we must go to the man himself.

The *Institutio*

This prospect, however, appears at first sight somewhat daunting. For Calvin's output was huge. His first theological work (*Psychopannychia*, a refutation of the Anabaptist belief in soul-sleep) was written in 1534, when he was twenty-five. Between then and his death thirty years later, he developed his *Institutio Christiana Religionis* from its original pocket-book size into a folio of eighty chapters and half a million words; wrote commentaries or preached expositions, later published, on all the major books of the Bible;[3] and composed controversial treatises on all the main doctrines of the faith against Romans, Lutherans, and Anabaptists, not to mention Socinus and the heady pantheist Servetus. His works fill fifty-nine thick volumes of the *Corpus Reformatorum*. Nor is there much padding in them; apart from his homiletic and satiric excursions, Calvin's thought moved fast, and his style was accordingly compressed, packing much thought into relatively few words. (He claimed to love brevity!) Confronted with so much material, the student might well quail. Yet two facts make it possible to grasp the substance of Calvin's theology with less labour than might have been expected. The first is his consistency; the second is the comprehensiveness of his *magnum opus*.

His consistency is remarkable. All that he wrote was homogeneous. He never changed his mind on any doctrinal issue. The only alteration in his published views that has been demonstrated to date is that whereas in *Psychopannychia* and the 1536 *Institutio* he ascribed the apocryphal book of Baruch to Baruch, he later concluded it to be pseudonymous.[4] Apart from this detail of criticism— not strictly biblical criticism, at that, and of no theological significance—all his opinions remained identical. 'Though he is of the number of those who grow old learning every day,' wrote Beza towards the end of Calvin's life, 'from the very beginning up to now, in all his many laborious writings, he has never set before the church one dogma about which he needed to alter his mind and part company with himself.'[5] Unlike Luther and Melanchthon, his contemporaries, and Augustine before him and Karl Barth after him, his outlook was truly formed before his literary career began, and though as time went on he was able to amplify and augment, he never needed to correct or retract. Among creative theologians there is hardly a parallel, save, perhaps, on a smaller scale, Athanasius.

Thus, any statement of view in any of Calvin's writings, early or late, may be taken as integral to his thought throughout. Those scholars who study particular themes in Calvin cross-sectionally have no need to raise questions of changing opinions from one work to another. No such changes took place. Calvin's theology, first to last, was a great tapestry of biblical strands of thought, master-fully woven, and all of a piece.

The second fact which simplifies the task of grasping Calvin's point of view is the comprehensiveness of the 1559 *Institutio*. This quality is explained by the book's history. Calvin's *Institutio* (the word means 'principles,' 'basic instruction') was first conceived as a vest-pocket-companion for Reformed Christians and an apologia for them against their detractors. The original (1536) edition contained only six chapters, on the law, the creed, the Lord's Prayer, the dominical sacra-ments, the five false sacraments of Rome, and Christian liberty. The first four of these chapters had links with Luther's catechetical writings, and both Calvin and his publishers (Platter and Lasius, of Basel) called the book a catechism, though it was not written in question-and-answer form.

For preface, it carried a letter to the French king, Francis I, explaining that Reformed Christians were not, as some supposed, disloyal citizens. Its title, con-sidering its limited size and scope, was, to say the least, grandiloquent: *Basic In-struction* [institutio] *in the Christian Religion, comprising almost the whole sum of godliness* [pietatis] *and all that needs to be known in the doctrine of salvation: a work very well worth reading for all who aspire to godliness.* It sold out within nine months, and a new edition was called for. Startled, as well as pleased, by its suc-cess, and uneasily conscious that it had not been all that its title claimed, Calvin set himself to revise and amplify, and the 1539 *Institutio* was almost three times as long as the first edition.

In a new preface, Calvin explained that part of his aim in enlarging it had been, first, to provide a textbook for theological students (apart from Melanchthon's *Loci Communes* and Zwingli's less systematic *Commentarius de Vera et Falsa Religione*, none such existed as yet on the Protestant side), and, second, to display the system of thought that would underlie the commentaries he proposed to write. With a clear allusion to the fulsome 'trailers' of the 1536 title page, Calvin named the en-larged volume *Basic Instruction in the Christian Religion, now at last truly answering to its description* [nunc vere demum suo titulo respondens]. The work still sold, and grew through further editions, till Calvin gave it final form in 1559. The 1559 tide ran thus: *Basic Instruction in the Christian Religion now first arranged in four books, and divided into particular chapters, according to the fittest method* [ad aptissimum methodum] *and so greatly augmented that it can almost be regarded as a new work.*

The *Institutio* was now five times its original length. Its four books were headed: (i) The knowledge of God the Creator; (ii) The knowledge of God the Redeemer in Christ; (iii) The way of coming to know the grace of Christ, and the benefits which thence derive to us, and the effects that follow; (iv) The external means or helps by which God calls us into the fellowship of his Son and keeps us there. The themes of this fourth book were the church, the sacraments, and civil government, all being regarded as means of grace. Thus Calvin's new arrangement (which, interestingly enough, was an almost point-for-point return to that of the catechetical booklet he wrote early on for use in Geneva, the 1537 *Instruction in Faith*) reproduced the order of the main topics in the Apostles' Creed—'I believe (i) in God the Father, maker of heaven and earth; and (ii) in Jesus Christ . . . ; (iii) I believe in the Holy Ghost; (iv) the holy catholic church.' Under these headings Calvin set out a complete statement of Christian truth as he understood it, and a full defence of it against Roman and Anabaptist alternatives.[6]

Calvin's *magnum opus,* therefore, came before the world as a Reformed *summa theologiae* and *summa pietatis* in one. Calvin himself saw it as the centrepiece of his life's work. He laboured at the definitive edition of 1559 at a time of extreme bad health, but the prospect of imminent death only spurred him to flog himself harder, in order to complete the task before life ended. He put into it all that he knew. Accordingly, it is supremely from the *Institutio* that we may, and should, take his measure as a theologian. Much is said today of the danger of oversimplifying and overpetrifying Calvin's thought if one reads the *Institutio* in isolation from his commentaries and catechisms, where polemics are not so obtrusive. The point is no doubt valid. Yet the heart of Calvin is in the *Institutio,* more than in any of his other works.

The harsh controversial passages, which cause modern readers much offense, are actually essential to its design. Just as the Bible, being the proclamation of God's truth to an intellectually warped world, is necessarily polemical at point after point, so Calvin, as a Christian and a minister, could not but be a fighting man; and the Reformation, as a renewal of biblical faith amid ecclesiastical paganism, could not but be a fighting movement; and the *Institutio,* as a Reformation manifesto and apologia, could not but be a fighting book. John Calvin was a peace-loving person who found controversy a tedious burden, and who worked tirelessly to bring Protestants together, yet any account of him which minimized the intensity of his commitment to the conflict of God's Word with human error, as well as sin, would be an injustice. We may not dismiss Calvin's polemics as mere appendages to his positive teaching, as unnecessary as they are unpleasant. Rather, we must reckon with Calvin's insistence that some notions ought to be fought for, and others fought against, to the death.

The Knowledge of God

The layout of the 1559 *Institutio* shows us at once its scope and range. As the opening chapter, dating from 1539, explains, it is a treatise on the knowledge of God, and the knowledge of ourselves which is bound up with it. As in Scripture, so in Calvin, 'knowledge of God' is a concept which unifies belief, experience, and conduct. It embraces both the knowing of God, which is religion, and what is known of, or about, God, which is theology. It denotes an apprehension of God, not merely as existing but as being 'for us' in grace, and of ourselves as

being 'for him' in worship and service. 'Properly speaking, we cannot say that
God is known where there is no religion or piety.' 'The effect of our knowledge (of
God) ought to be, first, to teach us reverence and fear; and, second, to induce us,
under its guidance and teaching, to ask every good thing from him, and, when it
is received, to ascribe it to him.' 'The knowledge of God does not consist in cold
(*frigida*) speculation, but carries along with it worship.' 'We are summoned to a
knowledge of God which does not just flutter in the brain, satisfied with empty
speculation, but to one which will prove firm and fruitful when it is duly grasped
by us and takes root in our heart.'[7]

In making the knowledge of God his central theme, and presenting the Reformed faith as a recovery of this knowledge—a truly religious theology, and a
truly theological religion—Calvin was picking up Luther's early polemic against
the scholastics, mystics, and merit-mongers, who thought to know God without
knowing Jesus Christ. With Luther, Calvin insisted that we only know God as
we listen to the Scriptures, and learn Christ from the Scriptures. The *Institutio*
assumes throughout the basic correlations by which Luther had maintained this
thesis. These were as follows.

The first was the correlation between *revelation* and *Scripture*, in the name
of which Luther had attacked transubstantiation, the mass-sacrifice, meritorious
works, purgatory, and current ideas of papal and conciliar authority, and had
anathematized all traditional tenets that lacked biblical support. The second was
the correlation between *the Spirit* and *the Word*, in the name of which Luther had
attacked Anabaptist illuminism and anathematized all 'spiritual' teaching that
diverged from the written Word, and its witness to Jesus Christ.

The third was the correlation between *the Word* and *faith*, in the name of
which Luther had attacked as superstitious all religious attitudes which did not
take the form of response to biblical truth and to the Christ of Scripture, the
incarnate Son of God who in his humanity and humiliation not merely spoke,
but was, God's word of grace to man. The fourth was the correlation between
faith and *works*, in the name of which Luther had insisted that there was no true
knowledge of God where there was not also active discipleship of Christ—that
is, faith spontaneously working in love to God and men, and in obedience to the
law. Calvin reproduced all these points.

Three questions may be asked to clarify Calvin's concept of the knowledge of
God. First, what does it mean to know God? To this question the *Institutio* replies,
in effect, that it means acknowledging him as Scripture reveals him; abasing oneself before him as a sinful creature; learning from his Word the law and the gospel;
believing the promise that he is our reconciled Father through the mediation and
blood-shedding of Jesus Christ; rejoicing in the reality of redemption, pardon, and
sonship; hoping in the promise of preservation and reward that God makes to all
who are Christ's; delighting in the prospect of a joyful resurrection; loving God for
all his love and mercy; obeying his law; practising daily self-denial; loving others

for his sake and seeking their good; submitting to his providential ordering of things; maintaining dependence on him by prayer and thanksgiving; and seeking to honour him in all commerce with the created order and all human relationships.

Calvin stresses that this knowledge of God as our God is his gift to us and the work of his Spirit within us, and that it is itself correlative to that union with Christ which is the means of our salvation. 'Christ, when he produces faith in us by the agency of his Spirit, at the same time ingrafts us into his body, that we may become partakers of all blessings.'[8]

Second, we may ask: what is the intellectual basis of this knowledge?—what, in other words, can be known about God by those who know him? To this question the *Institutio* offers its whole eighty chapters as a reply. They are arranged as a theology of the gospel, in an order evidently reflecting the structure of the Epistle to the Romans, which Calvin, like Luther, regarded as the key to Scripture.

Justification by faith stands at the centre of the *Institutio*, spatially as well as theologically; it occupies chapters xi–xviii of Book III. Calvin introduces it in a way which makes plain its central importance. 'We must now discuss justification thoroughly,' he writes, 'bearing in mind that it is *the mainstay for upholding religion,* and so giving it the more care and attention.'[9] Justification is in fact the focal centre of the *Institutio*.

What precedes it is a survey of things that must first be known before we can grasp it—namely, that we gain true knowledge of God only from Scripture (I.i–ix); that God is triune, Creator, and Sovereign, lord of history and disposer of all things (I.x–xviii); that godliness means humble love, reverence, submission, and dependence Godward (I.ii); that we are by nature guilty, blind, and helpless in sin (II.i–v); that Jesus Christ, the divine-human mediator, has procured salvation for us, and that both Testaments proclaim him to us (II.vi–xvii); what the law requires (II.viii); what faith is (III.ii); how God gives faith (III.i), and how faith begets repentance (III.iii–v) and a Christian life (III.vi–x). What comes after the section on justification is an account of what more the justified man needs to know to keep his faith in healthy exercise and to serve his God aright— namely, that his freedom from the law is not for lawlessness, but for free obedience (III.xix); that he must always pray (III.xx); that God's free election and gracious sovereignty guarantee his final salvation; that he has a hope of resurrection in glory (III.xxv); that he must wait on the ministry of word and sacrament in the church for his soul's good (IV.i–xix); and that he must be a loyal citizen, inasmuch as civil government exists to protect the church (IV.xx).[10]

The *Institutio*, however, like the Epistle to the Romans, is a many-sided book, and no one analysis can do justice to its total thrust. That given in the last paragraph brings out its practical, catechetical framework, but a further review is needed to set Calvin's pastoral concern in the perspective of his basic theocentrism. His concern that men should know grace was rooted in a deeper concern, that men should glorify God.

As Christian, pastor, and theologian. Calvin's ruling passion was that God, the source, stay, and end of all things, should receive the glory that was his due. What this meant positively was that men should live their lives in a spirit of adoring worship, conscious of the wonder of all God's work in creation, providence, and grace, bowing to his authority in every sphere of life, and sanctifying the secular by taking his thoughts as the rule of truth, his will as the rule of right, and his approval as the standard of value.

What the glorifying of God meant negatively was that men must neither cast off his rule nor intrude into his work. The slogans which served to circumscribe the understanding of Christianity for which Calvin and his fellow-reformers stood—*sola Scriptura; solo Christo; sola fide; sola gratia; soli Deo gloria!*—point to the radical self-denial to which we sinners are at this point called. Knowledge of God as Creator and Redeemer, holy, just, wise, and good, comes to us by Scripture *alone,* not by our own speculation. The benefits of redemption—reconciliation, righteousness, sonship, regeneration, glory—come to us by Christ *alone,* not by any fancied personal merit or any priestly mediation by the church. Christ and reconciliation are received by faith *alone,* not earned by works and effort; and that very faith is given to us and kept alive in us by grace *alone,* so that our own contribution to our salvation is precisely nil, and all the glory for it must therefore go to God *alone,* and none to ourselves. As in the *Institutio* Calvin controverts misconceptions of various kinds—idolatry, anti-Trinitarianism, illuminism, antinomianism, autosoterism, sacerdotalism, the mass-doctrine, papal supremacy, the finality of conciliar decisions, and so forth—his polemic is constantly spurred forward by the sense that these things dishonour God, and rob him of his glory and praise.

It is already clear that the focal centre of Calvin's concern with the intellectual structure of the knowledge of God was his anxiety that men should think biblically of Christ, and of grace. Like Luther, he stressed that Christ is the *scopus* of Scripture, the 'goal' to which it all points, and that grace is the uniting theme which binds the two Testaments together. Calvin, indeed, made more of the gracious covenantal basis of Old Testament legislation than ever Luther did. We may pinpoint Calvin's aim exactly by saying that he wanted men to know the grace of God in Christ as it is set forth in the Epistle to the Romans. And here lies the explanation of some features in his treatment of sin and salvation which are not always rightly understood.

No reader of the *Institutio* can fail to be struck by the intensity of Calvin's stress on the wretchedness of fallen man—corrupt, demented, defiled, beastly, vile, full of rottenness (these are his regular epithets). Why such violent denigration? we ask. We can dismiss the naive idea that Calvin's natural outlook was so jaundiced as to make all human life appear to him brutish and nasty. Everything we know about Calvin refutes that.

Nor are the true reasons for this language far to seek. They are not psychological, but theological. In the first place, writing against a humanistic background—we must remember that he was a child of the Renaissance before he became a son of the Reformation—Calvin wished to convey the sense which Scripture had given him of the tragic quality of the human predicament. Here was the noblest of this world's occupants, a creature made for fellowship with God and given great intellectual and moral potentialities, now spiritually ruined; he had lost his *rectitudo* (uprightness), the image of God in which he was made, and had been banished from God's favour; and yet in this condition he was so perverse as to be proud, and vainglorious, and self-satisfied! Calvin wished to bring out the tragic folly of the universal human attitude.

And then, in the second place, he wished to make men see and feel their own spiritual extremity. He knew that fallen man, just because sin has darkened his mind on moral and spiritual issues, is disinclined to take his fallen state seriously, and he knew too that shallow views of sin are a barrier to true faith. He who thinks himself still good at heart, still free to do good and please God, will trust in his own works for salvation, and never learn to look to Christ as his righteousness. So Calvin laboured the bondage of man to sin, and the vileness of man in sin, in order that his readers might learn to be realistic about themselves, and in self-despair go out of themselves to find peace with God through trusting the blood of Christ. In other words, his motive was to lead men from Romans 1:18ff. through to Romans 3:21ff. This was not misanthropy, but pastoral evangelism.

The main thrust of Calvin's treatment of salvation in Books II and III of the *Institutio*—a more thorough and systematic treatment than any previous theologian had written—is against the false gospel of synergism and self-help. Fallen men are spiritually helpless, Calvin insists; not only can they not obey God's truth, they cannot even properly understand it in their natural state; and the work of saving them must therefore be God's work entirely. We can sum up his contention thus: *God* (alone) *saves sinners* (however bad) *in and through Jesus Christ.*

God saves *sinners*. Here is the *wonder* of grace. Like Romans, the *Institutio* is dominated by the biblical thought of the judgement-seat of God, and of God himself as set to judge mankind retributively, giving evidence of personal pleasure or anger (as judges in Bible times were expected to do) according to the desert of the various parties before him. As in Romans 1–3, the present wrath of the Judge against all sin, and the coming day of reckoning for every man, appear in the *Institutio* as vivid realities, constantly to be kept in view. But if God is set to judge, what hope can any of us have? We are all sinners.

We have hope, says Calvin, because God has freely and undeservedly set his love upon us, and reconciled us to himself by propitiating his own wrath through the atoning sacrifice of his Son. 'Of his mere good-pleasure he appointed a mediator to purchase salvation for us.' 'Christ . . . was destined to appease the wrath of God by his sacrifice.' Calvin quotes John 3:16 and 1 John 4:10, and comments on the latter as follows: 'There is great force in this word 'propitiation'; for in a manner which cannot be expressed [*ineffabili quodam modo*] God, at the very time when he loved us, was hostile to us until reconciled in Christ.'[11] Here is the mystery of God's free grace—a wonder, not to be pried into by speculation but to be reverently adored.

God saves sinners *through Jesus Christ*—that is, through his cross. Jesus is the *mediator* of grace, the God-man, who took our place before God, bore the penalty of our sins, and by his resurrection conquered death on our behalf. Against the background of his doctrine of judgement, Calvin interpreted the atonement transactionally, in terms of penal substitution. Whereas Anselm had taught satisfaction for sin by, in effect, compensation, Calvin, following Luther, taught satisfaction by substitutionary punishment, the one suffering what the many deserved. Though Calvin stressed the unity of will and affection between the Father and the Son in carrying out the atonement, yet with Luther he held that on the cross Christ 'bore in his soul the dreadful torments of a condemned and lost man,'[12] and identified this with his descent into hell. Hasty criticism here will be unwise; Calvin was only seeking to spell out a divine mystery in terms of the biblical witness to it.[13]

God saves sinners *in Jesus Christ*—that is, by uniting them to him in his risen glory through the secret work of the Holy Spirit. Still following the sequence of Romans, Calvin adds to the thought of Christ for us (Romans 3–5) that of Christ in us (Romans 6–8). Through our incorporation into him, to which the sacraments point and the gift of faith is correlative, the benefits which he won for us are conveyed to us. This is the method of grace. In Christ we are justified (pardoned and accepted), adopted, given access to our heavenly Father, and progressively changed into Christ's image through self-denial and works of love. In Christ we have our hope of glory.

So God *saves* sinners. First to last, salvation is of the Lord. He who began the work by election, redemption, and the gift of faith can be trusted to complete it for all believers. Here is the *stability* of grace, and also the point at which knowledge of God's election brings comfort and strength. Why in the *Institutio* did Calvin treat of predestination and election, not in Book I, where he handled divine sovereignty in creation and providence, but later on in Book III, after dealing with the gospel and the Christian life? The reason seems to be that he wanted the theme to appear in the same evangelical context in which it appears in Romans. There it first enters in 8:29–30, not for any controversial purpose, but to encourage the people of God by assuring them that as their justification and calling sprang from free grace, so God's gracious purpose will stand, and they will be preserved to the end. If God resolved to save them, and gave his Son to that end before ever they turned to him, he will certainly not abandon them now that they have turned to him. This is the 'unspeakable comfort' which the doctrine of election brings in Romans 8:29–38; and it was in order that it might bring the same comfort to his readers that Calvin held it back till he could set it in an equivalent context in the *Institutio*.

Calvin and Scripture

The third question to be asked concerning Calvin's view of the knowledge of God is: by what means is this knowledge brought to us? Calvin's answer to this question, as we have seen, was: by Scripture alone. He did not deny that the whole natural order reveals God (though only as Creator, not as Redeemer), but he insisted that so far as this revelation is concerned sinful man is purblind: he may have an inkling that there is something—or Someone—there, but he cannot 'see' God revealed in creation till he has, as it were, put on the 'spectacles' of Holy Scripture (it is Calvin's own illustration)[14] and learned of God from the written Word. Scripture functions as 'spectacles' in this way by reason of both the content of its teaching and the ministry of the Spirit in connection with it. Here several questions arise.

First, how did Calvin regard Holy Scripture? As *Institutio* I.vi–ix and IV.viii.9 show, his concept of Scripture focused on two related ideas. The first is *os Dei,* 'the mouth of God'—that is, God's use of human language to address us. The second is *doctrina,* 'teaching'—that is, instruction conveyed by God's verbal utterances. 'Teaching from the mouth of God,' or, more simply and dynamically, 'God *speaking*'—'God *teaching*'—'God *preaching*'—this is the essence of Calvin's view of Scripture. 'Whoever wishes to profit in the Scriptures,' he wrote, commenting on 2 Timothy 3:16, 'let him first of all lay down as a settled point this—that the law and the prophecies are not teaching (*doctrinam*) delivered by the will of men, but dictated (*dictatam*) by the Holy Ghost . . . Moses and the prophets testified . . . that, as was actually the case, it was the mouth of the Lord that spoke (*os Domini loquutum esse*) . . . we owe to the Scripture the same reverence which we owe to God, because it has proceeded from him alone, and has nothing of man mixed with it.' Compare these sentences from the *Institutio*:

> The full authority which they [the Scriptures] obtain with the faithful proceeds from no other consideration than that they are persuaded that they proceeded from heaven, as if God had been heard giving utterance to them . . . Clear signs that God is its speaker [*manifesta signa loquentis Dei*] are seen in Scripture, from which it is plain that its teaching [*doctrinam*] is heavenly . . . Being enlightened by [the Spirit] . . . we are made absolutely certain . . . that [the Scripture] has come to us by the ministry of men from God's very mouth [*ab ipsissimo Dei ore*]. The apostles were the certain and authentic amanuenses of the Holy Spirit and therefore their writings are to be received as oracles of God, but others have no other office than to teach what is revealed and deposited in Holy Scripture.[15]

Calvin's thought is clear. The historic phenomenon of prophecy is the paradigm of all Scripture. All of it has the same unique character as did the original 'oracles . . . consigned . . . to public records' (see *Inst.* I.vi.2) *which formed its nucleus. The prophets prefaced their oracles by 'thus says the Lord', and the words they spoke were words from God: what came from their mouths actually issued from God's mouth, nor did it cease to be God's message when they wrote it down. In Calvin's view all Scripture, whatever its literary character, has the same double authorship: it all consists of words of men which are also words of God, and it is all God's doctrina,* given for our learning.

Calvin's reference to the Holy Spirit 'dictating' Scripture (a frequent phrase with him), and to the apostles as his 'amanuenses', does not, of course, imply anything as to the psychology of inspiration. Warfield, Doumergue, and others have shown that this is simply a theological metaphor conveying the thought that what is written in Scripture bears the same relation to the mind of God which was its source as a letter written by a good secretary bears to the mind of the man who dictated it—a relation that is of complete correspondence, and thus of absolute authenticity.[16]

It would have been strange indeed had this concept of Scripture not led Calvin to believe that everything laid down in Scripture is true, or, putting it negatively, inerrant. It is true that he never discussed this question directly; but he had no need to, for it was a matter of general agreement in his day. We cannot, therefore, deduce from his lack of emphasis on the point that he was either unclear about it or indifferent to it. Many since Doumergue have sought to find room in Calvin's thought for the possibility that biblical assertions may err in detail; but the evidence adduced proves the reverse—namely, that there was no such room.

The handful of passages in Calvin's commentaries which have sometimes been treated as admissions that biblical writers were astray in their teaching appear on inspection to fall into the following categories. (1) Some observe that at certain points God has accommodated himself to rough-and-ready forms of human speech, and tell us that in these cases God is evidently not concerned to speak with a kind or degree of accuracy beyond what such forms of speech would naturally convey. Thus, Calvin warns us not to expect to learn natural science (he specifies astronomy) from Genesis 1.

(2) Others tell us that by absolute biblical standards particular sentiments of inspired authors are deficient. The sentiments of Psalm 88:5, for instance, are 'apparently harsh and improper,' 'unadvised words' which 'the prophet . . . spoke less advisedly than he ought to have done.' But this created no difficulty for Calvin, for he did not regard the psalmist's prayer as didactic in intention. (What prayer, we may ask, ever was?) Calvin defined the Spirit's purpose of instruction in this psalm as, not to teach the doctrine of the after-life, but to give universal expression to the desperate feelings which men in spiritual distress actually have, and so to furnish 'a form of prayer for encouraging all the afflicted who are, as it were, on the brink of despair, to come to himself.'[17] Calvin would clearly have told us that to equate the Spirit's accommodation to the realities of human experience with false instruction was to fail to take seriously the fact that this was a prayer. It is not the purpose of prayers to give exact definitions of the faith.

(3) Others note that particular texts show signs of scribal error in transmission. Thus, for instance, Calvin tells us that 'by mistake' Jeremiah's name has

somehow 'crept in' (*obrepserit,* Calvin's regular word for unauthentic textual intrusions) in Matthew 27:9. There is a similar comment on 'Abraham' and the seventy-five souls in Acts 7:14–16. Elsewhere he writes that no 'reverence' prevents us from opining that 'a wrong number may have crept in from the carelessness of scribes.'[18] He was willing to consider the possibility of mistakes in all extant manuscripts.

(4) Others deal with cases where apostolic writers quote Old Testament texts loosely. Calvin's point in this group of comments is always that the apostles quote paraphrastically in order to bring out the true sense and application—a contention strikingly supported by modern discoveries about the *pesher* quotation-method of New Testament times.

(5) Others deal with a few points of what we might call formal inaccuracy by suggesting that in these cases no assertion was intended, and therefore no error can fairly be said to have been made. One example of this is Calvin's denial that the evangelists meant at every point to write a chronologically accurate narrative. Since on occasion they preferred a topical or theological principle of arrangement, Calvin argues, they cannot be held to contradict each other when they narrate the same events in a different sequence.

Another example is Calvin's suggestion that in Acts 7:14 (the seventy-five souls) and Hebrews 11:21 (Jacob's staff) the writer may have chosen to leave the Septuagint's mistranslation uncorrected, rather than risk distracting his readers from the point he was making. In these cases, Calvin implies, to allude to the incidents in the familiar words of the Greek Bible would not involve asserting either that the Septuagint translation was correct or that it expressed the true facts at the point where it parted company with the Hebrew. On neither issue would the New Testament writer himself be asserting anything, and consequently his formal inaccuracy in echoing the substantial inaccuracy of the Septuagint would not amount to error (false assertion) on his part.

Whatever be thought of Calvin's positions in the various passages cited, it seems clear that his basic assumption throughout is that Scripture, rightly interpreted, will not be found to make false assertions. This was the presupposition of all his exegesis. It is also clear that his concept of divine accommodation in Scripture was flexible enough amply to safeguard the full humanity of the inspired writings.

Calvin assumes without discussion that objectively the authority of Holy Scripture, that is, its claim to be believed and obeyed, rests on the fact of its inspiration. 'We owe to the Scripture the same reverence which we owe to God, because it has proceeded from him alone.' To acknowledge biblical authority is a way of confessing that the teaching of God's prophetic and apostolic spokesmen, and that alone, should rule the mind of his church. The only question in this field that he discusses in detail is the subjective ground on which our acknowledgement of biblical authority rests. Rejecting both the Roman contention that Scripture is to be received as authoritative on the church's authority, and the idea that Scripture could be proved divinely authoritative by rational argument alone, Calvin affirms Scripture to be self-authenticating through the inner witness of the Holy Spirit.

What is this 'inner witness'? Not a special quality of experience, nor a new, private revelation, nor an existential 'decision,' but a work of enlightenment whereby, through the medium of verbal testimony, the blind eyes of the spirit are opened, and divine realities come to be recognized and embraced for what they are. This recognition, Calvin says, is as immediate and unanalysable as the perceiving of a colour, or a taste, by physical sense—an event about which no more can be said than that when appropriate stimuli were present it happened, and when it had happened we knew it had happened. Through this inward enlightenment we perceive the truth of the deity and mediation of Jesus, as set forth in the gospel, and receive him as the Saviour of our souls; and through it we also recognize the divinity of the Scriptures, and receive them as the Word of the speaking God, still spoken to ourselves today. The proof that the 'inner witness' is a reality is that these transforming spiritual certainties really do dawn and abide, even against opposition, in human hearts. Of Christian certainty regarding the Scriptures, Calvin wrote, in words partly quoted already: 'Enlightened by him [the Spirit], we no longer believe that Scripture is from God either on our own judgment or on that of others; but, in a way that surpasses human judgment, we are made absolutely certain, just as if we beheld there the majesty [*numen*] of God himself, that it has come to us by the ministry of men from God's very mouth.'[19] 'I say nothing more than every believer experiences in himself,' Calvin adds, 'though my words fall far short of the reality.'

Authentication, as described, is the first part of the Spirit's ministry to the people of God in connection with the Scriptures; *interpretation* is the second. Calvin's approach to biblical interpretation may be summed up as follows. Being as truly human as it is divine, the Bible must be understood literally—that is, in the plain natural sense intended and expressed by its human writers. It is by getting into their minds that we get into the mind of God.

To get into their minds requires more than skill in grammar and logic and cultural forms; it requires some acquaintance with the God of whom they spoke, the spiritual realities with which they dealt, and the Christ to whom, in one way or another, their witness relates. This the Spirit alone can give. Moreover, when we have grasped the meaning of each passage for its author and first readers, we still have to ask what application it has to ourselves and our own situation, and what effect God means it to have on us here and now. Here, again, it is only the interpreting Spirit who enables us to discern the application, and thus effectively to learn God's will from his Word.

By this means, according to Calvin, the private reading and public exposition of inspired Scripture, through the attendant ministry of the Holy Spirit, conveys knowledge of God to sinful men.

Calvin's Theological Stature

Calvin's theological achievement was not to innovate, but to integrate. His mind, though independent, was not original; nor in any case was originality his aim. As a second-generation reformer, his object was to conserve and confirm the gains of his predecessors, Luther and Bucer (whom he admired greatly), Melanchthon (whom he valued as a friend rather than a mentor), and Zwingli (whom privately, however, he regarded as rather second-rate).[20]

> The system of doctrine taught by Calvin is just the Augustinianism common to the whole body of the Reformers [wrote Warfield.] And this Augustinianism is taught by him . . . fundamentally as he learned it from Luther, whose fertile conceptions he completely assimilated, and most directly from Martin Bucer, into whose practical, ethical point of view he perfectly entered. Many of the forms of statement most characteristic of Calvin—on such topics as predestination, faith, the stages of salvation, the church, the sacraments—only reproduce, though of course with that clearness and religious depth peculiar to Calvin, the precise teachings of Bucer, who was above all others, accordingly, Calvin's master in theology.[21]

But Calvin was able repeatedly to synthesize the ideas of his predecessors, and draw out their implications, with a systematic precision which in the world of Reformation theology was entirely new, and proved extraordinarily fruitful. It was no accident that the *Institutio* became the fountain-head of a great theological tradition. The major clarifications which Calvin achieved were perhaps the following.

He was the first to display the unity of the work of Christ under the rubric of his threefold office, as prophet, priest, and king. Earlier theologians from Eusebius on had mentioned these offices, sometimes all three together, but (in Calvin's view) 'frigidly and with no great profit, due to ignorance of what each title comprehends.[22] Luther had made some use of the thought of Christ as priest and as king, but it was left to Calvin to see that the third office must be added to show the full range of Christ's mediatorial ministry. All the Reformers had insisted that we are saved, not by our own works, nor by what the Church does for us, but by Christ alone. But it was Calvin who first perceived that the best and most biblical way to make this point was to present Christ as *prophet,* teaching his people by his word and Spirit: *priest,* securing their salvation by his blood-shedding and intercession: and *king,* ruling not them only, but all creation for their sake; thus, by his threefold ministry, compassing their whole salvation.

Also, Calvin was the first to offer a unified account of the work of the Holy Spirit. Warfield hails him as 'the theologian of the Holy Spirit,' and regards this as his foremost contribution.

> In the same sense in which we may say that the doctrine of sin and grace dates from Augustine, the doctrine of satisfaction from Anselm, the doctrine of justification by faith from Luther—we must say that the doctrine of the work of the Holy Spirit is a

gift from Calvin to the Church. It was he who first related the whole experience of salvation specifically to the working of the Holy Spirit, worked it out into its details, and contemplated its several steps and stages in orderly progress as the product of the Holy Spirit's specific work in applying salvation to the soul . . . What Calvin did was, specifically, to replace the doctrine of the Church as sole source of assured knowledge of God and sole institute of salvation, by the Holy Spirit.

Previously, men had looked to the Church for all the trustworthy knowledge of God obtainable, as well as for all the communications of grace accessible. Calvin taught them that neither function had been committed to the Church, but God the Holy Spirit had retained both in His own hands and confers both knowledge of God and communion with God on whom He will.

The *Institutes* is, accordingly, just a treatise on the work of God the Holy Spirit in making God savingly known to sinful man . . . Therefore it opens with the great doctrine of the *testimonium Spiritus Sancti* . . . that the only vital and vitalizing knowledge of God which a sinner can attain, is communicated to him through the inner working of the Spirit of God in his heart . . . And therefore it centres in the great doctrine of Regeneration—the term is broad enough in Calvin to cover the whole process of the subjective recovery of man to God—in which he teaches that the only power which can ever awaken in a sinful heart the motions of a living faith, is the power of the same Spirit of God moving with a truly creative operation on the deadened soul.[23]

This testimony, provided it be read Christocentrically (in terms, that is, of the fact that the Holy Spirit is Christ's Spirit, sent by him to bear witness of him and unite men to him), is true. Luther had at least adumbrated all the main points in Calvin's statement (those who doubt this should read Regin Prenter's *Spiritus Creator*),[24] 'but it was Calvin who welded Luther's insights into a whole and clarified their polemical thrust against the many-sided Roman claim that the church is the object and ground of faith—a claim which, at each point where it emerged, offered, as Calvin said, 'great insult to the Holy Ghost.'[25]

Again, Calvin was the first to bring out the Trinitarian character of the work of salvation, which Paul's epistles and John's gospel make so plain. On the basis of a sharp insistence on the full co-equality of the three Persons in the Godhead—an insistence which Warfield thought epoch-making in itself[26]—Calvin displays the saving of sinners as a single complex divine work in which all three Persons share, the Father choosing men to save and his Son to save them, the Son doing the Father's will in redeeming them, and the Spirit executing the will of both Father and Son in renewing them. This organic character of God's saving work was stressed more strongly and polemically by Calvin's successors in the Arminian controversy, but it is already explicit in Calvin's soteriology in *Institutio* II and III, which inspired the later development.

Then, too, Calvin brought clarity to the Protestant understanding of the Lord's Supper, which had become clouded through the Lutheran-Zwinglian debates. Calvin thought that both Luther and Zwingli had argued lopsidedly. Luther had held that the eucharistic bread actually contains Christ's body, thus seeming to identify our receiving of Christ at the Supper with the act of eating—one of Rome's mistakes. Zwingli had insisted that Christ's body, now glorified, is in heaven, not in the bread, and the eucharist is primarily a memorial of his death; thus seeming to imply that we do not receive Christ in his Supper at all. Calvin agreed that Christ's glorified body, being in heaven, is not physically and substantially in the sacramental elements, but maintained that in the Supper Christ, by his 'virtue'—that is, the Holy Spirit—communicates his 'flesh'—that is, himself, in the unity of his divine-human person and the power of his atonement—to all who receive the outward signs with faith in him whom they signify. By his method of integrating the idea of sacramental communion into the more basic concept of faith-union with Christ through Word and Spirit, Calvin blazed the trail later followed by Cranmer and Peter Martyr, and established among non-Lutheran Protestants lines of thought which have controlled their eucharistic theology ever since. Much work remains to be done on the eucharistic teaching of the Reformation, but it is unlikely that Calvin's pre-eminence in this field will be seriously challenged.

Calvin also clarified the idea of the church as a self-governing body, subject directly to Christ through his Word. Luther and Zwingli had been content, in effect, to reverse the medieval subordination of the state to the church: having defined the church as a company of believers, inwardly ruled by Christ, they had left the regulating of its outward life to the civil government. Calvin, by contrast, stressed that the church must fix its faith, order its life, and administer its discipline (with Bucer, Calvin held church discipline to be part of the cure of souls), through its own appointed officers. Magistrates, Calvin held, were not called of God to rule the church, but rather to maintain the church's right to rule itself. Of the way this principle kept the Reformed churches from falling prey to Erastianism, and of its later influence, both within and outside Presbyterianism, up to modern times, it is needless to speak.

Moreover, Calvin wrote what was in effect the first-ever theological study of the Christian life, the little treatise in *Institutio* III.vi–x. 'These chapters,' writes Schmidt, 'have had an influence on men of the Reformed faith more living, direct, and lasting than any other part of Calvin's writings.'[27] They view the life of the Christian pilgrim in terms of God's call (to holiness and good works) and God's ways (of discipline, through providential pressures). The main themes developed are self-denial, cross-bearing, 'meditation on the life to come' (the practice of hope—Quistorp calls Calvin 'the theologian of hope'),[28] the right use of earthly pleasures, and the serving of God in secular vocations. Schmidt characterizes Calvin's ideal as 'an austere and moderate asceticism, tempered by an underlying humanism'—'mortified cheerfulness.'[29] These chapters, with the rest of the material on the doctrine and life of faith which *Institutio* III contains, became the fountain-head of the massive and in many ways classical developments in the fields of ethics and sanctification which occupied Reformed theologians, particularly English-speaking ones, for a century after Calvin's death.

As for the doctrine of predestination, where Calvin is supposed to have sur-
passed his fellow-Reformers in boldness of speculation, the unexpected truth is
that he stated it more cautiously, biblically, and devotionally, than either Luther
or Zwingli had done—or, at any rate, had consistently done. All three (and all
their colleagues with them till the later period of Melanchthon) followed in Augustine's footsteps and maintained in some form double predestination (to life,
and to condemnation). But Zwingli handled the theme speculatively, and Luther
paradoxically, and it was left to Calvin to treat it in a consistently scriptural and
pastoral way. His vigour of assertion and debate on this issue must not blind
us to the essential sobriety of his exposition. As we have already hinted, Calvin
taught the *decretum horrible* (the adjective means 'awesome' not 'repulsive') for
the purpose for which, as he believed, God had revealed it—namely, to gladden
and strengthen the Christian, and with that to humble the proud and alarm the
self-reliant, in order to bring them through self-despair to faith in Christ. Predestination, the eternal purpose of God concerning grace, is not, as used to be
thought, the focal theme of Calvin's theology; rather, it is the undergirding of the
gospel, the ultimate explanation of why the Son of God became by incarnation
Jesus the Christ, and whence it is that some who hear the Word come to faith,
and how it is that Christians have a sure hope of heaven. Predestination, as Calvin
treats it, is merely a spelling out of the basic thesis about God in the Epistle to
the Romans, that 'in him, and through him, and to him, are all things: to whom
be glory for ever. Amen.' We only understand Calvin's predestinarianism when
we see its evangelical significance and motivation, as finally establishing the *sola
gratia* and thus compelling the *soli Deo gloria*.

Consistency

The main aim of this chapter has been not so much to catalogue Calvin's
tenets as to point out the structural principles of his thought. For Calvinism must
be understood as a way of thinking before it can be effectively estimated as a set of
beliefs. Calvin, who did not distinguish the theologian's task from the preacher's,
composed his *Institutio* in the same way that he prepared his sermons—namely,
by disciplining himself to echo and apply what he found taught in the inspired
Scriptures, and to exclude all lines of thought which, however attractive otherwise,
lacked biblical sanction. To him, the *doctrina* of the Bible was the self-testimony
of God, the Word of the Creator delineating himself to sinful men as their Redeemer through Jesus Christ, and teaching them how to acknowledge and serve
him in his dual capacity. The *Institutio,* which sets out and safeguards this knowledge, should accordingly be read as a vast expository sermon with the whole
Bible as its text, a systematic confession of divine mysteries learned from God's
own mouth. Its analytical structure, its sustained theocentrism, and its leading

themes—the unacknowledged majesty of the Creator; God's judgement-seat; the shame of sin; the quenching of God's wrath by the blood of Christ; the knowledge of God in Christ as a reconciled Father; the life of faith as the work in us of the Holy Spirit; the believer's hardships and hopes; predestination as guaranteeing glory; the church as the ministering fellowship of elect believers; the state as a servant of God; the unity of both Testaments in their witness to Christ—are sufficiently accounted for by reference to Calvin's key to Scripture, the Epistle to the Romans. The Calvin-critic's first task is to grasp Calvin's theological method, and to learn to see his tenets as its products. Failing this, our praise and blame of Calvin will inform men, not about him, but merely about ourselves. It is good that this century should be seeing the emergence of a better Calvin-criticism than that which, by its use of irrelevant non-theological criteria, has for so long obscured the true stature of 'the theologian.'

Such then, was Melanchthon's friend, 'the theologian.' Bible-centred in his method, God-centred in his outlook, Christ-centred in his message, he was controlled throughout by a vision of God on the throne and a passion that God should be glorified. His theological aim in the last analysis was to declare his vision, as he had received it from the Scriptures, in order that God might receive praise thereby. Warfield wrote:

> The Calvinist is the man who has seen God, and who, having seen God in His glory, is filled on the one hand, with a sense of his own unworthiness to stand in God's sight as a creature, and much more as a sinner, and on the other hand, with adoring wonder that nevertheless this is a God who receives sinners. He who believes in God without reserve and is determined that God shall be God to him, in all his thinking, feeling, willing—in the entire compass of his life activities, intellectual, moral, spiritual . . . is . . . a Calvinist . . . The Calvinist is the man who sees God behind all phenomena, and in all that occurs recognizes the hand of God . . . ; who makes the attitude of the soul to God in prayer the permanent attitude . . . ; and who casts himself on the grace of God alone, excluding every trace of dependence on self from the whole work of his salvation.[30]

Such a Calvinist was John Calvin. He lived as he preached and wrote, for the glory of God. Good theologians are not always good men, nor vice versa, but Calvin's life and theology were all of a piece. Consistency was his hallmark, both as a thinker and as a man.

CHAPTER 11

John Calvin and the Inerrancy of Holy Scripture

This chapter has a threefold aim. First, it seeks to determine what Calvin's view of Scripture actually was, with special reference to points on which scholars have disagreed. Second, it tries to show how Calvin's view relates to the questions that are currently debated among English-speaking evangelicals about biblical inerrancy. Third, it attempts a critique of the account of Calvin's bibliology and the suggestions as to its relevance that Jack Rogers and Donald McKim offered in 1979 in their widely, rather than deeply, learned essay *The Authority and Interpretation of the Bible*.[1]

Some preliminary discussion is called for if that threefold aim is to be achieved.

The Modern Inerrancy Debate

The arguments about inerrancy now in progress among evangelicals are the product of a century's interaction between confessional theology and critical biblical scholarship. The word 'inerrancy' (Latin, *inerrantia*) has a long history in Roman Catholic theological vocabulary but became a significant term in American Protestant usage only about a hundred years ago. Previously, the preferred term for expressing the conviction that Scripture never misinforms or misleads was infallibility,[2] but when Presbyterians began to construct reduced accounts of infallibility, those who still wished to confess the Bible's unqualified trustworthiness began to use the language of inerrancy for their purpose.[3]

That shift of vocabulary does not seem to reflect any hardening of response to the questions that biblical criticism raised (conservative response to critical scepticism about the factual truth of Scripture had in fact been firmly negative from the start). What it reflected, rather, was recognition that the word 'infallibility' was no longer clear enough to express what conservative Protestants still wanted to say to the world about the reliability of biblical affirmations.

However, there was a point about halfway through the nineteenth century when discussion of the truth of Scripture began to be dominated by the agenda, preconceptions, and claims of the historical-biblical criticism that had emerged in Germany, and at that point a watershed really was passed. Formerly, any queries about the truth of biblical statements had been part of direct attacks on the Bible's theology, made in the interests of rationalistic unbelief. But biblical criticism professed to be concerned only with the history and historicity of the records, not with dogma, and its exponents insisted (some perhaps naively, some perhaps disingenuously) that it was theologically neutral. Calvin, though himself as sensitive to the historical dimensions of Bible study as any scholar of his day, stands on the farther side of that watershed.

Heresy founded on misreading of Scripture he met in plenty, but nothing existed in his time like the modern biblical criticism that finds Scripture rich in errors of fact yet claims to aid faith. We should not, therefore, ever suppose him to be speaking to anything like the self-styled sheep in wolf's clothing we meet today.

The direct antecedents of the current evangelical debate[4] were: (1) Dewey M. Beegle's book *The Inspiration of Scripture* (1963, enlarged and reissued as *Scripture, Tradition and Infallibility*, 1973), an attack by a professed evangelical on the idea of inerrancy, (2) the view of Scripture taught (and the use of it modelled) in some professedly evangelical seminaries during the sixties and seventies, and (3) Harold Lindsell's strident *Battle for the Bible* (1976), the first blast of his trumpet against what he saw as the monstrous regiment of biblical errantists in the modern evangelical world.

Representative reassertions of the mainstream Protestant and, indeed, historic Christian view of Scripture in relation to current historical, scientific, and philosophical questions can be found on a grand scale in Carl F. H. Henry's magnum opus, *God, Revelation and Authority* (six volumes, 1976–1983) and more briefly in the Chicago Statement and other literature produced by the International Council on Biblical Inerrancy.[5] Lindsell understands inerrancy as the rallying point for evangelicalism's last stand in our time. Similarly, Francis Schaeffer has called it 'the watershed of the evangelical world.' In their view that inerrancy is crucial, they echo the opinion of such older authorities as John Wesley, who wrote: 'Will not the allowing there is any error in Scripture, shake the authority of the whole?' And, 'If there be one falsehood in that book, it did not come from the God of truth.'[6] Some today dismiss the inerrancy debate as trivial, but it is arguable, to say the least, that the estimate of Lindsell, Schaeffer, and Wesley has reason and common sense on its side.

In that debate, and in Protestantism generally, four types of positions regarding inerrancy can be distinguished. Each is best approached as belonging to a view about biblical authority, for that has always been the heart of Protestantism's theological and religious concern vis-à-vis the Bible, and historically it is in relation to authority that each view has been worked out.

First, some say that Scripture has divine authority because it is God's own testimony and teaching given in the form of human testimony and teaching, and they see its inerrancy as entailed by its divine origin. Twentieth-century exponents of that, the historic mainstream view, include B. B. Warfield, A. H. Strong, Herman Bavinck, Louis Berkhof, Geoffrey Bromiley, Cornelius Van Til, and Carl Henry.

Second, some, having affirmed biblical authority on the basis of the divine origin of what is written, go on to say that the God-given text may yet contain technical errors in history and science. They explain such errors as God's accommodation to the mental and cultural limitations of either his human messengers, his human audience, or both. That view is inherently dialectical, for it requires one to affirm that biblical affirmations are God's truth from one standpoint but not God's truth from another. (Whether such a dialectic does not induce unreality rather than understanding is a question waiting to be asked, but this is not the place to ask it.) Rogers and McKim apparently follow the later G. C. Berkouwer[7] in casting anchor here.

Third, some elucidate their claim that the Bible has authority by saying that though the text is no more than a fallible and sometimes fallacious human witness to God in history, God is pleased to use it as the means whereby he speaks to our minds and hearts today. That dialectical instrumentalism is a main motif in the bibliology of Karl Barth, Emil Brunner, and the neo-orthodox school of thought generally.

Fourth, some are illuminists, holding that the Holy Spirit in our consciences uses the human material of Scripture to trigger real theological and spiritual insight that may have only a loose, non-logical link with what the human writer meant the text originally to convey. That position agrees in principle with historic Quakerism, which trusts the inner light; it is the stance of various sorts of contemporary liberals and existentialists. Calvin's view, as we shall see, was in line with the first of the four positions, but he did not have the other three to contend with and so never stated it in antithesis to them as present inerrantists have to do.

Today, discussion of inerrancy is further complicated by the fears of some, based on things they have seen, heard, or read, that accepting inerrancy locks one into unscholarly exegetical practice, linked perhaps with the zany notion that belief in inerrancy makes one an inerrant interpreter.[8] When it is affirmed, as it sometimes is, that Calvin cannot have been an inerrantist because he was a brilliant scientific exegete, what is being said is that he did not conform to that stereotype. Indeed he did not, and it would be well for the world if no present-day inerrantists did either. The truth is (whatever some inerrantists' behaviour may have suggested to the contrary) that the confession of inerrancy is no more, just as it is no less, than an advance commitment to receive as from God everything without exception that the text of the Bible proves to be telling its readers.[9] What the text is in fact saying must, however, be settled inductively and a posteriori by grammatical, historical, and theological exegesis into which no a priori commitments enter, except the knowledge that the human writer wrote to be understood and the message that he sent to his own readers in their situation is precisely the message that the Holy Spirit here and now directs and applies to us in ours.

But it does not follow that he who is resolved to take whatever Scripture says as instruction to him from God will therefore prove the best exegete. One's quality as an interpreter cannot surpass one's linguistic and historical skills. There is, to be sure, a type of popular piety, rooted in a somewhat problematical blend of fundamentalist rationalism and pietist illuminism, that insists that those who do not venerate the whole Bible as God's truth will never truly grasp any of the things it is saying. In fact, however, as conservative scholars know well enough, though those who have a loose view of biblical authority cannot but fail to realize how biblical teaching bears on their own lives, they may nonetheless discern its content from a historical standpoint very clearly: more clearly, perhaps, than their evangelical counterparts. The best exegete, therefore, other things being equal, will be the erudite eclectic who knows the original languages and backgrounds, who can pick up and follow a writer's train of thought, and who has no prejudice against the work of scholars whose overall theology differs from his own.

Now that was Calvin's approach exactly. A man I knew who read and wrote copiously was once described to me as a 'literary bloke.' What one sees in Calvin is a 'literary bloke' as believer, pastor, and ecclesiastic—a scholarly saint who saw it as central to his Christian vocation to be a saintly scholar. Calvin believed that everything in Scripture is from God to us—that Scripture is God's word of address to all Christians, indeed to all mankind, in every age. He also believed that the way into the mind of God is by way of the minds of the human writers, in and through whose thoughts and words the Holy Spirit was fulfilling his role as the church's teacher.

As a humanist, Calvin already believed that the way to comment on any document was to follow and bring out the writer's flow of thought, and we see him already doing that with success in his first, prebiblical commentary, that on Seneca's *De Clementia*.[10] As a commentator on Scripture, Calvin's method was to do the same and present the result as the teaching of God, as instruction that the Holy Spirit had 'dictated' to God's faithful 'secretaries' (*amanuenses*) for the direction of Christian lives. The principle underlying Calvin's practice was that 'if the expositor reveals the mind of the writer, he is revealing the mind of the Spirit.'[11]

T. H. L. Parker has traced the way in which Calvin crystallized his strategy and goals as a commentator.[12] He would not focus on topics (loci) like Melanchthon but write running expositions of the text and confine topical analysis to the *Institutes*, which would thus serve as a preparation for and an aid in Bible study.[13] He would not run to words like Bucer, but go for *perspicua brevitas*, lucid brevity, crystal-clear terseness and relevance.[14] He started with Paul's letters, taking Romans first, and moved on to the rest of the New Testament and the major theological books of the Old. In the end, he wrote on all the New Testament except 2 and 3 John and Revelation (the last of which he claimed not to understand), and on the Pentateuch, Joshua, the Psalms, Isaiah, 1 Samuel, Job, Jeremiah, Ezekiel, Daniel, and the Minor Prophets.[15]

Time has done nothing to invalidate the verdict that B. B. Warfield passed in 1909 on the significance of that achievement:

> His expositions of Scripture . . . introduced a new exegesis—the modern exegesis. He stands out in the history of biblical study as . . . 'the creator of genuine exegesis.' The authority which his comments immediately acquired was immense . . . Richard Hooker—'the judicious Hooker'—remarks that in the controversies of his own time, 'the sense of Scripture which Calvin alloweth' was of more weight than if 'ten thousand Augustines, Jeromes, Chrysostoms, Cyprians were brought forward.' Nor have they lost their value even today. Alone of the commentaries of their age the most scientific of modern expositors still find their profit in consulting them.[16]

Calvin's contributions to exegesis were of epoch-making excellence because of the quality of insight that his knowledge of Greek, Hebrew, ancient history, and classical rhetorical technique, allied to his natural intelligence, gave him into the human writers' flow of expressed meaning. Yet Calvin presupposed throughout all his work both the divine origin and the inerrancy of all Scripture, as we shall see more fully in a moment.

The reputation of modern inerrantists for crude and unnatural exegesis rests on the idea that (1) they construe biblical statements about natural facts as teaching science, in the sense of answering the 'how' questions about the phenomena of the created order that are the natural scientist's concern; (2) they claim to find in prophetic Scriptures allegorically couched but currently recognizable predictions of specific present and impending world events prior to Jesus' return; (3) they impose on Scripture rationalistic theological grids that scale God down to the capacities of human minds (humanize him, we might say) and thus eliminate the mystery of his being and acts; (4) they deprecate enquiry into the human origins, backgrounds, and sources of the biblical books; and (5) they harmonize apparently inconsistent texts in ways that are not plausible from a literary or a historical standpoint.

This is not the place to discuss those allegations. Suffice it to say that Calvin was no less an inerrantist for being certainly free of the first four lapses and arguably of the fifth,[17] from which we may conclude that there is nothing necessarily unscholarly about inerrantist exegesis and that it darkens counsel to assume otherwise.

Approaching Calvin

Since publication of the fifty-nine volumes of Calvin's works in the *Corpus Reformatorum* series was completed,[18] Calvin research has become a lively international cottage industry among Christian scholars.[19] Out of that research has come an in-depth picture of Calvin in his own age that shows him to have been an even more outstanding literary man, churchman, pastor, and theologian than previous generations thought he was.

The Calvin of time-honoured caricature—Calvin the misanthrope, the power-hungry dictator of Geneva, the obsessive predestinarian speculator, the sadist who demonized God—has vanished,[20] and in his place, clear to view, stands a man of towering intellect and enormous mental energy, endowed with a magnificent memory, formidable eloquence both analytical and satirical, learning as wide, exact, and deep as that of any man of his day, unflinching moral courage, scrupulous fair-mindedness in applying his principles, and utter devotion to his God.

As to his personal crest—a burning heart held by a huge hand, with the French motto *prompte et sincere in opere Dei* [with readiness and honesty in the work of God] and the Latin legend *cor meum quasi immolatum tibi offero, Domine.* [I offer you my heart, Lord, as a sacrifice] speaks volumes.

A child of Renaissance humanism as well as a child of God, he was reared on the recognized humanities—grammar, logic, rhetoric, history, poetry, and what we would call moral philosophy, as set forth in Greek and Latin classics—plus legal studies for the juristic career planned for him by his father.[21] To that multiple expertise he later added biblical geography and Hebrew[22] and also historical theology, both patristic and medieval.

He seems to have known the Bible like the back of his hand, just as he did the theological world of his time. Most of his biblical insights first reached him, it appears, through the writings of Luther and Bucer, and the many controversial encounters that bulked-up the final version of the *Institutes* show that nothing of significance from professional, Latin-writing theological circles had escaped him. The combination of academic knowledge, mental skills, shrewd argument and good judgement, profundity of analysis, and absolute convictional consistency[23] that we see in Calvin over the thirty years of his literary career mark him out as one of the best minds ever. He was a moral, intellectual, and spiritual marvel, whose stature fresh study continues to enhance.

Calvin's *Institutes*[24] (fifth and last edition in Latin, 1559, in French, 1560) was his crowning achievement before he died, worn out at fifty-four, in May 1564. It won unqualified admiration in his own day and remains one of the world's great books.[25] It is a vast integrated web of catechetical, kerygmatic, confessional, apologetic, moral, devotional, and polemical theology, all based on what Calvin called grammatical (and what we would call theological) exegesis of texts in their literary and canonical context.[26] Organized around the concept of knowing God (Book 1 on knowing God the Creator, Book 2 on knowing God the Redeemer in Christ, Book 3 on knowing the grace of Christ by faith through the Spirit, Book 4 on the church's life and ordinances as the means of that knowledge), the *Institutes* follow roughly the order of topics in the Apostles' Creed and Paul's letter to the Romans.[27]

In his preface to the second and subsequent editions, Calvin spoke of the book as, among other things, an overview of biblical faith to prepare the way for study of the Scriptures themselves and of Calvin's own commentaries, whose *perspicua brevitas* would assume acquaintance with that, his basic work.[28] The widespread idea that the Calvin of the commentaries differs from and is somehow more authentic than the Calvin of the *Institutes* is a mistake; there is only one Calvin, and his *Institutes* and commentaries belong together, complementing each other in the manner described.

Calvin offered the *Institutes* as Christian philosophy.[29] We tend to think of it as his systematic theology (a term that did not exist in his day); we should note, however, that its scope is wider than that of most systematic theologies, for the life of faith (ethics and spirituality) is no less its theme than is the substance of faith (articles and dogmas). We should remember that its title is *Institutes of the Christian Religion,* which is more than Christian theology, and also that knowing God in Scripture embraces all aspects of our relationship with God, over and above our professed belief-system. The *Institutes* transcend any supposed dichotomy between the intellectual and moral aspects of Christianity and has the status of a devotional, no less than a theological, classic.

Calvin's Approach to Scripture

Calvin's concerns in bibliology (another word that he did not know) were not, as was said earlier, identical with ours. In his day the divine authorship of Scripture went unquestioned, and what was in debate was only its interpretation and authority as instruction from God through men. Hence Calvin centred his interest on the message-content of Scripture (when he spoke of Scripture as the Word of God, he always had in view its message-content) and on the function of Scripture in creating and sustaining faith and obedience.

In the *Institutes,* as elsewhere, we find him fighting about Scripture on four fronts. *First,* there was his running battle against medieval and Renaissance natural theology, with its assumption that reason (meaning, for practical purposes, thoughts lifted uncritically from Aristotle, Plato, and the Stoics) establishes things about God that Scripture does not say, which things then become a frame of reference that relativizes and blunts things that Scripture does say. *Second,* Calvin attacked various additions to biblical faith (diminishings of it, from one standpoint, since they diminish Christ) that rest only on post-biblical tradition. *Third,* he challenged the idea that the church gives Scripture its authority, insisting that the divine authority intrinsic to all that it says becomes known to us through the Spirit's inner witness (I.vii). *Fourth,* I.ix was a broadside against 'fanatics'[30] who appealed to the Spirit in themselves in disregard of and sometimes against the Spirit's instruction in the Word.

The main sources for studying Calvin's view of Scripture are three sections of the *Institutes*. In I.vi–ix, the basic passage, Calvin dealt with the necessity of Scripture for knowledge of God (vi) and its self-evidencing divine authority (vii)—authority that rational arguments fortify, though they cannot themselves convince us of it (viii), and authority from which God's Spirit will never lead us away (ix). In III.ii, especially sections 6–7 and 29–32, Calvin explained that true, God-given faith (defined as knowledge of God's gracious favour in and through Christ) is confidence based on and correlative to God's promises in Scripture. In IV.viii Calvin argued that the church's teaching should always be subject to the biblical Word of God. In addition to those passages, Calvin's views appear in his comments on relevant biblical texts, though as we saw he did not draw out the full dogmatic implications of those texts in the commentaries themselves, believing himself to have done that in the *Institutes*.

Calvin's approach to Scripture has perplexed some modern scholars. Parker analyses the perplexity as 'a question of relating the numerous passages where [Calvin] speaks of the Holy Spirit "dictating" the Scriptures to the prophets and apostles, his "*amanuenses*," and the no less frequent places where he treats the text as a human production and, as such, sometimes incorrect on matters of fact.' (We shall see reason to doubt whether Parker's last eight words are happily chosen, but let that pass for the present.)

> Some scholars [Parker continues,] emphasize the one side, some the other. Doumergue will distinguish between the form and content of Scripture and say with Gallican fervour: 'It is not the words that are important, it is the *doctrine,* the *spiritual doctrine,* the *substance.*' But Professor Dowey considers that Calvin 'believes the revelation to have been given word for word by the Spirit': Both views are quite right and can be supported easily by quotations from Calvin's writings.[31]

What should be said about that?

The perplexity reflects the unfortunate way in which Calvin has been interrogated by modern scholars. It is a fact that some scholars have felt unhappy with the doctrine, supposed to go back to Calvin, of the 'verbal inspiration' or 'verbal inerrancy' of Scripture, according to which God so overruled the mental and physical actions of the writers who produced the original Hebrew, Aramaic, and Greek documents that every single word they wrote should be seen as God-given, and every assertion they made on matters of fact, whether natural, historical, or theological, should be received as God-taught truth.

Such scholars have come to entertain a restricted view of God's overruling that makes it impossible that biblical documents should be *both* divine instruction in the sense affirmed *and* authentically human products, bearing the marks of each author's human idiosyncrasies and limitations. They have then brought their disjunction (*either* inerrant divine words *or* genuinely human reaction and expression, *but not both*) to Calvin and asked which alternative he embraced.

They have recognized that for Calvin biblical doctrine (*doctrina*, Latin for teaching) is from God. But their question has been, How far did he go in distinguishing between divine doctrine and its human formulations, and in particular, was he prepared to find factual, logical, and conceptual slips in the writers' proclamation of God?

Observing that Calvin certainly exegeted Scripture as human reaction and expression (witness, as we would say) and that he notes prima facie inconsistencies in the text and limitations of knowledge and attitude on the writers' part, they jump to the conclusion that in the back of his mind was a distinction, implicit if not explicit, between God's message in Scripture (his Word) and the sometimes defective form of human words in which we find it embodied. They thus, in effect, find Calvin reflecting their own views back to them, and sometimes they have praised him on that account.

But Calvin does not merit their praise. Having a clear concept of God's absolute sovereignty in foreordaining and overruling free (that is, psychologically self-determined) human acts, so that people say and do things of whose place in God's plan they are quite unaware,[32] Calvin could not with consistency have found any problem with the idea of verbal inspiration; it would have been an unprecedented lapse from his own theology had he done so, and there is not the least evidence that he ever did so. He did not work with the concept of non-decisive divine influence in human action, as Arminians and process theologians do; he was, after all, a Calvinist, and all the evidence suggests that at that point, as at all others, he thought like one.

So, though in exposition and debate he never stressed the thought that every single word of the text is from God (he did not need to; nobody in those days doubted it), and though, unlike some since, he always used the phrase *the Word of God* to signify the *doctrina* contained in Scripture or Scripture viewed as the bearer of that *doctrina*, rather than the uninterpreted text as such (which is only to say that he reproduced the ordinary usage of *ho logos tou theou* in the New Testament), and though he made much of the thought that God accommodates himself in the phraseology of Holy Scripture to our limited understandings (see below), never did he describe or treat the text as anything less than a flow of words that came from the Holy Spirit, carrying meaning that is God-given and that we learn as we enter into each human writer's expressed mind. What the writer says, God says.

And when the text appears to say something incorrect or unworthy, Calvin laboured to show that, rightly understood, it was both less and more than an error—less, because no mistake due to ignorance was actually made, and more, because the odd form of the statement itself yields us instruction in some way. If we ask why Calvin always took that line, rather than posit human error in the modern manner, the answer seems to be that since it was axiomatic for him that the text as given was the work of the Holy Spirit, he saw himself required by his very reverence for God as the author to try to show how at every point Scripture bears the marks of divine wisdom.

The idea that at any point it really does not bear those marks would have seemed to him irreverent to the point of blasphemy and in fact no less impossible than it was intolerable.[33] If we then ask how Calvin found it credible that sinful, fallible human beings should freely, spontaneously, and with all their idiosyncrasies showing, nonetheless have written material that was error-free and marked by divine wisdom in that way, his answer, drawn from prophecy as the paradigm case, is: 'They put forward nothing of their own';[34] 'they dared not announce anything of their own, and obediently followed the Spirit as their guide, who ruled in their mouth as in his own sanctuary.'[35] That God the Spirit had effectively overruled and guided their conscious obedience to his own prompting was Calvin's complete explanation of how it was that they genuinely 'spoke from God' (2 Pet. 1:21).[36] Gerrish's account of Calvin's approach to Scripture is thus entirely right.

> For Calvin, in fact, the whole Bible is the 'Word of God.' The expressions 'Scripture says' and 'The Holy Spirit says' are used synonymously (*passim*). In the Scripture God 'opens his own sacred mouth' (I.vi.I). We are sure that the Scriptures came to us 'from the very mouth of God' (*ab ipsissimo Dei ore ad nos fluxisse*: I.vii.5). Hence Calvin can introduce his exposition of the Decalogue with the invitation: 'Let us now hear God speaking in His own words' (*Nunc Deum ipsum audiamus loquentem suis verbis*: II.viii.12) . . . The human agents . . . are 'amanuenses' (IV.viii.9), 'organs of the Spirit' (*Comm.* on 2 Tim. 3:16), 'ministers' (*hominum ministerio*: I.vii.5). The writers did not speak *ex suo sensu*, nor *humano impulsu*, nor *sponte sua*, nor *suo arbitrio* [by their own understanding, human impulse, their own initiative or decision] (see on 2 Tim. 3:16 and 2 Pet. 1:21). The real 'author' of Scripture is God Himself (*authorem eius esse Deum*: I.vii.4). The writings of the apostles are to be regarded as the oracles of God (*pro Dei oraculis habenda sunt*: IV.viii.9). The Scripture comes from God alone and has no human 'admixture' in it (*ab eo solo manavit nec quicquid humani habet admixtum*: IV.viii.6). In a word, Scripture is produced by the dictation of the Holy Spirit (*dictante Spiritu sancto*: IV.viii.6) . . . Calvin is obliged by his view of inspiration to think of the Scriptures as inerrant.[37]

Some have thought that Calvin's frequent reference to the Spirit 'dictating' Scripture reflects a belief that in the process of inspiration the writers were psychologically passive, so that they wrote mechanically, like automata, without their own individuality finding expression.[38] But that is quite implausible, for many reasons. (1) Calvin never said anything like it; the hypothesis is built on the alleged implications of just the one word; (2) he did in fact regard the recording of God's revelations and the recounting of the events that surrounded them as part of the writers' active and conscious obedience to God, as we have seen; (3) his conviction that God sovereignly orders the psychologically free, spontaneous workings of men's minds everywhere and all the time made it needless for him to posit the suppressing of human spontaneity in that instance to guarantee divine content expressed in divinely chosen words; that we have also seen;[39] (4) his exegesis consistently highlights the writers' individuality no less than it stresses that God the Holy Spirit says for our learning all that they say;[40] (5) elsewhere he used 'dictate' metaphorically, speaking of experience, natural law, reason, and will 'dictating' conclusions and actions,[41] and there is no a priori likelihood that the meaning ceases to be metaphorical when it is the Holy Spirit who dictates (but if that is so, then 'dictates' means only 'suggests' and carries no implications about the psychological mechanics of the process); and (6) his contemporaries used 'dictate' in the same metaphorical way (the Council of Trent, for instance, said *dictante Spiritu Sancto* of the unwritten traditions that the Spirit was held to have given), so that if Calvin had wanted his readers to understand him as affirming something about the psychological mode of the biblical writers' inspiration, he would have had to say more than simply that the Spirit dictated (and it is hard to doubt that he was a good enough rhetorician, or 'communicator,' as we would say, to know that).

So, in the course of his frequent assertions that the Spirit gave the Scriptures, the fact that he never mentions this becomes decisive evidence against the idea that he meant us to gather more.[42] Calvin was not telling us what it felt like to be God's penman or how God made his messengers aware of what they had to pass on in his name: he was just telling us, over and over again, that the God-givenness of Scripture is a fact we must reckon with and should never lose sight of. Gerrish is again on the right track when he says:

> the term *dictare* scarcely supplies Calvin with a fully-articulated 'theory of inspira-
> tion.' Neither Luther nor Calvin devote much space to the 'mechanics' of inspiration:
> they are far more interested in the results. The real problem of the Reformers' teach-
> ing on this theme lies in their apparent assumption of an inerrant text: it is less [than]
> just to accuse them of holding to a mechanical view of inspiration. Several scholars
> have maintained that Calvin did not intend 'dictation' to be understood literally at
> all. This may be true: in any case, Warfield is surely right in saying that 'What Calvin
> has in mind is not to insist that the mode of inspiration was dictation, but that the
> result of inspiration is as if it were by dictation, viz., the production of a pure word
> of God free from all human admixtures.'[43]

So far, we have been focusing on Calvin's approach to Scripture in terms of his concept of inspiration. We are certainly not false to him when we do that, as his comment on 2 Timothy 3:16 ('all Scripture is inspired by God and profitable for teaching, for reproof, for correction, for training in righteousness') shows:

> He [Paul] commends the Scripture, first, on account of its authority, and second, on
> account of the usefulness that springs from it. In order to uphold the authority of
> Scripture, he declares it to be divinely inspired [*divinitus inspiratam*], for if it be so, it
> is beyond all controversy that men should receive it with reverence ... Whoever then
> wishes to profit in the Scriptures, let him first of all lay down as a settled point this,

that the law and the prophecies are not teaching [*doctrinam*] delivered by the will of men, but dictated [*dictatam*] by the Holy Spirit ... Moses and the prophets did not utter at random what we have from their hand, but, since they spoke by divine impulse, they confidently and fearlessly testified that, as was actually the case, it was the mouth of the Lord that spoke [*Domini loquutum esse*] ... We owe to the Scripture the same reverence which we owe to God, because it has proceeded from him alone, and has nothing of man mixed with it [*nec quicquam humani habet admixtum*].[44]

That passage shows how important the idea of inspiration was for Calvin. Yet perhaps a fuller grasp of his approach to Scripture emerges from exploring his concept of *doctrina*—'doctrine' in the sense of God's teaching conceived from the standpoint of God its teacher, in other words, truth divinely revealed in history and now set forth for our learning in Scripture.[45]

There is, said Calvin, one single divine *doctrina* that was given through the Son, God's personal Word, with more or less fullness at different times to different recipients.[46] It is known more fully and clearly under the gospel than it was before,[47] but it was no less truly embodied in the Old Testament than it is in the New.[48] Its content, first to last, concerns God's covenantal relationship with men, with all the gifts of grace and claims upon man's worship and service that the covenant brings. In its final, New Testament presentation, as was indeed the case clearly enough before, *doctrina* focuses on Jesus Christ, in and through whom this relationship is now a reality for those who believe. *Doctrina* in its original form was specific revelations given to individuals; now it takes the form of Holy Scripture, where all the revelations that God wanted to be passed on stand recorded.

Scripture, in its character as *doctrina,* is in effect God preaching, teaching, promising, admonishing here and now, for what is written is interpreted and authenticated to present readers by the Holy Spirit, who makes them aware that it is God's Word to them. Observe how Calvin used the concept of *doctrina* (the teaching) in the following key passage.

Whether God was known to the patriarchs through oracles and visions or put into their minds through men's labour and ministry what they should then hand on to posterity, it is beyond doubt that firm certainty of *the teaching* [i.e., certainty that it was God's teaching] was engraved on their hearts, so that they were convinced and knew that what they had learned came from God. For by his word God has always made faith to be beyond doubt [*indubiam*] and thus superior to all [mere] opinion. At length, so that his truth might survive in the world for ever as *the teaching* (i.e., God's communicating of revelation) constantly went forward [*continuo progressu doctrinae*] he willed that those same oracles which he had given to the patriarchs should be recorded as it were on public placards [*tabulis*]. For this purpose the law was published, and the prophets were thereafter added as its interpreters ... it was particularly laid upon Moses and all the prophets to teach the way of reconciliation between God and men, whence Paul calls Christ the end [*finem,* which Calvin takes to mean 'goal, end in view'] of the law (Rom. 10:4) ... yet I repeat that beside that particular teaching of faith and repentance, which sets forth Christ the mediator, Scripture picks out by sure marks and signs the one true God who created and governs the world, lest he be confused with the crowd of false gods . . . We must hold that for true religion to shine on us we have to make our start from the heavenly *teaching*, and that no one can get the tiniest taste of right and sound [*sanae*, healthy] *teaching* unless he is a pupil of Scripture. So the source [*principium*] of true understanding emerges when we reverently embrace what God willed to testify there about himself. For not only perfect, that is, fully equipped [*numeris suis completo*] Faith, but all right knowledge of God is born of obedience [sc., to God's testimony in Scripture].[49]

From that we see that Calvin's doctrine of divine *doctrina* was indeed the larger whole to which his assertions about the origin and nature of Scripture belong. Now we see that those assertions were part of Calvin's total presentation of God the Creator speaking in human language down the centuries to bring us sinners to know him through knowing Jesus Christ. We miss the overall thrust of Calvin's view of Scripture unless we see it in that frame of reference.

Calvin's Doctrine of Scripture

We have now reached the point from which we can view Calvin's account of Scripture as a whole. It is an impressive construct. Its theme is kerygmatic; it proclaims God graciously communicating with us so that we may commune with him. Its thrust is religious; it seeks to lead us into humble acceptance of God's instruction and obedient response to him by faith, repentance, worship, righteousness, and godly living. Its perspective, to achieve that pastoral goal, is polemical; Calvin developed it in contradiction to naturalistic paganism, authoritarian Romanism, and varieties of subjectivist (his word is 'fanatical') Protestantism, seeking to guide his readers into sounder ways. Its key points, briefly, are these.

The Necessity and Sufficiency of Scripture

Institutes I.vi is titled: 'Scripture is needed as guide and teacher for anyone who would come to God the Creator.' Chapters iii and iv are respectively titled 'The knowledge of God has been naturally implanted in the minds of men' and 'This knowledge is either smothered or corrupted, partly by ignorance, partly by malice.' Those titles together point up the first reason why Calvin held that we all need Scripture, namely, that the sinful perversity and blindness of heart that mark our fallen state are such that, left to ourselves, we constantly twist our Creator's self-disclosure in his works of creation and providence into some kind of lie.

God's 'general' or 'natural' revelation (to use the terms of later theologies) never of itself produces true apprehensions of God or due worship; our minds, however sharp in other ways, always tend to distort, more or less, those inklings and flashes of insight concerning God that come through to us from the outshining of revelation in the ongoing processes of the cosmos, which Calvin declares to be the theatre of God's manifested glory. And so the explicit verbal instruction of Scripture has to be brought in to set us straight.[50]

Second, knowledge of God as redeemer was set forth in history long past—history that began with the patriarchs and reached its climax and conclusion with Christ and the apostles—and to the revelation given in that history, Scripture, and Scripture alone, affords trustworthy access.[51]

Scripture, then, comes to us from God so that it may function as (to use Calvin's own images in I.vi) the thread that leads us out of the maze of our confusion about God,[52] the spectacles that enable us to see our maker clearly,[53] and the schoolmaster that ministers to our ignorance.[54] 'Scripture is the school of the Holy Spirit, in which, as nothing is omitted that is needful and useful to know, so nothing is taught but what is expedient to know.'[55] The Scriptures, though not offering answers to all the idle questions that might occur to us, are thus sufficient for their designed purpose; 'everything that relates to the guidance of our life is contained in them abundantly.'[56] Through them the Spirit leads us into 'all truth,' and to suppose that they need supplementing from other sources is 'to do grievous injury to the Holy Spirit.'[57]

The necessity and sufficiency of Scripture are the two bases on which Calvin's theological method rests. No reliance may be placed on the speculations and fancies of fallen men, Christians though they be; all our theology should find explicit validation from the Word or be judged illegitimate and false. The use of traditional ideas is to suggest questions to put to Scripture—no more—for such ideas have no intrinsic authority. But from Scripture the Spirit shows and teaches us all that we need to know for life and godliness, in fact vindicating older traditional ideas (patristic, as distinct from medieval scholastic) a great deal of the time.

The Clarity and Limits of Scripture

Scripture is clear, said Calvin, in the sense that those who persevere in humble, prayerful study of the text, who 'do not refuse to follow the Holy Spirit as their guide,'[58] and who look to official ministers to illuminate the Word by their teaching[59] will find that they come to understand it more and more.

Here, however, everything depends on one's spiritual disposition, whether one is impatient, self-willed, and self-reliant, or (to use one of Calvin's favourite words) docile.

> When we come to hear the sermon or take up the Bible, we must not have the foolish arrogance of thinking that we shall easily understand everything we hear or read. But we must come with reverence, we must wait entirely upon God, knowing that we need to be taught by his Holy Spirit, and that without him we cannot understand anything that is shown us in his Word.[60]

For clarity's sake, God in giving Scripture accommodated himself to our capacity [*captus*] condescending not only to talk man's language but to do so in an earthy and homespun way, sometimes

> with a contemptible meanness of words [*sub contemptibili verborum humilitate*][61]

> God lowers himself to our immaturity [*se ille ad nostram ruditatem demittit*]...When God prattles to us [*balbutit*] in Scripture in a clumsy, homely style [*crasse et plebeio stylo*] let us know that this is done on account of the love he bears us.[62]

It is a sign of love for a child to accommodate to his language and to be willing to use baby talk in conversing with him, and so it is, said Calvin, when God in Scripture speaks to us in a simple, not very dignified way. It helps us to understand him, and the very fact that he does it assures us of his affection and goodwill. Following Origen and Augustine, Calvin developed the thought that in Scripture God scales himself down, condescending to our limited capacity in the manner described. Calvin used that thought for a threefold purpose: apologetic and defensive, to counter the criticism that the biblical idiom and thought forms are not always worthy of God; exegetical and didactic, to explain what is and is not meant when the infinite, eternal, immutable Creator is said, for instance, to have a mouth, a nose, eyes, ears, hands, and feet, to rest, remember, yearn, laugh, and repent (change his mind); and pastoral and edificatory, to strengthen faith in the love of God who stoops to put himself on our level linguistically so that we may know him well.[63]

But the insight that God adapts his speech to our limitations, though assuring us that Scripture mediates to us real knowledge of him, reminds us also that we do not and cannot know him as he is in himself. What frames and surrounds God's self-revelation is the mystery, utterly dark or overwhelmingly bright (Calvin says both from time to time), of that which in God remains unrevealed, namely his incomprehensible life, power, and activity, as those are known to himself. God constantly warns us to stay within the bounds of revelation, not to stray outside the circle of God-given light into the darkness that lies beyond, not to try to penetrate by guesswork (what Calvin calls speculations, born of curiosity) into places where Scripture offers no thoughts for us to think.

Often Calvin reminds us, echoing 1 Timothy 6:16, that God dwells in unapproachable light where no man can see him, so that any speculative venture going beyond what he himself tells us in Scripture is a sort of Promethean presumption foredoomed to disaster. For instance, Calvin's introduction to the study of predestination is as follows:

> First let [curious persons] remember that when they enquire into predestination they enter the shrine of God's wisdom, where any who rush in with blithe self-confidence [*secure ac confidenter*] will not gain satisfaction for their curiosity and will enter a labyrinth from which they will find no way out ... If this thought prevails

with us, that the word of the Lord is the only road that can lead us to track down what is rightly to be held about him, and the only light that will illuminate us for discerning what ought to be seen concerning him, it will readily hold us back and keep us from all presumption [*temeritate*]. For we shall know that the moment we go past the limits [?] of the word our course is off the path and in the dark, where we are bound again and again to go astray, slip and come a cropper [?]. Let this, then, be the first thing before our eyes, that to seek any knowledge of predestination save that which is unfolded by the Word of God is as mad as to seek to travel where no road is or to see in the dark. Nor let us be ashamed to lack some knowledge about it when there is such a thing as well taught ignorance [*liqua docta ignoran*]. Rather let us gladly eschew that quest for knowledge, the craving for which is stupid, dangerous and even destructive.[64]

For Calvin, Wallace says, 'adoration rather than curiosity is the fitting attitude when searching out the secrets of revelation,'[65] and the humility of wisdom counsels us to keep most conscientiously within the bounds of what Scripture says.

The Authentication and Authority of Scripture

Here we explore that correlation of Word and Spirit that is rightly seen as methodologically decisive in all Calvin's theology. Calvin spelled it out in *Institutes* I.vii and ix. His basic claim was that the Spirit of God who 'dictated' Scripture also leads us by his own secret inward witness [*arcano, interiore Spiritus testimonio*] to acknowledge Scripture as the divine teaching that it truly is.[66]

The same Spirit who spoke by the mouth of the prophets must enter into our hearts to persuade us that they faithfully proclaimed what was divinely commanded ... Let this then stand as a fixed point, that those whom the Spirit has inwardly [*intus*] taught rest firmly upon Scripture, and that Scripture is self-authenticated, and that it is not right for it to be made to depend on [human] demonstration and reasoning, for it is by the Spirit's witness that it gains in our minds the certainty that it merits.[67]

The divinity of Scripture becomes evident to us as we become aware of the presence of God with us and realize that he is saying to us all that Scripture says. But because of sin's blinding and deafening effect, we remain unaware of the presence and utterance of God in and through Scripture until the Spirit restores to us mankind's lost ability to discern God's reality. But once that happens,

enlightened by his [the Spirit's] power [*virtute*] we believe that Scripture is from God, not on the basis of our own judgment nor that of others; but, rising above human judgment, we conclude with absolute certainty, as if we saw God's own majesty [*numen*] reside in it, that it came to us by the ministry of men from God's very mouth ... It is a conviction which does not call for rational proofs [*ratione*]: a knowledge with which the best reasoning agrees, in which indeed the mind rests more securely and steadily than in any rational proofs; an awareness which can only be born of heavenly revelation. I speak only of what every believer experiences, save that my words fall far short of a just account of the matter.[68]

The secret inner witness, then, is not the Spirit privately revealing to individuals information not publicly available but the Spirit renewing and actualizing that capacity to recognize God; that with which man was made but lost through sin. The dynamism of divinity that characterizes Scripture—known by the light that shines from it, the power that it exerts, the presentation of God that it offers, the presence of God that it communicates—is, so to speak, intrinsic to it, and what the Spirit does is to open the eyes of our understanding, so that we 'see' (that is, perceive and know) what is already there, objectively evidencing itself to us in the same immediate way in which, at a lower level, colours, sounds, and tastes also do.[69] 'Witness' in Calvin's phrase thus expresses not so much driving out ignorance by communicating information as eliminating doubt and double-mindedness by imparting certainty.

Calvin's concept of the Spirit's authenticating witness was his counter to the idea that the authority of Scripture strictly and properly depends on the say-so of the church. (The title of I.vii is: 'By what witness Scripture should be ratified, namely that of the Spirit: so that its authority may stand sure; and that it is an ungodly falsehood to suspend faith in it on the church's judgement.') He dismissed, as making the Holy Spirit a laughingstock [*Indibrio*], the supposition that the church must decide for us which books should be received as canonical,[70] and that would seem to show (though he does not discuss the matter further) that to his mind authenticating the canon as such was part of the Spirit's witnessing work.[71] Criticism of that view as impossibly subjective assumes that Calvin thought in terms of an atomic individualism, as if each Christian had to verify the canon for himself by the light of his own experience. That would indeed be a hazardous view to hold. Who on that basis could end up equally confident of each of our sixty-six books, neither more nor less?[72]

But Calvin, though he made much of personal Christian experience, thought theologically in terms of biblical corporateness, and plainly for him the shape of the question was, Can anyone justify rejecting the canonicity of any of the historically attested and accredited books, which over so many centuries have spoken to the church corporately with the accents of God and continue to do so today? Maybe the question merited more analysis than Calvin gave it, but that his final appeal on canonicity questions is to the historic witness of the Spirit in and to the church as a whole seems to be beyond doubt.

The authority of canonical Scripture has in modern times been construed in various ways: as the authority of the witnessing church, expert religious opinion, saving history, mystical intuition, honest experience, and so forth. None of those categories, however, was Calvin's. For him, the authority of Scripture was formally (as we should say) the authority of God instructing us and materially (our word again, not his) the authority of what God teaches—that is, of God's *doctrina,* which Scripture presents to us embedded in and illustrated by the flow of events of which God's particular verbal revelations were part. The narrating and the theologizing of which Scripture consists together constitute God's authoritative Word.

It should be noted here that Calvin showed a vivid sense of the historical progress of revelation and of the historical experience of Old Testament Israel, the first-century church, and the individuals whose personal story Scripture records. He was, of course, untouched by our present-day 'historical consciousness' (as some would call it), which tells us that the mentality and experience of former generations, especially in other cultures, was so different from our own as to be largely incomprehensible to us. Arguably, that was to his advantage since that modern idea has been taken to such extremes by certain sociologists and anthropologists that it has become a real blockage to any understanding of the past.[73]

But Calvin, being free from those sophisticated inhibitions, treating the nature of man, like the nature of God, as a constant, and viewing the historical facts of Scripture in the light of its revealed theological teaching, found *doctrina* in both the content and the manner of the Bible's historical narratives, as his commentaries and transcribed sermons abundantly show. Nor does the fact that verbally he distinguished revelations of truth from their historical matrix give any basis for supposing that those historical facts, and the factuality of the Bible narratives of them, were of less importance to him than were the revelations of theological truth that the apostles and prophets set forth. Everything in Scripture—narrative and theology together—was for him verbally God-given and substantively part of God's Word, the *doctrina* under whose authority Christians should live.

God's Word, then, functions as God's sceptre,[74] the emblem and instrument of his government over men. But that government is itself both the rule of the Spirit, who reigns by interpreting the Word to us and moulding our lives in obedience to it, and also the rule of Jesus Christ, whom the Word proclaims as incarnate Mediator, risen Saviour and enthroned Lord, and whose reign is an effective reality just so far as the Word of God is heeded. Of the Spirit in that connection Calvin wrote:

> The Holy Spirit so joins himself [*inhaerere*] to his truth which he expressed in Scripture that he shows his power in action precisely when reverence and respect for him come to be attached to the Word . . . as the sons of God see themselves bereft of all the light of truth without the Spirit of God, so they know that the Word is the instrument by which the Lord bestows the illumination of his Spirit on the faithful.[75]

Of Christ he wrote,

> Wherever the doctrine of the gospel (a phrase that for Calvin was equivalent to the full message of Scripture) is preached in purity, there we are certain that Christ reigns; but where it is rejected, his government is set aside.[76]

Thus the authority of the Word, the Spirit, and Christ belong together; indeed, they are one in the sense that if you do not acknowledge all three you do not in reality acknowledge any single one of them.

'Preached' in the last quotation is a reminder of Calvin's belief that oral instruction in the *doctrina* by duly accredited pastors and teachers is God's appointed way of ruling the church. The word also indicates the importance for Calvin of Scripture being competently interpreted (exegeted and applied). As Berkouwer said (and Calvin would have agreed), 'to confess Holy Scripture and its authority is to be aware of the command to understand and interpret it,'[77] for without proper interpretation, its authority is nullified. That leads to our next section.

The Understanding and Unity of Scripture

To say that Calvin subscribed to the Reformation tag 'Scripture interprets Scripture' [*Scriptura Scripturam interpretator*] is true, but more than just that must be said. Interpretation of Scripture was for Calvin a scholarly discipline of some complexity. It is convenient to follow the listing of Calvin's eight ideals as an interpreter that H. J. Kraus gives.[78]

Clarity and brevity—'a clarity of explanation that corresponds to the clarity of Holy Scripture'[79]—should be sought. The interpreter should not allow himself to lose sight of the wood among the trees.

The human author's intention (his *point*, as we would say) should be determined and kept in constant view. To make clear why the text says what it says is the main job of the commentator on any document, secular or sacred. Exegesis has to be directionally as well as grammatically correct. The way to enter into the mind of God is via the minds of the biblical writers, for both the substance and thrust of what each says are from God.

To that end the *historical, geographical, cultural, and situational background* of each document must be determined. In his commentaries Calvin did that most assiduously.

Linguistic knowledge should be added to knowledge of the background to determine the 'real,' 'true,' 'original,' 'literal,' 'simple' meaning (Calvin used all those terms) of each passage. As a good humanist, his aim was to read out of passages all that was in them and not to read into them what was not there. Calvin's linguistic knowledge embraced not only the grammar of Greek and Hebrew but also the classical theory of rhetoric (that is, effective *ad hominem* speech) as set forth by men like Cicero and Quintilian, and that enabled him to fix the flow of meaning in documents in the same way that modern linguistic and communication theory tells exegetes today to do.[80] (Indeed, a great deal of what current linguistic and communication theory tells exegetes Calvin already knew.)

The *context* of each biblical statement [*peristasin, hoc est complexum, vel
... circumstantiam*[81]] should be taken account of to see precisely what is and is
not implied by (and what does and does not follow from) the things that are
actually said.

Idioms and implications involved in the form of expression must also be
reckoned with or we shall miss some of what is meant. Idioms like *synecdoche*
(putting the part for the whole, or the whole for the part) are frequent in biblical language, as in all language, and should be identified where they occur.[82] The
Decalogue, in particular, is evidently synecdochic throughout and should be interpreted accordingly.

> There is always more in the commands and prohibitions than is expressed in words
> ... in just about all the commands synecdoches are displayed so plainly, that anyone
> who wants to limit the meaning of the law to the narrow confines of its words will
> rightly be laughed at. So it is plain that a responsible [*sobriam*] interpretation of the
> law goes beyond the words ... in each commandment we must look to see what it
> is about; then we must seek out its goal [*finis*] ... an argument to the opposite must
> be drawn out ... like this: if *this* pleases God, the opposite displeases him; if *this* dis-
> pleases him, the opposite pleases him; if he commands *this,* he forbids the opposite;
> if he forbids *this,* he commands the opposite.[83]

Calvin was here thinking in character as a professional jurist and man of letters;
he was as far as possible from the unnatural wooden literalism that equates the
verbal form with the meaning itself.

Other figures of speech should be recognized when they occur. *Metonymy,* for
instance, a use of one word for another reflecting a link between the things to
which the words refer (e.g., effect for cause, container for thing contained, material for thing made), is frequent in biblical as in all speech. It is neither to be literal-
ized nor allegorized but explained as calling attention to the link that produced it.
The total flow of thought of which it is part will fix its precise force.

Metaphor, again, is metonymy of a particular kind: it encapsulates a comparison with and thereby illuminates that to which it refers. An example of Calvin
finding metaphor is his argument that the fiery trial of 1 Corinthians 3:12–15
refers to divine testing here, not literal purgatory hereafter.[84] An example of his
finding metonymy in another form[85] is his argument against Lutheran and Zwing-
lian extremes that the eucharistic 'this is my body' is one of many biblical phrases
in which

> on account of the affinity that the things signified have with the symbols of them,
> the name of the thing was given to the symbol ... though in essence the symbol dif-
> fers from the thing signified, the one being spiritual and heavenly while the other is
> physical and visible, yet inasmuch as it does not just picture in the manner of a bare
> and empty token the reality it was consecrated to represent, but also truly holds forth
> that reality, why may not the name of the reality rightly attach to it?[86]

Those are typical examples of Calvin's care not to mishandle figures of speech that we can appreciate whether we accept the details of his exegesis or not.

Jesus Christ, the personal divine Word through whom all revelation and knowledge about God came and always will be given, should be regarded (Calvin often said) as the 'scope' of all Scripture—that is, its main subject, focal point, and centre of theological reference.

> We must read the Scripture with the purpose of finding Christ in it. If we turn aside from this end, however much trouble we take, however much time we devote to our study, we shall never attain the knowledge of the truth.[87]

For, as Calvin saw, the New Testament books identify themselves and the Old Testament Scriptures with them as witnesses to Jesus Christ and build up their account of Jesus in narrative and theology largely by displaying him as the fulfilment of Old Testament promises, prophecies, and types. So,

> the Christological interpretation in Calvin's Old Testament commentaries looks to the future for the fulfilment of promises and prophecies, and his New Testament commentaries have as the determining factor for exegesis a movement toward Christ.[88]

Though Calvin was careful not to read Christ into texts that did not certainly refer to him,[89] the commentaries and sermons are as a whole 'Christward' expositions to a very marked degree.

One further ideal reflected in Calvin's exegesis should be mentioned here. The interpreter should always show the naturalness of his choice between competing interpretative options. There should be no arbitrary refusal on a priori grounds of what appears as the plain meaning when the a posteriori criteria of scientific interpretation (those embodied in the eight ideals listed above) are applied. H. J. Forstman, having rightly said that for Calvin 'it is a foregone conclusion that all exegesis must uphold the divinity and, therefore, the unity and perfection of Scripture,' then states that 'because of this, Calvin as an exegete was free to read into a passage whatever might be necessary to arrive at the foregone conclusion.'[90] But that is wrong.

The truth is that Calvin not only declined to read into biblical passages anything that was not certainly there, he also argued to the unity of Scripture as much as from it, by showing over and over that common sense and disciplined care in exegesis can resolve seeming discrepancies with astonishing success. In other words, it seemed clear to Calvin that the natural meaning was also regularly and demonstrably the harmonious meaning and vice versa.

That needs stressing, for those conditioned by conventional modern scholarship are likely at first to find it hard to believe that Calvin seriously thought that, just as they may well find it hard to take the idea seriously themselves. Forstman, for instance, at one point looks away from the evidence that he himself has produced on Calvin's exegetical sensitivity to tell us that in pursuit of Bible harmony 'at times he [Calvin] had to depart from what seems to the contemporary reader the natural meaning of the text.'[91] With that opinion at least one contemporary reader, namely the present writer, totally disagrees, and he is confident that he is not alone in his disagreement. Take as an example Calvin's *Harmony of the Gospels*.[92] Anyone who works through it cannot but come to respect Calvin's honesty, intelligence, and alertness in facing the many superficially awkward problems that arise from differences of detail, wording, and order among the Evangelists.

More than that, however, he will in addition have to acknowledge that, though contemporary scholars doubt the usefulness of even trying to harmonize the Gospels, Calvin actually showed that once it is recognized that the Evangelists let themselves disrupt chronology for topical reasons, and reproduce more or less of Jesus' words for didactic reasons, simple, natural solutions for every apparent inconsistency suggest themselves. Calvin's introductory claim that 'the Holy Spirit has given (the evangelists) such wonderful unity in their diverse patterns of writing that this alone would almost be enough to win them authority if a greater authority from another source did not supply it'[93] is impressively substantiated by the *Harmony* as a whole.

Here, as in all his commentaries, Calvin's constant contention, expressed both by his actual arguments and by the rhetoric with which he clothed and presented them, is that it shows either perversity or stupidity or both to deny that the Bible, when naturally interpreted, is factually, theologically, and didactically self-consistent, for the evidence, point by point (so he urged), does in fact refute that denial. Thus Calvin earned himself the right to claim 'the beautiful agreement of all its parts with each other' as one of the arguments that are 'most suitable aids' to support faith in Scripture as the Word of God.[94]

Calvin and Inerrancy

It must seem obvious from what has been said that Calvin could never have consciously entertained the possibility that human mistakes, whether of reporting or of interpreting facts of any sort whatever, could have entered into the text of Scripture as the human writers gave it. Nor did he. As Dowey says, 'To Calvin the theologian an error in Scripture is unthinkable. Hence the endless harmonizing, the explaining and interpreting of passages that seem to contradict or to be inaccurate.'[95] Calvin would fault an apostle for poor style and bad grammar but not for substantive inaccuracy.[96]

When Scripture and secular sources diverge, Calvin held to Scripture, and the attribution to him by Emile Doumergue,[97] J. T. McNeill,[98] and Rogers and McKim,[99] among others, of willingness to admit errors of detail and form in the biblical text (what Rogers and McKim call 'technical errors') rests on a superficial misreading of what he actually said.[100]

The handful of passages in Calvin's commentaries that have sometimes been taken to show that he thought particular biblical writers had gone astray prove on inspection to fall into the following categories.

Some are reminders of points at which God accommodated himself to the rough-and-ready forms of human speech that simple people can understand. All that Calvin said about them is that in such cases God is evidently not concerned to speak with a kind or degree of accuracy that goes beyond what those forms of speech would naturally convey. The classic case is Calvin's handling of Genesis 1, where he described Moses as 'accommodating himself to the simplicity of ordinary people [*vulgi ruditati*]' and 'speaking popularly' [*populariter*],[101] and declared that he 'wrote in a popular style things which, without instruction, all ordinary persons endowed with common sense can understand . . . Had he spoken of things generally unknown, the uneducated might have pleaded in excuse that such subjects were beyond their capacity.'[102] On that basis Calvin defended Moses for speaking about created things as they appear rather than in scientific terms (when, for instance, he called the sun and moon 'two great lights,' though astronomers had since discovered that Saturn is a greater light than the moon). 'As befitted a theologian,' wrote Calvin crushingly, 'he had respect to us rather than to the stars.'[103]

Other passages state that particular texts show signs of having been changed—corrupted, as textual critics say—in the course of transmission. Thus for instance, commenting on Matthew 27:9, where the words of Zechariah 11:13 are ascribed to Jeremiah, Calvin wrote that 'by mistake' [*errore*] Jeremiah's name has somehow 'crept in' [*obrepserit*]. The verb is Calvin's regular word for inauthentic textual intrusions. Again, comparing Acts 7:16 with Genesis 23:9, he wrote, 'As for Luke's addition that they were laid in the tomb which Abraham bought from the sons of Hamor, it is plain that there is a mistake [*erratum esse*] in the word Abraham . . . hence this place must be emended [*corrgendus est*]. The roundabout 'there is a mistake,' with the use of *corrigo*, the ordinary word for emending a text corrupted in transmission, indicates that here also Calvin was talking about a copyist's error rather than an author's lapse. Rogers and McKim misread the latter comment, as J. T. McNeill did before them, and accuse Calvin of ascribing the error to Luke, but that is unwarrantable.[104] Similarly, having quoted Calvin's comment on Matthew 27:9, they go on to say, 'For Calvin, technical errors in the Bible that were the result of human slips of memory, limited knowledge, or the use of texts for different purposes than the original were all part of the normal human means of communication'[105]—as if Calvin had been saying that Matthew made a 'technical error' here.

But that reading of Calvin is also unwarrantable, unnecessary, unnatural, and altogether unlikely. Neither of those passages is evidence for their generalization, for which, in fact (to anticipate our conclusion), there seems to be no evidence at all. Technical error is not a concept that Calvin knew or used.

Other passages deal with cases where apostolic writers, appealing to Old Testament texts as proof or confirmation of New Testament truth, cite them loosely and paraphrastically. Calvin, however, stated over and over that when they did that, they never falsified the text's main point. Here is one generalized statement of his principle, occasioned by Matthew's report of how Micah 5:2 was quoted at Herod's court.

> We must always observe the rule, that whenever the Apostles quote a testimony from Scripture, though they do not render it word for word and in fact may move quite a way from it, they adapt it suitably and appropriately for the case in hand. So readers should always take care to note the object of the Scripture passages that the evangelists use, not to press single words too exactly, but to be content with the one message which they never take from Scripture to distort into a foreign sense, but suit correctly to its real purpose.[106]

Rogers and McKim say that Calvin thought Paul 'misquoted' Psalm 51:4 in Romans 3:4 and affirmed in his comment on Hebrews 10:5 (which they cite as 10:6—a 'technical error') that the saving message of Scripture is 'adequately communicated through an imperfect form of words.'[107] *Misquoted* and *imperfect* are, however, unjustified. Rogers and McKim are fathering onto Calvin the view (their own?) that quotations that are not verbatim are not correct, but what Calvin said in the passages they cite, as in many others too, is that quotations that genuinely apply at the level of principle are entirely correct, even when they are verbally loose. It is an odd freak that those two authors, who are elsewhere so insistent that Calvin's concern for Scripture focused on its intent, content, and function, rather than its verbal form,[108] should here accuse Calvin of criticizing the apostles' Old Testament quotations from an entirely verbal and formal standpoint. But their book contains several odd things.

Other passages deal with points of what Rogers and McKim might wish to call formal error or technical inaccuracy, by explaining that in those cases no assertion was intended and therefore no error can fairly be said to have been made. The inference is clearly cogent if its premise can be established, for where no assertion is attempted the question of falsehood and error cannot arise. One example is Calvin's insistence that the Evangelists never intended to present all that they reported about Jesus in an order that is chronologically exact but held themselves free to follow, on occasion, a topical or theological arrangement. From that it follows that they cannot be held to error or contradict each other when they narrate the same events in a different sequence.

Another example (that John Murray, perhaps rightly, thought unhappy and 'ill-advised,'[109] but that clearly comes in that category) is Calvin's suggestion that in Acts 7:14 (the seventy-five souls) and Hebrews 11:21 (Jacob's staff) the writer may have chosen to echo the Septuagint's mistranslation of the Hebrew of Genesis 46:27 and 47:31 rather than correct it, lest he disconcert his readers and so distract them from the point he was making, which was not affected by the mistranslation one way or the other. In those cases, so Calvin appears to imply, alluding to the incidents in the familiar words of the Greek Bible would not involve asserting either that the Septuagint translation was correct or that it expressed the facts at the point where it parted company with the Hebrew.

On neither issue would the New Testament writer himself be asserting anything, and hence his formal inaccuracy in echoing the substantial inaccuracy of the Septuagint would not amount to error (false assertion) on his part. Whether that line of explanation is accepted or not, it is clear that so far from admitting that biblical authors fell into error, Calvin's concern in his treatment of all those passages was to show that they did no such thing, and that is what matters for us at present.

At the start of this chapter we noted that Calvin was not the sort of inerrantist who held that (1) Scripture teaches science, in the sense of giving us concepts about nature that are logically alternative to those of the empirical disciplines, (2) biblical prophecy details future world history in a crackable pictorial code, (3) biblical theology dispels the mystery of God's essence and transcendence, (4) books of Scripture should not be looked at as human compositions at all, or (5) reasonableness is an irrelevant criterion when devising harmonistic hypotheses. What we have seen has confirmed those negative points and has also indicated what kind of inerrantist Calvin was when it came to interpreting God's written Word. He was a humanist exegete for whom every book and text of Scripture was a fully human piece of writing, a product of careful thought, often of hard study, and always of obedient attention to God on the writer's part. He was also a theological exegete for whom every passage was a divine oracle, dictated by the Holy Spirit.

In explaining Scripture he took note of both the cultural and historical factors that anchor each book in its own time and also the universal truths about God and men that make each book part of God's message for all time. He was a literary exegete, weighing, evaluating, and sometimes dissenting from the biblical elucidations of all his predecessors—from Origen, Chrysostom, and Augustine to his friend and peer Martin Bucer. He was also a churchly exegete, interacting throughout with the varied understandings of biblical faith that had at different times established themselves, more or less, in the Spirit-taught, though often fallible, fellowship of the people of God.

He was in no way a naive expositor, for his academic equipment was outstanding for his or any day, and he saw already a remarkable number of the questions that modern exegetes have raised, and worked through them with consistent academic rigor. At the same time he was a clear, down-to-earth Bible teacher, alert to the realities of religion no less than of theology and as far as can be imagined from the arcane subtlety that tends to afflict knowledgeable academics today. Calvin was, quite simply, a magnificent interpreter. His exposition was, and remains, coherent and penetrating and demonstrates the viability, by ordinary rational standards, of an inerrantist view of Scripture.

Postscript: A Flawed Account

All that remains of our agenda is to say something directly about the presentation of Calvin's approach to Scripture that Rogers and McKim offer on pages 89–116 of their book as part of a chapter called, very properly, 'Concentration on the Bible's Saving Function during the Reformation.' Much that those authors tell us about Calvin's humanistic education and orientation in theology, his contextual method of exegesis, the influence of his rhetorical training on his outlook, and his Christological and soteriological interest in the Bible is well informed and helpful. However, their book is a tract for the times with a case to make and an axe to grind, and their desire to claim Calvin as being on their side makes them squeeze him into the alien mould of their own mind-set, particularly in relation to two alleged antitheses that Calvin never contemplated and could not have accepted. They are as follows.

Antithesis number one is between concern for the *form* of Scripture and concern about its *function,* that is, between stressing and vindicating the God-givenness and factual truth of every word and phrase of the original text on the one hand, and on the other hand accepting and using Scripture as God-given instruction for leading us to Christ, feeding our souls, and teaching us to see life as it is under God and to worship God as Lord of all. Rogers and McKim, whose own explicit concern is with the latter matter rather than the former, deal with these as rival interests and present the major Reformed theologians as if each in resolving to highlight one had thereby resolved to downplay the other. Put that way, their historical thesis sounds unbelievably silly. So indeed it is. Only special pleading sustains it, and when they deal with Calvin, it leads them to ascribe to him, as a man like themselves, a recognition of 'technical errors' that is simply false to the facts, as we have seen already and shall in a moment see again.

But Calvin would have thought the antithesis itself absurd. As a literary man, he knew very well that it is through the particular words used and the particular nuances that their arrangement expresses that language fulfils its function of communicating the precise meaning that the speaker or writer has in mind; its function depends directly on its verbal form. For Calvin, Scripture was able to fulfil its God-given function precisely by virtue of its God-given form, and the Holy Spirit, through whose agency that function is fulfilled, was directly responsible for producing the words in that particular form. The Spirit teaches from a textbook that in effect he wrote himself. For Calvin, therefore, anyone who set the form and the function of Scripture, its givenness and its usefulness, in antithesis to each other, treating them as alternative rather than complementary theological concerns, would be talking a kind of nonsense, just as one would if one set food in antithesis to eating. The antithesis, Calvin would have said, is not a real one, and no one who is attending to Scripture itself would ever think of positing it.

We should note here that a further aspect of the antithesis as Rogers and McKim intend it is that those whose concern centres on the form of Scripture will attempt to show that God's book contains no historical or scientific inaccuracies, and those whose concern centres on its function will leave that question open or even allow that historical and scientific errors are actually there. By that criterion, however, Calvin was every bit as concerned about the form of Scripture as he was about its function, as we have already seen. Why should that be? We ask why Calvin should have had an interest here that Rogers and McKim make a point of not sharing. The pressure of that question brings us to the second antithesis, which for Rogers and McKim is really the fundamental one.

Antithesis number two is between *accommodation* and *inerrancy* in Scripture. The writers try to make Calvin party to their own view that God's gracious condescension in accommodating to our limitations the language in which he speaks to us in Scripture entailed features in the text for which 'technical errors' is the only proper name. They distinguish between 'technical errors'—non-verbatim quotations, non-expository quotations in which Old Testament words are used in an altered sense,[110] verbal slips, and evidence one way or another of limited factual knowledge—and intentional untruths and claim Calvin and Augustine as their authorities for allowing that Scripture contains the former, though not the latter.[111] To say that, they think, does justice to the religious concern that lay behind historic affirmations of biblical trustworthiness and evades unnecessary problems about biblical phenomena. So they embrace the thesis as their own. But leaving aside the question of whether Augustine is being fairly reported and whether in any case that is an acceptable view in itself, what is the evidence that Calvin took the position ascribed to him? As we saw, Rogers and McKim are prima facie wrong in supposing that Calvin ascribed an erroneous assertion to Matthew in Matthew 27:9 and to Luke in Acts 7:16 and thought of paraphrastic quotation from the Old Testament as error. And there seems to be no other evidence that Calvin's thoughts about the human phenomena of Scripture included any concept of error, 'technical' or otherwise.

In fact, the evidence points the other way. Calvin's concept of the unity of human and divine expression in the God-given Scriptures reaches further than Rogers and McKim and their mentor G. C. Berkouwer[112] seem to see. Calvin would certainly have criticized the positing of technical errors in Scripture as implicitly blasphemous because thereby error would be ascribed to the Holy Spirit. Whereas Rogers and McKim and the later Berkouwer, with Barth and most moderns, draw the instrumentalists' regular distinction between Scripture as human witness to God and God's Word spoken through it, Calvin made no such distinction; to him the two were one.

It is significant that immediately after the statement in the commentary on Genesis 1:16: 'Had he [Moses] spoken of things generally unknown, the uneducated might have pleaded in excuse that such subjects were beyond their capacity'—an explanation that Rogers and McKim quote[113] to explain why Moses did not launch into a technical discourse on astronomy—Calvin's very next sentence (which they do not quote!) is: 'Lastly, since the Spirit of God here opens a common school for everyone, it is not surprising that he should mostly select subject matter which would be intelligible to all.' Evidently for Calvin, what Moses teaches the Spirit of God also teaches, actively, deliberately, explicitly, so that if Moses or any other biblical writer made a technical error, the Spirit would be making it too. With that concept of the unity and identity of divine and human teaching in Scripture in his mind, it is no wonder that Calvin should have laboured to show the internal coherence and factual correctness of all that Scripture says. For him, the truthfulness and honour of God were directly involved in every single thing that Scripture expresses.[114]

There are other unreal and misleading antitheses in the mind-set of Rogers and McKim, notably that between what they see as the Augustinian-Platonist and Thomist-Aristotelian philosophical heritages, which also distort their presentation of the Calvin of history.[115] But enough, perhaps, has already been said to show that on this, as on other matters in their presentation of the Christian past, they are by no means reliable guides and that those who wish to understand Calvin's view of Scripture will on the whole be wise to look elsewhere.

CHAPTER 12

Predestination in Christian History

The subject of predestination is a high one, and to study it is like looking into the sun. When the sun is shining out of a bright blue sky we feel its warmth, but we are not able to look straight into it. It is simply too bright! In a similar way God dwells in light unapproachable (1 Tim. 6:16), and when we study the predestining purpose of God we are looking at that bright light. If we do not fully see what we are looking at, we ought not to be surprised. We do not have to be able to look into the sun in order to feel its warmth.

Before this conference ends I trust that every one of us will have appreciated what the Reformers used to speak of as the comfort (that is the support, encouragement and strength) of election, which is the side of predestination that most concerns us. But if at the end you still feel that there are aspects of the theme that are bewildering, do not worry. That need not in any way diminish the comfort which you may draw from it.

I have divided my material into four sections: (1) introductory questions, (2) the Reformed concept of predestination, (3) historical discussion, and (4) theological lessons from the ground surveyed.

Introductory Questions

The first question is: *What does Reformed theology mean by predestination?*

Answer: Reformed theology seeks to mean by predestination what the Bible itself means by predestination.

Romans 8:28 says, 'We know that in all things God works for the good of those who love him, who have been called according to his purpose.' The Greek word for 'purpose' could well be translated 'proposal' or 'plan.' In the next verse (v. 29), Paul tells us what God's proposal or plan is. That is why verse 29 begins with the word 'for.' It is Paul's regular way of beginning a statement of explanation. He says, in effect, 'When I speak of God's purpose I mean something specific, and this is it: Those whom God foreknew he also predestined to be conformed to the likeness of his Son, that he [the Lord Jesus] might be the firstborn among many brothers.' God's proposal was a decision determining people's destinies, predestining them to be conformed to the image of Jesus Christ. In verse 30 he continues this explanation: 'And those he predestined, he also called; those he called, he also justified; those he justified, he also glorified.' Here we see that the purpose of God was the source of that action on his part which actually saves us. He called us, justified us, and then, Paul says, glorified us. Note how Paul uses the past tense, as if glorification were already accomplished. He means that in God's plan the thing is settled already; he speaks of it as if it were done, because it is as good as done.

It is to this sovereign purpose of God that Reformed theology refers when it speaks of predestination. 'Pre' means 'before,' and expresses a double priority. God's plan is *chronologically* prior to anything that man does, for, as Paul tells us in another place, those who are saved were chosen in Christ 'before the creation of the world' (Eph. 1:4). The plan of God is also *logically* prior to any human response because it is his decision to save us and bring about our decision to accept Christ.

Nothing is said separately in verse 30 about any response of man to God's calling. This is because here, as elsewhere, Paul uses the word 'call' for that act of God whereby he evokes the responsive faith for which he asks. Calling is for Paul a work of power whereby God brings his promises to bear on us so that faith is drawn forth from us. Calling leads straight to justifying, because calling (*effectual* calling, as Reformed theology terms it) bestows the faith through which justification takes place.

There are two sides to God's predestinating purpose. This needs to be said at the outset because of the popular but erroneous doctrine of universalism. The Bible teaches that it is in God's plan that not all will be saved. One side of God's predestinating purpose is what Scripture calls election—God choosing those he will bring to eternal life in and through Christ. But the other side of God's predestinating decision is that he will judge the rest of men according to their rebellion and resistance to his ways.

I do not want to dwell on the dark side of predestination, but I would like to quote what Louis Berkhof says about the matter on page 118 of his standard textbook, *Systematic Theology*. He comments, 'Since the Bible is primarily a revelation of redemption, it naturally does not have as much to say about reprobation as about election. But what it says is quite sufficient.' Then this able theologian quotes a number of texts of which the leading ones are these:

Matthew 11:25–26—*I praise you, Father, Lord of heaven and earth, because you have hidden these things, from the wise and learned, and revealed them to little children. Yes, Father, for this was your good pleasure.*

Romans 9:18—*Therefore God has mercy on whom he wants to have mercy, and he hardens whom he wants to harden.*

Romans 9:21–24—Does not the potter have the right to make out of the same lump of clay some pottery for noble purposes and some for common use? What if God, choosing to show his wrath and make his power known, bore with great patience the objects of his wrath—prepared for destruction? What if he did this to make the riches of his glory known to the objects of his mercy, whom he prepared in advance for glory—even us, whom he also called, not only from the Jews but also from the Gentiles?

Romans 11:7—What Israel sought so earnestly it did not obtain, but the elect did. The others were hardened.

1 Peter 2:7–8—To those who do not believe, '[Jesus is] . . . a stone that causes men to stumble and a rock that makes them fall.' They stumble because they disobey the message—which is also what they were destined for.

Jude 4—Certain men whose condemnation was written about long ago have secretly slipped in among you. They are godless men, who change the grace of our God into a license for immorality and deny Jesus Christ our only Sovereign and Lord.

Though the Bible does not say much about it, the dark side is clearly there. Reformed theology seeks at this point to be biblical in acknowledging both aspects of predestination.

The second introductory question is: *Why is predestination important in Reformed theology?*

Answer: Because the doctrine of predestination resolves three vital questions. First, how is it that I am a Christian today? Second, what confidence can I have of getting to heaven? Third, what have I to thank God for?

What the truth of predestination teaches me is this:

First, I am a Christian today because God chose from eternity to make me one. He went the first mile when he sent his Son from heaven to die on the cross for my sins. He went the second mile when he called me by grace, working in my heart so that I responded to the gospel message in a way that I would not have done had he not so worked. It is thanks to God's predestination that I am a Christian.

Second, I have every confidence of getting to heaven. The doctrine of predestination says that once you have believed, God promises to keep you believing. Once he has brought you to faith according to his predestinating purpose, he will complete that purpose. It is all his doing, and it is guaranteed by his sovereignty. So I am safe in his hands, and my hope is secure.

Third, I owe God thanks for my entire Christian life—for the fact that I have been converted no less than for the fact that there was a Saviour for me to turn to. I must praise God for my conversion just as I praise him for Calvary.

The doctrine of predestination teaches us humility, the humility which acknowledges every spiritual benefit as God's gracious gift to me. Also, it reveals my security, telling me that God's purpose guarantees final glory for me. Finally, it prompts doxology, praise to God for the greatness of his grace to me.

Calvinists praise God for more than others do. They recognize more as God's gift to them. It is Calvinists who write hymns about 'amazing grace.' 'Amazing Grace' itself comes from John Newton, the eighteenth-century Anglican evangelical, who once said, 'I use Calvinism in my preaching as I use sugar in my tea, to sweeten the whole.' Here is a hymn about election which I would like you to hear. It is not great poetry, but it comes from a contemporary of Newton, the great Augustus Montague Toplady, who celebrated God's plan of grace in his hymns as vividly as anyone has ever done. Only a Calvinist would praise God in these terms, and I invite you to ask yourself whether these are not praises in which you too should join.

> How happy are we our election who see,
>   And venture, O Lord, for salvation on thee!
> In Jesus approved, eternally loved,
>   Upheld by thy power, we cannot be moved.
>
> 'Tis sweet to recline on the bosom divine
>   And taste of the comforts peculiar to thine,
> While born from above and upheld by thy love,
>   With singing and triumph to Zion we move.
>
> Our seeking thy face was all of thy grace;
>   Thy mercy demands and shall have all the praise;
> No sinner can be beforehand with thee;
>   Thy grace is preventing [prevenient], almighty and free.
>
> Our Saviour and Friend his love doth extend;
>   It knew no beginning and never shall end;
> Whom once he receives, his Spirit n'er leaves
>   Nor ever repents of the grace that he gives.
>
> This proof we would give that thee we receive:
>   Thou art precious alone to the souls that believe.
> Be precious to us, all beside us is dross
>   Compared with thy love and the blood of thy cross.

Such is the praise that springs from Reformed theology.

The third introductory question is: *Why is predestination emphasized by Reformed theologians?*

Answer: Because it is so often challenged, denied or, at the very least, ignored and evaded by Pelagians and Arminians. This makes the soul poor. Reformed people are distressed that others should make their souls poor, and try to stop it from happening; hence this emphasis. So Calvin approaches predestination in his *Institutes of the Christian Religion* (III.xxi.1), where he says that ignorance of God's election not only detracts from his glory because it robs him of his full measure of praise, but also impairs our humility because it robs him of his full measure of praise, but also impairs our humility because we do not realize our full dependence on God, and robs us of full confidence that we shall be kept in faith until we are brought into glory. If you do not know about God's predestination, says Calvin, you lose these things and so are impoverished in your spiritual life.

A person who denies predestination is likely to become self-reliant in the matter of faith. He will think of faith as his own contribution to salvation. He will say to himself: 'Well, I came to faith by my own wisdom and insight, and now I have to keep in faith by my own will-power. It all depends on me.' He will not be praising God for his conversion nor trusting God for his future Christian life, but will really be trusting himself. In practice he may well become anxious and self-absorbed, just because he does not trust God for his own future trusting. And he will be in a permanent muddle, because his heart tells him (as every regenerate person's heart does tell him) that he owes everything to God, and that his salvation is of the Lord, and when he prays he will acknowledge this; yet with his head he will deny it when he is discussing theology. Reformed theologians see these things and want to bring Christians to a better mind.

The Reformed Doctrine of Predestination

Now let me formulate in the theological language of historical discussion the full concept of predestination which Reformed theology draws from the Scriptures.

Reformed theologians speak of the 'decree' of predestination, from the Latin word *decretum*, meaning decision. This decision presupposes two 'mysteries,' using that word in the theologians' sense of realities which Scripture assures us are fact but concerning which we do not know how they can be. The first mystery is God's sovereign providence, which means his complete overruling of everything, including human actions, to ensure that what he has planned will come to pass. Paul speaks of this in Ephesians 1:11 when he says that God makes all things work 'in conformity with the purpose of his will.'

The second mystery is what we call human free will or free agency, which is part of our humanness and distinguishes us from computers and robots. It is a fact that in this world where God is in control of everything, nonetheless you and I are so made that our decisions really are our decisions, made, as we say, 'of our own free will,' and that remains true even when they are decisions which God works in us by grace—as when we come to repentance and faith, which by nature are impossible to us.

In conversion, our commitment to Christ is our own action and is done of our own free will, though it is God who works in us so that we want to repent and believe, and God who causes and enables us actually to do so. Free agency is always a reality; it is in fact part of God's image in us, and is the basis of human answerability to God at the final judgement.

In terms, now, of these given facts of total divine control and human free agency, the Reformed doctrine of predestination affirms that from eternity God has decided the course and destiny of every individual in this world. Every individual's life does in fact fulfil the course and enter into the destiny which God has appointed, whether that is salvation by grace through faith or condemnation by the God whom that person has rejected. Note, however, what this does *not* mean.

1. Predestination does not deny that human free agency and our consequent responsibility for what we do are realities. God does not compel people to sin against their will. He is not the author of their sins; they are, because they choose to sin. And, on the other side, as I said above, in conversion free will remains a reality. Men come to Christ 'most freely, being made willing by his grace' (Westminster Confession X.i). There is no denial of human free agency here.

2. Predestination does not mean fatalism, though it is often confused with fatalism. The only thing that predestination has in common with fatalism is the thought that the future is certain, but beyond that predestination and fatalism go in opposite ways. Fatalism is the idea that everything that happens is the product of blind, impersonal chance or, at the very least, a by-product of the actions of a God who does not care for us. It sees us as individuals caught in the cogs of a cosmic machine that is uncaring and pitiless so far as we are concerned. This is not the God with whom we have to do in Christianity.

3. Predestination does not mean commitment to any determinist theories in physics, metaphysics, or psychology. Determinist theories argue that present states are determined by past states within some defined and circumscribed system, either of the body or the mind or the cosmos as a whole. Whether any form of determinism is true is a question about the way the created order works, and the belief that the Creator ordains our ways and destinies is not bound up with any particular answer to it.

4. Predestination does not mean that anyone can be saved without Jesus Christ or apart from faith in him. Within God's predestining decree, means and ends are connected. Salvation is always through Christ by faith.

5. Predestination does not mean that the universal offer of pardon, adoption, and new life with God for everyone who responds to Jesus Christ—the offer, that is, which the gospel makes—is a fraud. On the contrary, it is a bona fide offer from God, guaranteed by the cross of Jesus Christ. When God says that whosoever will may come and take of the water of life freely, he means it. The offer is genuine, and those who reject it will one day realize that nothing kept them out of heaven save their own refusal to come in.

6. Predestination does not mean that the door of mercy is barred to anyone who actually wants to enter. To no such person does God say, 'No, you can't come in; there is no redemption, no mercy for you. You were predestined to stay outside, and outside you must remain.' The reason why this never happens is because no one ever wants to come in except God's chosen, whom he draws to Christ and brings to faith according to his predestining purpose. We are dealing, remember, with God's action towards our fallen race, in which nobody naturally seeks God. Nobody naturally wants to come to Christ. One who wants to come to Christ is already the subject of a work of grace, and will find the Saviour whom he or she is seeking.

7. Predestination does not mean that we can identify the reprobate. So far as we are concerned they are faceless people. None of us can be sure that we have ever met even one of them. When we have an opportunity of sharing Christ with somebody, we should conclude that God has given us that opportunity in order to bring his mercy into the life of that person. We should witness to them, therefore, with every confidence and no inhibitions, expecting to see God work in their lives.

8. Predestination does not mean that we can know that we are among God's elect before we believe in Jesus Christ, let alone that we dare not believe without enquiring about our election first. The basis for believing is the 'whosoever will' promise. You cannot know your election until you have believed. Scripture is clear on that.

9. Predestination does not mean that God's elect are a minority of the whole human race. We do not know one way or another whether they are a minority. Some theologians very much doubt if they are a minority. Certainly it is no part of the doctrine to assert that they are.

10. Predestination does not mean that those who know their election (or who believe they know their election) may allow themselves to be careless on moral matters. If a person says, 'Once saved, always saved; that is the predestining purpose of God; and since I know I am saved—for I once had an experience at an evangelistic meeting—it does not matter how I live now,' that statement merely proves he is a hypocrite and shows that his experience, whatever it was, was not true conversion. If you understand your election you know that you were chosen to be holy, and act accordingly.

One of the sweetest statements of the Reformed concept of predestination that I know is that given in the seventeenth of the Thirty-nine Articles of my own Anglican Church, first drafted by Archbishop Cranmer about 1550. I would like you to hear this in light of what I have said.

> Predestination to life is the everlasting purpose of God, whereby, before the foundations of the world were laid, he hath constantly [that is, firmly] decreed by his counsel secret to us, to deliver from curse and damnation those whom he has chosen

in Christ out of mankind, and to bring them by Christ to everlasting salvation, as vessels made to honour. Wherefore, they which be endued with so excellent a benefit of God be called according to God's purpose by his Spirit working in due season: they through grace obey the calling: they be justified freely: they be made sons of God by adoption: they be made like the image of his only-begotten Son Jesus Christ: they walk religiously in good works, and at length, by God's mercy, they attain to everlasting felicity.

As the godly consideration of predestination and our election in Christ is full of sweet, pleasant, and unspeakable comfort to godly persons, and such as feel in themselves the working of the Spirit of Christ mortifying the works of the flesh, and their earthly members, and drawing up their mind to high and heavenly things, as well because it doth greatly establish and confirm their faith of eternal salvation to be enjoyed through Christ, as because it doth fervently kindle their love towards God: so, for curious and carnal persons, lacking the Spirit of Christ, to have continually before their eyes the sentence of God's predestination, is a most dangerous downfall, whereby the Devil doth thrust them either into desperation, or into wretchlessness (*sic*) of most unclean living, no less perilous than desperation.

Furthermore, we must receive God's promises in such wise as they be generally set forth to us in Holy Scripture; and in our doings that will of God is to be followed which we have expressly declared unto us in the Word of God.

Historical Discussion

I turn now to the main historical debates which have surrounded this doctrine.

The story starts with Augustine opposing Pelagius and his followers early in the fifth century. Augustine maintained against Pelagius that there is no good in the life of fallen human beings apart from God's grace. This is because original sin, our heritage from Adam, expresses itself in the forms of pride (*superbia*), lust (*concupiscentia*), and self-absorption (for which Augustine's Latin phrase meant literally 'man bent back upon himself'), so that by nature we do not and cannot live for God as we were made to do. Augustine taught that this is where we are now through sin, and unless God changes our natures, we cannot respond to him in a positive way. So there must be grace, if there is to be faith in and love towards God.

Of course, this means that salvation depends on predestination, because it is from predestination that grace flows. Grace to believe and persevere is given to those who are chosen by God according to his predestining purpose.

The real battleground in Augustine's discussion with the Pelagians was whether the doctrine of original sin is true or not. This is the fundamental question in any discussion of predestination. Is it the case, as Augustine said, that as a result of sin man is by nature bad—to the core of his being? Or were Pelagius' people right to suppose that fallen man remains good, perhaps a little weaker in his responses to God than he was before, but not by much?

If you agree with Pelagius, you will reject Augustine's view that sovereign grace is necessary to bring men to faith in love towards their Creator. But I hope you do not agree with Pelagius at that point, for there is no question that Paul speaks as Augustine did. Remember Romans 8:7? 'The sinful mind is hostile to God. It does not submit to God's law, nor can it do so. Those controlled by the sinful nature cannot please God.' Augustine was merely echoing such statements as that.

In the one-thousand-year medieval period between Augustine and the Reformation, theologians oscillated between two opinions. They wanted to honour Augustine, but they wanted to go some distance with Pelagius as well. They wanted to say, 'Divine grace is needed because fallen man has been weakened through sin.' But they balked at saying, 'Fallen man is by nature thoroughly anti-God through sin.' As a result there were various compromise positions among these theologians, all starting from the thought that fallen man though weak is yet able still to desire God and to reach out after him. Semi-Pelagianism is the name by which such theories are usually known. They all carry the implication that God's election depends on his foresight of some spontaneous independent response on man's part to the divine Word.

At the time of the Reformation both Luther and Calvin insisted that you cannot do better than Augustine on this doctrine. Yet they did do better at one point. They organized their doctrine of predestinating grace around the gospel promise which God brings us to trust. Faith in God's promise of pardon and peace was central in their theology in a way that it did not ever quite become central in Augustine. They agreed with Augustine that God changes hearts. But Augustine had never said as clearly as they did that the very centre of our attention should be God's gracious promise to sinners sealed by the blood of Christ. It is this which his predestinating purpose leads his chosen to accept. Love and good works follow, but faith in the promise, and in the Christ of the promise, comes first.

After Calvin, Reformed theologians moved into a way of stating their theology different from that which Calvin had followed. Some think this meant a change of substance. I do not agree. I think it was only a rearrangement. Just as there is more than one way of arranging items in a shop window—you can put different items at the centre, arranging other items as background—so I think it was here.

Calvin and Luther had put the universal promise of the gospel at the centre of their shop window and set the doctrine of God's predestination behind it, undergirding it and explaining how it is that sinners like us are ever brought to trust Christ. In that they were following Paul's sequence of themes in Romans. We do not hear of predestination in Romans until chapter 8, verses 28–30. For seven and a half chapters Paul expounds the need for and the way of salvation, leading to new life in the Spirit; only then does he bring in predestination to explain how it is that we sinners come into and are kept in this new life. Luther and Calvin followed Paul's arrangement of these topics, and in Calvin's *Institutes* predestination is not treated until chapters 21–24 of book III, after everything about sin, law, atonement, faith, repentance, the Christian life, justification and prayer has been thoroughly covered. But Calvin's successors in Geneva and elsewhere, including those who drew up the Westminster Standards, put God's predestinating purpose in the centre of the shop window and set the gospel within the frame of reference which predestination provided. As I said, I do not think this was a change of substance at all. I think it was simply a change in the way of putting it.

For myself, I prefer Calvin's way of presenting predestination, because that is the way of Romans. It highlights the nature of election as grace to sinners, and cuts off at the root the hyper-Calvinism which is so mesmerized by predestination as to doubt whether the gospel invitation can properly be extended to all people. But I do not want to debate with my brethren about that.

In the early seventeenth century the battle erupted again. Arminianism, a latter-day form of semi-Pelagianism, affirmed a conditional election based on a foreseen response to the gospel offer, a response which men and women are put in a position to make by a grace that is universally given, but which no one is actually brought by God to make. According to Arminianism, God puts them in a position to make a response and then, as it were, stands back to see what they will do. What they do, either receiving Christ or not receiving Christ, is at that point their own doing in such a sense as not to be God's work in them. God chooses to save those who he foresees will of their own independent volition believe. By talking thus of conditional election, Arminians change the meaning of election from what it was in the Reformers, Augustine, and the New Testament.

Instead of looking to election as the source of the grace that saves, Arminians were now defining election as God's noting who of his or her own resources is going to believe and keep believing. Instead of election leading to faith as God's gift, faith leads to election as God's response. Instead of God saving us, first to last, we with his help save ourselves. This was a drastic reversal of biblical teaching.

The debate with the Arminians was synodically settled in 1618–19 at the Synod of Dort in Holland where the so-called 'five points' of Arminianism were answered by the 'five points' of Calvinism. As with Augustine, so here. The basic question was whether God sets the sinner in a position where he is able to decide for Christ in his own strength or not. Arminians said 'Yes.' The Reformed theologians stoutly insisted, 'No, it is God who must bring us to faith or we will never come to faith. The Arminian construction is a mistake; it assumes a false view of man; it does not take sin seriously enough. It is necessary to affirm predestination.'

In the eighteenth century a confused Calvinist named John Wesley (pardon me! but truth will out) muddled the discussion in a rather grievous way. He insisted that he was an Arminian because he wished to affirm the universal invitation of the gospel and the love of God expressed in the gospel. Well, Calvinists do that too! He also wished to affirm the necessity of holiness to final salvation—the need for those who come to faith then to live a life of obedience to God. That is something which Calvinists also affirm.

What John Wesley denied was that we can trust God for our continued trusting and look to him to preserve us in faith. He said that we must preserve ourselves in faith. That is the point at which he really parted company with Reformed theology. It was for this reason that he went with Arminians in affirming conditional election—holding that election is not God's decisive decision out of which our salvation comes, but is simply God's noting with approval who is going to believe and keep himself or herself in faith. Wesley wrote a number of sermons and tracts on the subject, one of which is called *Predestination Calmly Considered*. Many of its words are in capital letters and it is filled with exclamation marks! For some reason he found it hard to be calm when he discussed this subject. Others, too, have had this problem.

His brother Charles also said, 'I am an Arminian evangelical.' But, you know, he wrote Calvinistic hymns. Look at this:

> And can it be that I should gain
>   An interest in the Saviour's blood?
> Died he for me, who caused his pain?
>   For me, who him to death pursued?
> Amazing love! How can it be
>   That thou, my God, shouldst die for me?

That is what Calvinists call particular redemption: 'He loved me, and gave himself for me' (Gal. 2:20). Then in the same hymn we read:

> Long my imprisoned spirit lay
>   Fast bound in sin and nature's night;
> Thine eye diffused a quick'ning ray,
>   I woke, the dungeon flamed with light;
> My chains fell off, my heart was free,
>   I rose, went forth, and followed thee.

That is what Calvinists describe as effectual calling. No wonder 'Rabbi' Duncan said that Charles's hymns made him ask, 'Where's your Arminianism now, friend?'

The Wesleys were essentially Calvinistic in their basic thinking, and it is a pity that they made a point of insisting that they were not. The result was that in their own lifetime there was an estrangement between John Wesley and the clear-headed Calvinistic evangelist George Whitefield, which was a sad thing for the revival movement.

Ever since that time there has been estrangement between the Methodist constituency and the Reformed constituency, with many supposing that evangelical Arminianism asserts something which Calvinism denies, namely the universality of the gospel offer. That however is not true. The truth is that evangelical Arminianism is a denial of certain things that Calvinism asserts, namely, that election is the source of salvation and that God keeps in faith those whom he has brought to faith.

Theological Lessons

I pinpoint three theological lessons as I close.

First, come at predestination *biblically*, not only in matter but in manner also. Do not come at it speculatively. Do not be mesmerized by the doctrine of reprobation, about which the Bible says so little. The Scripture says, 'The secret things belong to the LORD our God, but the things revealed belong to us and to our children for ever, that we may follow all the words of [God's] law' (Deut. 29:29). Approach predestination in that spirit, taking to heart Calvin's warning that we must not go an inch beyond what the Bible says, for if we do, we can expect to find our heads going dizzy, our balance being lost and ourselves falling over the edge of an intellectual precipice into ruin. Come at predestination biblically and stay within the limits of Bible teaching.

Second, come at predestination *pastorally*, as the New Testament always does. Paul wrote in Romans 8 about God's plan to encourage believers under pressure. In Ephesians 1, he celebrates election in order to evoke praise of God from his readers. In Thessalonians he presents it as a doctrine which brings Christians assurance: 'We always thank God for all of you . . . [knowing] that he [God] has chosen you' (1 Thess. 1:2–4; cf. 2 Thess. 2:13–14). There is a matter for worship, encouragement, and praise in the doctrine of election. Pursue these concerns as you explore this theme.

Finally, come at the doctrine of predestination *Christ-centredly*. Meditate on John 6 and 10, where our Lord himself enunciates the truth of predestination.

> John 6:37–39—*All that the Father gives me will come to me, and whoever comes to me I will never drive away. For I have come down from heaven not to do my will but to do the will of him who sent me. And this is the will of him who sent me, that I shall lose none of all that he has given me, but raise them up at the last day.*

> John 6:44–45—*No one can come to me unless the Father who sent me draws him, and I will raise him up at the last day. It is written in the Prophets: 'They will all be taught by God.' Everyone who listens to the Father and learns from him comes to me.*

> John 10:14–16—*I am the good shepherd; I know my sheep and my sheep know me—just as the Father knows me and I know the Father—and I lay down my life for the sheep. I have other sheep that are not of this sheep pen. I must bring them also. They too will listen to my voice, and there shall be one flock and one shepherd.*

John 10:27–29—*My sheep listen to my voice; I know them, and they follow me. I give them eternal life, and they shall never perish; no one can snatch them out of my hand. My Father, who has given them to me, is greater than all; no one can snatch them out of my Father's hand.*

A doctrine which the Lord Jesus himself expresses should not be taken lightly by us, especially when the very heart of it is that the Father through his plan of predestining grace is securing a people for the Son, thus furthering the glory of the Son, which is his final purpose.

The glory of Jesus Christ as Saviour is directly bound up with this doctrine of predestinating grace, and God forbid that we should ever say anything or believe anything whose tendency is to rob Jesus Christ of his glory as the Saviour of men! May God give us understanding of these things.

CHAPTER 13

Justification in Protestant Theology

The Heart of the Gospel

'The confession of divine justification touches man's life at its heart, at the point of its relationship to God. It defines the preaching of the Church, the existence and progress of the life of faith, the root of human purity and man's perspective for the future.'[1] So wrote G. C. Berkouwer of the doctrine of justification by faith set forth by Paul and re-apprehended with decisive clarity at the Reformation; and in so writing he showed himself a true heir of the Reformers. For his statement is no more, just as it is no less, than a straightforward spelling out of what Luther had meant when he called justification by faith *articulus stantis vel cadentis ecclesiae*—the point of belief which determines (not politically or financially, but theologically and spiritually) whether the Church stands or falls.

With Luther, the Reformers saw all Scripture as being, in the last analysis, either Law or Gospel—meaning by 'Law' all that exposes our ruin through sin and by 'Gospel' everything that displays our restoration by grace through faith—and the heart of the biblical Gospel was to them God's free gift of righteousness and justification. Here was the sum and substance of that *sola fide—sola gratia—solo Christo—sola Scriptura—soli Deo gloria* which was the sustained theme of their proclamation, polemics, praises, and prayers. And to their minds (note well!) proclamation, polemics, praise, and prayer belonged together, just as did the five Latin slogans linked above as epitomising their message. Justification by faith, by grace, by Christ, through Scripture, to the glory of God was to them a single topic, just as a fugue with several voices is a single piece. This justification was to them not a theological speculation but a religious reality, apprehended through prayer by revelation from God via the Bible. It was a gift given as part of God's total work of love in saving us, a work which leads us to know God and ourselves as both really are—something which the unbelieving world does not know. And to declare and defend God's justification publicly as the only way of life for anybody was at once an act of confessing their faith, of glorifying their God by proclaiming his wonderful work, and of urging others to approach him in penitent and hopeful trust just as they did themselves.

So, where Rome had taught a piecemeal salvation, to be gained by stages through working a sacramental treadmill, the Reformers now proclaimed a unitary salvation, to be received in its entirety here and now by self-abandoning faith in God's promise, and in the God and the Christ of that promise, as set forth in the pages of the Bible. Thus the rediscovery of the Gospel brought a rediscovery of evangelism, the task of summoning non-believers to faith. Rome had said, God's grace is great, for through Christ's cross and his church salvation is possible for all who will work and suffer for it; so come to church, and toil! But the Reformers said, God's grace is greater, for through Christ's cross and his Spirit salvation, full and free, with its unlimited guarantee of eternal joy, is given once and for ever to all who believe; so come to Christ, and trust and take!

It was this conflict with the medieval message that occasioned the fivefold 'only' in the slogans quoted above. Salvation, said the Reformers, is by faith (man's total trust) *only*, without our being obliged to work for it; it is by grace (God's free favour) *only*, without our having to earn or deserve it first; it is by Christ the God-man *only*, without there being need or room for any other mediatorial agent, whether priest, saint, or virgin; it is by Scripture *only*, without regard to such unbiblical and unfounded extras as the doctrine of purgatory and of pilgrimages, the relic-cult and papal indulgences as devices for shortening one's stay there; and praise for salvation is due to God *only*, without any credit for his acceptance of us being taken to ourselves.

The Reformers made these points against unreformed Rome, but they were well aware that in making them they were fighting over again Paul's battle in Romans and Galatians against works, and in Colossians against unauthentic traditions, and the battle fought in Hebrews against trust in any priesthood or mediation other than that of Christ. And (note again!) they were equally well aware that the Gospel of the five 'onlies' would always be contrary to natural human thinking, upsetting to natural human pride, and an object of hostility to Satan, so that destructive interpretations of justification by faith in terms of justification by works (as by the Judaisers of Paul's day, and the Pelagians of Augustine's, and the Church of Rome both before and after the Reformation, and the Arminians within the Reformed fold, and Bishop Bull among later Anglicans) were only to be expected. So Luther anticipated that after his death the truth of justification would come under fresh attack and theology would develop in a way tending to submerge it once more in error and incomprehension; and throughout the century following Luther's death Reformed theologians, with Socinian and other rationalists in their eye, were constantly stressing how radically opposed to each other are the 'Gospel mystery' of justification and the religion of the natural man.

For justification by works is, in truth, the natural religion of mankind, and has been since the Fall, so that, as Robert Traill, the Scottish Puritan, wrote in 1692, 'all the ignorant people that know nothing of either law or gospel,' 'all proud secure sinners,' 'all formalists,' and 'all the zealous devout people in a natural religion,' line up together as 'utter enemies to the Gospel.' That trio of theological relatives, Pelagianism, Arminianism, and Romanism, appear to Traill as bastard offspring of natural religion fertilised by the Gospel. So he continued: 'The principles of Arminianism are the natural dictates of a carnal mind, which is enmity both to the law of God, and to the Gospel of Christ; and, next to the dead sea of Popery (into which also this stream runs), have, since Pelagius to this day, been the greatest plague of the Church of Christ, and its like will be till his second coming'[2]—a point of view entirely in line with that of Luther and his reforming contemporaries a century and half before. And all study of non-Christian faiths since the time of Luther and Traill has confirmed their biblically based conviction that salvation by self-effort is a principle that the fallen human mind takes for granted.

It has been common since Melanchthon to speak of justification by faith as the *material* principle of the Reformation, corresponding to biblical authority as its *formal* principle. That is right. Of all the Reformers' many biblical elucidations, the rediscovery of justification as a present reality, and of the nature of the faith which secures it, were undoubtedly the most formative and fundamental. For the doctrine of justification by faith is like Atlas. It bears a whole world on its shoulders, the entire evangelical knowledge of God the Saviour. The doctrines of election, of effectual calling, regeneration, and repentance, of adoption, of prayer, of the Church, the ministry, and the sacraments, are all to be interpreted and understood in the light of justification by faith, for this is how the Bible views them. Thus, we are taught that God elected men from eternity in order that in due time they might be justified through faith in Christ (Rom. 8:29–30). He renews their hearts under the Word, and draws them to Christ by effectual calling, in order that he might justify them upon their believing. Their adoption as God's sons follows upon their justification; it is, indeed, no more than the positive outworking of God's justifying sentence. Their practice of prayer, of daily repentance, and of good works springs from their knowledge of justifying grace (cf. Luke 18:9–14; Eph. 2:8–10). The Church is to be thought of as the congregation of the faithful, the fellowship of justified sinners, and the preaching of the Word and ministration of the sacraments are to be understood as means of grace because through them God evokes and sustains the faith that justifies. A right view of these things is possible only where there is a proper grasp of justification; so that, when justification falls, true knowledge of God's grace in human life falls with it. When Atlas loses his footing, everything that rests on his shoulders collapses too.

The Doctrine Analysed

A study of the expositions of justification in the works of the Reformers and the church confessions produced under their leadership in Germany, France,

Switzerland, the Low Countries, and Britain reveals such unanimity that the material may be generalised about as a single whole. The main points stressed are these:

1. The Need of Justification

The biblical frame of reference, within which alone justification can be understood and apart from which it remains, in the strictest sense, unintelligible, is created, said the Reformers, by two realities: human sin, which is universal, and divine judgement, which is inescapable. The basic fact is that the God who made us intends to take account of us, measuring us by his own standards, and from his imminent inquisition nothing can shield us. All stand naked and open before the searcher of hearts, and all must prepare to meet their God. But that being so, all hope is gone; for, being morally and spiritually perverse throughout, we are forced to recognise that in God's eyes we are hopelessly and helplessly guilty, justly subject to his condemning sentence and to that judicial rejection which the Bible calls his *wrath*. The pride which prompts us to rail at this judgement as unjust is itself part of the perversity which makes it just. Anyone who knows anything of his own inner corruption and of the holiness of his judge will find Luther's question, 'How may I find a gracious God?' rising in his heart unbidden—but to this question the unaided human mind can find no answer. To persons convicted of sin, efforts for self-justification appear as the abortive products of self-ignorance; those who have become realistic about themselves see clearly that there is no road that way. Luther in the monastery sought perfect *contritio* (sorrow for sin, out of love for God), without which, so the theology of his day told him, there was no forgiveness. No man ever worked harder than Luther to make himself love God, but he could not do it. When, later, Luther said that Romans was written to 'magnify sin,'[3] what he meant was that Romans aims to induce a realistic awareness of moral and spiritual inability, and so create the self-despair which is the anteroom of faith in Christ.

When the Reformers insisted that the Law must prepare for the Gospel, this was what they meant. Conviction of sin, springing from God-given self-knowledge, is, they said, a necessary precondition for understanding justification, for it alone makes faith possible. The Augsburg Confession of 1531 states: 'this whole doctrine [of justification] must be related to the conflict of an alarmed conscience, and without that conflict it cannot be grasped. So persons lacking this experience, and profane men, are bad judges of this matter.'[4] Calvin makes the same point in *Institutio* III.xii, a chapter on the theme that justification must be studied in the solemnising light of God's judgement seat.[5] And John Owen preserves this perspective when at the start of his classic treatise *The Doctrine of Justification by Faith* (1677) he writes:

> The first inquiry ... is after the proper relief of the conscience of a sinner pressed and perplexed with a sense of the guilt of sin. For justification is the way and means, whereby such a person doth obtain acceptance before God ... And nothing is pleadable in this cause, but what a man would speak unto his own conscience in that state, or into the conscience of another, when he is anxious under that inquiry.

And again:

> It is the practical direction of the consciences of men, in their application unto God by Jesus Christ, for deliverance from the curse due unto the apostate state, and peace with him, with the influence of the way thereof unto universal gospel obedience, that is alone to be designed in the handling of this doctrine. And therefore, unto him that would treat of it in a due manner, it is required that he ... not dare to propose that unto others which he doth not abide by himself, in the most intimate recesses of his mind, under his nearest approaches unto God, in his surprisals with dangers, in deep afflictions, in his preparations for death, and most humble contemplations of the infinite distance between God and him. Other notions ... not seasoned with these ingredients ... are insipid and useless.[6]

Luther would have graduated Owen *summa cum laude* for that!

2. The Meaning of Justification

What justification is, said the Reformers, must be learned from Paul, its great New Testament expositor, who sees it clearly and precisely as a judicial act of God pardoning and forgiving our sins, accepting us as righteous, and instating us as his sons. Following Augustine, who studied the Bible in Latin and was partly misled by the fact that *justificare*, the Latin for Paul's δικαιοῦν, naturally means '*make righteous*,' the medievals had defined justification as pardon plus inner renewal, as the Council of Trent was also to do; but the Reformers saw that the Pauline meaning δικαιοῦν is strictly forensic. So Calvin defines justification as 'acceptance, whereby God receives us into his favour and regards us as righteous; and we say that it consists in the remission of sins and the imputation of the righteousness of Christ.'[7] Justification is decisive for eternity, being in effect the judgement of the last day brought forward. Its source is God's grace, his initiative in free and sovereign love, and its ground is the merit and satisfaction—that is, the obedient sin-bearing death—of Jesus Christ, God's incarnate Son.[8]

Behind Calvin's phrase, 'the imputation of the righteousness of Christ' lies the characteristic 'Christ-and-his-people' Christology which was the centre of reference—the hub of the wheel, we might say—of the Reformers' entire doctrine of grace. The concern of this Christology, as of the New Testament Christology which moulded it, is soteriological, and its key thought is participation through exchange. This idea is spelled out as follows. The Son of God came down from heaven in order to bring us to share with him the glory to which he has now returned. By incarnation he entered into solidarity with us, becoming through his Father's appointment the last Adam, the second head of the race, acting on our behalf in relation to God. As man, he submitted to the great and decisive exchange set forth in 2 Corinthians 5:21: 'For our sake he [God] made him to be sin who knew no sin, so that in him we might become the righteousness of God.'

> This [said Luther], is that mystery which is rich in divine grace to sinners, wherein by a wonderful exchange our sins are no longer ours but Christ's, and the righteousness of Christ is not Christ's but ours. He has emptied himself of his righteousness that he might clothe us with it; and fill us with it; and he has taken our evils upon himself that he might deliver us from them. So that now the righteousness of Christ is ours not only objectively (as they term it) but formally also it is not only an ontological reality, 'there' for our benefit in some general sense, but it actually imparts to us the 'form,' i.e., the characteristic, of being righteous in God's sight.[9]

Our sins were reckoned (imputed) to Christ, so that he bore God's judgement on them, and in virtue of this his righteousness is reckoned ours, so that we are pardoned, accepted, and given a righteous man's status for his sake. Christians in themselves are sinners who never fully meet the Law's demands; nonetheless, says Luther, 'they are righteous because they believe in Christ, whose righteousness covers them and is imputed to them.'[10] On this basis, despite all the shortcomings of which they are conscious, believers may be sure of eternal salvation, and rejoice in hope of the glory of God. And this, said the Reformers, is what it means to know Christ; for we do not know him, however much else we may know about him, till we see him as Christ *pro nobis,* dying, rising, and reigning for us as our gracious Saviour.

The Reformers were explicit in grounding our justification on Christ's penal substitution for us under the punitive wrath of God. According to Anselm, whose view had been standard in the West for four centuries before the Reformers, Christ's death was a satisfaction for our sins offered to God as an alternative to the punishment of our persons. The Reformers assumed this formula, but added two emphases which went beyond Anselm—first, that the Son's offering was made at the Father's bidding; second, that Christ's death made satisfaction precisely by being the punishment of our sins in his person.[11] Satisfaction, in other words, was by substitution; vicarious sin-bearing by the Son of God is the ground of our justification and hope. In saying this, the Reformers were not offering a speculative rationale of Christ's work of reconciliation, but simply expounding and confessing the scriptural reality of it. They did not discuss, as later generations were to do, why, or indeed whether, God must judge sin retributively as a basis of pardoning it, or how vicarious punishment can be shown to be meaningful and moral, or any of the other questions which the Socinian critique of the Reformed doctrine was to raise; their concern was just to enter fully into biblical thinking on this matter, and to relay it as clearly and precisely as possible. Luther, commenting on Galatians 3:13, 'Christ redeemed us from the curse of the law, having become a curse for us,' states penal substitution like this:

> We are sinners and thieves, and therefore guilty of death and everlasting damnation. But Christ took all our sins upon him, and for them died upon the cross . . . all the prophets did foresee in spirit that Christ should become the greatest transgressor, murderer, adulterer, thief, rebel, blasphemer, etc., that ever was . . . for he being made a sacrifice, for the sins of the whole world, is now an innocent person and without sins . . . our most merciful Father, seeing us to be oppressed, overwhelmed with the curse of the law, and so to be holden under the same that we could never be delivered from it by our own power, sent his only Son into the world and laid upon him the sins of all men, saying: Be thou Peter that denier; Paul that persecutor, blasphemer and cruel oppressor; David that adulterer; that sinner which did eat the apple in Paradise; that thief which hanged upon the cross; and, briefly, be thou the person which hath committed the sins of all men; see therefore that thou pay and satisfy for them. Here now cometh the law and saith: I find him a sinner, and that such a one as hath taken upon him the sins of all men, and I see no sins but in him; therefore let him die upon the cross. And so he setteth upon him and killeth him. By this means the whole world is purged and cleansed from all sins, and so delivered from death and all evils.[12]

Calvin speaks less vividly and dramatically, but to the same effect:

> Because the curse caused by our guilt was awaiting us at God's heavenly judgement seat . . . Christ's condemnation before Pontius Pilate . . . is recorded, so that we might know that the penalty to which we were subject had been inflicted on this righteous man . . . when he was arraigned before a judgement-seat, accused and put under pressure by testimony, and sentenced to death by the words of a judge, we know by these records that his role was that of (*personam sustinuit*) a guilty wrongdoer . . . we see the role of the sinner and criminal represented in Christ, yet from his shining innocence it becomes obvious that he was burdened with the misdoing of others rather than his own . . . This is our acquittal, that the guilt which exposed us to punishment was transferred to the head of God's Son . . . At every point he substituted himself in our place (*in vicem nostram ubique se supposuerit*) to pay the price of our redemption.[13]

This is the characteristic doctrine of the Reformation concerning the death of Christ. It was an act of obedient substitution on his part, an acceptance in his own person of the penalty due to us, in virtue of which the holy judge declares guilty sinners immune from punishment and righteous in his sight. The great exchange is no legal fiction, no arbitrary pretence, no mere word-game on God's part, but a costly achievement. The divinely established solidarity between Christ and his people was such that he was in truth 'made sin' for us, and 'bore in his soul the dreadful torments of a condemned and lost man,'[14] so that in our souls the joy of knowing God's forgiveness and favour might reign for ever. This, to the Reformers, was the heart and height of the work of divine grace, not to be wrangled over, but to be trusted and adored.

3. The Means of Justification

Justification, said the Reformers, is by faith *only*. Why so? Not because there are no 'good works' in the believer's life (on the contrary, faith works by love untiringly and the knowledge of justification is the supreme ethical dynamic),[15] but because Christ's vicarious righteousness is the *only* ground of justification, and it is *only* by faith that we lay hold of Christ, for his righteousness to become ours. Faith is a conscious acknowledgement of our own unrighteousness and ungodliness and on that basis a looking to Christ as our righteousness, a clasping of him as the ring clasps the jewel (so Luther), a receiving of him as an empty vessel receives treasure (so Calvin), and a reverent, resolute reliance on the biblical promise of life through him for all who believe. Faith is our act, but not our work; it is an instrument of reception without being a means of merit; it is the work in us of the Holy Spirit, who both evokes it and through it ingrafts us into Christ in such a sense that we know at once the personal relationship of sinner to Saviour and disciple to Master and with that the dynamic relationship of resurrection life, communicated through the Spirit's indwelling. So faith takes, and rejoices, and hopes, and loves, and triumphs.

One of the unhealthiest features of Protestant theology today is its preoccupation with faith: faith, that is, viewed man-centredly as a state of existential commitment. Inevitably, this preoccupation diverts thought away from faith's object, even when this is clearly conceived—as too often in modern theology it is not. Though the Reformers said much about faith, even to the point of calling their message of justification 'the doctrine of faith,' their interest was not of the modern kind. It was not subject-centred but object-centred, not psychological but theological, not anthropocentric but Christocentric. The Reformers saw faith as a relationship, not to oneself, as did Tillich, but to the living Christ of the Bible, and they fed faith in themselves and in others by concentrating on that Christ as the Saviour and Lord by whom our whole life must be determined. A. M. Stibbs echoed the Reformers' 'object-centred' account of faith with precision when he wrote:

> The faith of the individual must be seen as having no value in itself, but as discovering value wholly and solely through movement towards and committal to Christ. It must be seen as simply a means of finding all one's hope outside oneself in the person and work of another; and not in any sense an originating cause or objective ground of justification. For true faith is active only in the man who is wholly occupied with Christ; its practice means that every blessing is received from another. For this reason faith is exclusive and intolerant of company; it is only truly present when any and every contribution towards his salvation on the part of the believer or on the part of the Church is absolutely and unequivocally shut out. Justification must be

seen and received as a blessing dependent wholly and exclusively on Christ alone, on what he is and what he has done—a blessing enjoyed simply through being joined directly to him, through finding one's all in him, through drawing one's all from him, without the interposition of any other mediator or mediating channel whatever.[16]

The Doctrine Distorted

To the Reformers' doctrine of justification by faith alone Reformed theology has held down the centuries, maintaining it to be both scriptural in substance and life-giving in effect.[17] This tenacity has, however, involved constant conflict, as it still does. Two things have long threatened the truth as stated: first, the intruding of works as the ground of justification; second, the displacing of the cross as the ground of justification. Both are familiar weeds in the Church's garden; both express in very obvious ways the craving for self-justification which lurks (often in disguise!) in the fallen human heart. Something may be said about each.

First, *the intruding of works.* This happens the moment we look to anything in ourselves, whether of nature or of grace, whether to acts of faith or to deeds of repentance, as a basis for pardon and acceptance. Reformed theology had to fight this tendency in both Romanism and Arminianism. The Council of Trent (1547, Session VI) defined justification as inner renewal plus pardon and acceptance, the renewal being the basis of the pardon, and went on to affirm that the 'sole formal cause' (*unica formalis causa*) of justification, in both its aspects, was God's righteousness imparted through baptism as its instrumental cause.[18] 'Formal cause' means that which gives a thing its quality; so the thesis is that the ground of our being pardoned and accepted by infused grace is our having been made genuinely righteous in ourselves. (This links up with the Roman idea that 'concupiscence' in the regenerate is not sin till it is yielded to.[19]) In reply, a host of Reformed divines, continental and British, episcopal and non-episcopal, drew out at length the Reformers' contention, discussed above, that the 'sole formal cause' of justification is not God's righteousness imparted, but Christ's righteousness imputed. The same point was pressed against the seventeenth-century Arminians, who held that faith is 'counted for righteousness' because it is in itself actual personal righteousness, being obedience to the Gospel viewed as God's new Law, and being also an act of self-determination that is in no sense determined by God. The argument against both Romans and Arminians was that by finding the ground of justification in the believer himself they contradicted the Scriptures; nourished pride and a spirit of self-sufficiency and self-reliance in religion, so encouraging self-ignorance; destroyed assurance by making final salvation depend upon ourselves rather than on God; obscured the nature of faith as self-renouncing trust; and robbed both God's grace and God's Son of the full glory that was their due. It is not enough, declared the Reformed writers, to say that without Christ our justification could not be; one must go on to say that it is on the ground of his obedience as our substitutionary sin-bearer, and that alone, that righteousness is reckoned to us, and sin cancelled. The Westminster Confession (XI.i) has both Romanism and Arminianism in its eye when it declares, with classic precision and balance:

> Those whom God effectually calleth he also freely justifieth; not by infusing righteousness into them, but by pardoning their sins, and by accounting and accepting their persons as righteous; not for anything wrought in them, or done by them, but for Christ's sake alone; not by imputing faith itself, the act of believing, or any other evangelical obedience, to them as their righteousness; but by imputing the obedience and satisfaction of Christ unto them, they receiving and resting on him and his righteousness by faith; which faith they have not of themselves; it is the gift of God.

Second, *the displacing of the cross* as the ground of justification. This happens when the correlation between Christ's sin-bearing and our pardon is lost sight of. It can occur, and has occurred, in various ways. The truth of biblical teaching may be queried, in which case one may say (for instance) that though judicial notions meant much to Paul, because of his rabbinic conditioning, and to the Reformers, in whose culture legal concepts were dominant, they are really unfit for expressing God's forgiveness, and the idea that our heavenly Father's pardon had to be paid for by the blood of Christ is in any case monstrous. Or the objective reality of God's wrath against sin may be specifically denied, and the cross be construed in terms other than penal substitution. But in every case where the correlation breaks, the effect is to shut us up to supposing that God, after all, pardons and accepts us for something in ourselves—our repentance, or the righteousness of which it is the promise. So we return by a new route to the idea that the ground of justification is, after all, our own works, actual or potential. The history of the older rationalism and liberalism over two centuries shows many instances of this.

A third disruptive notion, more recently launched, is *the eliminating of faith* as the means of justification. This happens in universalism, which affirms that through God's love in creation and redemption all men have been redeemed and justified already, and the only question is whether they yet know it. So justification is before faith and apart from it, and faith is no more than discovery of this fact. Clearly, neither on this view nor on those noted in the two previous paragraphs can faith be given its biblical significance as the means whereby a sinner lays hold of Christ, and from being under wrath comes to be under grace.

Justification by faith only, as Reformed Christians know, is a 'Gospel mystery,' a revealed secret of God which is a wonder of grace, transcending human wisdom and indeed contradicting it. No wonder, then, if again and again it is misunderstood, or objected to, or twisted out of shape! But, as we have seen, to those who know anything of God's holiness and their own sinfulness the doctrine is in truth a lifeline and a doxology, a paean of praise and a song of triumph—as it was to the judicious Richard Hooker, with whose majestic and poignant declaration of it we close this section.

> Christ hath merited righteousness for as many as are found in him. In him God findeth us, if we be faithful; for by faith we are incorporated into him. Then, although in ourselves we be altogether sinful and unrighteous, yet even the man who in himself is impious, full of iniquity, full of sin; him being found in Christ by faith, and having his sin in hatred through repentance; him God beholdeth with a gracious eye, putteth away his sin by not imputing it, taketh quite away the punishment due thereto, by pardoning it; and accepteth him in Jesus Christ, as perfectly righteous, as if he had fulfilled all that is commanded him in the law: shall I say, more perfectly righteous than if himself had fulfilled the whole law? I must take heed what I say: but the Apostle saith, 'God made him which knew no sin, to be sin for us; that we might be made the righteousness of God in him.' Such we are in the sight of God the Father, as is the very Son of God himself. Let it be counted folly, or phrensy, or fury, or whatsoever. It is our wisdom, and our comfort; we care for no knowledge in the world but this, that man hath sinned, and God hath suffered; that God hath made himself the sin of men, and that men are made the righteousness of God.[20]

The Reformed Doctrine in the Church of England[21]

Had the post-Reformation Church of England held to Hooker's view of justification, there would today be no uncertainty as to whether Anglican soteriology is Reformed or not. What actually happened, however, has created much uncertainty at this point. The convulsions of the mid-seventeenth century threw up a generation of teachers whose views embodied the first two of the distortions described above, while the past century and a half has seen Anglican theologians exploring the third. The Reformed and evangelical status of the Church of England has often been called in question by reason of ideas about ministry and sacraments that have surfaced within it, but a profounder reason for the query would be the un-Reformed notions about justification on which these views rest.

To be more specific: under Dutch Arminian and Greek patristic influences and with the laudable purpose of highlighting the need for holiness as the path to final salvation, men like William Forbes, Henry Hammond, Jeremy Taylor, Herbert Thorndike, and George Bull reacted against the position spelled out by Hooker and upheld during the century after him as both biblical and officially Anglican by, for instance, Bishops George Downame (Downham), Lancelot Andrewes, John Davenant, Joseph Hall, James Ussher, and Thomas Barlow, those Anglicans who framed the Irish Articles (1615) and the Westminster Confession (1647), and theologians William Perkins, and William Whitaker, John Donne, John Bramhall, Robert Sanderson, William Beveridge, plus the great Independent John Owen. Reaction took these later Carolines in different directions on points of detail, but in their goal of seeking an accommodation of, or a *via media* between, Protestant and Tridentine positions without transgressing the Anglican formularies they were at one, and the same theological perspectives appear in them all, as follows:

First, they accepted the Socinian contention that the Reformed doctrine of Christ's righteousness imputed to believers is logically antinomian in the sense that it makes personal holiness unnecessary and irrelevant for final salvation. Recoiling from the bogy of antinomianism, they sought to show that personal holiness is the direct ground of God's acceptance of the Christian at the last.

Second, they accepted the Arminian idea that God's new covenant proclaimed in the Gospel is essentially a conditional promise, based on Christ's death as its presupposition, to give pardon and life in heaven to those who practise repentance and faith to the very end. Repentance and faith thus constitute their personal righteousness, and are the ground of God's award.

Third, they accepted the Tridentine teaching that sinful impulse (concupiscence) is not a guilty thing in God's sight till it is yielded to, and that a grace-aided sinner is capable of unflawed acts of faith, repentance, and obedience which he himself may properly regard as his own righteousness, just as, according to this teaching, God does.

Fourth, they accepted the redefinition of faith which Arminians and some Puritans had come up with, according to which faith is essentially volitional (active) rather than intellectual (passive), as the Reformers had conceived it to be. Instead of being a God-given certainty of one's acceptance here and now for Jesus' sake, faith thus became a resolute commitment to obey Christ; instead of being a fiducial reception through the Spirit of a divine assurance, based on God's promise in Scripture, that one is this moment and for ever justified in Christ, it became in effect a meritorious work whereby justification is sought; instead of being the root of repentance, it became indistinguishable from repentance, so that it could now actually be equated with one's 'new obedience' in Christ.

The effect was to disrupt the correlation between Christ's obedience to death and our present justification, and to make justification by faith appear as a new form of justification by works, the difference from the old form being simply that less is now asked for as a condition of justification than was formerly the case. Once, perfect obedience to the law was required; now, a sustained act of faith will do the trick. 'Our Saviour hath brought down the market,' wrote Henry Hammond.[22] But this is not the Reformed doctrine, even though it is sometimes heard today on evangelical lips. The nature of faith in its relation to God's own justifying word needs more study among evangelical Christians than it commonly receives.

As a result of the Caroline heritage, variously adapted, taking a permanent place in the Anglican mix, and prompting a persistent critique of *sola fide* teaching as if it means that one is justified through feeling justified(!), Anglican thinking about justification is today in a state of some confusion. Space forbids further discussion of its cross-currents here; suffice it to say two things only. First, the foundation of the Reformed doctrine is belief in the total inability of fallen man ('those who are in the flesh cannot please God' [Rom. 8:8]), the particularity of Christ's redemption ('who loved me and gave himself for me' [Gal. 2:20]), and the sovereign mercy of God in effectual calling ('those whom he called he also justified' [Rom. 8:30]), and it cannot be stated in any other context or frame of reference. Second, assurance of final salvation is integral to the Reformed doctrine of God's justifying gift in Christ, and this is something which no form of semi-Pelagianism, whether Protestant (Arminian) or Roman Catholic (Tridentine), can accept. It is greatly to be hoped that the Reformed doctrine will reassert itself within Anglicanism in these days.

CHAPTER 14

Thomas Cranmer's Catholic Theology

The white-bearded, shabby old man (he was sixty-six) who had till lately been Primate of England stood on the platform by the pulpit weeping uncontrollably while the preacher flayed him as a traitor and heretic, patronised him as a penitent, and argued the need for his immediate execution. The sermon, two hours long, was brutally smug, and the packed congregation was fidgeting by the end of it. But the proceedings had not finished yet. The preacher now called on the old man to profess his faith, ' "that all men may understand that you are a catholic indeed." "I will do it," said the archbishop, "and that with a good will." '[1]

He took out a piece of paper containing a prayer and a speech, prayed, and then began reading the speech to the silent crowd. Its first words were familiar to some standing by; they had seen Cranmer's original draft, sent to the printer three days before. They did not know that Cranmer was reading from a later version with an altered last paragraph.[2] The first draft had ended with Cranmer repudiating his eucharistic writings as 'untrue books' and asserting transubstantiation. But the speech that Cranmer actually delivered that March morning in 1556 finished like this:

> And now I come to the great thing, which so much troubleth my conscience, more than any thing that ever I did or said in my whole life, and that is the setting forth of a writing contrary to the truth; which now here I renounce and refuse, as things written with my hand contrary to the truth which I thought in my heart, and written for fear of death, and to save my life if it might be. And that is all such bills and papers which I have written or signed with my hand since my degradation, wherein I have written many things untrue. And forasmuch as my hand offended, writing contrary to my heart, my hand shall first be punished therefor; for, may I come to the fire, it shall be first burned. And as for the Pope, I refuse him, as Christ's enemy, and antichrist, with all his false doctrine. And as for the sacrament, I believe as I have taught in my book against the Bishop of Winchester, the which my book teacheth so true a doctrine of the sacrament, that it shall stand at the last day before the judgement of God, where the papistical doctrine contrary thereto shall be ashamed to show her face.[3]

Pandemonium broke out, drowning the last words. 'Stop the heretic's mouth, and take him away!' shouted the preacher. Cranmer went white as a sheet, but it was noticed that his distraught look had gone. An upsurge of nervous energy (God-sent, he would have told us) was sustaining him. The officials pulled him down from the platform to lead him to the stake, but in the event he led them, going out of St. Mary's and down Turl Street so fast that they could hardly keep up with him.

The friars who had presided over his last two recantations trotted beside him, remonstrating with him in a fine Spanish fury; the scene, if less pathetic, would have been comic. Cranmer was unmoved. At the stake he ignored the friars, but wished some senior dons a courteous good-bye, shaking hands with as many as would shake hands with him. In the fire he stood still holding his right hand steady in the flames so that all might see it burn first. His mind was on Stephen. Once he cried, 'I see heaven open and Jesus at the right hand of God' (and why should he have said that, if it were not true?). Several times he said, 'Lord Jesus receive my spirit.'

Otherwise his passing was quiet. Opinions differed, then as since, as to whether his was a good life, but none could ever deny that he made a good end.[4] As with Samson, his dying did even more for his cause than his living had done. 'By his death,' wrote C. H. Smyth with justifiable rhetoric, 'he damned the Marian Counter-Reformation, and lit, more signally than even Latimer and Ridley, a candle that should never be put out.'[5]

The Quest for Catholicity

Foxe's *Acts and Monuments,* four times reprinted in full (on six thousand large quarto pages) between 1837 and 1877, and read in most pious Victorian homes in a standard one-volume abridgement known as *Foxe's Book of Martyrs,* has stamped on the English mind the image of Thomas Cranmer as a martyred Protestant. This is not false; but it would be nearer Cranmer's own mind to say that he was burned for being a catholic. It was a happy irony that allowed him to make his last speech in response to an invitation to show himself 'a catholic indeed': for that was just what he believed he was doing when he abjured his recantations, the papal claims, and the real presence. To him, as to all the Reformers, Protestantism (unlike Anabaptistry) was precisely a quest for Catholicism—that is, for solidarity with the catholic church that Jesus founded. The Reformation was the work of churchmen, and as such was neither a lay-minded reaction against ecclesiastical superstition and graft, nor an outbreak of nationalistic sectarianism, but a conscious attempt to restore to the church of the West the catholicity that it had so long lost.

To the Reformers, as to the Fathers, catholicity was a theological and historical concept before it was a geographical or statistical one; they saw the essence of catholicity as lying in faithfulness to the gospel word and sacramental usage given to the church by Christ through the apostles at the beginning. Thus catholicity was to them in the first instance a matter of apostolicity, and apostolicity was in the first instance a matter of doctrine. Where apostolic teaching had been corrupted, there catholicity was wanting.

Cranmer judged that for three or four centuries before his time, due to papal absolutism, priestcraft, the theology of the mass, and neglect of the Bible, the church in England, as throughout Europe, had lapsed grievously from the catholic norm, and his overriding concern as churchman, theologian, and praying Christian was to see this deviation corrected. Cranmer's passion to regain and hold fast catholicity gave unity to his work as Archbishop of Canterbury, and is the clue to understanding both him and it.

His approach to this task comes out in the title of his first book on the eucharist: *A Defence of the True and Catholic Doctrine of the Sacrament . . . grounded and stablished upon God's Holy Word, and approved by the consent of the most ancient Doctors of the Church.* Cranmer held that the Fathers had, on the whole, been faithful expositors of the biblical faith, and that it was only since the twelfth century that the church had fallen into substantial error. It was not that he axiomatically accepted the tradition of the early centuries as showing what Scripture means or assumes or implies, even when it goes beyond what Scripture can be shown actually to say (the typical Anglo-Catholic position): it was, rather, that having studied Scripture in its 'literal' (i.e., natural, grammatical, intended) sense, letting one text comment on another and relating each author's statements to his overall scope, as the humanists taught all the Reformers to do, and having studied patristic theology by the same method, he had come to see that what the Fathers said coincided for substance with what the Scriptures said on each point dealt with.

Thus he was able to appeal to both Scripture and the Fathers in the same breath, and to profess his entire solidarity with 'the most ancient doctors.' This was no mere controversial device for anti-Roman polemics: it reflected a scholar's verdict that the Fathers had demonstrably been expounding the essence of biblical Catholicism, and that therefore they fully deserved the regard traditionally paid them as authoritative guides in doctrine. One of his charges against the uncatholic teaching of the three previous centuries was that it wrested the Fathers no less than the Scriptures. In his appeal 'unto a free general council' at his degradation, he was able to say:

> And touching my doctrine of the sacrament, and other my doctrine of what kind
> soever it be, I protest that it was never my mind to write, speak, or understand any
> thing contrary to the most holy word of God, or against the holy catholic church
> of Christ; but purely and simply to imitate and teach those things only, which I
> had learned of the sacred scripture, and of the holy catholic church of Christ from
> the beginning, and also according to the exposition of the most holy and learned
> fathers and martyrs of the church . . . I am ready in all things to follow the judge-
> ment of the most sacred word of God and of the holy catholic church . . . I mean
> and judge those things as the catholic church and the most holy fathers of old, with
> one accord, have meant and judged.[6]

Cranmer the Theologian: His Development

How did he reach his mature views? He was at the opposite extreme from Calvin, his younger contemporary, whose mind on everything was perfectly formed by the time he was twenty-five; intellectually as cautious and conservative as he was painstaking and thorough, his convictions ripened only slowly, after long and deliberate study. We know a little of his theological development.

He went up to Cambridge in 1503, took his B.A. in 1511 and, his M.A. in 1514, and was elected a fellow of Jesus. From an anonymous but clearly well-informed biographer we learn that as an undergraduate he was 'nosseled in the grossest kind of sophistry . . . chiefly in the dark riddles and quidities of Duns and other subtle questionists.'[7] From this, the ordinary arts course, he emerged a young man of studious habits with wholly conventional religious opinions. In 1551 he wrote regretfully of the time 'many years past' when he had held

> that error of the real presence . . . as of transubstantiation, of the sacrifice propitiatory of the priests in the mass, of pilgrimages, purgatory, pardons, and many other superstitions and errors that came from Rome; being brought up from youth in them, and nousled therein for lack of good instruction from my youth, the outrageous floods of papistical errors at that time overflowing the world.[8]

After graduating, he pursued humanist studies ('Faber, Erasmus, good Latin authors') till Luther set Christendom arguing in 1517: but then, 'considering what great controversy was in matters of religion (not only in trifles, but in the chiefest articles of our salvation), he bent himself to try out the truth herein: and . . . applied his whole study three years to the . . . Scriptures' (using, no doubt, Erasmus' 1516 New Testament for that purpose). 'After this he gave his mind to good writers, both new and old, not rashly running over them, for he was a slow reader, but a diligent marker of whatsoever he read; for he seldom read without pen in hand . . .'[9] Three crucial developments of opinion, resulting from these enquiries, were the milestones of his theological career.

First, he came to hold that the traditional papal claim to ecclesiastical jurisdiction everywhere was null and void; that Luther was right to call the Pope antichrist for making it; and that the Scriptures vest all ecclesiastical power under Christ in the person of the supreme civil magistrate—in England, the King. Foxe reports that at his examination before Brokes in 1555, Cranmer told how in 1533 he had informed Henry that he scrupled becoming Archbishop of Canterbury, because

> if he accepted the office, then he must receive it at the pope's hand; which he neither would nor could do, for that his highness was only the supreme governor of this church of England, as well in causes ecclesiastical as temporal, and that the full right and donation of all manner of bishopricks and benefices . . . appertained to his grace,

and not to any other foreign authority ... Whereat the king, said he [Cranmer], staying a while and musing [Cranmer had certainly given him something to muse on!] 'asked me, how I was able to prove it. At which time I alleged many texts out of the scriptures, and the fathers also' [the characteristic Cranmerian conjunction] 'approving the supreme and highest authority of kings in their realms and dominions, disclosing therewithal the intolerable usurpation of the pope of Rome.'[10]

Cranmer had reached this position well before 1533: in 1536 he wrote to Henry that he had daily prayed for many years that he might see the power of Rome destroyed, and now rejoiced that in England, at any rate, his prayers had been answered.[11]

As archbishop, Cranmer conscientiously respected the royal supremacy in church affairs, even when regretting particular royal enactments, such as Henry's Act of Six Articles: for 'I must obey the king by God's laws': 'Christ biddeth us to obey the king, *etiam dyscolo*' ('even if froward'—a reminiscence of 1 Pet. 2:18).[12] Humanly speaking, Cranmer would never have survived the closing years of Henry's reign on any other terms. His principle eventually created for him a terrible problem of conscience, for when Mary bade him accept the Pope she was asking him to affirm the royal supremacy by abjuring it. Bewildered, isolated, and under strain, he wavered: his six recantations, each more abject than the last, tell the sad story. But at length, perhaps because he was also required to affirm transubstantiation and so (as he believed) endanger the true knowledge of Christ, he saw his way out of the wood, and bore his final witness to the principle of royal supremacy by dying in defiance of the Crown.

The second theological milestone in Cranmer's career was his acceptance of the Lutheran view of faith and justification. The first clear dateable expressions of this are in the *Institution of a Christian Man* (1537), of which Cranmer was the main author; his notes on Henry's revision of it (1538); and the fourth of the 1538 Articles which he drafted, or, at any rate, agreed upon, in conference with the Lutherans;[13] though the manuscript *Notes on Justification,* a collection of biblical, patristic, and scholastic citations illustrating the main points in Cranmer's mature doctrine, may well be earlier than any of these.[14] But probably Cranmer was clear about justification before visiting Nuremberg in 1532, unless he became clear about it while there, for Osiander, the Lutheran pastor, not yet embroiled in the speculations which Calvin censured in the 1559 *Institutes* (III.xi.5–12), would hardly have consented to marry off this wife's niece to this not-very-distinguished foreign visitor, whom he had only known a few weeks, had the foreigner in question lacked sympathy with the basic Lutheran thesis.

Cranmer was never involved in large-scale debates about justification, nor did he ever introduce the theme formally into his sacramental discussions. But it is clear that for him, as for all the Reformers, the doctrine of justification by faith alone compelled a drastic rethinking of the sacraments. For if sacraments are really means of grace (as all Reformation theologians, Zwingli included, agreed they were), and if grace means the apprehended reality of one's free forgiveness, acceptance, and adoption, in and through Christ, and if grace is received by faith, and if faith is essentially trust in God's promise, then the sacraments must be thought of as rites which display and confirm the promises of the gospel, and as occasions for faith's exercise and deepening.

From this it will follow that, instead of the gospel being really about the sacraments as means for conveying specific spiritual blessings given no other way (the medieval thesis), the sacraments are really about the gospel, in the sense that they hold forth visibly the same promises, and the same Christ, that gospel preaching holds forth audibly, and they call for the same response of active, appropriating faith. The use of faith as a key-concept in sacramental theology thus led Cranmer, in company with Reformation theologians generally, to assimilate the two sacraments to each other, and both to the gospel word.

We find Cranmer first committing himself to these convictions about the sacraments in the ninth of the 1538 Articles, *Of the Use of Sacraments*.

> We teach that sacraments, which were instituted through the word of God, are not only marks of profession among Christians, but are rather certain sure witnesses and efficacious signs of grace, and of God's good will towards us, by which God works invisibly in us, and sheds his grace invisibly into us, if so be that we receive them rightly [*rite*]; and we teach that faith is stirred up and strengthened through them in those who use them. We teach, moreover, that the due use of sacraments involves that in adults, in addition to true contrition, faith must needs be present also, to believe the present promises which are shown, set forth, and offered, by the sacraments. For it is not true, as some say, that sacraments confer grace *ex opere operato* without a good movement of heart on the part of their user; for when persons in their reason use the sacraments, the user's faith must be present also, to believe the promises, and receive the things promised, which are conveyed through the sacraments.[15]

These ideas, which underlay all Cranmer's later theological and liturgical work in connection with the sacraments, were direct corollaries of his understanding of justification by faith.

The third milestone was a change of mind about the nature of the eucharistic presence, to which he came in 1546 when 'doctor Ridley did confer with me, and by sundry persuasions and authorities of doctors drew me quite from my opinion.'[16] At his trial, Cranmer insisted that he had only ever held two views on this: first, 'the papists' doctrine,' that Christ came to be corporally present in the elements through priestly consecration, and second, that to which Ridley led him, that Christ came to be spiritually present to and in the faithful communicant through his participation in the rite as a whole. Transubstantiation was to Cranmer one of several competing theories of the mode of the corporal presence: he had himself rejected it by 1538, as appears from his letter to Cromwell on August 15 of that year explaining that Adam Damplip, whose eucharistic teaching had caused trouble at Calais, did not question the real presence, but only the theory of transubstantiation—'and therein I think he taught but the truth.'[17] *Pace* Foxe, Strype, Burnet, and many since. Cranmer never held the alternative Lutheran theory of consubstantiation: in 1538 he wrote to Cromwell that he had described it to a Lutheran ambassador as 'that error of the sacrament.'[18]

His view after he abandoned transubstantiation must have been similar to the (to Rome, heretical) scholastic doctrine of impanation, which is not so much a theory of the mode of the presence as a refusal to have a theory. It has been questioned whether Cranmer abandoned belief in the real presence before the end of 1548, on the grounds that in the English version of Justus Jonas's catechism, which he published in June of that year, Lutheran eucharistic doctrine is taught. But Cranmer insisted more than once that in fact the catechism taught no such thing: although 'divers ignorant persons, not used to read old ancient authors, nor acquainted with their phrase and manner of speech,' misread it as asserting the real presence and the corporal reception of a corporally present Christ, and 'did carp and reprehend for lack of good understanding.'[19]

We must allow Cranmer to have known his own mind in 1548; and a study of his unobtrusive changes in Jonas's original text shows that, while keeping as close as he could to Jonas's words, he had edited out all that pointed to an unambiguously Lutheran doctrine as distinct from his own 'catholic' teaching.[20] Later in 1548, Cranmer spoke against the real presence in the House of Lords, and from then on there was no doubt where he stood. It was his reformed view of the eucharistic presence that Cranmer expounded in his *Defence* (1550), vindicated in his *Answer unto a Crafty and Sophistical Cavillation devised by Stephen Gardiner* (1551), and expressed in his two communion services of 1549 and 1552.

Cranmer the Theologian: His Stature

What calibre of theologian was this man? In his lifetime his powers were regularly underestimated, and the same habit has persisted for four centuries since his death. We are suggesting in this essay that he was in fact, in his unobtrusive way, a theologian of the first rank. It is true that he was neither prolific nor original nor argumentative, but this does not of itself mark him down as a second-rater. Then as now, it was hardly possible for a conscientious Archbishop of Canterbury to be a prolific writer, certainly not in years of wholesale ecclesiastical overhaul. We know that during the last three years of Edward's reign Cranmer had to retire almost completely from his ordinary public duties in order to get through his work on the second Prayer Book, the reply to Gardiner, the Articles, and the revision of canon law.

As for originality, Cranmer had no interest in it; his only wish was to be a faithful catholic theologian, finding lines of thought and forms of words that would express fully and accurately, in positive form, the consensus of biblical, patristic, and Reformation teaching. It was to this task that he dedicated his extraordinary erudition and his outstanding, if slow-going, gifts of penetration, discrimination, and synthesis. His finished work is thus refreshingly free from the narrowing personal quirks and idiosyncrasies that disfigure the output of even theological titans like Luther. Instead, it displays an astonishing largeness, universality, and pregnancy, of idea. The major theological notions with which Cranmer worked are all big and seminal; plant them in your mind, and they grow—and grow—and grow.

Nor do they date, even when their verbal clothing does. For they are not recognizably the product of any single age, certainly not of Cranmer's own age. Cranmer took over his conceptual raw material in the catholic form in which (as he believed: and he had a right to an opinion) it had been distilled out of the Bible through centuries of Christian thought and prayer. This is the secret of the perennial power of his Prayer Book. He was able to give his services a timeless, universal quality just because he was willing to traverse the whole field of historic Christian exposition in order to sift out and bring into proper focus the eternities and immensities of the biblical faith.

Cranmer's theological genius was not for system-building, nor yet for polemics (into which he could never put much heart), but for crystallizing a stock of tested material into confessional definitions (the Articles), forms for worship (the Prayer Books), and plain practical expositions, like the three great homilies of 1547 (on Salvation, Faith, and Good Works) and the *Defence.* By common consent, he was at his greatest in liturgical composition.

This in itself, however, is indirect testimony to his strength as a theologian, for creative liturgical work only succeeds when the liturgist knows exactly what theological content should go into each service. Here Cranmer excelled: his superb architectural sense in service-building, his gift for constructive adaptation and fusion of old forms, and his mastery of language, were all at the service of a mature theology, massive, simple, clear, and biblical. A man can easily be a worse liturgist than he is a theologian, because of the extra skills that service-writing requires, but he cannot possibly be a better. If Cranmer's services pass muster as masterpieces of Christian worship, there is at least a presumption that the theology behind them is also in the master class. It will, therefore, be worthwhile to review the main themes of Cranmer's theology somewhat more closely.

Scripture, Justification, the Church

The theological life's-work to which Cranmer gave himself was, first, to verify whether the upsurging theology of Luther and his followers, with its radical challenge to existing ideas, was the catholic faith or not, and second, when he had settled this to his satisfaction, and been providentially thrust into the primacy, to carry through in the English church a reordering of faith, worship, and discipline which would restore full catholicity to it. His method of tackling the first part of this task was mentioned earlier: three years' Bible study, to see what the Scriptures, taken in their plain historical sense, did and did not say, followed by a note-taking examination of the whole range of Christian theology, ancient and modern, so far as it bore on the questions in hand.

> He seldom read without pen in hand, and whatsoever made either for the one part or the other of things being in controversy, he wrote it out if it were short, or, at the least, noted the author and the place, that he might find it, and write it out by leisure.[21]

He had in his library most of the major Fathers, schoolmen, and contemporary divines,[22] and his topically arranged commonplace books, now in the British Museum, show that he made good use of them. Thus it was that whenever Henry VIII wanted an orientation on a theological question (for he fancied himself as a theologian) 'he would but send word to my Lord overnight, and by the next day the King should have in writing brief notes of the doctors' minds, with a conclusion of his own [Cranmer's] mind which he [Henry] could never get in such readiness of none, no, not of all his clergy and chaplains about him, in so short a time.'[23] Cranmer was, in fact, an exceedingly erudite divine, and he tested the Reformation theses in a most painstaking, thorough, and broad-based way.

The undated *Notes on Justification* show us his method in operation. They consist of a set of propositions summing up between them the reformed understanding of justification by faith alone, each confirmed by a long list of citations, first from Scripture (chiefly Paul), then from the Fathers (including Irenaeus, Origen, Basil, Ambrose, Jerome, Theodoret, Augustine, and Chrysostom), and some finally from the main scholastics (among them Peter Lombard, Thomas Aquinas, Anselm, and Bernard). The layout of the material shows that what Cranmer was looking for was a coincidence between the plain sense of Scripture, as he read it, and the teaching set forth as expository of Scripture, and in professed subjection to Scripture, by the leading divines of Christian history. He believed that where he perceived such a coincidence, there he could be sure that his own understanding of Scripture was not just a private eccentricity, but that he had found the true catholic faith. He said in 1534 that 'when all the fathers agreed in the exposition of any place of Scripture . . . he looked on that as flowing from the Spirit of God.'[24] Hence 'every exposition of the scripture, whereinsoever the old, holy, and true church did agree, is necessary to be believed.'[25] This attitude reflects, not an ascription to the Fathers of independent personal authority (as he often pointed out, the Fathers themselves 'always appealed to the scriptures, as the common and certain standard'[26]), but rather a certainty that the Holy Spirit has over the centuries been actively leading Christ's people into a common understanding of biblical truth.

Thus Cranmer sought for the catholic consensus on teaching on the various controverted questions of the Reformation. A further example of the same method, this time put to polemical use, is found in *A Confutation of Unwritten Verities,* apparently a set of extracts from one of Cranmer's commonplace books, with introduction and concluding chapter added posthumously by 'E. P.' the editor.[27] Here, Cranmer first adduces twenty-four biblical texts to prove that 'the word of God written, contained within the canon of the Bible, is a true, sound, perfect, and whole doctrine, containing in itself fully all things needful for our salvation,' and then deploys a mass of quotations, mainly patristic, to confirm the negative corollaries that neither Fathers, nor councils, nor angels, nor apparitions, nor miracles, nor custom, can establish articles of faith apart from Scripture. Here, again, Cranmer's method reveals his aim: he is seeking to show the coincidence of what the Bible seems to teach with what the great body of Christian theologians have taught from the beginning, in order that, on the one hand, he may identify the catholic faith beyond all peradventure, and, on the other, he may show how un-catholic Rome really is. From the list of sixty-five topics on the contents page of Cranmer's commonplace books we find that he had dealt in this fashion with virtually every major issue of faith and order which the Reformation had raised.[28]

What were these issues? Formulated against the background of acceptance of the ecumenical creeds, they centred upon four main subjects. The first was *Scripture.* How does the Bible stand related to the church? Who may venture to interpret it? What should be made of extra-biblical traditions, set forth in conciliar or papal pronouncements, or in canon law, and hallowed by custom and usage? What is the Bible's proper place in the life of the church and the Christian?

The second subject was *salvation,* which was discussed in connection with the battle-cry *sola fide,* 'by faith alone.' What is justification? On what is it grounded? What is faith? In what sense does it justify and save? On what terms are sins forgiven? What is the importance for salvation of good works, merit, priestly absolution, penances, pilgrimages, relics, indulgences, works of supererogation, monastic vows, confirmation, masses for the living and the dead, and the prayers of departed saints? What is the truth about purgatory and praying for the dead?

The third subject was *the church.* What are the true marks of the church? What validates, and what invalidates, the claim to be a church? What ecclesiastical authority belongs to Popes, general councils, and magistrates? By what method should churches be reformed? How may the separation of national churches from the Roman obedience and communion be defended against the charge of schism? How may the church's unity be safeguarded and shown forth?

The final subject was *the eucharist.* In what sense is the minister a priest and the eucharist a sacrifice? In what sense is Christ present and received at it? What constitutes true eucharistic devotion? On all these questions, save that of the eucharistic presence and reception of Christ, Cranmer took a substantially Lutheran line, though his statements in each case reflect his own special interests and angle of approach.

With regard to Holy Scripture, the issues that concerned Cranmer were those of his age, not of ours. To modern debates about biblical inspiration and inerrancy he has little to contribute. It was enough for him, as for all sixteenth-century theologians, to revere all Holy Scripture as prophetic writing, in the sense that, like the prophets' oracles, its human words were divine words also, and its teaching was all of it divine instruction. Hence Cranmer's careful regard for the wording of the text. On Henry's proposal to substitute 'suffer us not to be led into temptation' for 'lead us not . . .' in the English version of the Lord's Prayer in the *Institution,* Cranmer commented revealingly: 'we should not alter any word in the scripture, which wholly is ministered unto us by the Ghost of God (2 Pet. 1:21), although it shall appear in many places to signify much absurdity: but first, the scripture must be set out in God's own words'—and then the explanatory comment added after, quite separately.[29] This reverence for Scripture as 'God's own words' marks all Cranmer's theological writing.

On the canon, Cranmer maintained what was in essence the common Protestant position. In the anonymous tract *Of Unwritten Verities,*[30] he (if it is he: but it is entirely in his style) explains that the New Testament had been written and, with the Old Testament, 'authorised' in the church (he means recognised and declared to be authoritative) under the powerful influence of the Holy Spirit in the 'golden time' that followed Pentecost—'the time of the most high and gracious shedding out of the mercy of God into the world, that ever was from the beginning of the world unto this day.'

Involved here is a triple claim: first, that the witness of Christ's apostles, uniquely inspired as it was by the Holy Spirit, provides a norm and standard of faith for the church in all after ages; second, that the authority of the New Testament is not the conferred authority of an ecclesiastical enactment, but the intrinsic authority of the apostolic witness which it enshrines; third, that the catholic canon is guaranteed to us, not by an infallible church's say-so, but by the Holy Spirit's faithfulness to his Pentecostal mission to glorify the exalted Christ before men's eyes.

Having inspired written apostolic accounts of the glory of Christ, the Spirit did not omit to move the infant church to acknowledge their truth, authority, and edifying power. Cranmer was sure that the early church drew up its lists of authoritative writings in conscious dependence on the Spirit of Christ. 'Who may think but that they [the clergy] and all the people, at the said authorising of the Scripture, prayed devoutly for the assistance of the Holy Ghost, that they might have grace to authorise such as should be to his honour, to the increase of the faith, and to the health of the souls of all his people?' The unanimity which the church eventually reached in its quest for the canon was, Cranmer held, the

Spirit's answer to these prayers. Thus, desirous as he was to believe 'as the catholic church doth believe, and ever hath believed from the beginning,'[31] he received the historic canon (not the Apocrypha[32]) as a fixed element in catholicity. 'And more receive we not, because these old fathers of the first church testify in their books, that there was no more than these required to be believed as the scripture of God.'[33]

Cranmer consistently stressed two facts about Scripture. The first was its *sufficiency for salvation*. This was a patristic way of stating the principle of biblical authority, which focused attention on the Bible's religious significance. The sufficiency of Scripture meant that, whereas all that the Bible lays down concerning faith and morals must be observed, and each man's spiritual welfare depends upon his doing so, the same is not true of any other tenets whatsoever. So the extra-biblical traditions ('unwritten verities') which Rome claimed to have received by oral transmission from the apostles could not be regarded as in any sense necessary to salvation: for, on the one hand, their apostolicity could not be proved, and, on the other, to made them essential was to represent Scripture as insufficient—a wholly un-catholic view.

In this connection, mention must be made of the sharp distinction (some might say, too sharp) which Cranmer drew between the realm of faith and morals and that of church order and ceremonies. In the former realm, he held, Scripture is a direct and universal rule, from which no variation is lawful: but in the latter realm it leaves churches free to make whatever arrangements local circumstances require for maintaining good order and furthering godliness. There is no revealed church order, only a general demand that no biblical truth should be endangered or denied, and no biblical obligation neglected, in the church's outward life. This distinction (easy to state and defend in general terms, hard to apply in particular cases, as the dispute with Hooper about the vestments showed) had for Cranmer a threefold importance.

First, it disposed of Rome's claim to preserve essential catholic ceremonies, by showing that there were no such things. Secondly, it made it possible to assert the unity of Protestant Christendom, despite the great differences between various Reformation churches in the realm of government and order. Thirdly, it gave a basis for demanding the observance of prescribed church order in England through each successive stage of its reformation (a demand which Cranmer, who feared anarchy, was always anxious to make) without seeming to treat man-made ceremonies as indispensable means of grace, and thereby encouraging superstition. Cranmer was always careful to stress that the established order should be observed for the sake of unity and peace, not because any part of it was necessary to salvation.

Cranmer's other main stress was upon the *usefulness* (*utilitas*) of Scripture— that is, its value as a means of grace. Nothing, he held, matters more for the Christian than to read, mark, learn, and inwardly digest the Bible.

It containeth fruitful instruction and erudition for every man: if any things be necessary to be learned, of the holy scripture we may learn it . . . In the scriptures be
the fat pastures of the soul; therein is no venomous meat, no unwholesome thing;
they be the very dainty and pure feeding . . . Here may all manner of persons, men,
women, young, old, learned, unlearned, rich, poor, priests, laymen, lords, ladies, officers, tenants, and mean men, virgins, wives, widows, lawyers, merchants, artificers,
husbandmen, and all manner of persons, of what estate or condition soever they be,
may in this book learn all things what they ought to believe, what they ought to do,
and what they should not do, as well concerning Almighty God, as also concerning
themselves and all other.[34]

Hence Cranmer's efforts, from the time he became Primate, to get the English
Bible authorised and read; hence, too, the conscientious packing of his reformed
liturgy with biblical material; hence also his admirable lectionary, covering the
whole Bible (the New Testament three times) each year. To make the Church
of England a Bible-reading, Bible-loving church was Cranmer's constant ideal:
Anglicanism owes him at this point an incalculable debt.

Cranmer's doctrine of justification may be learned from his manuscript *Notes
on Justification*, his private comments on Henry's alterations of the *Institution of a
Christian Man*, and—the most important source—his three homilies, on Salvation, Faith, and Good Works.[35] He regarded the homily on Salvation as having
confessional status, as appears from Article 11 of his Forty-two: 'Justification
by faith alone in Jesus Christ, *in the sense in which it is explained in the homily on
justification,* is a most sure and salutary doctrine of Christian men.' (The reference
to the homily remains in Article 11 of the Thirty-nine.) Cranmer agreed with
Luther, both in regarding the doctrine as of crucial importance ('this is the strong
rock and foundation of Christian religion . . . this whosoever denieth is not to be
counted for a Christian man'[36]), and also in his analysis of its content.

To expound justification by faith in a way that leads to piety without pietism
and assurance without antinomianism is never easy, and the necessity of speaking to a situation in which men's minds were possessed with a truncated idea of
faith as mere credence, and a firm belief that its whole significance in salvation
was as a meritorious work, could only make the task harder. But Cranmer proved
equal to its demands.

He rooted the doctrine in two basic realities. The first is man's sinfulness and
impotence to do God's will, which brings him into a state of failure, guilt, and
condemnation. (This is the theme of the homily on the Misery of Man, which
precedes Cranmer's on Salvation.) The second reality is God's mercy to sinners,
the measure of which is his gift of his Son to be crucified for them. Justification
itself is the bestowal upon them of righteousness (forgiveness and acceptance)
for Christ's sake. It is 'free unto us, yet it cometh not so freely unto us, that there
is no ransom paid therefor at all':[37] the price was paid on our behalf by Christ
upon the cross.

The merits of Christ in his life and death are the sole grounds of our justification—not any merits of our own, for we have none, only demerit and ill-desert. The homily speaks of Christ's merit in three ways: first, as 'a sacrifice and satisfaction or, as it may be called, amends to his Father for our sins; to assuage his wrath and indignation conceived against us for the same';[38] second, as a ransom-price, paid to meet the claim against us of divine justice; third, as righteousness, a representative fulfilling of the law in virtue of which we law-breakers are given the status of law-keepers. 'Christ is now the righteousness of all them that truly do believe in him. He for them paid their ransom by his death. He for them fulfilled the law in his life. So that now in him, and by him, every true Christian man may be called a fulfiller of the law: forasmuch as that which their infirmity lacked, Christ's justice hath supplied.'[39]

Cranmer wrote to Henry that he valued the word 'satisfaction' in connection with Christ's death 'to take away the root, ground, and fountain of all the chief errors, whereby the bishop of Rome corrupted the pure foundation of Christian faith and doctrine . . . satisfactory masses, trentals, *scala coeli,* foundations of charities, monasteries, pardons, and a thousand other abuses . . .'[40] The truth, according to Cranmer, is that Christ's 'full, perfect and sufficient sacrifice, oblation and satisfaction, for the sins of the whole world' makes all human endeavours to satisfy for sin and gain merit before God as needless as they are futile.

Cranmer defines faith fiducially, contrasting 'dead' faith (barren orthodoxy), which, he says, is not real faith at all, with 'the very sure and lively Christian faith,' 'the true faith which the Scripture doth so much commend,' which is,

> not only to believe all things of God which are contained in Holy Scripture; but also is an earnest trust and confidence in God, that he doth regard us, and that he is careful over us, as the father is over the child whom he doth love; and that he will be merciful unto us for his only Son's sake; and that we have our Saviour Christ as our perpetual Advocate and Priest; in whose only merits, oblation, and suffering we do trust that our offences be continually washed and purged, whensoever we, repenting truly, do return to him with our whole heart . . .[41]

Faith trusts, not in itself, as a meritorious virtue, but in Christ only, for acceptance with God: 'our faith in Christ, as it were, saith unto us thus: It is not I that take away your sins, but it is Christ only: and to him only I send you for that purpose.'[42] Justification by faith only, therefore, 'according to the meaning of the ancient authors' (of whom Cranmer cites eleven in the course of the sermon) is this: 'We put our faith in Christ, that we be justified by him only . . . Christ himself only being the cause meritorious thereof.'[43]

Faith, God's gift to his elect, brings assurance of final preservation. The believer is confident that

> if by fragility and weakness he fall again, God will not suffer him to lie still, but put his hand to him and help him up again, and so at the last he will take him up from death unto the life of glory everlasting.[44]

Believers rely for final salvation on God's faithfulness, not their own; Cranmer makes this point several times in criticism of various of Henry's proposed alterations to the *Institution,* which implied the contrary. Yet assurance does not make believers careless or lazy, for indolence and inaction are a contradiction of faith's nature. 'A true faith . . . will break out and shew itself by good works';[45] that is how you tell it is there. And no man has a right to think that he has faith unless he is actively obeying God's laws, out of thankfulness for grace and redemption. By stressing this, Cranmer, like Luther, cut off antinomianism at the root.

Belief in the sufficiency of Christ's sacrifice for full acceptance with God, both here and hereafter, led Cranmer, still following in Lutheran footsteps, to reject purgatory and the mass-sacrifice on Christological grounds. Of purgatory he wrote:

> What a contumely and injury is this to Christ, to affirm that all have not full and perfect purgation by his blood, that die in his faith! Is not all our trust in the blood of Christ, that we be cleansed, purged, and washed thereby? And will you have us now to forsake our faith in Christ, and bring us to the pope's purgatory to be washed therein, thinking that Christ's blood is an imperfect lee or soap that washeth not clean?[46]

Similarly, Cranmer judges the idea of the mass-sacrifice to be

> injurious to the sacrifice of Christ . . . it is an abominable blasphemy to give that office or dignity to a priest, which pertaineth only to Christ; or to affirm that the church hath need of any such sacrifice: as who should say, that Christ's sacrifice were not sufficient for the remission of our sins, or else that his sacrifice should hang upon the sacrifice of a priest.[47]

Accordingly, all suggestion that clergy were being ordained to a ministry of priestly sacrifice was eliminated from Cranmer's reformed ordinal.

Cranmer's view of justification by faith as central to Christianity controlled his liturgical work. In each of the main services in the 1552 Prayer Book, the basic structural pattern is a sin-grace-faith sequence, out of which all praises are made to rise; and this is simply the gospel of justification in liturgical form. Thus, Morning and Evening Prayer were made to start penitentially, with confession of sin, followed by the proclaiming of God's pardon and the Lord's Prayer used as a plea for forgiveness and newness of life; out of which comes psalmody, praising God for salvation, followed by further exercises of faith in profession (the creed), prayer, and the hearing of God's word. Also, the Holy Communion service was recast from the traditional shape of the 1549 rite into a new mould, which was essentially just a threefold repetition of the sin-grace-faith cycle: the first in the Ante-communion, from the opening collect to the intercession (the focal points being the law, the gospel, and the creed), and the second and third in the communion proper, the second running from the longer exhortation to the Sanctus (in its context, praise for salvation) and the third from the prayer of humble access to the Gloria (also praise for salvation).

Cranmer's use of this cycle as the basic structural principle for his eucharistic liturgy reflects his conviction that justification by faith, in and through Christ, is what the sacrament is about—the message that it proclaims, and the promise that it seals. The repetition of the cycle within the communion itself apparently expresses the principle that, since the function of the sacraments is to confirm the gospel word to believers, a complete verbal presentation of the gospel (done here by confession, absolution, and comfortable words) is the proper liturgical preparation for administering the sacrament. So too in Cranmer's baptismal office the sin-grace-faith (= vows) sequence is presented first, and then the sacrament is administered as a sign and seal of the grace promised and claimed.

Of the 1552 communion service, Gregory Dix (no friend of Cranmer's theology as he understood, or rather misunderstood, it although he was a sound judge of liturgical quality) wrote thus:

> As a piece of liturgical craftsmanship it is in the first rank . . . It is *not* a disordered attempt at a catholic rite, but the only effective attempt ever made to give liturgical expression to the doctrine of 'justification by faith alone.'[48]

Cranmer's comment on this would doubtless have been that, since he only left the traditional shape of the liturgy in order to bring out better the true theological meaning of the sacrament, his service was actually more catholic than any medieval rite had been; also, that there is in any case no such thing as a catholic liturgical norm, only a normative catholic theology, which different churches may and must express in their worship in different ways, as seems most edifying and acceptable in each situation. But he would have applauded Dix's insight into his intentions.

Over four centuries (for the 1662 Prayer Book is Cranmer almost unchanged) Anglican worshippers have rejoiced in the nourishing and uplifting power that they have found in Cranmer's liturgical forms. It is true that the literary quality of his services is superb, but this is not the secret of their strength. It is Cranmer's embodiment in their structure of the evangelical sequence, sin-grace-faith, so that on every occasion they lead worshippers into the refreshing reality of apprehended justification and bold fellowship with a great and gracious God, that gives them their invigorating force.

Of Cranmer's doctrine of the church little need be said, for he never dealt with this subject very thoroughly. What is clear is that he endorsed the main stresses of Reformation ecclesiology. Thus, against Richard Smith's conventional 'catholic' assertion of the church's authority and inerrancy, we find Cranmer summarising the conventional Lutheran line of thought about the church visible and invisible (though neither here nor elsewhere does he actually use the word 'invisible': perhaps he saw, as many have seen since, how easily misunderstood it can be). The real, holy church of the elect—the church, that is, which God acknowledges as such—is 'but a small herd or flock,' dispersed among, and sometimes oppressed, suppressed, or even expelled by, the 'open known church.' The 'open church,' however, invalidates its claim to be the church when it casts off the control of Scripture:

> then it is not the pillar of truth, nor the church of Christ, but the synagogue of Satan, and the temple of antichrist, which both erreth itself, and bringeth into error as many as do follow it.[49]

This was the case with Rome: so it was no schism to forsake her. All claims to be the church must be tested before they are admitted. 'The visible church of Christ is a company of faithful men, in the which the pure Word of God is preached, and the Sacraments be duly administered according to Christ's ordinance'[50] No group not answering to this description can be allowed to belong to the catholic church, however godly individuals within it may be. The line of continuity by which the catholic church in history is known is that of sound faith, not of sacramental or sacerdotal succession divorced from catholic truth. Indeed, so far is apostolic succession from being essential to the ministry that, in an emergency, ordination is dispensable altogether; mere appointment by the civil governor will establish a true and valid ministry, and if there is no possibility of word and sacrament being ministered otherwise it becomes his duty to make such appointments.[51]

Ironically, the principle of royal supremacy in church affairs, on which Cranmer laid such stress, was one of the least successful features of his theology. The idea that in a Christian country the reformation of the church's order and external life should depend on the Christian magistrate—in Tudor England, the king— was a Reformation commonplace and the principle remains defensible. But it can hardly be denied that Cranmer developed it in an unbalanced way. Because the church was coterminous with the state, Cranmer treated the two as virtually identical, laying no stress on the distinction between civil and ecclesiastical authority. Hence in his thinking the former simply swallowed up the latter, and benevolent royal despotism in the ecclesiastical sphere, on the Henrician pattern, came to be viewed as the biblical norm of church government. Here, more than anywhere else, Cranmer shows the limitations of his age—although (to be fair to him) even here he believed he had recovered a genuine element in catholicity, witnessed to by the Old Testament monarchy and confirmed by the example of such emperors as Constantine and Theodosius.

On the credit side, however, must be set Cranmer's ecumenical concern, which in 1552 led him to moot a pan-Protestant Synod, at which the reformed national churches of Europe should compose their differences, especially about the eucharist, and testify to their unity of faith by producing a common confession.[52] He must have known that it was doubtful whether the Lutherans and Calvinists would be able to reach agreement, but he was sure that for the sake of peace and love among themselves, and of a clear witness to the world, they ought to get together and try. That the plan came to nothing was chiefly due to the apathy of Melanchthon, not to any lack of effort on Cranmer's part.

The Lord's Supper

It was in connection with the doctrine of the Lord's Supper that Cranmer's major contribution to theology was made. His *Defence* is a theological classic. Inevitably, it has a polemical slant: in the Preface Cranmer announces that part of its object is to pull up 'two chief roots' of Roman error which obscure the gospel and glory of Christ—'the real presence of Christ's flesh and blood in the sacrament of the altar (as they call it)' and 'the offering of Christ by the priest for the salvation of the quick and the dead.'[53]

But its main purpose is constructive and pastoral: to lead English Christians, even 'the very simple and unlearned people,' into a right understanding and valuation of the sacrament, for their souls' health. 'For the more clearly it is understood, the more sweetness, fruit, comfort, and edification it bringeth to the godly receivers thereof.'[54]

As a piece of constructive theological exposition, the work has great value in its own right. Nothing so quickly reveals a theologian's calibre as his sacramental teaching, for this is, so to speak, the roof of his theological house; it rests squarely upon his beliefs about God, man, creation, redemption, the church, the ministry, the work of Christ, and the work of the Spirit, and its shape provides an immediate clue to the structure and adequacy of the theological edifice which it crowns. The richness of Cranmer's sacramental teaching is impressive testimony to his overall theological acuteness and power.

Two presuppositions directly control Cranmer's approach to the eucharist. The first is his doctrine of justification by faith on the basis of the perfect, finished, all-sufficient sacrifice of Christ on the cross: a doctrine which, as we have seen, undercuts the medieval idea of the mass-sacrifice from the start. The work of putting away sins is Christ's alone, and Christians have no part in it; their sole part (and this, as we saw, is the meaning of 'faith only') is to rely on Christ's merits, and receive his benefits. The second presupposition is that the sacraments are visible words, rites ordained by Christ to confirm to our other senses the gospel promises which preaching proclaims in our ears. So Cranmer writes:

> Our Saviour Christ hath not only set forth these things [sc., concerning his saviourhood] most plainly in his holy word, that we may hear them with our ears, but he has also ordained one visible sacrament of spiritual regeneration in water, and

another visible sacrament of spiritual nourishment in bread and wine, to the intent that, as much as it is possible for man, we may see Christ with our eyes, smell him at our nose, taste him with our mouths, grope him with our hands, and perceive him with all our senses. For as the word of God preached putteth Christ into our ears, so likewise these elements of water, bread, and wine, joined to God' word, do after a sacramental manner put Christ into our eyes, mouths, hands, and all our senses.[55]

A passage like this brings out the point that what the gospel offers us is not Christ's merit and righteousness simply, but Christ himself. The benefits of his work are enjoyed only in union with his person: we must be *in* him to be saved *through* him. Cranmer's expositions of justification, directed as they are against the notion of human merit, focus attention on the benefits of Christ but make little of the thought of personal union with him. This, however, is the central theme in Cranmer's sacramental teaching, just as it is basic to the symbolism of the sacraments themselves.

At this point, therefore, the *Defence* is a necessary complement to Cranmer's homilies. Cranmer's account in the *Defence* of the convicted sinner's longing for pardon as hunger and thirst for Christ, and of Christ himself, in the power of his atonement, as the sinner's meat and drink (for 'the scripture calleth the same thing that comforteth the soul meat and drink'), shows us, in a way that the homilies scarcely do, that it is to the person of Christ that Cranmer's conceptions of justification and faith are really orientated; and that in proclaiming justification Cranmer is not offering us a mere theological abstraction or legal fiction, but inviting us to personal closure and union with a living Saviour.[56]

In his *Answer* to Gardiner, Cranmer stresses the parallelism of the two dominical sacraments with each other, and both with the word of the gospel message. It is axiomatic to him that what cannot be said of baptism and of the preaching of the gospel ('the sacrament of the word'—Forsyth's phrase would have pleased Cranmer) cannot be said of the eucharist either. In both sacraments, as in the word preached, Christ is present, in the sense that 'he worketh mightily by the same' in men's hearts; but he is not present or received in the eucharist in a different, or fuller, sense than in baptism, or, for that matter, in the sermon. So Cranmer writes (to quote a typical passage):

> Where you say that in baptism we receive the Spirit of Christ, and in the sacrament of his body and blood we receive his very flesh and blood; this your saying is no small derogation to baptism, wherein we receive not only the Spirit of Christ, but also Christ himself, whole body and soul, manhood and Godhead, unto everlasting life, as well as in holy communion.[57]

—and as we do also in and by the word preached.

Cranmer roundly denies that he is asserting the 'real absence' of Christ from the eucharist:[58] he insists that his own understanding of the eucharistic presence is in fact richer and more edifying, as well as more biblical and reverent, than that of his opponents. He denies that Christ is present corporally, substantially, carnally, or naturally in the consecrated elements—present, that is, under the forms of bread and wine, in the same physical, localised sense in which he was present in the world before his ascension, and will be present once more at his coming again: to say such a thing, Cranmer insists, is grotesque Christological nonsense. But Cranmer affirms that Christ is truly, 'in deed,' and 'really' (in the sense of veritably) present when the eucharistic rite is performed. His formula for the presence is that Christ is there sacramentally in the elements and spiritually in the participants.

By 'sacramentally' he means figuratively: Christ is 'there' in a sense analogous to that in which the subject of a portrait is 'there' when his picture hangs on the wall. The elements, and the action performed with them (breaking the bread, pouring the wine, consuming both), constitute a sign symbolically presenting to us Christ's passion, making the cross vivid to our minds ('real,' as we say), and assuring us that as believers we do in fact 'dwell in him, and he in us,' so that the benefits of his passion are all ours.

Following Christ's example at the institution, we speak of the sign as if it were the thing signified, calling the bread his body, and the wine his blood: this is sacramental language. When the Fathers called the elements Christ's body and blood, and the rite his sacrifice and passion, they were not speaking realistically, but sacramentally. Thus their testimony confirms Cranmer's 'catholic doctrine' of the eucharist, rather than Rome's.

But this is only half the story. Christ is also present in faithful communicants spiritually—that is, by the Holy Spirit. The Christ who comes to them in the sacramental rite is the same Christ who comes to them through the preaching of the word—'whole Christ,' the God-man, crucified, risen, glorified, enthroned, coming in the authority of his offices and the power of his atoning work.

The presence of this Christ, according to his promise, with those who meet in his name is the fundamental reality of the Christian life, and it is enjoyed at the communion table, where the Holy Spirit mediates it through the sacramental sign, just as it is enjoyed on other occasions when the Holy Spirit mediates it through the preached word. In both cases, the presence of Christ, effected by the Spirit, is correlative to our exercise of faith, which is also Spirit-wrought: it is not that Christ's glorified body comes to be present on the table, but that through faith Christ himself is made present to our hearts.

> My doctrine is that the very body of Christ, which was born of the virgin Mary, and suffered for our sins, giving us life by his death, the same Jesus, as concerning his corporal presence, is taken from us, and sitteth at the right hand of the Father; and yet he is by faith spiritually present with us, and is our spiritual food and nourishment, and sitteth in the midst of all them that be gathered together in his name.[59]

It is in terms of communion with this present Christ that Cranmer explains the meaning of eating Christ's flesh and drinking his blood. John 6, which uses this imagery, is not, he maintains, a sacramental discourse: rather, it is a discourse about the reality that the sacrament itself is about—namely, trusting in Christ and his cross for salvation, and being assured by divine promise that this trusted Christ is actually in one, to keep, and nourish, and bring one to glory. This is what feeding on Christ is: a spiritual communion, guaranteeing present and unending union and coming transformation. Believers enjoy it apart from the sacrament, as well as in the sacrament; unbelievers never enjoy it at all. Writes Cranmer:

> The true eating and drinking of the said body and blood of Christ is, with a constant and lively faith to believe, that Christ gave his body, and shed his blood upon the cross for him, and that he doth so join and incorporate himself to us, that he is our head, and we his members . . . having him dwelling in us, and we in him. And herein standeth the whole effect and strength of this sacrament[60]

—namely, in the fact that God uses it to further this feeding. In the sacrament, Christ invites thus:

> Consider and behold my body crucified for you; that eat and digest in your minds. Chaw you upon my passion, be fed with my death. This is the true meat, this is the drink that moisteneth . . . The bread and the wine which be set before our eyes are only declarations of me, but I myself am the eternal food.

And the true feeding is that in response

> lifting up our minds, we should look up to the blood of Christ with our faith, should touch him with our mind, and receive him with our inward man; and that, being like eagles in this life, we should fly up into heaven in our hearts, where that Lamb is resident at the right hand of his Father, which taketh away the sins of the world . . . being made the guests of Christ, having him dwelling in us through the grace of his true nature, and through the virtue and efficacy of his whole passion . . .[61]

Lastly, if the mass-idea is false, in what sense is the eucharist a sacrifice? In a double sense, says Cranmer: it is an occasion for both commemorating Christ's sacrifice, and offering our own. His sacrifice was his high priestly self-offering for sins: we make a representation of it, but we do not in any sense offer it. Our sacrifice, distinct from his, though made by virtue of it, and in dependence upon it, is our responsive thank-offering of worship and service. In the broadest sense, the Christian sacrifice is the Christian life, 'our whole obedience unto God, in keeping his laws and commandments.'[62]

As offered in the communion service, it takes the form of praise, thanksgiving, and self-oblation. The sacrificial language of the Fathers about the Supper should be explained in terms of this distinction: if they refer to it as a sacrifice for sin, that is not because it taketh away our sin, which is taken away only by the death of Christ, but because the holy communion was ordained of Christ to put us in remembrance of the sacrifice made by him upon the cross.[63]

If they refer to it as the sacrifice of Christian people, they mean that it is an offering of praise and devotion to God.[64] In no case, however (so Cranmer claims), do they countenance the intrusion into Christ's high-priestly ministry which Rome claims for the priest in the mass.

On the Right Road

Such, in outline, was the theology of Thomas Cranmer. Three concerns ran through it all, giving it shape and direction, and imparting to it a stimulating and suggestive quality which is matched by no other English theology of the Reformation period, not even that of the learned jewel.

The first was to seek a biblical catholicity by learning from the past. We suggested earlier that Cranmer's approach here was determined by his doctrine of the Holy Spirit: knowing that the Spirit who inspired the Scriptures had remained with the church to interpret them, Cranmer *expected* to get help from the great theologians of Christian history in understanding them, and to find that in essentials, and at the level of theological intentions, these theologians were at one. Cranmer's concern to find a catholic consensus of biblical understanding running down the ages stands as a valuable corrective to the methods of facile antithesis— the Fathers and Reformers set against each other, and sometimes the Bible against both—which are so widely current today, and have reduced so much modern theology to a state of unstable sterility.

Cranmer's second concern was to think through the doctrine of salvation Christologically—in terms, that is, of the biblical and catholic understanding of the person and work of Christ. It was through considering the meaning of Christ's cross that he became clear what justification meant, and that faith was not a meritorious work, and that purgatory, the place of temporal punishment for sin, must be a fiction, and that the idea of the mass-sacrifice was a dishonouring of the cross. It was through considering what Jesus Christ is—risen, ascended, glorified, reigning, absent in body, but coming again, and meantime present with his people in all the power of his atonement by the Holy Spirit, and vitally united to them for life eternal—that he came to his understanding of the eucharistic presence and our feeding on Christ in the Supper.

He tells us himself that this was how he reached his final eucharistic conceptions: 'after it had pleased God to show unto me, by his holy word, a *more perfect knowledge of his Son Jesus Christ,* from time to time *as I grew in knowledge of him,* by little and little I put away my former ignorance.'[65] Cranmer reduced the questions what is salvation? what is justification? what is the eucharist? to this question: what, according to Scripture, is our Lord Jesus Christ? We learn what these things are from discovering what he is. This Christological method of studying salvation and the sacraments is still the only sound one.

Cranmer's third concern was to do justice to the ministry of the Holy Spirit, as the one who mediates experiential knowledge of the presence, power, and grace of Jesus Christ to the people of God. The *Institution,* the Prayer Book, and Cranmer's weighty and glowing expositions of Christ's spiritual presence at the sacrament (on which Bishop Neill well comments that to make Cranmer's sense clear we might 'use a capital, and write "Spiritual presence" '[66]), all testify to this concern. Cranmer's reflection upon the doctrine of the Holy Spirit gave him his understanding of the canon of Scripture and catholicity on the one hand, as we saw, and also of the nature of faith in Christ, and union and communion with him, on the other. It is a pity that Cranmer nowhere fully worked out his insights into the Spirit's work. But what he left us is a standing admonition of the need to give the Spirit his due place in both theology and devotion, and of the impossibility of avoiding ecclesiastical authoritarianism, barren formalism, and superstitious sacramentalism, unless we do.

No doubt many of Cranmer's insights remained fragmentary and undeveloped. No doubt he misread some patristic texts (though not, perhaps, many). No doubt his appeal to the Fathers was one-sided. No doubt he had less theological energy than some of his great contemporaries. No doubt he over-simplified some issues, and on others failed to carry his thinking quite far enough. No doubt his use of language was sometimes over-subtle, mystifying to others and inhibiting to his own exercise of mind. All this may be freely admitted. But it remains true that Cranmer's deepest theological instincts were right, and his best work, though now four centuries old, seems still to point the way ahead.

CHAPTER 15

Richard Baxter on Heaven, Hope, and Holiness

One of the many pleasures of being Jim Houston's colleagues at Regent College is team-teaching with him an annual seminar on Cistercian and Puritan spirituality, studied from original texts. Among the Puritans, Richard Baxter always figures large, as one whose writings and life express Puritan godliness at its noblest. Seminar members are invited to choose from three Baxter projects: an exploration of part one of *A Christian Directory*, where the basic principles of Puritan piety are brought together; a study of Baxter's view of what it means to be a minister, as focused in *The Reformed Pastor*, and an enquiry into the discipline of meditation on one's hope of glory, the subject of Baxter's sprawling masterpiece, *The Saints' Everlasting Rest*. Over the years, the third project has proved the hardest for students to do well, since they start so far away from Baxter's sense of reality. That, I hasten to say, is not a put-down for Regent students, many of whom are superb; it is, rather, a comment on the late-twentieth-century Christian culture of the West, which bequeaths to its children its own blind spots. The following pages attempt to bridge the gap between our mind-set and Baxter's at this point, so that we may get close enough to him to learn from him on this momentous biblical theme. With my purpose, at least, I think Jim Houston will be pleased, whatever the quality of my attempt to carry it out.

In describing Baxter's theme as 'momentous' and 'biblical' I was already declaring an interest, about which I had better now come clean. I bring to this piece of writing three convictions. The first is that rejoicing in the 'living hope' of 'an inheritance that can never perish, spoil or fade—kept in heaven for you, who through faith are shielded by God's power' and 'set[ting] your hope fully on the grace to be given you when Jesus Christ is revealed' (1 Pet. 1:4–5, 13) are integral elements in New Testament spirituality; and I see New Testament spirituality as the norm for all subsequent Christian devotion, just as New Testament doctrine is the norm for all subsequent Christian belief. My second conviction is that a good deal of what is involved in being 'alive to God' in this or any age depends directly on having this 'living hope' vivid in one's heart. I think here of the qualities of zeal, enterprise, energy, and persistence in well-doing for God; of loving, adoring worship as a daily habit; of meekness, sweetness, and selflessness under pain and disappointment; of a sense of proportion, a due appreciation of pleasure, and realism about death. My third conviction is that we Western Christians, by and large (Jim Houston being a shining exception), are to our shame a sluggish, earthbound lot compared with our Puritan predecessors, and that lack of long, strong thinking about our promised hope of glory is a major cause of our plodding, lacklustre lifestyle. A change for the better is needed at this point, and I believe Baxter can help us towards it; and that, I confess, is my main reason for choosing to write about him now.

Baxter the Puritan

Baxter claimed to be, and indeed was, a Puritan to his fingertips. The hindsight of history shows him to have been an outstanding example of that outstanding Anglo-Saxon type. Some, acknowledging his astonishing saintliness, reasonableness, breadth of ecumenical sympathy, and freedom from the bigotry and party spirit that besmirched so much seventeenth-century history, have thought of him as standing apart from the Puritan movement as a whole. But nobody in the seventeenth century thought that, nor would any today, did they not picture Puritanism in terms learned from such as Macaulay, Hawthorne, Belloc, and Chesterton, as an essentially morbid movement, fed by a barbarous crypto-Manichaean theology that opposed grace to nature, revelation to rationality, godliness to good manners, and purity to pleasure—a movement, in short, that pitted Christianity against culture, and was shaped by a judgemental group mind that saw legalistic rigidity and pharisaic morality as marks of true religion. Certainly, Baxter was not like that! But then, neither was the Puritanism of history, and it is high time that this venerable caricature, 'distressingly and stridently recurrent' as it still is,[1] was finally laid to rest.

What, then, was the nature of historical Puritanism, the movement with which Baxter identified and that valued him as its best writer on the Christian life and, later, as the leading apologist for its ecclesiastical non-conformity?[2] The question is not too hard to answer. Puritanism according to Baxter, and as modern scholarship, correcting centuries of past misrepresentation, portrays it,[3] was a total view of Christianity, Bible-based, church-centred, God-honouring, Christ-exalting, Reformational, internationalist, literate, orthodox, and pastoral. It saw personal, domestic, professional, political, churchly, and economic existence as aspects of a single whole, namely society viewed as a *corpus Christianum*, and it taught everyone to order all departments and relationships of their life according to the Word of God, so that everything would be sanctified and become 'holiness to the Lord.' Puritanism's spearhead activity was pastoral evangelism and nurture through preaching, catechizing, and counselling (which Puritan pastors

called 'casuistry', the resolving of 'cases of conscience'). Puritan pulpit instruction, which we can assess from the vast number of devotional books containing
written-up sermons that were published by something like a hundred Puritan
authors, highlighted the realities of a Reformed Augustinianism in the inner life—
self-knowledge; self-humbling for sin, and repentance; faith in, and love for, Jesus
Christ the Saviour; the need for regeneration, and for sanctification (holy living,
by God's power) as proof of its reality; the call to conscientious conformity to all
God's laws, and to a disciplined use of the means of grace; and the blessedness
of the assurance and joy from the Holy Spirit that all faithful believers under
ordinary circumstances may know. Puritans saw themselves as God's pilgrims,
travelling home through rough country; God's warriors, battling the world, the
flesh, and the devil; and God's servants, under orders to worship, fellowship, and
do all the good they could as they went along. Of this Christianity Baxter was a
masterful teacher and shining example throughout the more than fifty years of
his ministerial career. (Ordained in 1638, he died in 1691.)

Diligence in 'duty' and wise use of time were basic Puritan virtues, and here
Baxter was phenomenal. Though a sick man living in pain throughout his working life,[4] he was an omnivorous polymath, always studying, reading quickly and
remembering well what he had read, and consistently thoughtful, knowledgeable,
and judicious in the opinion he expressed on what the books had set before him.
He was in fact the most voluminous English theologian of all time, who in addition to approximately 4 million words of pastoral, apologetic, devotional, and
homiletic writing reprinted in his *Practical Works*,[5] produced some 6 million on
aspects of the doctrine of grace and salvation, church unity and non-conformity,
the sacraments, Roman Catholicism, antinomianism, millenarianism, Quakerism,
politics, and history, not to mention a massive autobiography and a systematic
theology in Latin. And all these writings show the mature judgement of a clear,
sharp, well-stocked mind, very honest and spiritually very alert. The mental and
literary vigour of this chronic, often housebound invalid, like the evangelistic and
pastoral vigour of his spectacular fifteen years in Kidderminster (1641–1642 and
1647–1661) during which most of the town came to faith, seems incredible but
Baxter's vigour is a matter of recorded fact.

Whence, we ask, came Baxter's energy? How did he manage it all? What
kept him going? In an unfinished autobiographical poem he gives us part of the
answer:

> A life still near to Death, did me possess
> With a deep sense of Time's great preciousness;

so that

> I Preach'd, as never sure to Preach again,
> And as a dying man to dying men.[6]

It is clear that, with one foot in the grave as he believed, Baxter enjoyed through-out his ministry that wonderful concentration of the mind that Dr Samuel John-son thought would flow from knowing one was going to be hanged in a fortnight. But it is also clear that the enhanced sense of urgency and responsibility and of the importance of the present moment that his expectations of death called forth was only half the story. Though Baxter worked up to the limit ('I doe [*sic*] as much as I can'[7]) and took no vacations, he was not tense and frantic, driven by guilt; rather, he was joyful and thankful, being drawn by love. The secret is not he was a workaholic, but that he was if I may coin a word, a praiseaholic. This is clear from what follows.

Death, Rest, Perfection

That death is for believers the gate of life; that our living in this world should be seen as preparation for dying out of it into a better one; and that wisdom says, in Alexander Whyte's phrase, 'forefancy your deathbed' so as to retain a sense of reality were three Christian truths that Baxter understood very well, and as a man living at death's door he practised assiduously two habits of mind that these truths prompt.

The first habit was to estimate everything—values, priorities, possessions, relationships, claims, tasks—as these things will appear when one actually comes to die. This was Baxter's antidote to the creeping infection of worldly greed in its various forms.

The second habit was to dwell on the glory of the heavenly life to which one was going. This was Baxter's antidote to aimlessness, sluggishness, and drift.

During the winter of 1646 as he lay sick and lonely in a country house far from his Kidderminster home, broken in health and 'sentenced to Death by the Physicians,' Baxter the wordsmith and preacher started to write out homiletically 'for my own use' his meditations on 'the Everlasting rest which I apprehended myself to be just on the Borders of.'[8] So he began his first and in some ways great-est book. Recovered, he saw what benefit his meditations had brought him, and made it a rule henceforth to meditate on heaven specifically for half an hour or more each day.[9] Also, it became a regular part of his ministry to encourage oth-ers to follow his example, as the fourth part of *The Saints' Everlasting Rest* most passionately does. In 1676 he wrote 'one of the most beautiful of his books'[10] a long admonitory address to himself that was printed in 1683 under the title *Mr. Baxter's Dying Thoughts upon Philippians* 1:23. The text is 'For I am in a strait betwixt two, having a desire to depart, and to be with Christ; which is far better.' Baxter's theme is, once again, the substance and ground of the Christian hope of glory, and the soliloquy centres this time on seeing the life to come not as rest from toilsome labour so much as the perfecting and fulfilling of human nature.

At the end of his life he loved to meditate on the description of heavenly Jerusalem in Hebrews 12:22–24, a passage which, so he declared, 'deserves a thousand thousand thoughts.'[11] It was Baxter's habit of holding heaven at the forefront of his thoughts and desires that goes furthest to explain why, 'when he spake of weighty Soul-concerns, you might find his very Spirit Drenched therein,'[12] and whence over the years, pain-racked bag of bones that he was, he drew the motivation and mental energy that sustained his ministry. The hope of heaven brought him joy, and joy brought him strength, and so, like John Calvin before him and George Whitefield after him (two verifiable examples) and, it would seem, like the apostle Paul himself (see 1 Cor. 15:10; 2 Cor. 11:23–30; Col. 1:29), he was astoundingly enabled to labour on, accomplishing more than would ever have seemed possible in a single lifetime.

Baxterian heavenly mindedness is something that late-twentieth-century Christians find it extraordinarily hard to tune into, for several reasons over and above our low-level spirituality across the board. One reason is that our affluent culture is too comfortable and in the short term too gratifying. Life for English Christians, whatever their convictions, in the tortured and unhappy seventeenth century was harsh, full of pain, and in the end disappointing and indeed brutalizing, whereas modern Western culture conspires to massage everyone into feelings of dreamy contentment with things as they are, and has great and alarming success in so doing. Artificially induced inability to see this world as a wilderness drains away from us the joy and excitement about the hope of heaven's glory that marked New Testament Christians, patristic Christians, medieval Christians, Reformation and Puritan Christians, Wesleyan and Victorian Christians, and still marks Christians in black Africa. Indeed, our Western worldliness dulls our sense of God at every point, and where the sense of God is dim thoughts of heaven grow dim also.

A second reason is Western cultural prejudice against hopes of a better, celestial world as being escapist, and against the biblical imagery of heaven (robes, crowns, thrones, gold, jewels, and so on) as being jejune and repellent to civilized taste. Having shared these prejudices as an unconverted teenager, squirming when congregations sang 'Jerusalem the golden / With milk and honey blest,' I think I am now entitled to nail them as stupidities, the first a mental miasma spun off from Marxist materialism, the second a sign of the unbeliever's inability to 'cash' pen-pictures of Near Eastern splendour in terms of the joyous fellowship with Christ for which they are metaphors and analogies. But the sad fact is that these prejudices are widespread, and the materialist, no-nonsense mind-set of our technological Titanism reinforces them every day.

A third reason why heavenly mindedness fails to register nowadays, even with Christians, might be labelled the misdirection of desire. As C. S. Lewis, expanding on Augustine, maintained, the pangs of joy, in the special sense of sweet desire and longing, are universally felt, and are really a natural, built-in craving for God and heaven.[13] But because original sin has twisted all our desires in an egocentric direction, and because our technologically oriented culture shrinks our souls and erodes our capacity for moral and spiritual discernment, we imagine that the hunger of our hearts will be satisfied by sexual activity, aesthetic experience, making money, gaining and using power, or something similar, and we dismiss the idea that God and heaven are what our hearts seek as old-fashioned, unenlightened fantasy. Some Christians are only half-way to wisdom at this point, supposing that the God who satisfies and gives rest to the heart is one whom they can manage, deploy, and exploit in the interests of these secular objectives, rather than one whom they must worship, adore, trust, love, thank, and give themselves up to in radical self-denial: so far has original sin retained its corrupting influence in their lives. Misdirected, earthbound desire is so much part of life today that not even Christians are interested in heaven, and Baxter's statement, made a year before he died, 'I live in almost continual thoughts of heaven,'[14] is likely to prompt no more than a yawn.

But it is worth learning to swim against the secularist stream (which nowadays often flows as strongly within as outside the churches) and to grasp Baxter's wisdom about heavenly mindedness as a basic dimension of being alive to God; so I proceed.

Heaven in the Head and the Heart

First question, then: Why should one meditate on heaven? Baxter gives a series of reasons in *The Saints' Everlasting Rest*:

> Consider, A heart set upon heaven will be one of the most unquestionable evidences of thy sincerity ... A heart in heaven is the highest excellency of your spirits here, and the noblest part of your Christian disposition ... A heavenly mind is a joyful mind; this is the nearest and truest way to live a life of comfort ... A heart in heaven will be a most excellent preservative against temptations, a powerful means to kill thy corruptions ... The diligent keeping of your hearts on heaven, will preserve the vigor of all your graces, and put life into all your duties ... The frequent believing views of glory are the most precious cordial in all afflictions ... It is he that hath his conversation in heaven, who is the profitable Christian to all about him ... There is no man so highly honoureth God, as he who has his conversation in heaven ... There is nothing else that is worth the setting our hearts on ... (4.3).

In short, the practice of meditation on the prospect of heaven will both honour God and do one good. As a cherishing of hope, it will reinforce the holiness of life whereby the hope is laid hold of; as a following of the Holy Spirit's lead, it will increase knowledge of the love of God, who has granted us heaven by his grace, and so increase our love for God in response. 'We fall in with the heavenly Spirit in his own way, when we set ourselves to be most heavenly. Heavenly thoughts are the work which he would set you on; and the love of God is the thing which he works you to thereby.'[15] Meditating on heaven is a headclearing, heartwarming, invigorating discipline, hard work and ungratifying to the flesh, no doubt, but very enriching to the spirit. So Baxter had proved in his own life, and so he presented the matter to the Christian world.

Second question: How should one form ideas of heaven, to shape one's meditation?

One way is to analyse the idea of personal perfection. Basic to the Christian's self-knowledge, as God mediates it through the Scriptures, is the awareness of one's current imperfection, with which goes that other aspect of self-knowledge, awareness of one's desires that lack fulfilment at present. In *Dying Thoughts* particularly, Baxter pursues this method of building up a notion of heaven. He describes heaven as a state in which every faculty is made faultless and is wholly occupied in knowing, adoring, loving, and enjoying God. 'What is heaven to me but God? God, who is light, and life, and love, communicating himself to blessed spirits, perfecting them in the reception, possession, and exercise of life, light, and love for ever ... God ... is heaven and all to me.'[16] 'It is the presence of God that maketh heaven to be heaven.'[17] Heaven begins here: 'the knowledge and love of God in Christ is the beginning or foretaste of heaven.'[18] Full heavenly experience, however, remains future, 'we ask for perfection, and we shall have it, but not here.'[19] How, when, and where we shall enter heaven, how the soul will exist without the body in the intermediate state, what its experience will then be, and how soul and body will unite again, or the soul be freshly embodied, at the general resurrection if not in some way before, are matters completely opaque to us ('a hundred of these questions are better left ... Had all these been needful to us, they had been revealed'[20]). But revelation and reason unite to assure us of the certainty of that future fulfilment for which heaven is the God-given name.

Baxter spells this out in personal terms. The perfecting of his mind means that his omnivorous appetite for knowledge will be satiated at last, understanding will be perfect. He will know everything, and know it thoroughly, by direct intuition, as God knows it. 'I shall quickly, in heaven, be a perfect philosopher.'[21] To arouse his eagerness, he reviews the celestial curriculum:

> I. I shall know God better. II. I shall know the universe better. III. I shall know Christ better. IV. I shall know the church, his body, better, with the holy angels. V. I shall know better the methods and perfection of the Scripture ... VI. I shall know the methods and sense of disposing providence better. VII. I shall know the divine benefits, which are the fruits of love, better. VIII. I shall know myself better. IX. I shall better know every fellow-creature ... X. And I shall better know all that evil, sin, Satan, and misery, from which I am delivered.[22]

As one who aspired always to mental clarity on earth, Baxter rejoices to anticipate the full mental clarity of heaven.

Also, his will will be perfected. As external distractions from righteousness will be no more, so inner conflict will be over: 'there will be nothing in me that is cross to itself; no more war or striving in me; not a law in my mind, and a law in my members, that are contrary to each other . . . all will be at unity and peace within.'[23] Frustration will be a thing of the past: 'I shall have all whatsoever I would have, and shall be and do whatsoever I would be and do.'[24] Unimpeded and undistracted, the whole person will be joyfully devoted to the absorbing and joyous activity of loving the triune God. 'Perfect, joyful complacency in God is the heaven which I desire and hope for';[25] 'seeing and loving will be the heavenly life.'[26] Baxter's capacity for action will be perfected too: 'There are good works in heaven, and far more and better than on earth.[27] Perfect praise and perfect service, and both without end, are the realities in prospect. Much of this is necessarily wrapped in obscurity while we live on earth; the soul's 'thoughts about its future state must be analogical and general, and partly strange.'[28] Certainly, however, 'in heaven we shall have not less, but . . . more excellent sense and affections of love and joy, as well as more excellent intellection and volition; but such as we cannot now clearly conceive of.'[29]

So far, Baxter has been forming his idea of heaven by extrapolating from the Christian's present relationship with God, other intelligent beings, and the world of things, and by eliminating from the scene pain, evil, and all frustration factors. The idea thus gained may now be amplified by introducing 'analogical collections.' In *The Saints' Everlasting Rest* Baxter gives the following rationale of this next move:

> It is very considerable, how the Holy Ghost doth condescend in the phrase of Scripture, in bringing things down to the reach of sense; how he sets forth the excellences of spiritual things in words that are borrowed from the objects of sense . . . doubtless if such expressions had not been best, and to us necessary, the Holy Ghost would not have so frequently used them; he that will speak to man's understanding, must speak in man's language, and speak that which he is capable to conceive . . .
>
> But what is my scope in all this? . . . that we make use of these phrases of the Spirit to quicken our apprehensions and affections . . . and use these low notions as a glass, in which we must see the things themselves, though the representation be exceeding imperfect, till we come to an immediate perfect sight.[30]

The purpose of the biblical imagery is to make thoughts of heaven concrete, dramatic, and attractive, and the Christian's wisdom is to let his regenerate imagination feed on it accordingly, so that the significance of each pictorial item comes home to his heart.

So, in the first part of *The Saints' Everlasting Rest*, Baxter pictures Christ's return, the general resurrection, the final judgement, and the entry of God's people into the full glory of their promised inheritance; and he imagines the redeemed recalling their earthly pilgrimage:

To stand in heaven, and look back on earth . . . how must it needs transport the soul and make it cry out . . . Is this the end of believing? Is this the end of the Spirit's workings? Have the gales of grace blown me into such a harbour? Is it hither that Christ hath enticed my soul? . . . Is my mourning, my sad humblings, my heavenly walking, groanings, complainings, come to this? . . . So will the memory of the saints for ever promote their joys.[31]

He goes on to imagine the delights of fellowship with the universal church, with Israelite saints and Christian saints, Fathers, Reformers, and Puritans, in a passage so striking that it must be quoted at length:

It cannot choose but be comfortable to me to think of that day, when I shall join with Moses in his song, with David in his psalms of praise, and with all the redeemed in the song of the Lamb for ever, when we shall see Enoch walking with God, Noah enjoying the end of his singularity, Job of his patience, Hezekiah of his uprightness . . . Will it be nothing conducible to our comforts to live eternally with Peter, Paul, Austin [Augustine], Chrysostom, Jerome, Wickliffe, Luther, Zuinglius, Calvin, Beza, Bullinger, Zanchius, Paraeus, Piscator, Camero[n]; with Hooper, Bradford, Latimer, Glover, Saunders, Philpot; with Reighnolds [Rainolds], Whitaker, Cartwright, Brightman, Bayne, Bradshaw, Bolton, Hall, Hildersham, Pemble, Twisse, Ames, Preston, Sibbs?[32]

Baxter often refers to the communion of saints as a principal ingredient in heaven's joy. His bitter experience, as pastor and statesman, of the pride and party spirit that sets Christians at each other's throats made him long for the perfect peace and love of heaven. The triumph at the Restoration of sectarianism over catholic principles in the restored Church of England, from which two thousand Puritan pastors were summarily ejected, was to him the greatest tragedy of his life, and as his hopes for church peace in England grew fainter thereafter, he dwelt more and more on the truly catholic churchmanship that he would enjoy in the new Jerusalem. Though Puritanism has sometimes been represented as a form of religious individualism, a cult of the isolated believer, and though a highly developed individuality, such as we see in Baxter himself, was certainly a mark of the movement, a passage like that just quoted highlights the corporate and churchly frame within which this individuality blossomed. The Puritan movement was in fact communal and societal in its very essence, and we should not wonder that this apotheosis of church fellowship should have bulked large in Baxter's concept of heavenly glory.

The importance of clarity about what lies at the end of the Christian pilgrimage seemed to Baxter incalculable. Human beings are rational creatures, and rationality is a matter, among other things, of choosing means to ends. The more strongly one desires an end, the more carefully and diligently will one use the means to it. 'The Love of the end is it that is the *poise* or spring, which setteth every Wheel a going.'[33] But an unknown end will not be loved. 'It is a known, and not merely an unknown God and happiness, that the soul doth joyfully desire.'[34] Such desire will then give wings to the soul. 'It is the heavenly Christian that is the lively Christian. It is strangeness to heaven that makes us so dull. It is the end that quickens to all the means; and the more frequently and clearly this end is beheld, the more vigorous will all our motion be . . . We run so slowly, and strive so lazily, because we so little mind the prize.'[35] So let Christians animate themselves daily to run the race set before them by practising heavenly meditation, 'the delightfulest task to the spirit, and the most tedious to the flesh, that ever men on earth were employed in.'[36]

This brings us to the third question: How are we to meditate on heaven? How, that is, are we to set about this task?

The Discipline of Heavenly Meditation

The first step, says Baxter, is to fix a time. In authentic Puritan fashion he advocates an evangelical rule of life. 'A Christian should have a set time for every ordinary duty, or else when he should practice it, it is ten to one but he will put it by. Stated time is a hedge to duty.'[37] The time allotted must not be too short, for 'as I cannot get me a heat without walking, no nor running neither . . . unless I *continue* some considerable time, no more can I in Prayer and Meditation.'[38] Baxter's advice is to 'set apart one hour or half hour every day.'[39]

The task, as presented in part four of *The Saints' Everlasting Rest,* is 'set and solemn acting of all the powers of the soul upon this most perfect object, rest, by meditation.'[40] This means that Christians are 'to use your understandings for the warming of your affections, and to fire your hearts by the help of your heads'[41]— in other words, to turn their light into heat. 'He is the best Christian who hath the readiest passage from the brain to the heart.'[42] The procedure, modelled loosely on the method set out by Joseph Hall in *The Arte of Divine Meditation* (1606), assumed, as we see, what Hall also affirmed, that the arousing of the affections is 'the very soul of meditation whereto all that is past [i.e., all that precedes] serveth but as an instrument.'[43] Meditation consists of consideration (discursive thought) followed by soliloquy (speaking to oneself in the presence of God). Baxter structures the exercise as follows.

Stage one, says Baxter, is to bring the truth about our promised rest before our minds as clearly and fully as possible and then to awaken ('act') the various affections—love, desire, hope, courage, and joy—in appropriate responses to this truth. When by this means our object of contemplation has become an object of love, desire, and delight, then is the time to enter upon the second stage, 'pleading the case with our own souls . . . Soliloquy is a preaching to oneself.'[44] The aim of this is to move oneself to resolute Christian practice. Soliloquy thus corresponds to the 'improvement' of 'doctrine' by 'uses' (applications) in a Puritan sermon. If heaven is so desirable, the Christian must say to himself, should I not be exerting myself much more to make sure of reaching it? The following passage shows what Baxter had in mind.

> In thy meditations upon all these incentives ... preach them over earnestly to thy heart, and expostulate and plead with it by way of soliloquy, till thou feel the fire begin to burn ... Dispute it out with thy conscience ... There is much more moving force in this earnest talking to ourselves, than in bare cognition, that breaks not out into mental words. Imitate the most powerful preacher that ever thou wast acquainted with ... There is more in this than most Christians are acquainted with, or use to practice. It is a great part of a Christian's skill and duty, to be a good preacher to himself ... Two or three sermons a week from others is a fair proportion; but two or three sermons a day from thyself, is ordinarily too little.[45]

Finally, believers should pass on 'from this speaking to ourselves, to speak with God' in prayer, which is 'the highest step that we can advance to in the work.'[46] Earnest desire and hearty resolution, poured out in petition, will never lack God's blessing.

This habit of meditation, leading to prayer, will, says Baxter, be greatly promoted by hearing sermons about heaven ('happy the people that have a heavenly minister!'[47]), by talking to other believers about heaven, and by reading the books of creation and providence—another typical Puritan emphasis.

> Make an advantage of every object thou seest, and of every thing that befalls in thy labour and calling, to mind thy soul of its approaching rest. As all providence and creatures are means to our rest, so do they point us to that as their end. Every creature hath the name of God, and our final rest, written upon it ... O learn to open the creatures, and to open the several passages of providence, to read of God and glory there ... We might have a fuller taste of Christ and heaven in every bit of bread we eat, and in every draught of beer we drink, than most men have in the use of the sacrament.[48]

Such, then, in outline is heavenly meditation according to Richard Baxter, the mainstay, as he saw it, of Christian motivation, and the power-point of ongoing sanctification. Space forbids us to explore it further, but the essence of it is now clear, and anyone who wishes to follow up on Baxter's teaching can consult *The Saints' Everlasting Rest* directly. What has been reviewed, however, must leave us with some nagging questions. Could it be that here is a devotional secret we need to learn, and an inner discipline we need to recover? We have seen what Baxter believed that heavenly meditation did for him, and there can be no doubt as to his spiritual stature. Was he right to think it was heavenly meditation that made the difference? Would the practice benefit us as he claimed it benefited him? Does it bear at all on what is involved in being 'alive to God' in these days? I leave my readers to face these questions as I close. What, I wonder, will Jim Houston have to say about them? I eagerly look forward, I confess, to finding out.

CHAPTER 16

Arminianisms

Within the churches of the Reformation, the terms 'Calvinism' and 'Arminianism' are traditionally used as a pair, expressing an antithesis, like black and white, or Whig and Tory, or Roman and Protestant. The words are defined in terms of the antithesis, and the point is pressed that no Christian can avoid being on one side or the other. Among evangelicals, this issue, though now 350 years old (if not, indeed, 1900 years old), remains live and sometimes explosive. 'Calvinism' and 'Arminianism' are still spat out by some as anathematizing swearwords (like 'fundamentalism' on the lips of a liberal), and there are still places where you forfeit both fellowship and respect by professing either. There remain Presbyterian churches which ordain only Calvinists, and Methodist and Nazarene bodies which ordain only Arminians, and the division between 'general' or 'free-will' (Arminian) and 'particular' or 'Reformed' (Calvinistic) still splits the Baptist community on both sides of the Atlantic.

In evangelism, cooperation between evangelicals is sometimes hindered by disagreement and mistrust over this matter, just as in the eighteenth century the Calvinistic evangelicals and John Wesley's party found it hard on occasion to work together. Nor is it any wonder that tension should exist, when each position sees the other as misrepresenting the saving love of God. The wonder is, rather, that so many Christians who profess a serious concern for theology should treat this debate as one in which they have no stakes, and need not get involved.

This article seeks to understand and evaluate the Calvinist-Arminian antithesis. To that end, we shall address ourselves to three questions. First, what is Arminianism? Second, how far-reaching is the cleavage between it and Calvinism? Third (assuming that by this stage we shall have seen reason to regard Arminianism as a pathological growth), what causes Arminianism? and what is the cure for it? Before we tackle these questions, however, one caveat must be entered.

Our concern is with things, not words. Our subject matter will oblige us to speak of Calvinism and Arminianism frequently, but it is no part of our aim to revive bad habits of slogan-shouting and name-calling.[1] What matters is that we should grasp truly what the Bible says about God and his grace, not that we should parade brand labels derived from historical theology. The present writer

believes, and wishes others to believe, the doctrines commonly labelled Calvinistic, but he is not concerned to argue for the word. One who has received the
biblical witness to God's sovereignty in grace is blessed indeed, but he is no better off for labelling himself a Calvinist, and might indeed be the worse for it; for
party passion and love of the truth are different things, and indulgence in the one
tends to wither the other.

What Is Arminianism?[2]

Historically, Arminianism has appeared as a reaction against the Calvinism
of Beza and the Synod of Dort, affirming, in the words of W. R. Bagnall, 'conditional in opposition to absolute predestination, and general in opposition to
particular redemption.'[3] This verbal antithesis is not in fact as simple or clear as
it looks, for changing the adjective involves redefining the noun. What Bagnall
should have said is that Calvinism affirms a concept of predestination from which
conditionality is excluded, and a concept of redemption to which particularity
is essential; and Arminianism denies both. The difference is this. To Calvinism,
predestination is essentially God's unconditional decision about the destiny of
individuals; to Arminianism, it is essentially God's unconditional decision to
provide means of grace, decisions about individuals' destiny being secondary,
conditional, and consequent upon foresight of how they will use those means
of grace. To Calvinism, predestination of individuals means the foreordaining of
both their doings (including their response to the gospel) and their consequent
destinies; to Arminianism it means a foreordaining of destinies based on doings
foreseen but not foreordained. Arminianism affirms that God predestined Christ
to be man's Saviour; repentance and faith to be the way of salvation; and the gift
of universal sufficient inward grace to make saving response to God possible for
all men everywhere, but it denies that any individual is predestined to believe. On
the Calvinist view, election, which is a predestinating act on God's part, means
the efficacious choice of particular sinners to be saved by Jesus Christ through
faith, and redemption, the first step in working out God's electing purpose, is an
achievement which actually secures certain salvation—calling, pardon, adoption,
preservation, final glory—for all the elect. On the Arminian view, however, what
the death of Christ secured was a possibility of salvation for sinners generally, a
possibility which, so far as God is concerned, might never have been actualized
in any single case; and the electing of individuals to salvation is, as we said, simply
God noting in advance who will believe and so qualify for glory, as a matter of
contingent (not foreordained) fact. Whereas to Calvinism, election is God's resolve to save, and the cross Christ's act of saving, for Arminianism salvation rests
in the last analysis neither on God's election nor on Christ's cross, but on a man's
own co-operation with grace, which is something that God does not himself

guarantee. Biblically, the difference between these two conceptions of how God in love relates to fallen human beings may be pinpointed thus.

Arminianism treats our Lord's parable of the Supper to which further guests were invited in place of those who never came (Luke 14:16–24; cf. Matt. 22:1–10) as picturing the whole truth about the love of God in the gospel. On this view, when you have compared God's relation to fallen men with that of a dignitary who invites all needy folk around to come and enjoy his bounty, you have said it all. Calvinism, however, does not stop here, but links with the picture of the Supper that of the Shepherd (John 10:11–18, 24–29) who has his sheep given him to care for (vv. 14, 16, 27; cf. 6:37–40; 17:6, 11–12), who lays down his life for them (10:15), who guarantees that all of them will in due course hear his voice (vv. 16, 27) and follow him (v. 27), and be kept from perishing for ever (v. 28). In other words, Calvinism holds that divine love does not stop short at graciously inviting, but that the triune God takes gracious action to ensure that the elect respond. On this view, both the Christ who saves and the faith which receives him as Saviour are God's gifts, and the latter is as much a foreordained reality as is the former. Arminians praise God for providing a Saviour to whom all may come for life; Calvinists do that too, and then go on to praise God for actually bringing them to the Saviour's feet.

So the basic difference between the two positions is not, as is sometimes thought, that Arminianism follows Scripture while Calvinism follows logic, nor that Arminianism knows the love of God while Calvinism knows only his power, nor that Arminianism affirms a connection between believing and obeying as a means and eternal life as an end which Calvinism denies, nor that Arminianism discerns a *bona fide* 'free offer' of Christ in the gospel which Calvinism does not discern, nor that Arminianism acknowledges human responsibility before God and requires holy endeavour in the Christian life while Calvinism does not. No; the difference is that Calvinism recognizes a dimension of the saving love of God which Arminianism misses, namely God's sovereignty in bringing to faith and keeping in faith all who are actually saved. Arminianism gives Christians much to thank God for, and Calvinism gives them more.

Arminianism was born in Holland at the turn of the seventeenth century, and synodically condemned by the whole Reformed world at Dort in 1619. In England, an Arminian tradition of teaching lasted into, and right through, the eighteenth century. Arminianism was part of the Wesley family heritage, and John and Charles fought the Calvinists by prose and poetry throughout their evangelical ministry. The Arminian evangelical tradition has been maintained by Methodists and others up to the present day.

It is important to realize that both in its general tenor and in its practical effect the Arminianism of the 'Belgic semi-Pelagians,'[4] as John Owen called the Remonstrants and their supporters, was not by any means identical with the Arminianism of John Wesley, his *Arminian Magazine* (1778–),[5] and his colleague

John Fletcher. The following account of Wesley's doctrine, taken from Fletcher's
First Check to Antinomianism (1771), will alert us to the difference:

> ... he [Wesley] holds also *General Redemption,* and its necessary consequences,
> which some account *dreadful heresies.* He asserts with St. Paul that Christ *by the
> GRACE of God, tasted death for every man;* and this *grace* he calls *free,* as extending
> itself *freely* to all ... He frequently observes with the same apostle, that *Christ is the
> Saviour of ALL men, but specially of them that believe;* and that *God will have ALL men
> to be saved,* consistently with their moral agency, and the tenor of his gospel. With St.
> John he maintains, that *God is love,* and that *Christ is the propitiation not only for our
> sins, but also for the sins of the WHOLE WORLD* ... and with St. Peter, that *the Lord
> is not willing that any should perish, but that ALL should come to repentance;* yea, that
> God, without hypocrisy, *commandeth ALL men, EVERYWHERE, to repent.*

Thus far, Wesley's position coincided completely with that of the Remonstrants;
but Fletcher's next point is this:

> Thus far, Mr. W. agrees with Arminius, because he thinks that illustrious Divine
> agreed thus far with the Scriptures, and all the early Fathers of the Church. But if Ar-
> minius (as the Author of *Pietas Oxoniensis* affirms in his letter to Dr. Adams) 'denied
> that man's nature is totally corrupt, and asserted that he hath still a freedom of will to
> turn to God, but not without the assistance of grace,' Mr. W. is no Arminian, for he
> strongly asserts the *total* fall of man, and constantly maintains that by nature man's
> will is only free to evil, and that divine grace must first prevent, and then continually
> further him, to make him willing and able to turn to God.[6]

These sentences point us to the basic difference between the Remonstrant and
the Wesleyan Arminianisms. In seeing man's acts as contingent so far as God
is concerned, and in thinking that moral agency presupposes 'free will' in the
special and particular sense of indeterminacy of action under God, the two were
agreed. In claiming that all men actually have power to respond to such revelation from God as reaches them, and that revelation sufficient to save actually
reaches every man, whether he hears the gospel or not, they were agreed also.
(Historic Calvinism would query all these positions.) But the two Arminianisms divided over the question whether capacity for response to God had been
wholly lost at the Fall. Wesley said it had, but held that it was now restored to
every man as a gift of grace. The Remonstrants (not, it seems, Arminius himself)
said it had never been wholly lost, and 'total inability' had never been a true diagnosis of man's plight in Adam. Sin, said the Remonstrants in effect, has made
man *weak* in the moral and spiritual realm, but not *bad;* he still has it in him to
reach out, however sluggishly, after what is right, and God in fact helps him, powerfully if not decisively, in each particular right choice. Wesley agreed that God
helps to actualize an existing capacity in every right choice, but maintained that
this capacity only existed now because it had been supernaturally restored to all

the race in consequence of the cross. While accepting Remonstrant synergism, in the sense of seeing man's cooperation in right action as something distinct from, and independent of, God's energizing, Wesley insisted that the capacity to cooperate was itself a love-gift from God to sinners, and that the Calvinistic doctrine that original sin involves loss of this capacity entirely had not been a whit too strong.

The effect of this difference was to give the two Arminianisms contrasting thrusts. The Remonstrant thrust was to upgrade fallen nature, minimize sin, and recast Christianity as a moralism of grace (that is, a system, like Roman Catholicism, in which grace makes possible saving moral endeavour: in New Testament terms, a Judaizing Christianity which is really 'another gospel'). The end of this road, as the century following Dort showed, was Deism—salvation by merit of morality without internal grace at all. The Wesleyan thrust, however, was explicitly anti-deistic and in intention, if not entirely in effect, anti-moralistic too. Wesley maximized sin in order to magnify grace. He challenged the then standard Anglican moralism, of which he had himself once been a victim, by affirming present justification through faith in Christ alone, and by adding that true Christian morality was the fruit of justifying faith, and that self-abandoning trust was of this faith's very essence. Where Remonstrant Arminianism had been humanistic and rationalistic in motivation, delimiting God's sovereignty of set purpose in order to assert man's autonomy and self-determination, and so show that he, not God, was the author of his sins, and could properly be called to account for them, Wesleyan Arminianism was directly religious in motivation—more religious than theological, in fact—seeking only to exhibit the love of God in salvation and the power of faith in everyday life and practice. Remonstrant Arminianism, like later Baxterianism, took a voluntaristic view of faith as essentially commitment to new obedience, a view which assimilates faith to repentance and makes it both look and feel like a human work determining salvation. Wesleyan Arminianism, however, like earlier Reformation theology, both Lutheran and Calvinist, distinguished faith from repentance, defining it as assured trust in Christ, correlative to the witness of the Holy Spirit, and springing from the sense of hopelessness and helplessness which God's law induces. Having thus excluded all self-reliance from the psychology of faith, Wesley seems never to have seen the oddity of continuing to profess a theology which obliged him to view faith as man's own work of response to God. There was, in truth, beneath the surface clearness and practicality of his mind, a great deal of muddle at the theoretical level. Certainly, however, his view of the nature of faith made his professed Arminianism as fully evangelical, and as little legalistic, as it is possible for a synergistic system to be.[7] We shall mark the difference between it and the Remonstrant position by calling them *evangelical* and *rationalistic* Arminianisms respectively. We shall now glance at their history, taking the latter first.

Rationalistic Arminianism

Rationalistic Arminianism was in effect, if not in intention, a revival of the semi-Pelagian reaction to Augustinianism which was developed in the fifth century by John Cassian and Faustus of Ries. It was a movement of recoil from the high doctrine of predestination taught by Luther, Calvin, and their reforming contemporaries[8] and systematized—perhaps too neatly—by Beza, Calvin's successor and first appointed as head of the Geneva Academy. Arminianism emerged in Holland, but not as an isolated phenomenon; similar reactionary theologies appeared at about the same time in England, as we shall see, and in German Lutheranism. It was part of a Europe-wide encroachment on the theology of the Reformation by the rationalism of the Renaissance.

The story is this. In 1589 a brilliant young Amsterdam clergyman, who had studied for a year with Beza, Jakob Harmenszoon (Arminius[9]) by name, was asked to respond to an attack by a humanist layman named Koornhert, of Delft, on the supralapsarian view of predestination, and also to a pamphlet by two clergy who, under pressure from Koornhert's arguments, had moved to the position later called infralapsarianism or sublapsarianism. (Supralapsarianism, as spelled out by Beza and the many who went with him in the last third of the sixteenth century, was the view that God's pre-mundane election of some to salvation and his passing by of others had respect to men, not as fallen, but simply as rational creatures whom God planned to create, and so was logically prior in God's thinking to his decision to permit the Fall. Infralapsarianism, as expressed by the Synod of Dort and most English-speaking Calvinists since, viewed the subjects of election as vessels of mercy chosen from a race envisaged as fallen and ruined.) It was assumed that Beza's pupil would hammer the defectors hard, but Arminius' detailed studies in preparation for writing led him to give up supralapsarianism for good.[10] The expected reply never appeared. Instead, for the next twenty years till his death of tuberculosis in 1609, at the age of forty-nine, Arminius maintained, discreetly but decidedly, the 'Arminian' view of election and the state of fallen man.[11]

In 1610, a group of his followers issued a *Remonstrance,* stating five theological positions for which they claimed toleration and protection. The first was that predestination is not the cause of the faith which saves or the unbelief which damns; the second was that Christ died to redeem all men, not just the elect; the fifth was that believers through negligence can fall out of the state of grace (through ceasing to believe); while the third and fourth disclaimed pure Pelagianism by affirming that neither faith nor good works exist apart from internal grace. Eventually, after much debate, the international Synod of Dort (1617–19) pronounced against these semi-Pelagian formulations, as we must call them, and affirmed in opposition five counter-theses of its own. These 'five points of Calvinism,' made memorable in English by the mnemonic T-U-L-I-P, are: the Total depravity and inability of man in sin; the Unconditional and decisive character of God's election of sinners to salvation; the Limited scope (but definite and effective nature) of Christ's redemptive sin-bearing on the cross; the Irresistible, efficacious quality of the grace which, by renewing sinners' hearts, leads them to faith and repentance through a calling that is truly effectual; and the certain Perseverance, through divine preservation, of all regenerate persons to final glory.[12] The overall thrust of the Dort deliverances is to make the double point that it is God who saves us by fulfilling his plan of election, which means that it is Christ who saves by his effective purchase of us on Calvary and the Holy Spirit who saves by instilling faith, and that in no sense do we save ourselves; salvation is wholly of the Lord, first to last a gift of free sovereign mercy. A. W. Harrison rightly calls the canons of Dort 'rather one of the classic statements of Calvinism than an exposition of Arminian error';[13] their significance lies in their positive affirmations, which controlled the presentation of the Reformed faith in Europe for more than a century.

Dort having spoken, the plea for toleration went to the wall and the Arminians were temporarily exiled; but in 1626 they were able to return and open a theological seminary at Amsterdam, where Simon Episcopius, Stephanus Curcellaeus (Etienne de Courcelles), and Philip von Limborch, three outstanding men, taught in succession. Philip Schaff's description of Arminianism as standing for 'an elastic, progressive, changing liberalism'[14] was, however, true of the seminary. The continental Arminian school drifted into undogmatic moralism and pietism, with Arian, Socinian, deist, and immanentist flavouring from time to time.

In England, where Bezan Calvinism was part of accepted orthodoxy for a generation from the 1570s, Peter Baro (Baron), a French refugee who had become Lady Margaret Professor of Divinity at Cambridge, caused a stir in 1579 by arguing from the case of Nineveh, in the book of Jonah, the position which Melanchthon had taught and which in substance Arminius was to maintain ten years later—that 'God predestined all men to eternal life on condition of their faith and obedience.'[15] William Barrett, Baro's student, preached the same doctrine in 1595, and the resulting furor led to the composing of the nine Lambeth Articles. These, the nearest English counterpart to the Dort canons, were a semi-official statement of what was then taken as Anglican and Christian orthodoxy on predestination and grace.[16] At the Hampton Court Conference of 1604, John Rainolds of Oxford went so far as to ask for the Lambeth Articles to be added to the Thirty-nine, but Bishop Bancroft and Dean Overall vigorously opposed the idea, and King James, who in any case was resolved to give the Puritans nothing of substance, said no.

The seventeenth century saw, however, a widespread English recoil from Calvinism, both supra- and infralapsarian, along the lines that Baro and Barrett marked out. Though in Elizabeth's last years it looked as if the Bezan Calvinism of Cambridge's William Whitaker (died 1595) and William Perkins (died 1602), the only two British theologians of international reputation, was carrying all before it, men such as Lancelot Andrewes and John Overall, like Hooker before them, were already standing quietly apart, thinking it a provincial and uncatholic development, and their viewpoint made steady headway. James I, though himself a Calvinist in soteriology, with a robustly Calvinist Archbishop of Canterbury, George Abbot, favoured 'High Churchmen' who accepted his doctrine of the divine right of kings, and these tended to be Arminian in sympathy. Laud, who became Archbishop of Canterbury under Charles I, was one of them. Led by Laud, and greatly disliking Puritans, Charles promoted many Arminians,[17] and the net result was to set Anglican theology moving away from the world of Bezan scholasticism. Interest in the Greek Fathers, which blossomed at that time, confirmed the trend. In the middle of the century, the Cambridge Platonists, who interestingly had personal links with the Dutch Arminians,[18] began spreading their attractive combination of moralism and natural theology, and this became a fountainhead of later latitudinarianism. Absolute personal predestination had come to be thought of as a distinctly Puritan assertion, and when after 1660 the Restoration set the pendulum swinging against all that Puritanism had stood for, Calvinism had the status only of an oddity maintained by non-conformists. Anglican theologians with few exceptions were Arminian in type, as indeed they are still.

Justification and God

It is now clear that rationalistic Arminianism, so far from being a creative advance upon the Bezan formulation of God's sovereignty, was rather a reaction against it, narrowing and impoverishing as reactions usually are, and that its concern was less to assert what Calvinists were denying than to deny what they were asserting. But we have not yet fully mapped the gulf that divides Arminian from mainstream Reformed theology. Two more areas of divergence call for notice. The first is the doctrine of justification.

The Reformers' doctrine of justification can be summed up in the following seven points.[19] (1) Every man faces the judgement-seat of God, and must answer to God there for himself; nothing can shield him from this. (2) Every man is a sinner by nature and practice, a non-conformist so far as God's law is concerned, and therefore all he can expect is God's wrath and rejection. Thus far the bad news; now the good news. (3) Justification is God's judicial act of pardoning a guilty sinner, accepting him as righteous, and receiving him as a son and heir. (4) The sole source of justification is God's grace, not man's effort or initiative. (5) The sole ground of justification is Christ's vicarious righteousness and blood-shedding, not our own merit; nor do supposed works of supererogation, purchase of indulgences, or multiplication of masses make any contribution to it; nor do the purgatorial pains of medieval imagination have any significance, or indeed reality, in relation to it. Justification is not the prize to work for, but a gift to be received through Christ. (6) The means of justification, here and now, is faith in Christ, understood as a pacifying and energizing trust that Christ's sacrificial death atoned for all one's sins. (7) The fruit of faith, the evidence of its reality and therefore the proof that a man is a Christian as he claims to be, is a manifested repentance and life of good works.

The Council of Trent met the Reformers' doctrine by defining justification as inner renewal plus pardon and acceptance and affirming that the 'sole formal cause' (*unica formalis causa*) of justification, in both its aspects, was God's righteousness (*iustitia*) imparted through baptism as its instrumental cause.[20] 'Formal cause,' in the language of the schools, denoted that which gave a thing its quality (thus, heat was the formal cause of a thing being hot, or having the quality of hotness). The Tridentine thesis thus was that the ground of our being pardoned was the quality of actual divine righteousness infused into us: God declares us righteous, not liable to punishment for our sins, because we have been made genuinely righteous in ourselves. In the more biblical terminology of Protestantism, this was to make regeneration, or the start of sanctification, the ground of justification. In reply, a host of Reformed divines, continental and British,[21] drew out at length the position already explicit in Calvin,[22] that the 'sole formal cause' of justification is not God's righteousness *imparted,* but Christ's righteousness *imputed*; and to make their meaning more clear, they developed the habit of distinguishing between Christ's *active* obedience to God's law, in keeping its precepts, and *his passive* obedience to it, in undergoing its penalty, and insisted that our acceptance as righteous depends on the imputing to us of Christ's obedience in both its aspects.[23] The same polemic was directed at the Arminians, who were regularly accused of being crypto-Romans because they held that our faith is itself actual, personal righteousness, being obedience to the gospel viewed as God's new law, and as such is not only the condition but also the ground of our justification. Faith is 'counted for righteousness,' on this view, because it is righteousness. The Reformed men argued against both Romans and Arminians that by finding the ground of justification in the believer himself, they ministered to human pride on the one hand and on the other hand robbed the Son of God of the glory which is his due. It is not enough, they urged, to say (as both Romans and Arminians did say) that without Christ our justification would be impossible; one must go on to say that it is on the ground of his obedience, as our representative and substitutionary sin-bearer, and that alone, that righteousness is reckoned to us and sin cancelled. The analysis of justification in the Westminster Confession reflects the precision and balance of thought, as well as the polemical thrusts, that came to focus in these exchanges.

> Those whom God effectually calleth he also freely justifieth; not by infusing righteousness into them, but by pardoning their sins, and by accounting and accepting

their persons as righteous; not for anything wrought in them, or done by them, but for Christ's sake alone, not by imputing faith itself, the act of believing, or any other evangelical obedience, to them as their righteousness; but by imputing the obedience and satisfaction of Christ unto them, they receiving and resting on him and his righteousness by faith; which faith they have not of themselves—it is the gift of God. (XI.i)

Why did the Arminians take the line they did concerning the ground of justification? The answer is that they were driven to it by the inescapable logic of their basic denial that the individual's salvation is wholly God's work, through the effectual calling and sovereign preservation whereby he executes his eternal unconditional decree. The same logic characteristically operates in Roman Catholic thinking too. That the particular denials out of which the Arminian doctrine of justification was built are corollaries of that basic denial becomes clear as soon as they are set out. There were five of them.

The first denial was that man's act of faith is wholly God's gift.

The second denial was that there is a direct correlation in God's plan between the obtaining of redemption by Christ's obedience to death and the saving application of redemption by the Holy Spirit—direct, that is, in the sense that the former secures and guarantees the latter. The Arminian view was that the atonement made salvation possible for all but not necessarily actual for any. This meant abandoning any precise concept of Christ's death as *substitutionary,* for substitution is, by its very nature, an effective relationship, securing actual immunity from obligation for the person in whose place the substitute has acted:

Payment God will not twice demand
First from my bleeding Surety's hand
And then again from mine.

Grotius' famous, or infamous, theory of the atonement as an *example* of the punishment sinners would receive if they did not come to their senses and repent was one of several ways in which the Arminian conception was spelled out.

The third denial was that the covenant of grace is a relationship which God imposes unilaterally and unconditionally, by effectual calling, saying to his elect, 'I will ... and you shall ...'. The Arminian idea was that the covenant of grace is a new law, offering present pardon on condition of present faith and final salvation on condition of sustained faith.

The fourth denial was that faith is essentially *fiducial* (a matter of trustful knowledge, assured and animating, of what another has done). The Arminian alternative was that faith is essentially *volitional* (a matter of committing oneself to do something, i.e., live by the new law which Christ procured). Pietists from the seventeenth to the twentieth century have so regularly fastened onto the Arminian conception as to make it appear an evangelical axiom, but the fact remains that it marks a shift from the original Reformation teaching,[24] and one which can quickly breed both anti-intellectualism and the idea of faith as a meritorious work.

The fifth denial was that the ground of justification is Christ's righteousness imputed. The Arminian notion, as we saw, was that faith itself is the ground of justification, being itself righteousness (obedience to the new law) and accepted by God as such. Arminius' formula was that Christ's righteousness is imputed to us not for righteousness, but as a basis on which faith may be imputed to us for righteousness.[25] Appeal was made to the phraseology of faith being reckoned for righteousness in Romans 4:3, 5, 9 (cf. 11, 13; all echoing Gen. 15:6); but Paul's insistence that the Christian's righteousness is God's gift (5:15–17), and his emphatic declarations that sinners, though ungodly (4:5; 5:6–8), are justified by faith through Christ's blood irrespective of their own works, make this exegesis really impossible.

The Arminian teaching on justification is in effect, if not in intention, legalistic, turning faith from a means of receiving from God into a work that merits before God. As such, it corresponds in principle with the doctrine of the Council of Trent; at this point its critics were right. But it, or perhaps we should say, the way of thinking which it represented, had a wide influence, not least in England. Anti-Puritan, anti-Calvinist Anglicans such as Henry Hammond, Herbert Thorndike, and Jeremy Taylor taught justification on the basis of a personal righteousness which God accepts, despite its shortcomings, for Jesus' sake. They spell out the nature of this righteousness in terms of repentance and effort for holiness, and their concept was canonized after the Restoration by the (unhappily) influential Bishop George Bull, who interpreted Paul by James and understood both as teaching justification by works. (The trick was done by defining faith moralistically, as 'virtually the whole of evangelical obedience,' and 'all the obedience required by the gospel.'[26]) Teaching of this kind led inevitably to a new legalism of which the key thought was that the exerting of steady moral effort now is the way to salvation hereafter. By Wesley's day the true meaning of justification by faith had been forgotten almost everywhere in the Church of England.

Within Puritanism, too, the Arminian doctrine of justification made inroads. The only Arminian Puritan of ability was John Goodwin, author of *Imputatio Fidei* (on Romans 4), *The Banner of Justification Displayed, An Exposition of Romans 9* and *Redemption Redeemed.*[27] Goodwin was a stormy petrel, and although much noticed, he does not seem to have converted many to his opinions. But Richard Baxter, perhaps the greatest of all Puritan devotional writers, urged the Arminian doctrine of justification (for that is what it was) as part of his Amyraldean understanding of the gospel (we shall glance at Amyraldism shortly), and as a result of a generation's campaigning by him in its interest his position had become influential among the heirs of the Puritans in both England and Scotland by the end of the seventeenth century. In the 1690s it was referred to as 'Baxterianism' and (because of the prominence it gave to the 'new law' idea) 'Neonomianism.'[28]

Baxter's view was rooted in a rather quaint natural theology; with Grotius, he thought Bible teaching about God's rule and kingdom should be assimilated to current political theory, or, as he put it, theology should follow a 'political method.' God should be viewed as governor, and the gospel as part of his legal code. Our salvation involves a double justification, one here and a second here-after, and both justifications require a twofold righteousness, Christ's, the meri-torious cause of the enacting of God's new law, and our own, in obeying that new law by genuine faith and repentance. Jesus Christ, who procured the new law for mankind by satisfying the prescriptive and penal demands of the old one, should be thought of as head of God's government, exalted and enthroned to administer the law which his death secured and under it to pardon true believers. Faith is imputed for righteousness here and now because it is real obedience to the gospel, which is God's new law and the new covenant. Faith, however, involves a commit-ment to keep the moral law which was God's original prescriptive code, and every believer, though righteous in terms of the new law, needs pardon every moment for his shortcomings in relation to the old one.

Baxter did battle constantly against those who held the mainstream Re-formed view that the ground and formal cause of our justification is the imput-ing to us of Christ's own righteousness (i.e., his fulfilment of the precept and penalty of the moral law on our behalf). He was certain that this view logically entails antinomianism (i.e., the needlessness of our keeping God's law), on the 'payment-God-will-not-twice-demand' principle: what Christ has done for us we cannot be required to do again for ourselves. At this point in his thinking Baxter assumed, as his Roman Catholic, Socinian, and High Anglican contemporaries also did, that law-keeping has no relevance for God or man save as work done to secure salvation. It is an odd mistake for him to have made, but he never got this streak of legalism out of his theological system.[29] His views had crystallized dur-ing his traumatic time as a chaplain in the 1640s countering real antinomianism in the army, and from then on antinomianism was his *bête noire,* right up to his last months on earth, when by assaulting as antinomian the reprinted sermons of Tobias Crisp, he effectively wrecked the 'Happy Union' between Presbyterians and Independents almost before it had been contracted.[30]

The Crispian controversy of the 1690s produced much heated writing, but the best contribution was the coolest—Robert Traill's *Vindication of the Protestant Doctrine concerning Justification, and of its Preachers and Professors, from the unjust charge of Antinomianism. In a Letter from the Author to a Minister in the Country.* Traill notes, first, that Baxter's scheme does not come to terms with the repre-sentative headship of Christ, the last Adam, as set forth in Romans 5:12ff.—the unique relationship on which the imputing of Christ's righteousness to his people is based—and, second, that the scheme is spiritually unreal, for a sinner pressed in conscience by the burden of uncleanness and guilt finds relief, not by remind-ing himself that his faith is evangelical righteousness according to the new law, but by looking to Christ and his cross. Talk of one's faith and one's righteousness at such a time would be at best a frivolity and at worst a snare. There seems to be no possible answer to that. Not even Baxter's 'politicized' version of the Arminian doctrine of justification will do.

This brings us to the last divergence between Arminian and Calvinist thinking that we shall notice, namely, their different views of God's character. This is a distinct issue from whether he is sovereign in men's response or lack of response to him, and whether he unconditionally elects to salvation or not. The difference emerges as we reflect on the view of the atonement which lay behind Baxter's teaching on justification. Taking a leaf out of Grotius' book, Baxter held that when God purposed to restore fallen man, he carried out his plan not by satisfying the law, but by changing it. In consideration of Christ's death a new law was brought in, waiving the penal requirement of the old law. To be sure, Baxter sees Christ's death as satisfaction (compensation) to the Father for our sins, in a manner reminiscent of Anselm, rather than as a penal example for man's instruction in the fashion of Grotius; yet he is with Grotius in assuming that the demand for retribution in the original law was grounded not in the nature of God, but only in the exigencies of government. What is at issue here is the divine holiness. Mainstream Reformed theology sees both the precept and the penalty of the law of God as permanently expressing his unchangeable holiness and justice, and holds that God does not save sinners at the law's expense; instead, he saves them by satisfying his law on their behalf, propitiating his own wrath by diverting it upon the Son as man's substitute, so that he remains just in judging all sin as it deserves even when he justifies him who has faith in Jesus. The schemes of Grotius and Baxter make the wrath of God against sin a public gesture which is something less than a revelation of God's abiding character; thus they open the door to the idea that a wise benevolence is the real essence of God's moral nature. In due course Unitarians and Liberals latched onto this idea, some of them with grateful backward glances to the Arminians and to Baxter for having pointed the way to their position.[31]

One last fruit of rationalistic Arminianism calls for notice: the modified Calvinism (a 'half-way house between Calvinism and Arminianism,' A. W. Harrison calls it[32]) which the Scot John Cameron developed at the Saumur Seminary, and which history knows as Amyraldism, from Moise Amyraut (Amyraldus), its most copious exponent. Amyraldism affirmed that as Arminianism erred in thinking that unconditional predestination has no place in God's decree to save believers, so supra- and infralapsarians erred in thinking that the Father sent the Son to redeem only the elect. Instead, God first appointed the Son to redeem our fallen race without distinction and then chose whom he would effectually call and preserve to glory. Amyraldism thus fused the Arminian view of indefinite (universal) redemption and of the covenant of grace as identical with the whosoever-will promise of the gospel with the Calvinistic belief in particular election, effectual calling, and final preservation. Baxter found Amyraldism congenial to his 'political method' and lifelong quest for a unitive theology, but Reformed theologians generally have judged it incoherent and lame, and positively anti-biblical in its way of relating the mission of Christ to men's salvation. Certainly, such a view could hardly ever have emerged had there been no felt need for a pacifying synthesis of Calvinism and Arminianism which would give a sense that all had won, and all must have prizes.

Now we move to *evangelical* Arminianism, which had as part of its purpose the reinstating of the Reformation truth of justification which rationalistic Arminianism had so effectively turned out of doors.

Evangelical Arminianism

John Wesley learned moralistic Arminianism from his parents as part of the family doctrine. Both Samuel and Susanna had moved out from Calvinistic non-conformity into Arminian Anglicanism, and were sharply hostile to the teaching they had left behind. (The psychology of such attitudes is well known.) A letter from Susanna to John in 1725, when he was twenty-two, states exactly the view of predestination, and of the meaning of Article 17 of the Thirty-nine, which he always upheld in later life:

> The doctrine of predestination as maintained by rigid Calvinists, is very shocking ... because it charges the most holy God with being the author of sin ... I do firmly believe that God from all eternity hath elected some to everlasting life, but then I humbly conceive that this election is founded in His foreknowledge, according to Romans viii, 29, 30 ... *Whom* in his eternal prescience God saw would make a right use of their powers, and accept of offered mercy, He *did predestinate* ... nor can it with more reason be supposed that the prescience of God is the cause that many finally perish than that our knowing the sun will rise tomorrow is the cause of its rising.[33]

However, John's association with the Moravians, which led to his Aldersgate Street experience of 1738, knocked all the moralism and self-effort out of his Arminianism, and brought in its place a clear emphasis on instantaneous justification through faith[34] as part of an instantaneous new birth, without which there was no true religion. As we hinted earlier, Wesley's stress when presenting conversion as the entrance to authentic Christian life (unlike that of some today who would see themselves as Wesley's successors) was on man's utter and helpless dependence on God to give faith and bring about new birth. This was because Wesley thought of faith, not as decision (to use the modern catchword), but as a compound of trust and assurance, the subjective expression of the Spirit's inner witness. What the Spirit witnessed to in giving faith was the promise of pardon and adoption as applying to oneself. Calvin, speaking here for all the Reformers, had defined faith as 'a firm and sure knowledge of the divine favour toward us, founded on the truth of a free promise in Christ, and revealed to our minds, and sealed on our hearts, by the Holy Spirit.'[35] Wesley's teaching on faith represents a return to this; a return from the world of synergism and self-determination to that of monergism and sovereign grace.

It was Wesley's Aldersgate Street experience that determined his view of faith. There, as his heart was 'strangely warmed' through the reading of Luther on Romans, he entered into what his Moravian friends had told him that real faith was: namely, assurance of pardon and acceptance through the cross. 'I felt I did trust in Christ, Christ alone, for salvation; and an assurance was given me, that he had taken away my sins, even *mine* . . .' Habitually (though not in perfect verbal consistency), Wesley taught that this assurance is an integral element in the faith that God gives—the faith, that is, that saves.[36] Repentance was to him faith's precondition, manifested by sorrow for sin and reform of manners. Sometimes, indeed, as in his 1744 Conference Minutes, he would describe repentance as 'a low state of faith,' or as the faith of a *servant* in contrast with that of a son (compare Gal. 4:1–7; Rom. 8:1ff.); his basic thought, however, was that, whereas repentance is a state of *seeking* God, faith is the state of finding him, or rather of *being found* by him. A person seeking God can do no more than wait on God, showing the sincerity of his quest by the earnestness of his prayers and the tenderness of his conscience, till the light of assurance dawns in his heart. Such teaching is similar to the Puritan doctrine of 'preparatory works,' and led to similar practice in counselling troubled souls: it is a far cry from Dutch Arminianism.

As for Wesley's view of justification itself, it was as far as Wesley knew a return to the Reformers. He spoke of Christ's atoning death in penal and substitutionary terms, and insisted that it was on the grounds of his death, and that alone, that we are forgiven and accepted by God. With perfect sincerity he declared himself in 1765 to have believed about justification for twenty-seven years, 'just as Mr. Calvin does.'[37]

Yet Wesley would never let the world forget that he wanted his teaching taken in an Arminian sense, because Calvinism in all its forms was anathema to him; and this caused him much trouble, mostly unnecessary and of his own making. He always caricatured Calvinism in the same three ways: as antinomian, making holiness needless; as restricting the preaching of God's love to the world (for some reason he was always sure that according to Calvinism only 'one in twenty' is elect); and as fatalistic, destroying moral responsibility, and denying the connection between means and ends in the spiritual realm. At the end of his life he wrote:

Q. 74. What is the direct antidote to Methodism, the doctrine of heart-holiness?

A. Calvinism: All the devices of Satan, for these fifty years, have done far less toward stopping this work of God, than that single doctrine. It strikes at the root of salvation from sin, previous to glory, putting the matter on quite another issue, [i.e., Wesley takes Calvinism to say that men may be saved without holiness by virtue of their election].

Q. But wherein lie the charms of this doctrine? What makes men swallow it so greedily?

A. It seems to magnify Christ, although in reality it supposes Him to have died in vain. For the absolutely elect must have been saved without Him; and the non-elect cannot be saved by Him.[38]

Misrepresentations like this, from a godly man who over fifty years had had many Calvinistic friends and abundant opportunity to read Calvinistic books, argue a degree of prejudice and closed-mindedness which is almost pathological. Perhaps John's invincible ignorance (shared by Charles) as to what Calvinism really was should be seen as a lifelong haunting by the ghost of Susanna. At all events, it became a rod for his back, and for the backs of many others too.

Wesley's first anti-Calvinist eruptions were occasioned by troubles in the Fetter Lane and Kingswood Societies in 1740–41. There were some sharp exchanges, and John, with Charles's help, produced a volume entitled *Hymns on God's Everlasting Love,* in which, along with some vintage Wesley paeans, ditties of this sort were reeled off:

> *God, ever merciful and just*
> *With new-born babes did Tophet fill;*
> *Down into endless torments thrust,*
> *Merely to show his sovereign will.*
> *This is that* Horrible Decree!
> *This is that wisdom from beneath!*
> *God (O detest the blasphemy!)*
> *Hath pleasure in the sinner's death.*[39]

Comment on the tone and content of such lines, and on the degree of pastoral wisdom which they show as a contribution to domestic debate within a young evangelical movement, is surely superfluous.

For all the inflammatory gestures made on both sides, the 1741 debate died down; but in 1770 came bigger trouble. Wesley's Conference Minutes, wishing to make the point (against real or supposed Calvinistic antinomians), that salvation through faith is also, and necessarily, salvation in holiness, were so drafted as to appear to teach, Roman-style, that a man's own works are the ground of his acceptance with God. Having reaffirmed that 'we have leaned too much toward Calvinism' in playing down the fact that a man must be faithful and labour for life and bring forth works of repentance if he is to be saved, the Minutes proceed thus:

Once more review the whole affair.
(1) Who of us is now accepted with God? He that now believes in Christ with a loving obedient heart.
(2) But who among those that never heard of Christ? He that, according to the light he has, 'feareth God and worketh righteousness.'

(3) Is this the same with 'he that is sincere'? Nearly, if not quite. [The Arminian doctrine of 'universal sufficient grace' here comes to the surface.]

(4) Is not this salvation by works? Not by *merit* of works, but by works as a condition.

(5) What have we been disputing about for these thirty years? I am afraid about words . . .

(6) As to *merit* itself, of which we have been so dreadfully afraid. We are rewarded according to our works, yea because of our works. How does this differ from *secundum merita operum*? which is no more than, 'as our works deserve.' Can you split this hair? I doubt [i.e., I rather think] I cannot.

(7) Does not talking . . . of a justified or sanctified state, tend to mislead men; almost naturally leading them to trust what was done in one moment? Whereas we are every moment pleasing or displeasing to God, according to our works . . .[40]

These Minutes sparked off the heated and tragic controversy of the next five years, in which Wesley's lieutenants John Fletcher and Thomas Olivers exchanged fierce literary punches with Toplady, the Hill brothers, and Berridge, while the Calvinist and Arminian segments of the revival movement drifted further and further apart. One comment only, however, is relevant for us: it is no more right to dismiss these Minutes as theologically inept (even though the 1771 Conference admitted that they had been unguarded), than it is right, with A. W. Harrison, to call them, 'apparently innocuous.'[41] They are in truth an object lesson on the tensions and incoherences that necessarily arise as soon as an Arminian, committed as he is to treating man's response to the gospel as man's own contribution, and continuance in grace as contingent on his continued response, tries to state the Reformation doctrine of justification by grace through faith without works. The doctrine he states, whatever he calls it, will appear as justification by works in fact. No man, however confident in manner, can really square this circle. Wesley's various attempts to do so (and he made quite a number) put one in mind of the parody of the Scout song:

> *They said it couldn't be done:*
> *He said, 'There's nothing to it!'*
> *He tackled the job with a smile—*
> *And couldn't do it.*

Which brings us to our next section.

How Far-Reaching Is the Cleavage between Calvinism and Arminianism?

Views differ here. Some maximize the cleavage in terms of theological black and white. In the seventeenth century, for example, Prynne spoke of 'Arminian thieves and robbers,' and Francis Rous told Parliament that 'an Arminian is the spawn of a Papist.' In the eighteenth century the Wesleys, as we saw, told the world that Calvinism was blasphemous, devilish, and spiritually ruinous. Many since have echoed both estimates, and left the matter there. A more discerning approach, however, is that exemplified by William Ames, one of the *periti* of Dort, who wrote: 'the view of the Remonstrants, as it is taken by the mass of their supporters, is not strictly a heresy that is, a major lapse from the gospel, but a dangerous error tending toward heresy. As maintained by some of them, however, it is the Pelagian heresy, because they deny that the effective operation of inward grace is necessary for conversion.'[42] Ames's words alert us to the fact that Arminianisms vary, so that blanket judgements are not in order: each version of post-Reformation semi-Pelagianism must be judged on its own merits. Ames is right. The facts surveyed in this article show clearly the need for discrimination. Thus, it is surely proper to be less hard on Wesleyanism than on any form of Dutch Arminianism, just because (to the loss of clarity and consistency, yet to the furtherance of the gospel) Wesley's teaching included so much Reformation truth about the nature of faith, the witness of the Spirit, and effectual calling. Wesley's Arminianism, we might say, contained a good deal of its own antidote! Its evangelical and religious motivation, also, puts it in a different class from the Remonstrant position.

But why should Arminianisms vary in this way? The final answer is: not because Arminians are personally erratic, but because all Arminian positions are intrinsically and in principle unstable. Arminianism is a slippery slope, and it is always arbitrary where one stops on the slide down. All Arminianisms start from a rationalistic hermeneutic which reads into the Bible at every point the philosophic axiom that to be responsible before God, man's acts must be contingent in relation to him. All Arminianisms involve a rationalistic restriction of the sovereignty of God and the efficacy of the cross, a restriction which Scripture seems directly to contradict. All Arminianisms involve a measure of synergism, if not strong (God helps me to save myself) then weak (I help God to save me). All Arminianisms imply the non-necessity of hearing the gospel, inasmuch as they affirm that every man can be saved by responding to what he knows of God here and now. The right way to analyse the difference between Arminianisms is to ask how far they go in working out these principles, and how far they allow evangelical checks and balances to restrain them.

On all this, we have just three comments to make.

First: the Bible forbids us to take a single step along the Arminian road. It clearly affirms the positions which Dort highlighted: God's absolute sovereignty; human responsibility without any measure of contingency or indeterminacy (look at Acts 2:23!); and a direct connection between the work of Christ in obtaining and applying redemption. The very name of Jesus is itself an announcement that 'he shall save his people from their sins' (Matt. 1:21 KJV). It does not tell us that he will make all men savable, but that he will actually save those who are his. And it is in these terms that the Bible speaks throughout.[43]

Second: if we travel the Arminian road, there are three precious things that we necessarily lose. These are: the clear knowledge of God's sovereignty in our salvation, the clear sight of Christ's glory as the Saviour of his people, and the clear sense of the Christian's eternal security in the covenant of grace. Also, our piety, unless inconsistent with and superior to our principles (as John Wesley's, for instance, seems to have been), must centre on the thought that at each present moment everything—future salvation, present blessing, current usefulness to God—depends on the use I make of opportunities and resources already given, for God, having made me able to do what I should do, is standing back, so to speak, waiting to see if here and now I shall do it. Self-reliance rather than dependence, strain rather than spontaneity, and an anthropocentric fixity on dedication which inhibits the theocentric instinct for doxology will thus become characteristic of our Christian lives, and the inner relaxation and gaiety witnessed to by such outstanding workers for God as Paul, George Whitefield, and C. H. Spurgeon, who knew themselves to be carried along and kept every moment by divine power, is something to which we are likely to be comparative strangers. These are sad, and saddening, losses, which impoverish the children of God in the same way that Roman Catholicism impoverishes them. There is more comfort and joy for God's children set forth in the Scriptures than the Roman and Arminian theologies allow them to possess. At this point, at least, Rous's verdict stands: Romanism and Arminianism show themselves to be all too much akin.

Third: we must acknowledge that professed Calvinists bear some blame for the pilgrimage of others along the Arminian road, both in the seventeenth and eighteenth centuries and since. Arminianism, we have seen, is a reaction, and it seems undeniable that one factor producing it has been Calvinistic theological provincialism, in the sense defined by Mildred Bangs Wynkoop—'any partial truth raised to the status of a whole truth, or any over-emphasis of one segment of theology to the neglect of other emphases.'[44]

What is a Calvinist? Basil Hall speaks of 'that careful balance of [Calvin's] theological doctrines and his organisation of the Geneva Church in relation to the civil power, which constitutes what should properly be called "Calvinism,"'[45] and notes how both Beza and Perkins, the architect of Puritan theology, 'distorted' (there is a value judgement in that word, so it would be better simply to say 'changed') 'that balance of doctrines which he had tried to maintain.'[46] Beza saw Calvinism as a heritage of church doctrine to be preserved, an orthodoxy best thought through in Aristotelian categories and analysed with Aristotelian detachment; thus he became the pioneer Reformed scholastic. He articulated with exact precision the formulae of supralapsarianism, original guilt, and particular redemption, which Calvin had not done, however true it may be that his

thought points in these directions. In his arranging and interrelating of theological doctrines Beza removed predestination back from where Calvin put it in
his final (1559) revision of the *Institutes*—in book III, after the gospel and the
Christian life, so that it appears as undergirding a known salvation, as in Romans
8:29–38—and subsumed it once more under the doctrine of God and providence, as the medievals had done: which was an invitation to study the gospel
promises in the light of predestination, rather than vice versa (an invitation also
given—regrettably, it may be thought—by the Westminster Confession). Perkins based Christian assurance not on Scripture, Christ, being in the church, and
receiving the sacraments, as Calvin had done, but on discerning in oneself signs
of election. Thus Perkins and Beza moved on from Calvin, whether or not they
are judged to have moved contrary to him. Again, many who style themselves
Calvinists today mean hereby to advertise that they accept Beza's scholastic development of Calvin's view of sin and grace, as confessionally restated by the Synod
of Dort and the Westminster divines, and that they value the pastoral, devotional,
and evangelistic use of this development found in the Heidelberg Catechism,
English Puritanism, and the revival tradition from Whitefield and Edwards to
Spurgeon: which too is a moving on from Calvin, however direct or deviant. It
would take a bold man to deny that any theological provincialism might have
entered into this vigorously developed tradition.

Specifically: can it be denied that any stress on God's sovereign predestination which overshadows or makes doubtful the *bona fide* universality and truthfulness of Christ's invitation in the gospel, and man's genuine responsibility before
God for his reaction to it, is an example of theological provincialism? Can it be
doubted that any stress on the believer's continuing sinfulness which undermines
or excludes expectations of present power against temptation and progress in
holiness is another example of it? But it is certain that the sense of being confronted by just these irreligious-seeming provincialisms gave strength and won
adherents to the seventeenth- and eighteenth-century Arminianisms, which both
saw themselves as called to supply the rational, reverent corrective that was then
needed. We must acknowledge that it was in part bad Calvinism that encouraged
this unhappy mistake.

We still conclude, therefore, that Arminianism should be diagnosed, not as
a creative alternative to Reformation teaching, but as an impoverishing reaction
from it, involving a partial denial of the biblical faith in the God of all grace.

The lapse is less serious in some cases, more so in others, but in every case it
calls for responsible notice and compassionate correction. The logical conclusion
of Arminian principles would be pure Pelagianism, but no Arminian takes his
principles so far (otherwise one would call him a Pelagian, and be done with it).
Calvinists should therefore approach professed Arminians as brother evangelicals trapped in weakening theological mistakes, and seek to help them to a better
mind. So we move to our final brief section.

What Are the Causes of Arminianisms, and What Is the Cure for Them?

Satanic malice and the natural darkness of the human mind are, no doubt, contributory causes of Arminianism in its various forms; but what has directly produced it in history, as we have already begun to indicate, is reaction against an image (not necessarily correct) of Calvinism. Arminians appear as men concerned to do justice to four biblical realities: the love of God, the glory of Christ, the moral responsibility of man, and the call to Christian holiness. The reason why they affirm universal redemption, universal sufficient grace, man's ability to respond to God, man's independence in responding, and the conditional character of election, is that they think these assertions necessary as means to their avowed end. Calvinists believe that the Arminian method of safeguarding these four realities actually imperils them, and can argue strongly to this effect; but they can only expect to be listened to if they are showing actual concern for these realities themselves. And if their Calvinism appears hard, cold, and academic, lacking love for God and man, lacking passion for evangelism, lacking both the tender conscience and the burning heart, they must not wonder if their arguments fail to carry conviction. It is to be feared that much of the Arminianism in this world has been due in part, at any rate, to recoil from an unspiritual Calvinism. We are deliberately, in this article, avoiding any attempt to generalize about our situation today; but those who find themselves up against Arminianism (or perhaps it calls itself anti-Calvinism) at the present time would do well to ask whether Calvinists themselves have not had something to do with bringing it into being, by not advancing their doctrine with holy and loving attitudes and actions.

How can Arminianisms be cured? Only God can finally set men's heads right, just as only he can ever set our hearts right. But if we, who stand on the Calvinist side, can learn afresh to explain that true theology must be confessional, a faithful echo of the Bible, neither adding nor subtracting; and that the reality of human moral agency and responsibility in a world where God is Lord is one of the mysteries of creation, which we reverently acknowledge, but do not pretend fully to understand; and that total inability to respond to God is indeed part of the human tragedy; and that the redeeming love of God is not an impotent goodwill that can be thwarted, but a sovereign resolve that not even Satan can stop; and that there is in every regenerate heart a testimony confirming the biblical insistence that it is the triune God, and he alone, who saves us; and that God in the gospel offers pardon and life to every man who hears it, and that none who hears it misses this blessing save by his own unbelief; and that expectant evangelism is every Christian's duty; and that it is the very knowledge that it is God who saves, and that he does not send his word forth for nothing, that upholds our expectancy; and that the reprobates are faceless men so far as we are concerned, so that we can never be sure we have met even one of them—then we may hope to see the children of God returning in increasing numbers from the dry places of Arminianism to the 'old paths, wherein is the good way,' where they will find rest for their souls and power for their lives.

CHAPTER 17

British Theology in the First Half of the Twentieth Century

It is not British theology that has led the world during the twentieth century. The real epoch-makers, those whose work has actually become a theological watershed for Protestantism generally, have been, rather, men like Schweitzer, Barth, and Bultmann—none of them British. Of the greatest British theologians of this century—by common consent, Bishop Charles Gore (d. 1932), Peter Taylor Forsyth (d. 1921), and Archbishop William Temple (d. 1944)—the most that can be said is that they influenced some people inside and outside their immediate circle but few beyond the bounds of the British Isles.

Introduction

British theology last led the world in the seventeenth century when Puritan teaching on the Christian life was the envy of Lutheran and Reformed divines and the stock-in-trade of the New England pulpit. Since then, however, British theology has been consistently insular, occupied with its own internal dialogue, viewing continental and, in this century, transatlantic developments with a sense of detachment, learning from them rather tardily, and contributing little of importance to their discussion. This situation reflects, in part, a difference of cultural and theological background: British theology as a whole, having mainly historical interests and caring nothing for Kant, has never, like German theology, been haunted by the spectre of nihilism nor, like American theology, been infected with the fever of relativism. Also, the British distaste for extremism prompts prejudice against antithetical thinking—such as marks German and American theology—as necessarily unbalanced. Aloofness is a British national characteristic, moreover, that manifests itself in other realms as well. British theology thus stands apart. It lacks insight into the existentialist angst and Kantian phenomenalism which mould German theology, and it does not sympathize with the American habit of treating symbol and myth, rather than truth and fact, as the basic theological categories. British theology, accordingly, has contributed little to the central debates of twentieth-century Protestantism.

It has not been without significance, however, for it has contributed much to the thought of the ecumenical movement. Being conciliatory and pacific, it has preferred a 'both-and' over an 'either-or' formula, and synthesis over antithesis. Continuity, comprehensiveness, and flexibility have been its ideals. Most modern British theologians see themselves as either conservative liberals or (in the case of High Anglicans) liberal Catholics. Many, by latching on to Alec Vidler's distinction between liberalism, a set of nineteenth-century opinions, and liberality, a temper of enquiry and intellectual generosity ('the opposite not of conservative, but of fanatical or bigoted or intransigent'[1]), have made clear their espousal of the latter rather than the former. W. M. Horton's phrase 'adaptive traditionalism' well describes the present British theological temper.

Characteristics of Modern British Theology

Three constant features have marked British theological work during this century: its historical orientation, its ideal of rationality, and its churchly consciousness.

1. *Its historical orientation.* Anglicans are sometimes accused by non-Anglicans of knowing no theology but historical theology, and, although exaggerated, the charge has some validity. But British theologians as a whole tend to prefer an historical to a strictly local or dogmatic method of investigation. While continental writers produce systematic theologies, British divines ponder on the history of doctrine, seeking to adapt and modify traditional views in a way that commends itself to the 'modern mind' (the unacknowledged hero of much modern British theology in this century). And the inevitable danger that arises of compromising opportunism and unprincipled relativism is not always avoided. Yet this approach in modern British theology has produced some of the most scholarly and useful studies of particular doctrines—works, for example, by H. R. Mackintosh, *The Person of Jesus Christ* (Presbyterian, 1912); J. K. Mozley, *The Doctrine of the Atonement* (Anglican, 1916); N. P. Williams, *Ideas of the Fall and Original Sin* (Anglican, 1927); K. E. Kirk, *The Vision of God* (Anglican, 1931); R. Newton Flew, *The Idea of Perfection in Christian Theology* (Methodist, 1934).

The penchant of British divines for the historical approach reflects an instinct for tradition and a sense of history which are as British as they are Christian—perhaps more so! British apologetics, too, are historically slanted: the argument regularly proceeds as if the historicity of the Christian facts is the main thing in dispute, and once their historicity is granted no serious question about their meaning can arise. This naiveté perhaps reflects the fact that British intellectual life is still largely nourished by Christian ideas: secularism has not yet gone so far in Britain as in some other places.

2. *Its ideal of rationality.* Rationality here does not mean rationalism, that spirit which refuses to grant the existence of mystery and the supernatural, and which admits the reality of only what it can comprehend to its own satisfaction; rather, rationality here signifies coherence, both metaphysical and moral. This is the real point of the characteristic 'appeal to reason' in British theology. It is one expression of the above-mentioned love of synthesis. The purpose of this 'appeal to reason' is to show how theology fits in with, illuminates, and perfects the rest of knowledge, and how it integrates and gives meaning to all the experiences of life. The feeling that theological work should have apologetic value in an age of wide defection from Christianity has strengthened this purpose. The quest for rationality has marked British theology in this century in at least the following ways:

(1) It has led theologians to seek a concordat with philosophy, and for nearly forty years to ally themselves with idealism which, first in its monistic form and then as 'personal idealism' (a pluralistic version which replaced Hegel's universal spirit with finite individual spirits), dominated Oxford and the Scottish universities until the 1930s. The theologians embraced idealism because, as a 'spiritual' philosophy which found in personality its highest categories of valuation and interpretation, it seemed to favour theism, and certainly opposed materialism. In 1912 one Anglican enthusiast, R. C. Moberly, called the idealist notion of God as the Absolute 'at once the most refutable and the most religious view of God that has ever been framed.' But this was really inept. Hegelianism means pantheism, and makes a biblical view of creation and sin impossible. Personal idealism implies a finite God in the image of an ideal man. Immanence, taken as an ultimate category of theological explanation, as it is by all forms of idealist theology, implies continuity and correspondence between God and man and leaves no room for anything else. Thus it points away from incarnation to a divinity in every man, away from reconciliation and atonement to the moral and spiritual evolution of the race, away from special revelation to a universal religious consciousness, away from faith in a historical Christ to naturalistic mysticism ('in tune with the Infinite'). Idealism could not, therefore, be other than a systematically distorting factor in all thought about God and the world, man and sin, revelation, miracles, Christology, and the gospel. But this distortion was not seen at first.

Between the two World Wars the needed lessons were learned—but slowly. This learning process William Temple reveals in his theological pilgrimage of over thirty years. Starting from idealism, with a weak Christology,[2] and seeking a philosophical unification of experience under theological auspices (*Mens Creatrix*, 1917), he was driven over the years to a sort of realism by a growing concern to stress features of Christianity which idealism obscures—God's transcendence, the gravity of sin, and hence the rationality of a particular redemptive revelation, and of a personal Incarnation as that revelation.[3] It was a triumph of Christian instinct over philosophical conditioning, a triumph which, by Temple's own admission, the Johannine writings did most to bring about. By 1937 Temple was insisting that sin is an irrational factor in God's world which precludes explanatory syntheses, and in that year he called theologians to 'renewed devotion of their labour to the themes of Redemption, Justification, and Conversion,' as the realm where 'our need lies now and will lie in the future.'[4] In 1942, in a private letter, he explained how through deeper appreciation of the biblical outlook his approach to the ideal of synthesis had been transformed:

> What we must completely get away from is the notion that the world as it now exists is a rational whole—we must think of its unity not by the analogy of a picture, of which all the parts exist at once, but by the analogy of a drama where . . . the full meaning of the first scene only becomes apparent with the final curtain; and we are in the middle of this. Consequently the world as we see it is strictly unintelligible. We can only have faith that it will become intelligible when the divine purpose which is the explanation of it is accomplished.
>
> Theologically, this is a greater emphasis on eschatology . . .[5]

Temple's words effectively mark the end of the idealist epoch in British theology. British theologians as a body are not now committed to immanentism in any form. Yet they retain their rational temper and synthetic instincts, and would never indulge in anything like the Barthian polemic against natural theology (which polemic, indeed, they tend to regard as a sign of shallowness!). Antitheses between theology and particular philosophies they regretfully recognize, but that there is a necessary opposition between theology and philosophy as such they would not admit. (Of course, there are one or two Barthians in Britain, but there are one or two neo-Thomists too!—and at this point they tend to cancel each other out.)

(2) The quest for rationality has led Anglican divines in particular to explore the 'incarnational' approach pioneered in the liberal Catholic manifesto *Lux Mundi* (1889; subtitled 'A Series of Studies in the Religion of the Incarnation'). In this book, Gore and his colleagues used the Alexandrian identification of the incarnate Son with the cosmic Logos, ever active in all nature and all people, as grounds for claiming as Christian such current trends of thought as evolution and socialism. Since *Lux Mundi,* liberal Catholics generally have maintained that it is the incarnation, the taking of manhood into God, rather than the atonement, which throws most light on the meaning of human life, for the incarnation crowned the creative work of the Logos by bringing human nature to the height of its perfection, unattainable otherwise, and demonstrated how, through union with the Incarnate One, our humanity may be perfected also. This consciously anti-Protestant, pro-patristic line of thought has led some Anglo-Catholics to view the church as the extension of the incarnation and to analyse salvation not as forgiveness and co-resurrection with Christ through faith, but as a progressive divinizing of nature through the sacraments. This 'incarnational' approach

fascinated for more than a generation because of its seeming possibilities for synthesis (super-naturalizing the natural). The chief monuments to its influence are Temple's *Christus Veritas,* which argues 'from the emerging series Matter, Life, Mind, Spirit, to the Incarnation as the grade of reality in which humanity is fulfilled,'[6] and Lionel Thornton's *The Incarnate Lord*[7] which uses Whitehead's philosophy of organism to present the incarnation, Scotist-fashion, as the climax of creation. Einar Molland points to this 'incarnational' interest when he comments that if the Orthodox is the 'Church of Easter' and the Lutheran the 'Church of Good Friday,' the Anglican is the 'Church of Christmas.'[8]

(3) Since reason operates in the moral no less than in the metaphysical realm, the quest for rationality has prompted much reflection on the moral coherence of God's ways with man. The desire for a moral rationale of revelation for apologetic purposes goes back through Butler at least to Anselm. But the suggestion that dogmatics itself should consciously follow a moral method of inquiry and exposition was not made until Forsyth put in his famous plea for a 'moralising of dogma,' that is, for reconstructing theology as a 'metaphysic of the conscious' which 'starts with the conviction that for life and history the moral is the real, and that the movements of the Great Reality must be morally construed as they are morally revealed.'[9] No doubt the background of this plea was the anti-metaphysical bias which Forsyth learned from Ritschl; but the actual warrant for it (so Forsyth claimed) is just the Christian revelation itself, which discloses not an impersonal cosmic principle, but a living God who is holy love. Moreover (Forsyth argued), this method is of great importance for commending Christianity to a generation for whom the notion of truth guaranteed by external authority (church or Bible) has become unconvincing: the gospel must be trained on the conscience, and then by its own moral power will evidence itself as truth. In all this Forsyth was voicing something which modern British theologians in general have felt. The moral as well as the metaphysical coherence of the Christian revelation must be shown. Much British doctrinal exposition in recent years has been consciously 'moralized,' but none, perhaps, as successfully as Forsyth's own work.

(4) The ideal of rationality has predisposed British theologians against all dialectical modes of theological thought. The appeal to paradox as an ultimate category finds no response among them, and teaching which multiplies paradoxes finds no favour. The thought of Barth, Niebuhr, and even Brunner (the one neo-orthodox theologian who is widely read in Britain) has made little direct impact in England and not much more in Scotland. The ideal of rationality at the same time prompts British theologians to impute irrational obscurantism to any who are content to be naively biblical, who state and apply what the Bible says simply on the grounds that the Bible says it. This, it seems, rather than any particular doctrinal quarrel, explains why British theologians as a body remain doubtful about Billy Graham, and why the resurgent British evangelicalism of the

post-war years, which by and large is content with naive biblicism, is not much respected in theological circles.

3. *Its churchly consciousness.* Neither in England nor in Scotland is modem theology in any potent sense confessional; yet modem British theologians of all churches and schools have shown a deep awareness that they speak to the church from within the church, and with a responsibility towards the church. This sober awareness has marked not only Anglo-Catholics, with their deep sense of the church's organic life; it has manifested itself also to quite a remarkable degree among liberal thinkers. Between the wars, Schleiermacher's program of distilling doctrine from the church's corporate experience, although out of fashion elsewhere, was widely taken up by British liberal theology. This approach, it was held, was the way to rehabilitate Christianity. In their editorial preface to the volumes of the liberal *Library of Constructive Theology,*[10] W. R. Matthews and H. Wheeler Robinson wrote: 'The authors (in the series) have a common mind ... with regard to the starting-point of reconstruction. They desire to lay stress on the value and validity of religious experience and to develop their theology on the basis of the religious consciousness. In so doing they claim to be in harmony with modern thought ...' The dangers of subjectivism and relativism in such a method are obvious, yet most of the liberals of this period, because of their strong sense of unity with the universal church, were kept from leaving conventional paths very far. Their aim, like Schleiermacher's own, was to reconstruct the old faith from within, and not to recast it into something new from without.

These facts show why British theology during this century, as compared with its German and American counterparts, has been so remarkably stable. Despite weakened conceptions of revelation and inspiration, and persistent shakiness in handling the central doctrines of the gospel—the atonement, justification, faith, the Holy Spirit, the Lord's return—it has remained steady, and potentially disruptive continental developments (in the areas, for instance, of gospel eschatology and form-criticism) have been neutralized before being swallowed. The conservatism of British liberalism, by and large, has been astonishing. There were some extremists, of course, and the limelight they enjoyed sometimes conveyed the impression that the older theology was about to collapse. Since almost all of the most powerful British theologians of the century have been on the side of the creeds, however, such fears have not been well founded at any time. Conservative evangelicals, often oblivious to everything but the place of Scripture, have sometimes been puzzled that, with the prop of an infallible Bible removed, British theology has not collapsed into complete unbelief. But twentieth-century British theology has at no point been a monolithic structure. By its own constant claim, made by all schools of thought (except the conservatives themselves), it has rested on a threefold appeal: (1) to Scripture (as at least a record of revelation, if not a revelation in itself), (2) to the church (creeds, traditions, and corporate experience, however interrelated), and (3) to reason (the mind's eye for coherence and congruity). In this broad-based and nicely balanced structure, the weakening of one buttress has not sufficed to topple British theology. Indeed, the eclipse of idealism, the 'biblical theology' movement, and the growth of an apologetic for special revelation based on the inner coherence of Scripture, plus a growing sense that an evangelical theology focused on grace is at the present time more necessary than a theological philosophy focused on nature, have brought British theology today closer to the faith of the Reformation than it was at the beginning of the century.

Let us now examine some of the changes that have taken place.

Movements in Modern British Theology

For our purposes, the British theological scene at the turn of the last century may be described as follows:

First, Old Testament higher criticism (that is, Wellhausenism) had clearly come to stay. In an age when idealism and Darwinism joined hands to affirm evolution as the only valid category for scientific and philosophical explanation, the scientific status of an evolutionary account of Old Testament theology and religion seemed beyond question. Wellhausenism had captured the British universities and most of the theological colleges, and was rapidly being embodied in standard commentaries and reference books.[11] The magic names in Old Testament study were S. R. Driver, Regius Professor of Hebrew at Oxford, and W. Robertson Smith (d. 1894), higher criticism's martyr, who after losing his Aberdeen chair for heresy became Professor of Arabic at Cambridge, and whose *Religion of the Semites,* according to a first-hand observer, 'was regarded almost as a sort of Bible in itself' by Oxford theological students in the early nineteen-hundreds.[12] The only major attempt to turn the higher critical flank was James Orr's *Problem of the Old Testament* (London: Nisbet, 1906), which won respect for its scholarship but not assent to its argument. In 1907 Orr himself wrote wryly that critical scholarship 'is for the present so settled on its lees in its confidence in its immovable results that little anyone can say will make any impression on it.'[13]

In the New Testament field, however, historical conservatism was the order of the day. It was generally held that the work of the Cambridge Three, B. F. Westcott (d. 1901), J. B. Lightfoot (d. 1889), and F. J. A. Hort (d. 1892), had conclusively vindicated the main outlines of the gospel story. 'Their lasting contribution,' wrote Alan Richardson (his adjective is empirically justified), 'was to show that the Church's ancient faith in Christ Incarnate, Crucified, Risen and Ascended, was in no way imperilled by the most scrupulous employment of critical historical methods but was rather established by it.'[14] Confidence in the substantial historicity of the gospel narrative has persisted throughout this century. Rationalistic gospel criticism, still a live issue in other places, has really been a dead issue in Britain since the century opened. The opinions of Harnack, Schmiedel,

Bultmann, and others who oppose the 'Jesus of history' to the 'Christ of faith' have been respectfully noted and considered; but though their scepticism about the virgin birth, miracles, and bodily resurrection of Jesus has been taken up by some able scholars, the main body of British theologians and New Testament scholars have always opposed them. Before the Second World War, while the Fourth Gospel was somewhat suspect, the reliability of the 'artless' synoptics was steadily maintained; today, the synoptics are suspected of being more midrashic than was once thought, but the historicity of John is affirmed with more conviction than for many years. One British book after another on the Gospels has used the tools of the critical trade to modify sceptical continental extremes. It is this persistent confidence in the essential factuality of the gospel story which largely explains why, on the one hand, British theologians still value historical apologetics, and why, on the other, they do not feel closely involved in the apologetic problems besetting those who, with Bultmann, think that the historical Jesus was totally unlike the Christ of the New Testament.

The main theological question at hand when the century began concerned the nature and status of the Bible. Wellhausenism rules out inerrancy. What, then, becomes of biblical inspiration and authority? Can they be retained, if inerrancy is given up? Scholars laboured to show that they could. Following William Sanday,[15] they remodelled the idea of inspiration by arguing that not the words of Scripture but its authors were inspired. Inspiration (or revelation, for, according to this view, the two words were synonymous) means moral and spiritual illumination, or religious insight. This God gave to the biblical writers as they were able to bear it; they received it more or less faithfully, and verbalized it as best they could. The Bible is thus the record of God's progressive self-disclosure to their conscience and consciousness, and of their own apprehension of him, evolving correlatively. Although not verbally inspired, the Bible may be called the Word of God inasmuch as it contains a record of revelation as given in history. It is the only record of this revelation that we have, and as such is indispensable.

But if the Bible is not all true, how can it be authoritative? This question was answered in terms of the principle that authority in religion has the nature of a moral claim, and does not require for its reality the bestowal of inerrant factual information. The traditional polemic against Roman belief in an infallible church was turned against the doctrine of the infallible book. The true authority of the Bible, it was said, is known in the experience of being 'found' by that in the Bible which evidences itself to us as having the nature of the ethically highest. This experience of moral and spiritual authority should satisfy us. The desire for an infallible Bible, we are now told, is just as improper and irreligious as the belief that we have one is false.

To stop there, as the liberals usually did, leaves unanswered two questions of some urgency. First, different things 'find' different people: how may we know what ought to 'find' us? Second, what is the relation between the moral and spiritual insight enjoyed by the biblical writers and the beliefs about matters of fact with which, to their thinking, all knowledge of God—be it theirs or anyone else's—was bound up? How far may we sit loose to the latter without imperilling our receptiveness to the former? To these questions liberal Protestantism really has no answer. Gore, the liberal Catholic, had one, however. He held that the authority of Scripture, moral and spiritual as it is, is mediated to us, and the necessary area of factual belief circumscribed for us, by the normative witness to essential Christianity which was given by the early church's corporate life and in particular by the ecumenical creeds. On this basis, Gore contended tirelessly and with good effect against those who queried the virgin birth, the dominical miracles, and the resurrection. Critics were quick to point out the peculiarity of a view which ascribes an infallibility to the creeds which it denies to the Scriptures; yet Gore's position was clearly more satisfying to the spirit than the liberal alternative. It is not surprising that in the vacuum created by the rejection of biblical infallibility, and by the liberal failure to offer any certainty in matters of faith, or even to see that man's cry for certainty was any more than weakness of the flesh, Gore's point of view made great headway in the Church of England.

Other features of the situation may be more briefly described. In Christology, two opposite trends were in evidence: the one, humanitarian (Jesus was a God-indwelt man), the other, kenotic (Jesus was God the Son, who, in becoming man, renounced his omniscience, omnipotence, and omnipresence, at least for the period of his earthly life). The latter view was more than an apologetic device for explaining why Jesus' view of the Old Testament differed from Wellhausen's, although it was in this connection that Gore introduced it to England (in *Lux Mundi*). The deepest motive of the kenotic trend was to do justice to Jesus' humanity, and to the moral grandeur of his life and death as man, something which (it was held) classical Christology, concentrating on his deity and ignoring his human limitations, had never done. This motivation is obvious in the three major expositions of the kenotic theme produced in the early years of the century by Frank Weston (*The One Christ*, 1907), H. R. Mackintosh (*The Person of Jesus Christ*, 1912), and P. T. Forsyth (*The Person and Place of Jesus Christ*, 1909). It is in Forsyth, according to Ramsey, that 'kenotic doctrine comes nearest to vindicating itself.'[16] Perhaps it is significant that this very un-Johannine Christology, which divides the indivisible Trinity and changes the unchangeable Word, should have flourished in England just at the time when the Fourth Gospel was under a cloud; that its sternest critic should have been that most Johannine thinker, William Temple;[17] and that during the past twenty-five years, when the Fourth Gospel has been better appreciated, little has been heard of the kenotic theory.

On the atonement, Ritschlian and immanentist influences were inclining men to abandon objective theories for Abelardianism. The chief monuments to this tendency, which began to be reversed soon after the First World War, are H. Rashdall's *The Idea of Atonement in Christian Theology* (1918) and R. S. Franks's two books, *History of the Doctrine of the Work of Christ* (1918) and *The Atonement* (1934).

Eschatology was not seriously studied, except as a biblical curiosity. Universal progress until the kingdom of God had come on earth was assumed by all except the evangelicals. (Most of these were premillennialists, and some held, following J. N. Darby, that the preparousia apostasy had already begun; these views had no influence outside evangelical circles, however.)

From the standpoint of our present concern, the main movements in British theology during this century may be pinpointed under three heads:

1. *The eclipse of evangelicalism.* While the word 'evangelical' may be variously applied, its meaning in Britain was quite definite at the beginning of the twentieth century. It denoted the position of those in all the churches who, in opposition to rationalism on the one hand and sacramentalism (Roman and Anglo-Catholic) on the other, maintained the theology of the Reformation, the piety of the Puritans, and the evangelistic ideals of the eighteenth-century Revival, basing these tenets on a robust belief in the plenary inspiration, entire truth, final authority, and vitalizing power of Holy Scripture as 'God's Word written' (Thirty-nine Articles, 20). In the mid-nineteenth century, evangelicalism was the norm in all British churches except the Church of England, where latitudinarians ruled and Tractarian 'catholics' crusaded. But before the century ended most non-Anglican evangelicals had accepted higher criticism. This proved disastrous, for evangelical theology had been conscientiously monolithic, seeking to be wholly Bible-based and Bible-controlled, and to judge everything by the biblical standard. As a result, when the formal principle of the divine truth of biblical teaching, as such, was given up, evangelical theology literally fell to pieces. Its sharply defined traditional tenets—verbal inspiration, total depravity, sovereign grace, penal substitution, imputed righteousness, final perseverance—dropped from the picture and its doctrinal outlines were blurred beyond recognition. Within a generation, classic evangelical theology, at least at the ministerial level, had almost vanished. The strongest resistance occurred in the Church of England, where many evangelicals rejected higher criticism and preserved their historic position intact. Throughout the first half of the century men like H. C. G. Moule, W. H. Griffith Thomas, and T. C. Hammond maintained a theological testimony to the old paths which, to say the least, was very respectable. But they had little influence on Anglican theological life. J. K. Mozley makes a fair and perceptive comment on this situation:

> The Anglican Evangelicals have had a far more distinguished record in theology than is apt to be recognised. But their influence on the general thought of the Church suffered from, among other causes, their attitude on the subject of the Bible and their inattention to the problems arising in connexion with the philosophy of religion. They were far more rigid in face of the results which were claimed to follow from the methods of Higher Criticism than were . . . the *Lux Mundi* school, while they made no attempt to construct a Christian philosophy of religion, which could appeal on purely intellectual grounds to minds conversant with modern movements in science and metaphysics. It is, of course, possible to hold that in both these respects

the Evangelical theologians were in the right; but it can hardly be doubted that their doctrinal appeal was lessened owing to what seemed to many to be a narrowness in their outlook.[18]

Does this seeming 'narrowness' deserve praise or blame? If praise, perhaps it should be qualified. The evangelicals must certainly be praised for seeing that Wellhausenism cut across Christ's teaching about Scripture, and also for refusing the kenotic explanation thereof, which, as they realized, completely undermines our Lord's authority as a teacher. And they can hardly be blamed for thinking it more important to continue in the evangelistic and pastoral work to which they had given themselves continuously since the awakening of 1859 than to construct religious philosophies. On the other hand, there is no denying that the cultural isolationism into which evangelicals had been falling for half a century was now coming home to roost; they were simply not equipped for the kind of philosophical as well as critical counter-attack that the situation required. Even if they had been—if, shall we say, there had been twenty James Orrs to do battle instead of just one—it is doubtful whether the evangelical impact on an evolution-fixated age would have been any greater than in fact it was.

Just as the first liberal Catholics had wedded Tractarian tradition to current secular trends in *Lux Mundi,* so some Anglican evangelicals left their conservative moorings to champion a parallel synthesis in a book entitled *Liberal Evangelicalism* (1923). They embraced higher criticism and renounced inerrancy; also, they 'sat loose' to the substitutionary doctrine of the atonement. They held that the 'evangelical experience' could be conserved independent of the precise view of Scripture and the Cross that historically had produced it. This contention was wrong, as forty years' trial has shown. The idea is in fact self-contradictory, since 'evangelical experience,' if it means anything at all, means specifically experience which is generated and fed by evangelical doctrine. While liberal Catholicism prospered, liberal evangelicalism languished theologically and, like other mediating theologies, proved to be barren and unstable, or, to use Archbishop Ramsey's polite phrase, 'somewhat viable to the superficial liberal and progressive ideas of the time.'[19] It is not hard to see why this should have been so. Liberal Catholicism is a comparatively stable structure; it has a fixed credal minimum and also a characteristic theological method—a sustained dialectic between the Bible and ecumenical tradition, and between these and current philosophy as well. This approach gives continuity to liberal Catholicism through all its reassessments and reshapings of detail. But liberal evangelicalism was simply an opportunist compromise. Unlike liberal Catholicism, and the older evangelicalism with its biblical method, it had no methodological basis of its own; it merely offered on a pietistic basis an enlarged area for intellectual license. This, perhaps, is the best explanation for what puzzled Mozley, namely, that the liberal evangelicals have made no distinctive contribution to theology at all.[20]

So far, evangelicalism has been discussed purely from the standpoint of its view of Scripture. But in one sense, of course, even if their view of the Bible is unsatisfactory, all who affirm man's helplessness in sin, and salvation by faith in Christ and his atonement, are evangelicals. Two such evangelicals, both Scotsmen, must be cited here: Principal James Denney, of Glasgow, and Principal P. T. Forsyth, of Hackney College, London. They were Britain's greatest theologians of the Cross in this century. Both were self-consciously 'modern men,' committed to biblical criticism and sharing Ritschl's prejudice against 'metaphysical' theology.

But both had revolted as adults against current immanentist, sacramentalist, and un- or anti-dogmatic fashions in theology and religion, and both sought in all that they did to recall men from these barren wastes to the apostolic message of faith in a crucified Saviour. Forsyth had been converted out of liberalism while in the ministry; Denney (so his friend W. R. Nicoll tells us) had been led by his wife to study Spurgeon, whence came 'the great decision of his life,' namely, to centre his ministry wholly on the cross of Christ.[21] Both Denney and Forsyth had the spirit of crusaders, and valued each other as comrades in arms. Denney wrote of Forsyth: 'He has more true and important things to say, in my opinion, than anyone at present writing on theology.' And Forsyth called Denney 'the greatest thinker we have on our side.'[22] Their cast of mind differed, however. Denney, the New Testament exegete, excelled in exact analysis, and his writing was lucidity itself, whereas Forsyth, the theological prophet, used a method of synthetic impressionism and had a written style once unkindly described as 'fireworks in a fog.' But their aims were the same, and their views substantially identical, as their books on the atonement show.[23]

In the first place, both saw the word of the Cross as itself the solution to the problem of authority. Both affirmed that it is simply and precisely the apostolic gospel, and the God and the Christ of that gospel, that are authoritative. What humbles and compels assent and response, they say, is and must be the grace of God in the apostolic apprehension and expression of it, that is, God himself coming to us in Christ, summoning and moving us to faith in the Reconciler and in his finished work. Both thus explain the authority of the Bible in terms, not of the formal factor of inspiration (divine origin) but of its material content and of prevenient grace.

Both stress that, as the gospel is the heart of the Bible, so the atonement is the heart of the gospel. Both point to Calvary for the solution of all spiritual and theological problems. Both view Calvary as the act of a holy God who judges sin, and who saves us from sin through his act of judging it. Both Denney and Forsyth were wary of the forensic categories of an older orthodoxy (which, perhaps, they understood in too external a way). Forsyth, stressing Christ's solidarity with his people as their representative and surety, called the atonement penal (since Christ bore what our sins deserved) but not substitutionary; Denney, on similar grounds, called the atonement substitutionary but not penal. But the difference here was merely verbal. Finally, both emphasized the finished character of Christ's reconciling work, and invoked the resurrection as proof of it.

It is true that their method of analysing Christianity in terms of the apostolic religious consciousness, and reading the New Testament as an expression of this rather than as a written revelation from God, cast such a rationalistic and ultimately agnostic haze over their theology that no amount of stress on the witness of the apostolic consciousness to the objectivity of the atonement and the prevenience of grace could dispel it. Their method was evidently intended to secure the status of the Cross as a redemptive revelation of God, and to establish the normative character of the apostolic preaching, without ever raising the question of whether or not God has *spoken* (verbally, propositionally). What they considered to be the strength of their method might more truly be judged its weakness. Nonetheless, their reassertion of the gospel of atoning grace was one of the finest things that twentieth-century British theology has seen.

But these men were swimming against the stream. While they had many admirers in their lifetime, they had few disciples and no one to carry forward their emphasis. The New Testament gospel was as much out of fashion as biblical inerrancy, and evangelicalism was heavily eclipsed.

2. *The retreat from immanentism.* When this century began, divine immanence, as we saw, was the accepted key-feature for any account of the relations between God and man. But, as indicated above, this immanentist incubus had been shaken off before the middle of the century by a development due to several converging factors.

First, strongly criticized by Cambridge realists (G. E. Moore, B. Russell) in the twenties, and by Oxford logical empiricists (G. Ryle, A. J. Ayer) in the thirties, idealism lost its standing in the universities as a respectable philosophy.

Second, immanentists provoked reaction by running their favourite idea to death, and by putting it to heterodox use in Christology. Thus, in 1907, in a swashbuckling manifesto, *The New Theology*, R. J. Campbell explicitly reduced the incarnation to an instance of immanence, or divine indwelling. Similarly in the early twenties, the leaders of the Modern Churchmen's Union (Anglican) proclaimed a Christology of mere immanence, and claimed a measure of such immanence-incarnation in every man. 'It is impossible to maintain that God is fully incarnate in Christ, and not incarnate at all in anyone else,' said H. Rashdall in 1921. Gore, who had previously criticized Campbell in *The New Theology and the Old Religion* (1908), saw that the root of the trouble in both cases was immanentism pushed to its logical conclusion, that is, the assimilating of divine to human, and human to divine. H. D. A. Major blandly admitted Gore's charge as follows: 'Dr. Gore is correct in affirming that we believe that there is only one substance of the Godhead and the Manhood, and that our conception of the difference between Deity and Humanity is one of degree. The distinction between Creator and creature, upon which Dr. Gore and the older theologians place so much emphasis, seems to us to be a minor distinction ... It is not a moral distinction at all.'[24] But, according to J. W. C. Wand, a first-hand observer, when once the Modernists (as they were called, although their movement had no links with Roman modernism) brought their views into the open, 'public opinion was revolted by the revelation. The movement ... dwindled ... to a position of comparative insignificance.'[25] Immanentism was thus discredited.

Third, the category of transcendence was re-established as fundamental to that of immanence. By their own method (analysis of the religious consciousness) philosophical theologians were driven to stress the 'otherness' of the Immanent, and its felt discontinuity, as well as continuity, with man. Otto's *Idea of the Holy*[26] was influential here. John Oman laboured impressively to vindicate the idea of a personal Supernatural.[27] Temple's work, as we saw, tended in a similar direction. Gore's remarkable apologetic trilogy, *The Reconstruction of Belief*,[28] complemented these developments. Gore's appeal was to divine revelation in history, in the prophets and in Christ, and not at any point to the religious consciousness.[29] His running fight with immanentism, as he built up an orthodox account of God transcendent and triune from biblical history, helped to lead thinkers away from immanentist theory to a different mental method and set of conclusions. The immanentist tide was running out.

Fourth, the Barthianism and neo-Thomism of the thirties, both stressing God's transcendence, knocked further nails into the coffin of immanentism.

Fifth, there was more and more stress on the principle that biblical categories must control the theologian's use of philosophical concepts (such as immanence), and not vice versa. This emphasis was a direct result of the 'biblical theology' movement.

3. *The rise of 'biblical theology.'* Like the discovery of penicillin, the 'biblical theology' movement was in a sense accidental, that is, it was merely the by-product of some other research, in this case gospel study by a Cambridge college chaplain, Sir Edwyn Hoskyns. Pursuing 'the quest of the historical Jesus' as all students of the Gospels had been doing for decades, Hoskyns was led to challenge the liberal Protestant reading of the evidence in a more radical way than had been done for some time. Men like Harnack had presented the historical Jesus as an ethical teacher whose followers deified him and had grafted a mystery cult onto his teaching. But, Hoskyns argued, all the identifiable literary strata of the Synoptic Gospels deal with the same themes: the presence of the Messianic kingdom in Jesus' words and works; the divine necessity of Jesus' death and future return in glory, according to Old Testament prophecy; and the calling of his disciples to share his humiliation now, that they might share his glory hereafter. Denney had anticipated these conclusions in *Jesus and the Gospel* (1908), but without making much impact. When Hoskyns published them, however,[30] their importance was seen at once. They were valued as closing three troublesome gaps which the liberal view had opened.

First, they closed the gap between the Jesus of history and the Christ of faith. The contrast which underlies the synoptic tradition at this point, Hoskyns argued, is not between the Jesus of history and the Christ of faith, but between Christ humiliated and Christ returning in glory.[31] The Christ of apostolic faith is indeed the Jesus of history, risen and exalted as foretold.

Second, Hoskyns's conclusions closed the gap between Palestinian disciple-ship and the developed churchmanship of the apostolic age. The contrast which the evidence offers us here, Hoskyns wrote, is 'not between the disciples of a Jewish prophet and the members of an ecclesiastically ordered sacramental cultus, but between the disciples of Jesus who are as yet ignorant of his claims and of the significance of their own conversion, and the same disciples, initiated into the mystery of his Person and of his life and death, leading the mission to the world.' The faith of the apostolic church is thus a 'spontaneous Christian development' out of Palestinian discipleship. What caused the development was not Hellenism but Pentecost.

Third, Hoskyns's conclusions closed the gap between the two Testaments. Christ and his disciples read the Old Testament as a Christian book, as part one of the story of the acts of God, that looks prophetically towards part two, towards the events which formed the theme of the apostolic witness. The two Testaments, therefore, belong together. Since the New depends on the Old, the two must be read as a theological unity, and read 'from within,' not as records of fitful insights garnered by religious adepts, but as believing testimony to the action of God in fulfilling his plan of history.

Hoskyns's work began a new era in British theology. For a generation now British biblical and theological study has proceeded on his principles, and seems likely to continue to do so. Of *The Riddle of the New Testament,* Professor C. F. D. Moule of Cambridge wrote in 1961: 'The general direction in which the argument moved was ahead of its time then and seems to be more than ever coming into its own now.'[32] Few would disagree. Never, since Hoskyns gave them an approach to the New Testament which shows it to be coherent both internally, part with part, and externally, with the Old Testament, have British biblical scholars as a whole been attracted to views which would divide one part of Scripture from another. Here, as elsewhere, the British theologian holds that the most coherent view is the one most likely to be right. And it is against this background of Hoskyns's solution to the problems of the historical Jesus, and to the unity of the Bible, that British theologians do their work today.

British Theology Today

Because of its complex dialogical method, and its motivating passion for co-herence and continuity, modern British theology is not likely to become seriously unsteady in the foreseeable future. With the Anglicized neo-Thomism of E. L. Mascall and the Scotticized Barthianism of T. F. Torrance as lookouts, no return to immanentism is to be expected. Today everyone stresses the reality of revelation; revelation by divine action is universally affirmed, and room is slowly being made again for its biblical and necessary presupposition, that is, revelation by speech. Although plenary biblical inspiration is not generally admitted, it is a matter of common consent that the Bible is a record of revelation, a witness and response to revelation, and a revealing medium. Many books have been written in recent years expounding its inner unity. That authority belongs extensively to the total biblical interpretation of the total biblical narrative, and within this, supremely to the gospel would be axiomatic with most British theologians today, although the value of this admission must remain problematic so long as biblical facts like the Fall are begrudged factual status. Man's guiltiness and perversity in God's sight is, however, recognized by all, at any rate in general terms. The influential 'social' Trinitarianism of Leonard Hodgson[33] has displaced the implicit Sabellianism of the idealist era. The two-nature Chalcedonian Christology, long maligned by persons who disliked the 'metaphysical' categories of nature and substance, is now widely accepted again, chiefly through Anglo-Catholic advocacy. Kenoticism smoulders, but it has been some time since its ashes were stirred. Abelardianism has virtually vanished: that Christ died as man's representative, that his death was a sacrifice offered on man's behalf that changed man's situation for the better would be generally agreed. There would be disagreement as to how this was accomplished, however, most theologians shying away from the ideas of penalty and substitution. Against a broad ecumenical background the church and the sacraments are themes for sustained debate between 'catholics' and 'protestants.'

This situation, and the conservative tendencies which still operate within British theology, offer some encouragement for evangelicals. Things are better, or at least less bad. Nevertheless, British theology still has two great weaknesses. First, its typical idea of biblical authority (dialectically related to that of church and conscience) lacks the precision which a clear grasp of inspiration, inerrancy, and the relationship between the Spirit and the Word would give. Hence, subjectivist impressionism and unreformed traditionalism frequently mar British discussion of the details of doctrines; also, as long as doubts remain as to whether biblical assurances, purporting to be divine promises, really are so, the door is barred against an entrance, theological or experiential, into the biblical view of the life of faith as a matter of 'standing on the promises of God.' Second, British theology is not evangelical enough in its interests. The concentration on redemption, justification, and conversion, for which Temple called in 1937, has not been forthcoming. Tomorrow's theologians will evaluate today's work on the atonement as undistinguished; and for more than a century no British theologian has written a treatise on justification or regeneration. When asked, 'What is the gospel?' the trumpets of British theology give a very uncertain sound. But this is no wonder, when those who walk in the old paths of evangelical faith have been out of the British theological conversation for so long. It is greatly to be hoped that they will regain their place in this conversation, for the indicated weaknesses in British theology are such as only evangelicals themselves are ever likely to correct.

CHAPTER 18

The Theological Challenge to Evangelicalism Today

Let me begin by commenting on the title that I have chosen. My title speaks of a *challenge.* This is an overworked word; perhaps I should apologise for using it. My only defence is that I am using it in its strict and full meaning, and for this there seems no alternative word available.

What is a challenge? It is a demand, and a demand of a particular kind. It is a demand that measures a man. It is a demand that one is in honour bound to meet. It is discreditable to fail to respond to a challenge. I am going to suggest that our present situation issues a challenge to us—that it makes a demand upon us which we are in duty bound to meet; and that it will be to our discredit as evangelical churchmen if we fail to meet it.

My title speaks of a challenge to *evangelicalism.* This is a cheapened word; many use it to mean nothing more than low churchmanship, or some general interest in evangelism. But I am using it here in a sense corresponding to that which 'evangelical' bears in the title of this Fellowship. In other words, I am thinking of evangelicalism within the Church of England, and I mean by evangelicalism in the first instance adherence to a definite doctrinal position, on which one's churchmanship, evangelism, and pastoral practice are based. The rest of the Church calls this position 'conservative' evangelicalism, and we may for the moment accept the title.

My title speaks of a *theological* challenge to evangelicalism. Now some would tell me straight away that it is a waste of time talking to evangelicals about theology. Evangelicals, they would tell me, are not interested in theology; they never have been; theological interest is not part of the evangelical ethos; evangelicals are practical people, and therefore(!) impatient of theology. Give them an evangelistic or pastoral challenge, and they will rise to it; but talk to them about a theological challenge, and you are asking for the cold shoulder. 'Theology is not our business,' they will say, 'we leave all that to others.' So I should be told by certain people; but frankly I do not believe a word of it.

Outstanding Theologians

To start with, it is not true as a statement of past history that evangelicals have never been interested in theology. Not to speak of the Reformers of the sixteenth century, and the Puritans of the seventeenth, let us just think of the century and a half between 1840 and 1990—a century and a half which from some standpoints was a time of evangelical decline. Consider these names: Dean Goode; E. A. Litton; R. B. Girdlestone; T. P. Boultbee; Nathaniel Dimock; John Stott; Bishops Ryle, Moule, and Knox; and in Australia, T. C. Hammond, Leon Morris, and D. B. Knox.

Were these not evangelicals? And were they not theologians? In all seriousness, I ask: did any other section of the church produce twelve theologians of equal calibre during those 150 years? I do not think so.

Nor do I believe it to be true as a statement of present fact that evangelicals are not interested in theology. For what is theology? Theology is just the systematic, scientific study of Holy Scripture regarded as a written revelation of truth from God. Theology is just seeking to know the whole mind of God on every subject on which he has spoken.

And what is theology for? Theology is for the purpose of deepening our faith and increasing our knowledge of God, and preserving us from errors of belief and behaviour, so that we may save both our own souls and the souls of others.

And why is theology necessary? Because being human, we must think; and, being Christians, we must think about God; and if our thoughts about God are not true—good theology—then they will be false—bad theology. The only alternative to good theology is bad theology; and the only cure for bad theology is better theology. I do not believe that evangelicals are unaware of these things, or unconcerned about them, and therefore when I am told that evangelicals are not interested in theology I refuse to believe it. I do not believe, therefore, that it will be impossible to interest you in my present subject!

Two Questions

What, then, is the theological challenge that faces us today?

May I introduce it in a general way, by putting two questions.

First: *What is evangelicalism?*

In a word, evangelicalism is Bible Christianity, gospel Christianity, apostolic Christianity, mainstream Christianity. It is an understanding of the Christian revelation based upon two principles: the final authority of Holy Scripture in all matters of faith and life, and the centrality of justification by faith in the Lord Jesus Christ.

Second: *When is evangelicalism challenged theologically?*

A theological challenge is issued to evangelicalism whenever the church loses, or threatens to lose, its grip on the gospel, or whenever Christians cease to walk according to the truth of the gospel.

Consider these two types of situation separately.

(1) The Church loses its grip on the gospel whenever it falls under the sway of an outlook that would swallow up the gospel by assimilating it into a larger, non-evangelical whole. The New Testament provides illustrations of this. For instance: Paul wrote to the Galatians because there the gospel was in effect being swallowed up by *legalism*. Certain people were teaching that faith in the Lord Jesus Christ was certainly a good start for Gentiles, but that obedience to the Jewish law must be added to it if Christian Gentiles were to be counted among the seed of Abraham in an unqualified way and receive the full promised blessings of the Abrahamic covenant.

Or again: Paul wrote to the Colossians because there the gospel was in effect being swallowed up by *polytheism*. Certain people were teaching that faith in the Lord Jesus Christ was certainly an excellent thing, but that the worship of angels must be added to it if Christians were to enjoy the fullness of salvation.

The most fundamental fault of both heresies was that they sought to add to the gospel of salvation by faith in Christ, thus treating it as no more than a part of a larger and more comprehensive whole. Paul answered both in the same way, by asserting the sufficiency of Christ as Saviour and the completeness of the salvation that believers have in him.

(2) Christians cease to walk according to the truth of the gospel either when they let their lives be governed by doctrinal error (as when the Galatians kept 'days, and months, and seasons, and years' [Gal. 4:10 RV] according to the Jewish ceremonial law and the Colossians worshipped angels [Col. 2:18] as their mentors taught them to do), or when they compromise the truth in practice under pressure from an influential body of non-evangelical opinion (as when Peter withdrew from table-fellowship with Gentile Christians at Antioch under pressure from the Jerusalem party [Gal. 2:12]). Paul withstood such errors of practice no less vigorously than he opposed deviations from evangelical doctrine.

Now, what I want to suggest to you is that evangelicals today face a situation in which all these tendencies appear in modern dress, and that this situation issues to us a theological challenge.

Ecumenical Outlook

The dominant factor in the present church situation is undoubtedly the ecumenical outlook. This has popularly given rise to the idea that Christian truth has been 'fragmented,' by reason of the divisions of Christendom, into a series of isolated and partial 'insights,' at present scattered abroad through the various theological traditions within the Christian church; and that what is needed is to gather them all together and construct from them a grand synthesis in which all will find a place—a sort of theological rissole, or Irish stew. The common ecumenical estimate of evangelicalism is that it is one among these many traditions, due in time to be assimilated into the larger whole.

The first consequence of this estimate is pleasing and encouraging. It is to create a new respect for some of the things that evangelicals say. On the subjects of personal religion and evangelism, many non-evangelicals now freely admit that evangelicals have much to teach that they and the churches generally need to learn.

This is in happy contrast with the situation fifty, sixty, and seventy years ago, when evangelicalism was widely regarded as a fossilized relic, having nothing to contribute to the contemporary situation, and doomed soon to peter out and become extinct.

But the second consequence of this estimate is neither pleasing nor encouraging. It is to create the feeling that evangelicals ought to take as well as to give. Evangelicals are addressed (as, for instance, by the Anglo-Catholic Gabriel Herbert, in *Fundamentalism and the Church of God*[1]) in terms that amount to something like this:

> The exchange has got to be a two-way business. We have been willing and glad to learn from you the things that you have to teach us; now you must be ready to learn from us the things that we have to teach you—about the priesthood, for instance, and the sacraments, and the eucharistic sacrifice, and other things in which the 'catholic' tradition has specialised. It would be very proud and standoffish on your part if you refused to let us enrich your tradition from our tradition. It would be like the standoffishness of the Corinthian schismatics; it would be sinful, and wrong. And it would hinder our common advance towards the richer ecumenical theology that is to come, which is going to be catholic and evangelical and everything else too.

Now we see the nature of the theological challenge which faces evangelicals today. It is to discern what reply we should make to these rather patronising ecumenically minded overtures. We are asked to enter into conversation about these things—very well, we must not refuse to talk when others are anxious to talk with us, but we must be clear as to what we ought to say, and what points need to be made for the safeguarding of the gospel in our present situation.

The suggestion is that evangelicalism should be regarded, and should learn to regard itself, as one tradition among many, both in Christendom and in Anglicanism, and that the way ahead is for evangelicalism to be assimilated into a larger whole in which all traditions unite. Should we accept this estimate, as a basis for discussion with non-evangelicals?

Evangelicalism Is Christianity

We should not. On the contrary, in all such conversations and exchanges we should seek to maintain and vindicate the following two principles.

(1) The first principle is that *evangelicalism is Christianity*. This is a big thing to say, but nothing less than this is big enough to counter the ecumenical estimate of evangelicalism. As against the view that evangelical theology is a fragment of truth, needing to be filled out from other sources, we must maintain that, in principle at any rate, evangelical theology is the whole truth, and that, to the extent that you deviate from the evangelical position, you deviate from Christianity itself. And we have a solid argument in our hands to prove that. The argument is drawn from the nature of evangelical theology itself.

What is the nature of evangelical theology? It crystallises in the little word 'only.' Its axioms are the principles of justification by faith *only*, apart from human works; and of acceptance through Christ *only*, without human merit and indeed in defiance of human demerit; and of salvation by grace *only*, not by human endeavour; and of glory to God *only* for salvation, without man having anything of which to boast; and of saving knowledge: by Scripture *only*, without human tradition or speculation coming in to supplement it.

Now the argument is this: that you cannot add to evangelical theology without subtracting from it. By augmenting it, you cannot enrich it; you can only impoverish it. Thus, for example, if you add to it a doctrine of human priestly mediation, you take away the truth of the perfect adequacy of our Lord's priestly mediation. If you add to it a doctrine of human merit, in whatever form, you take away the truth of the perfect adequacy of the merits of Christ. If you add the idea that the essence of sacramental worship (and especially at the Lord's Supper) is receiving Christ and his benefits by faith in the 'visible word' of the sacramental sign. And so we might go on. The principle applies at point after point. What is more than evangelical is less than evangelical. Evangelical theology, by its very nature, cannot be supplemented; it can only be denied. And all attempts to supplement it are in effect denials of it at one point or another.

The way ahead, therefore, is the way, not of synthesis, but of reformation. Our ecumenical programme, as evangelicals, must take the form of a summons to all traditions in Christendom that have lost touch with evangelical faith and theology to do as we have sought to do, and submit: to being reformed—corrected and reshaped—by Holy Scripture. This is a large demand, admittedly, but theologically it is the only demand that we can make with a good conscience. To be cowed into asking non-evangelical Christendom for anything less would be to compromise the truth. We should not be meeting the challenge of our situation if as evangelicals we asked merely to be tolerated and left in peace. This is a time for thinking big, and talking on an ecumenical scale. And what we have to say when we talk on this scale is that Christianity, in its own nature, is just evangelicalism, and evangelicalism, in its own nature, is just Christianity: neither more, nor less.

Evangelicalism Is Anglicanism

(2) The second principle for which we have to stand is that *evangelicalism is Anglicanism.*

Numerically, it is of course true that evangelicals make only a minority in the Anglican Communion, and some are inclined to speak of them as having only at best squatters' rights there. By right of history and theology, however, evangelicals have a title to the whole estate, and our situation challenges us to state, and prove, that this is so. In order to make out our claim, there are two things in particular that we need to contend for at the present time.

(a) *A confessional definition of Anglicanism.*

It is habitual today to define Anglicanism in terms of the Anglican Communion as a whole, and to do so on the principle that 'whatever is, is right'—in other words, to equate Anglicanism with whatever the Anglican Communion happens to have become. What sort of definition is produced by this method? The most that can be said is that Anglicanism is a diversified liturgical ethos growing on a family tree of Orders. (Pardon the odd metaphor—it describes an odd thing.)

What the Anglican Communion has in common is the fact that all its prayer books have some genealogical link with 1662, and all its Orders can be traced back to Archbishop Matthew Parker. Beyond this, there is no common factor; for most of the churches in the Anglican Communion have ceased to demand clerical subscription to any part of the Thirty-nine Articles, and some do not even print them in their Prayer Book.

Properly speaking, of course, Anglicanism means the religion of what Magna Carta called the *ecclesia Anglicana,* the Church of England. To find out what this religion is, one ought to look at the constitution of the Church of England, as historically settled. However, the desire to define Anglicanism in terms of what the Anglican Communion is today has led some to dabble in the black art of hindsight, and to rewrite the relevant history retrospectively, in order to make out that what the Anglican Communion is today the Church of England always was. Here, for instance, are some remarkable statements taken from an editorial in *The Times* commenting on the plea made last year (1960) by the Dean of St. Paul's for a revision of the Thirty-nine Articles. (I quote them, may I say, not because they are in any way authoritative, but because they are representative of accepted ways of thinking. An opinion has to be pretty respectable, and pretty well established, before it gets into an editorial in *The Times!*) Now note what is said.

> It is part of the essence of Anglicanism [affirms the writer] to hold that [what Christians believe] is better expressed in the forms of corporate worship than in

theological definitions . . . It is the Book of Common Prayer . . . and not the Articles, in which Anglicanism consists.

What is the significance of the Articles, then? we ask. And this is what we are told.

Their (the Articles) essential merit is that they were the work of politicians concerned to find formulae which would enable men of diverse theological opinions to maintain a common religious practice.

This is smooth and confident speaking. The writer evidently has no qualms as to the truth of what he is saying. But the facts of history tell a completely different story.

Were the Articles drawn up by politicians? No; they are the work of theologians, chiefly Archbishop Cranmer.

Were they meant to function as ambiguous compromise formulae, holding together men of really divergent convictions? No; to start with, they are not ambiguous at all in their historical setting; and furthermore, it is clear that the intention of those who drew them up and required subscription to them was to ensure that nobody who did not believe as much as the Articles asserted should be able to officiate in the Anglican ministry. Bishop Pearson correctly characterised their aim and nature when he wrote, three centuries ago, as follows:

The book [of Articles] is not, nor is pretended to be, a complete body of divinity . . . but an enumeration of some truths, which upon and since the Reformation have been denied by some persons; who upon denial are thought unfit to have any cure of souls in this Church and realm; because they might by their opinions either infect the flock with error or else disturb the Church with schism or the realm with sedition.[2]

What, then, of the much-vaunted comprehensiveness of the Articles? It consists precisely in the fact that they are minimal in what they require, and leave free to differ on many subjects on which other Reformation creeds laid down a precise determination. But it was never intended that the Church of England should accommodate clergy who fell short of the minimum which the Articles define.

In view of these facts, it seems unhistorical nonsense to say that the Articles are not of the essence of Anglicanism. The truth (unquestioned in the Church of England till a century ago) is that the Articles are basic to the life and outlook of the Church of England, for they constitute the Church of England's confession of its faith.

Three Things Follow

But if this is so, then three things follow at once.

It follows, *first,* that Anglicanism, the religious position of the Church of England, is essentially a confessional position, to be defined in terms of the Thirty-nine Articles.

It follows, *second,* that Anglicanism is evangelicalism, and evangelicalism is Anglicanism, inasmuch as the faith defined in the Thirty-nine Articles is the evangelical faith, founded on the twin principles of biblical authority and justification by faith.

It follows, *third,* that the Anglican Communion, so-called, is theologically a very problematical phenomenon; for most of the daughter churches in the Anglican family have formally dropped the mother church's confession of faith, and then gone on to revise their prayer books on non-evangelical principles. What significance can be held to attach to the concept of a 'Communion' in these circumstances? The answer is not obvious.

But the one thing that does seem obvious in our present situation is that it is part of our responsibility as evangelicals to insist on a confessional definition of Anglicanism, in terms of the Thirty-nine Articles.

That means that we must continue to maintain the positive significance of clerical subscription. For a century the Church of England has been asking itself the wrong question about clerical subscription—the question, namely, how little subscription need mean. But surely the right question to ask is how much the act of subscription ought to mean. We must raise this question, and answer it by insisting that the act of subscription ought to imply a true and hearty endorsement of the doctrine, and the proportions, and the stresses, of the Articles, and a firm intention of teaching their doctrine, and living by it, and seeking to order everything in the Church's outward life in accordance with it.

Prayer Book Revision

This brings us to the second thing that we need to stand for in the present situation.

(b) *A confessional check on Prayer Book revision.*

We live in an era of liturgical change and experiment. We cannot change that fact, even if we would. Nor, surely, is it necessarily a bad thing to try and revise and perhaps amplify our statutory services, provided that this is done in the light of the doctrine of the Articles, and with the intention of expressing that doctrine more fully and effectively in our public worship today. Unfortunately, however, that is not how it is being done.

It is most disturbing to find ourselves offered new services which represent a deliberate attempt to get away from truths that the Articles teach, and which our present services clearly embody. It is disturbing, for instance, to find that in the proposed new baptism services the doctrine of original sin fails to appear, and, though they speak explicitly of the water as mystically washing away sin, they make no clear reference to the death of Christ as the ground on which sins are forgiven: and that despite the emphatic assertions of original sin in Article 9 and of the meaning of Christ's death in Article 2. It is disturbing also to read in the 1958 Lambeth Report how desirous the bishops are to have a new eucharistic liturgy for the whole Anglican Communion which will make the essential action of the service, not the sacramental receiving of Christ, but the symbolical self-offering of the worshippers in Christ: and this despite the emphasis on receiving in Article 28. How, we ask, can clergy who have cordially subscribed the Thirty-nine Articles be expected to approve of such services? It would be scandalous if they could.

What we need to plead for, in the present situation, is that the work of Prayer Book revision should be governed at each stage by the relevant teaching of the Thirty-nine Articles. In the realm of liturgical revision, the Church of England is at the moment allowing itself to behave in a way which is not merely irrational, but positively schizophrenic; for the new Canon II affirms that the Articles are 'agreeable to the Word of God, and may be assented to with a good conscience by all members of the Church of England,' and yet here is this endeavour being made to enrich our worship by means of new services which represent a retreat from the Articles! This sort of thing will make the Church of England a laughing-stock. In the name of common sense, as well as of revealed truth, evangelicals are challenged by this situation to raise their voices against the threatened separation of our liturgy from our Articles, and to demand a full acceptance of the principle that the faith of the Articles must decisively control any attempted revision of the Prayer Book.

Such are some of the main ways in which the present situation seems to me to issue a theological challenge to evangelical churchmen. I hope and pray that under God we may be enabled to meet the demands which it makes upon us.

Notes

Notes to Chapter 1

LUTHER was an address originally published in *Approaches to the Reformation of the Church,* Puritan and Reformed Conference Reports, 1965, pp. 25–33. Reprinted by permission.

Notes to Chapter 2

JOHN CALVIN AND REFORMED EUROPE was originally published in *Great Leaders of the Christian Church,* ed. John Woodbridge (Chicago, Moody Press, 1988), pp. 208–15. Reprinted by permission.

Notes to Chapter 3

A MAN FOR ALL MINISTRIES was originally presented as the St. Antholin's Lectureship Charity Lecture, 1991, and published by the Charity in London by Needham's. Reprinted by permission.

1. Preface to *Reliquiae Baxterianae (RB),* sec. 2, p. 2.

2. Quotations are from *The Autobiography of Richard Baxter,* ed. J. M. Lloyd Thomas (London: J.M. Dent, 1931), *RB,* pp. 106, 107–8, 112, 115, 117, 118–19, 125, 130–31.

3. The details are from an eye-witness account reproduced in *Autobiography,* pp. 58–264.

4. Quoted from *Autobiography,* p. 298.

5. *RB,* part 1, pp. 21, 84–85.

6. Ibid., p. 89.

7. Ibid., pp. 93–94.

8. *Practical Works* (Soli Deo Gloria, 1991), III; pp. 585–86.

9. *Autobiography,* p. 293.

10. Hugh Martin, *Puritanism and Richard Baxter* (London: SCM Press, 1954), p. 173.

11. Published as *The Reverend Richard Baxter's Last Treatise,* ed. F. J. Powicke (Manchester: John Rylands Library, 1926).

12. *Richard Baxter and Margaret Charlton: A Puritan Love Story,* ed. J. T. Wilkinson (London: George Allen and Unwin, 1928), pp. 110, 152; Baxter's memoir has now been reprinted as J. I. Packer, ed., *A Grief Sanctified* (Ann Arbor: Servant Books, and Leicester: Crossway, 1998).

13. See now *A Grief Sanctified.*

14. Matthew Sylvester, *Elisha's Cry after Elijah's God,* appended to *RB,* p. 1.

Notes to Chapter 4

THE SPIRIT WITH THE WORD: THE REFORMATIONAL REVIVALISM OF GEORGE WHITEFIELD was originally published in *The Bible, the Reformation and the Church: Essays in Honour of James Atkinson,* W. P. Stephens, ed., Journal for the Study of the New Testament, Supplement Series 105 (Sheffield: Sheffield Academic Press, 1995), pp. 166–89. Reprinted by permission.

1. Wesley's journal (actually, a sequence of twenty-one journals) fills the first four volumes of his *Works* (ed. T. Jackson; 14 vols.; repr. Grand Rapids: Baker Book House, 1986). See also *The Journal of John Wesley* (ed. N. Curnock; 8 vols.; London: Epworth Press, 1938).

2. The writings in question are *A History of the Work of Redemption* (sermons preached in 1739; book published in 1744); *The Distinguishing Marks of a Work of the Spirit of God* (1741); *Thoughts on the Revival of Religion in New England in 1740* (1742); *A Treatise on the Religious Affections* (1746); all contained in *Works* (ed. E. Hickman; 2 vols.; repr. Edinburgh: Banner of Truth, 1974).

3. A. Dallimore, *George Whitefield* (2 vols.; I, London: Banner of Truth, 1970; II, Edinburgh: Banner of Truth, 1980), II.521.

4. Wesley, *Works,* III.238. Other similar comments: 'Humanly speaking, he is worn out' (p. 133; May 1763). 'His soul appeared to be vigorous still, but his body was sinking apace' (p. 354; March 1769). Whitefield died on September 30, 1770.

5. Ibid., VI.177.

6. Dallimore, *George Whitefield,* I.381–83.

7. Ibid., II.149–59.

8. H. S. Stout, *The Divine Dramatist: George Whitefield and the Rise of Modern Evangelicalism* (Grand Rapids: Eerdmans, 1991), pp. 144–47. Whitefield's paper was called *The Weekly History; or, An Account of the Most Remarkable Particulars Relating to the Present Progress of the Gospel.*

9. Dallimore, *George Whitefield,* II.531.

10. Dallimore calls it 'St Mary's' (*George Whitefield,* I.50) and 'the de Crypt School' (II.528), but is wrong both times. It was always 'the Crypt school' *simpliciter.* Stout, *The Divine Dramatist,* p. 2, moves the school, with the Bell Inn, Whitefield's home (almost next door), and Southgate Street where both stood, from Gloucester to Bristol—a spectacular slip.

11. 'There is no end to the interest which attaches to such a man as Whitefield. Often as I have read his life, I am conscious of a distinct quickening whenever I turn to it. *He lived.* Other men seem to be only half alive; but Whitefield was all life, fire, wind, force.

My own model, if I may have such a thing in due subordination to my Lord, is George Whitefield' (quoted from L. Drummond, *Spurgeon, Prince of Preachers* [Grand Rapids: Kregel, 1992], p. 219).

12. See Lloyd-Jones's appreciation of Whitefield, 'John Calvin and George Whitefield,' in *The Puritans: Their Origins and Successors* (Edinburgh: Banner of Truth, 1987), pp. 101–28. 'I could imagine no greater privilege, than to speak on George Whitefield,' p. 102.

13. *George Whitefield's Journals* (London: Banner of Truth Trust, 1960).

14. *Letters of George Whitefield, 1734–42* (Edinburgh: Banner of Truth, 1976).

15. See n. 3 above. The adjective 'filiopietistic' comes from Stout.

16. London: Hodder & Stoughton, 1973.

17. See n. 8 above.

18. Published quarterly by Christianity Today, Inc., 465 Gundersen Drive, Carol Stream, IL 60188.

19. 'He had a most peculiar art of speaking personally to you, in a congregation of four thousand people' (Cornelius Winter, who was Whitefield's factotum and travelling companion, 1767–70, in Dallimore, *George Whitefield*, II.482).

20. Lloyd-Jones, 'John Calvin and George Whitefield,' p. 117. I cannot track down Lloyd-Jones's reference to Wesley; but his journal for February 1750 contains this equally condescending comment: 'Mr. Whitefield preached . . . Even the little improprieties both of his language and manner were a means of profiting many, who would not have been touched by a more correct discourse, or a more calm and regular manner of speaking' (Wesley, *Works*, II.172). And later that year: 'I have sometimes thought Mr. Whitefield's action was violent' (*Works*, II.195).

21. Lloyd-Jones, 'John Calvin and George Whitefield,' p. 117.

22. Stout, *The Divine Dramatist*, pp. 9–10.

23. Ibid., p. xix.

24. Compare Winter's observations, from the end of Whitefield's life: 'It was truly impressive to see him ascend the pulpit. My intimate knowledge of him admits of my acquitting him of the charge of affectation. He always appeared to enter the pulpit with a significance of countenance, that indicated he had something of importance which he wanted to divulge, and was anxious for the effect of the communication.' 'I hardly ever knew him go through a sermon without weeping, and I truly believe his tears were the tears of sincerity. His voice was often interrupted by his affection.' 'His freedom in the use of his passions often put my pride to the trial [i.e., embarrassed me]. I could hardly bear such unreserved use of tears, and the scope he gave to his feelings, for sometimes he exceedingly wept, stamped loudly and passionately, and was frequently so overcome, that for a few seconds, you would suspect he never could recover' (Dallimore, *George Whitefield*, II.482–83).

25. Stout, *The Divine Dramatist*, p. xxii.

26. Ibid., p. xxiii.

27. Dallimore, *George Whitefield*, II.286.

28. *Evangelical Dictionary of Theology*, ed. W. Elwell (Grand Rapids: Baker Book House, 1984), *s.v.* 'Pietism,' pp. 855–56.

29. See D. Crump, 'The Preaching of George Whitefield and His Use of Matthew Henry's Commentary,' *Crux* 25.3 (September 1989), pp. 19–28. 'Usually, for an hour or

two, before he entered the pulpit, he claimed retirement; and on a sabbath morning more particularly [when in London, where he had two pulpits to serve, and a new sermon was needed each Sunday], he was accustomed to have [Samuel] Clarke's Bible [a Puritan product, reprinted in 1759 with "A Preface to the Serious Reader" by Whitefield: see *Works of George Whitefield* (ed. J. Gillies; London, 1771), IV.275ff.], Matthew Henry's Commentary, and Cruden's Concordance within his reach' (Winter, in Dallimore, *George Whitefield,* II.481).

30. *Letters of George Whitefield,* 1734–42, pp. 98, 79.

31. Ibid., p. 442.

32. *Works,* IV.306.

33. *The Revived Puritan. Select Works of the Rev. George Whitefield, Containing a Memoir . . . Thirty Sermons . . . Fourty Seven Discourses . . . A Compendium of his Epistolary Correspondence . . . In One Volume* (Lewes: Sussex Press, John Baxter, 1829).

34. See the biographies, especially those of Tyerman, Pollock, and Dallimore. All the biographies are captivated, more or less, by Whitefield's personal qualities.

35. Dallimore, *George Whitefield,* II.222.

36. Ibid., II.453.

37. Ibid., II.295–303.

38. 'I was stunned to see his amazing wisdom, wherein he is taught to manage the Church, doing all calmly and wisely, following the Lord' (*Howell Harris, Reformer and Soldier,* ed. T. Beynon [Carnarvon: Calvinistic Methodist Bookroom, 1958], p. 41).

39. It should be noted that the publishing of Whitefield's journals began without his consent. On his return to England from Georgia in 1738 he found that James Hutton, an ardent supporter, had at this point jumped the gun. 'Whitefield had sent his diary of the journey from London to Georgia to Gibraltar, for private circulation. [He had made friends in Gibraltar during the three weeks his ship had stopped there on the outward journey.—J.I.P.] A printer called Cooper saw it, scented profits and put it in print; but as he could not always decipher Whitefield's handwriting the text was corrupt and Printer Hutton had decided the absent author would approve if he published an accurate version' (Pollock, *George Whitefield,* p. 69). Finding this journal already a best-seller Whitefield followed it up over the next three years with half a dozen more. For more details, see Iain Murray's introduction to *George Whitefield's Journals,* pp. 13–19.

40. Dallimore, *George Whitefield,* II.241.

41. Ibid., II.352.

42. Ibid., chs. 17, 23, II.247ff., 335ff.

43. To John Wesley, 12 Sept. 1769; to Robert Keen (Whitefield's last letter), 23 Sept. 1770; Dallimore, *George Whitefield,* II.475, 498.

44. Reprinted in one volume, *Sermons on Important Subjects* (London: Henry Fisher, Son, and P. Jackson, 1832).

45. *Works,* IV.307, 278.

46. For details, see Dallimore, *George Whitefield,* I.405. Dallimore corrects the mistake, traceable to Tyerman, of supposing that Whitefield learned his Calvinism from Jonathan Edwards, whom he first met in 1740. On the voyage to America, a year before, he recorded that he had been 'greatly strengthened by perusing some paragraphs out of a book called *The Preacher,* written by Dr. [John] Edwards, of Cambridge, and extracted

by Mr. Jonathan Warn, in his books entitled, *The Church of England-Man turned Dissenter,* and *Arminianism the Backdoor to Popery.* There are such noble testimonies . . . of justification by faith only, the imputed righteousness of Christ, our having no free-will, &c., that they deserve to be written in letters of gold' (*Journals,* p. 335). Tyerman and others seem to have confused Jonathan with John Edwards.

47. See, on this, C. F. Allison, *The Rise of Moralism* (London: SPCK, 1966).

48. 'The Righteousness of Christ, an Everlasting Righteousness,' in *Sermons on Important Subjects,* pp. 207ff.

49. *Sermons on Important Subjects,* pp. 664–65.

50. *Works,* VI.178.

51. *Sermons on Important Subjects,* p. 489.

52. Dallimore, *George Whitefield,* II.534.

53. I have presented the morphology of revival in *Keep in Step with the Spirit* (Old Tappan, NJ: Revell, and Leicester: InterVarsity Press, 1984), pp. 235–62, and in *God in Our Midst* (Ann Arbor: Servant Books, and Milton Keynes: Word Books, 1987).

54. Letters of George Whitefield, 1734–42, p. 277.

55. See J. I. Packer, *Among God's Giants: The Puritan Vision of the Christian Life* (Eastbourne: Kingsway, 1991), ch. 18, 'Puritan Evangelism,' pp. 383–407; = *A Quest for Godliness.* (Wheaton: Crossway, 1990), pp. 291–308.

56. See M. Luther, *The Bondage of the Will,* trans. O. R. Johnston and J. I. Packer (London: James Clarke, 1957), pt. 7, pp. 273–318.

57. Stout, *The Divine Dramatist,* ch. 13, 'Dr. Squintum,' pp. 234–48.

58. *Sermons on Important Subjects,* no. 8, 'The Necessity and Benefits of Religious Society,' pp. 107–18. This was actually Whitefield's first sermon.

59. M. Noll, 'Father of Modern Evangelicals?' *Christian History* (spring 1993), p. 44. Noll's generalisation, though too sweeping and simplistic (for the Puritans both sides of the Atlantic preached about God's plans for the church and the individual with equal emphasis), has significant substance.

60. *Among God's Giants,* ch. 3, pp. 41–63.

61. Dallimore, *George Whitefield,* II.392–93.

Notes to Chapter 5

A KIND OF PURITAN: MARTYN LLOYD-JONES was originally published in *Martyn Lloyd-Jones: Chosen by God,* ed. Christopher Catherwood (Crowborough, Sussex: Highland Books, 1986), pp. 33–58. Reprinted by permission.

1. 'Puritanism and Its Origins,' in *The Good Fight of Faith* (Westminster Conference Report, 1971), p. 72.

2. 'John Bunyan: Church Union,' in *Light from John Bunyan* (Westminster Conference Report, 1978), p. 86.

3. *The Good Fight of Faith,* p. 73.

4. 'John Knox—the Founder of Puritanism,' in *Becoming a Christian* (Westminster Conference Report, 1972), p. 102.

5. *The Good Fight of Faith,* p. 86.

6. Ibid., pp. 89–90.

7. 'Henry Jacob and the First Congregational Church,' in *One Steadfast High Intent* (Puritan and Reformed Studies Conference Report, 1966), pp. 59–60.

Notes to Chapter 6

DAVID MARTYN LLOYD-JONES was originally published in *Heroes*, ed. Ann Spangler and Charles Turner (Ann Arbor: Servant Books, 1985), pp. 285–99. Reprinted by permission.

1. Iain H. Murray, *David Martyn Lloyd-Jones: The First Forty Years, 1899–1939* (Edinburgh: Banner of Truth Trust, 1982), pp. 135ff.

Notes to Chapter 7

NO LITTLE PERSON: REFLECTIONS ON FRANCIS SCHAEFFER was originally published as the foreword to *Reflections on Francis Schaeffer*, ed. Ronald W. Ruegsegger (Grand Rapids: Academie Press, 1986), pp. 7–18. Reprinted by permission.

1. Edith Schaeffer, *L'Abri* (London: Norfolk, 1969), pp. 226–27.

Notes to Chapter 8

1. LUTHER AGAINST ERASMUS was originally delivered to the pastoral conference of the English Evangelical Lutheran Church, Oct. 30, 1964, and first published in *Concordia Geological Monthly*, XXVII.4, April 1966. Reprinted by permission.

2. Desiderius Erasmus, 'Erasmus Roterodamus Regi Angliae Henrico Octavo S. D.' *Opus Epistolarum Des. Erasmi Roterodami*, ed. P. S. Allen, V (Oxonii: In Typographeo Clarendoniano, 1924), 541, no. 1493.

3. [Ernest] Gordon Rupp, *The Righteousness of God: Luther Studies* (London: Hodder and Stoughton, 1953), p. 268.

4. Desiderius Erasmus and Martin Luther, *Erasmus–Luther: Discourse on Free Will*, trans. and ed. Ernst F. Winter (New York: Frederick Unger, 1961), p. 12. (This book contains a full English translation of the *Diatribe*.) The two treaties are also now available in trans. and ed. E. Gordon Rupp and Philip Watson, *Luther and Erasmus: Free Will and Salvation* Library of Christian Classics (Philadelphia: Westminster, 1969).

5. Ibid., p. 20.

6. Ibid., pp. 86–87.

7. Ibid., pp. 92–93.

8. [Desiderius] Erasmus, 'Erasmus to Zwingli,' *Luther's Correspondence and Other Contemporary Letters*, trans. and ed. Preserved Smith and Charles M. Jacob II (Philadelphia: The Lutheran Publication Society, 1918), p. 198; cited from P. G. Schwiebert, *Luther and His Times* (St. Louis: Concordia, 1950), p. 687.

9. Martin Luther, *The Bondage of the Will*, trans. and ed. J. I. Packer and O. R. Johnston (Westwood, NJ: Revell, and London: James Clarke, 1957), pp. 319–20.

10. Margaret Mann Phillips, *Erasmus and the Northern Renaissance* (New York: Macmillan, 1950), p. 197.

11. Benjamin Breckenridge Warfield, 'The Theology of the Reformation,' in *Studies in Theology* (New York: Oxford University Press, 1932), p. 471.

12. Rupp, *The Righteousness of God*, p. 283.

13. Martin Luther, 'Luther and Wolfgang Capito in Strassburg,' *D. Martin Luthers Werke*, Br. 8 (Weimar: Herman Böhlaus Nachfolger, 1938), p. 99 (Cited as *WA, Weimarer Ausgabe*). *De Servo Arbitrio* is in *WA* 18, pp. 600–787.

14. Luther, *The Bondage of the Will*, pp. 64–65.

15. Philip S. Watson, *Let God Be God! An Interpretation of the Theology of Martin Luther* (London: Epworth, and Philadelphia: Muhlenberg, 1947), p. 9.

16. Luther, *The Bondage of the Will*, p. 319.

17. Ibid., p. 78.

18. Ibid.

19. Erasmus and Luther, *Erasmus–Luther: Discourse on Free Will*, p. 6. Cf. Luther, *The Bondage of the Will*, pp. 66, 68.

20. Luther, *The Bondage of the Will*, pp. 66–67.

21. Ibid., pp. 73–74.

22. Ibid., p. 70.

23. Ibid., p. 67.

24. Ibid., p. 107.

25. Ibid., p. 140.

26. Ibid., p. 162.

27. Ibid., p. 100.

28. Ibid., p. 204.

29. Ibid., pp. 103–104.

30. Ibid., p. 103.

31. Ibid., pp. 313–14.

32. Ibid., p. 217.

33. Ibid., pp. 170–71.

34. Ibid., pp. 175–76.

35. Ibid., p. 317.

Notes to Chapter 9

'SOLA SCRIPTURA' IN HISTORY AND TODAY was originally published in *God's Inerrant Word*, ed. J. W. Montgomery (Minneapolis: Bethany House Publishers, 1974), pp. 43–62. Reprinted by permission.

1. Luther, *Weimarer Ausgabe (WA)*, ed. J. C. F. Knaske et al. (Weimar, 1883–), 3.14; 4.318 (Commentary on the Psalms, 1513–15).

2. *WA*, 2.279 (Disputation with Eck, 1519).

3. *WA*, 7.838. On the question whether the words 'Here I stand, I cannot do otherwise' which were added in the first printed version, were really spoken by Luther on that occasion, see R. Bainton, *Here I Stand: A Life of Martin Luther* (New York: New American Library Mentor Books, 1955). In any case, Luther put these words into print in the following year in a striking passage from his reply to 'King Heinz' (Henry VIII of England!): 'For me it is enough that King Heinz cannot quote a single Scripture ... I place against the sayings of all Fathers, and every artifice and word of angels, men and devils, the Scripture and the gospel. *Here I stand, here I bid defiance, here I strut about and say, God's Word for me is above everything.* I will not give a hair though a thousand Augustines, a thousand Heinz-churches' (a reference to Henry's position as 'supreme head' of the Church of England) 'were all against me, and I am certain that the true church with me holds fast to the word of God' (*WA*, 10.256).

4. B. A. Gerrish writes, 'We must carefully distinguish: (1) natural reason, ruling within its proper domain (the Earthly Kingdom); (2) arrogant reason, trespassing upon the domain of faith (the Heavenly Kingdom); (3) regenerate reason, serving humbly in the household of faith but always subject to the Word of God. Within the first context reason is an excellent gift of God; within the second, it is Frau Hulda, the Devil's Whore; within the third, it is the handmaiden of faith' (*Grace and Reason: A Study in the Theology of Luther* [Oxford: Oxford University Press, 1962], p. 26). Gerrish notes that Calvin's *Institutes* II.ii 'amounts to a summing-up' of Luther's view of reason in fallen man (p. ix).

5. Arthur Skevington Wood, *Luther's Principles of Biblical Interpretation* (London: Tyndale Press, 1960), p. 7.

6. Cf. the following remark of Luther's: 'I will not waste a word in arguing with one who does not consider that the Scriptures are the Word of God: we ought not to dispute with a man who thus rejects first principles' (cited without reference by A. M. Renwick, in *Evangelical Quarterly*, XIX/2 [April 1947], p. 114).

7. *WA*, 7.97.

8. Augustine was by far the most admired and influential of the fathers among the Reformers, particularly for his doctrine of grace formulated against Pelagianism. Misled by the meaning of 'justificare' in Latin, he understood justification as God's work of making sinners subjectively righteous by pardoning their sins and infusing into them the grace of love (*caritas*).

9. This was the patristic view of tradition, which medieval divines did not wholly abandon: see R. P. C. Hanson, *Tradition in the Early Church* (London: SCM, 1962), and G. Tavard, *Holy Writ or Holy Church* (London: Burns & Oates, 1959). The later theory that Scripture and tradition are two distinct and complementary sources of doctrine was not explicitly taught by the Council of Trent, though following Melchior Cano, Canisius, and Bellarmine, most Roman Catholics from the sixteenth century till very recently have assumed the contrary. See J. R. Geiselmann in *Christianity Divided*, ed. D. J. Callahan, H. A. Obermann, D. J. O'Hanlan (London and New York: Sheed and Ward, 1962), pp. 39ff.

10. Cf. Westminster Confession I.x: 'The supreme Judge, by which all controversies of religion are to be determined, and all decrees of councils, opinions of ancient writers, doctrines of men, and private spirits are to be examined, and in whose sentence we are to rest, can be no other but the Holy Spirit speaking in the Scriptures.'

11. B. B. Warfield, *Calvin and Augustine* (Philadelphia: Presbyterian & Reformed, 1956), p. 484. Warfield continues: 'It was [Calvin] who first related the whole experience

of salvation specifically to the working of the Holy Spirit, worked it out in its details, and contemplated its several steps and stages in orderly progress as the product of the Holy Spirit's specific work in applying salvation to the soul . . . What Calvin did was, specifically, to replace the doctrine of the Church as the sole source of assured knowledge of God and sole institute of salvation, by the Holy Spirit . . . The *Institutes* is, accordingly, just a treatise on the work of God the Holy Spirit in making God savingly known to sinful man and bringing sinful man into holy communion with God' (pp. 485ff.).

12. The reader can begin to verify this by consulting R. Prenter, *Spiritus Creator* (Philadelphia: Muhlenberg, 1953).

13. *WA*, 54.187.

14. Wood, *Luther's Principles*, p. 7.

15. *Institutes* I.vii.3.

16. Ibid., I.viii.1.

17. Ibid., I.ix.3.

18. Cf. Article 6 of the Anglican Thirty-nine Articles: 'Holy Scripture containeth all things necessary to salvation: so that whatsoever is not read therein, nor may be proved thereby, is not to be required of any man, that it should be believed as an article of the Faith, or be thought requisite or necessary to salvation.'

19. Article 20.

20. James Barr, *The Bible in the Modern World* (London: SCM, 1973), p. 27.

21. *The Bondage of the Will*, trans. and ed. J. I. Packer and O. R. Johnston (London: James Clarke, and Old Tappan, NJ: Revell, 1987), p. 71. (*WA*, 18.607).

22. T. H. L. Parker, *Calvin's New Testament Commentaries* (London: SCM Press, 1971), pp. 79–80.

23. *The Church's Use of the Bible Past and Present*, ed. D. E. Nineham (London: SPCK, 1963), p. 162.

24. Barr, *The Bible in the Modern World*, p. 6. It seems that this view is now embedded in the World Council of Churches, at any rate at the secretariat level. Peter Beyerhaus blames 'the breakdown of the exegetical preparation for Bangkok' on 'the depth of the hermeneutical crisis in the WCC. There is no common conviction that the Bible is the authoritative and reliable basis for Christian faith and ministry. Scripture is seen by many as a collection of different historical documents justifying the experiences of salvation and understandings of the divine will at the time they were written. But these witnesses, it is felt, do not necessarily agree among themselves' (*The Evangelical Response to Bangkok*, ed. Ralph Winter [South Pasadena: William Carey Library], pp. 110–11). See also p. 58.

25. The phrase comes from T. H. L. Parker's account of Calvin's exegetical method in *Calvin's New Testament Commentaries*, p. 68.

26. Warfield, *Calvin and Augustine*, p. 481.

27. Cf. *Institutes* II.ix–xi.

28. Luther's sense of the unity of the New Testament comes out vividly when he writes in the preface to his German translation of it: 'we must get rid of the delusion that there are four gospels . . . the New Testament is one book . . . there is only one gospel, only one book in the New Testament, only one faith, and only one God' (*WA*, 6.2).

29. This is where both differ from many modern exponents of the unity of the Bible who view the matter in terms of a 'biblical theology' or '*Heilsgeschichte*' standpoint. The

latter commonly treat the biblical witness to God's saving acts in history as spotty and unreliable, more or less; Luther and Calvin, however, put implicit trust in it, as the teaching of the Holy Spirit.

30. Barth will not attempt a Christian view of history, and is equivocal on the continuity of God's saving act in Christ with the rest of world history. Bultmann's rejection of the physical miracles ascribed in the gospels to Christ, and of his virgin birth and bodily resurrection, reveal a mechanistic, uniformitarian view of nature as rigid as that of any Deist. For both, wherever else God's control may be a reality, it does not seem to be so in the material order.

31. Cf. Nineham, *The Church's Use of the Bible*, and 'The Use of the Bible in Modern Theology,' in *Bulletin of the John Ryland's Library,* lii (1969), pp. 178–99; Evans, *Is 'Holy Scripture' Christian?* (London: SCM, 1971); Barr, *The Bible in the Modern World.*

32. Barr, *The Bible in the Modern World*, p. 113.

33. Ibid., p. 147.

34. Ibid., p. 114.

35. The phrase is from Anglican Article 20.

36. For an excellent and conclusive example of such a battle see the critique of Dewey M. Beegle's view of Scripture by Cornelius Van Til in his mimeographed class syllabus *In Defense of the Faith,* I: *The [Protestant] Doctrine of Scripture* (Ripon, CA: Den Dulk Christian Foundation, 1967), pp. 72–87.

Notes to Chapter 10

CALVIN THE THEOLOGIAN was originally published in *John Calvin,* ed. G. E. Duffield (Abingdon: Sutton Courtenay Press, 1963), pp. 149–75. Reprinted by permission.

1. Modern books which show this include T. H. L. Parker, *Portrait of Calvin* (London: SCM Press, 1954), and *John Calvin: a Biography* (London: Dent, 1977); J. Cadier, *The Man God Mastered* (London: Inter-Varsity Press, 1960); A-M. Schmidt, *Calvin and the Calvinistic Tradition* (New York: Harper, 1968); F. Wendel, *Calvin* (London: Collins, 1963); William J. Bouwsma, *John Calvin* (New York and Oxford: Oxford University Press, 1988). Emile Doumergue's *Jean Calvin: Les hommes et les choses de son temps,* 7 vols. (Lausanne: G. Bridel, 1897–1927), was the pioneer work rehabilitating Calvin; it remains indispensable for the serious student.

2. On the grounds for this judgement see W. Cunningham, *The Reformers and the Theology of the Reformation* (Edinburgh: T. and T. Clark, 1862), pp. 95–102. This is not, however, to say that he would have acquitted of the charge of speculation the developed supralapsarian scheme against which Arminianism was a reaction, and on the basis of which the Synod of Dort conducted its deliberations. Wendel notes (*Calvin,* p. 129) that in Calvin redemption is 'logically subordinated' to election: he suggests that this shows dependence on Scotus, but since Calvin never makes Scotus' nominalist point, that Christ's sacrifice has no value other than that which God chooses to set on it, this must be held doubtful.

3. Only the Solomonic writings, Judges, Ruth, Kings, Chronicles, Ezra, Nehemiah, Revelation (which Calvin professed not to understand), and 2 and 3 John, were omitted.

Calvin preached through Judges in 1561, and Kings in 1563–64, but the sermons have not survived. See T. H. L. Parker, *The Oracles of God* (London: Lutterworth, 1947), pp. 162, 164.

4. B. B. Warfield, *Calvin and Calvinism* (New York: Oxford University Press, 1931), p. 389, n. 21. See clarification in ch. 11, n. 23 in this volume.

5. Beza, *Abstersio Calumniarum*, p. 263.

6. On the growth of the *Institutio* from the first edition to its final form, see Wendel, *Calvin*, pp. 112ff.; Warfield, *Calvin and Calvinism*, pp. 373ff.

7. *Institutes* I.ii.1; I.ii.2; I.xii.2; I.v.9.

8. Ibid., III.ii.35.

9. Ibid., III.xi.1, my italics.

10. The practical bearing of each of these topics on Christian living is indicated in the paragraphs which introduce them: cf. *Institutes* III.xix.1, xx.1–2, xxi.1, xxv.1; IV.i.1, xiv.1, xx.1.

11. Ibid., II.xvii.1,2. Cf. II.xvi.4: 'in a wondrous divine way he loved us even when he hated us.'

12. Ibid., II.xvi.10.

13. For a full analysis of Calvin on the atonement, see P. van Buren, *Christ in Our Place: The Substitutionary Character of Calvin's Doctrine of Reconciliation* (Edinburgh: Oliver and Boyd, 1957).

14. *Institutes* I.vi.1. Chapters iii–vi deal with this whole subject.

15. Ibid., I.vii.1,4,5; IV.viii.9. Scripture is an 'official record (*consignatio*: almost, "affidavit") of heavenly *doctrine*' (I.vi.3).

16. Cf. Warfield, *Calvin and Augustine* (Philadelphia: Presbyterian & Reformed, 1956), pp. 62ff.; Doumergue, *Jean Calvin*, III.725, IV, 73ff.; R. E. Davies, *The Problem of Authority in the Continental Reformers* (London: Epworth Press, 1946), pp. 114ff.; E. A. Dowey, *The Knowledge of God in Calvin's Theology* (New York: Columbia University Press, 1952), pp. 101ff.; K. S. Kantzer, 'Calvin and the Holy Scriptures,' in *Inspiration and Interpretation* (Grand Rapids: Eerdmans, 1957), pp. 137ff. There is a valuable review of evidence, and of scholars' readings of it, in J. K. S. Reid, *The Authority of Scripture* (London: Methuen, 1957), pp. 49–55. Reid would apparently regard our view of Calvin's teaching on the Bible as an oversimplification. But his argument that because Calvin did not identify the Spirit with the Word, or Christ with the Scriptures, therefore he did not accept the theory of verbal 'inspiration' (pp. 18, 54) gives the latter phrase a decidedly Pickwickian (Barthian!) sense.

17. *Commentary on the Psalms* (*CTS* III.410–11, 407). Calvin comments similarly on Psalm 39:13: 'he errs . . . his mind was so affected with the bitterness of his grief that he could not present a prayer pure and well seasoned with the sweetness of faith . . . he could not lift up his heart with so much cheerfulness as it behoved him . . . the desires of the flesh . . . forced him to exceed the proper limits in his grief' (*Commentary* II.88).

18. *Harmony of the Pentateuch* (*CTS* II.304).

19. *Institutes* I.vii.5; see the whole chapter.

20. Wendel, *Calvin*, p. 136.

21. Warfield, *Calvin and Augustine*, p. 22. On the details of Calvin's debt to Bucer, which Warfield, writing in 1909, perhaps slightly exaggerated, see Wendel, *Calvin*, pp. 137–44. On Calvin's debt to Luther, Wendel quotes A. Lang and J. Koestlin. Lang wrote:

'In the first edition of the *Institutes* [Calvin] seems almost to be a Lutheran of southern Germany. But afterwards too, Calvin was entirely in agreement with Luther with regard to all the fundamental doctrines bearing upon justification, upon the total perversion of sinful man, upon sinning and original sin, upon Christ the unique Saviour and mediator, upon the appropriation of salvation through the Holy Spirit, the Word and the sacraments. We have even authority to claim that the central teaching of Luther on the justification of faith and regeneration by faith was preserved more faithfully and expressed more forcibly by Calvin than by any other dogmatician of the Reform.' Koestlin wrote: 'In the developments [in the 1536 *Institutio*] concerning the Christ who made himself wholly one of us, who overcame death, who interceded for us with his whole person and his entire work, by his obedience and by the fact that he took his (?) sins upon himself, one perceives an intimate relatedness to Luther . . . Upon the subject of predestination, one would discover nothing that Luther might not have written at the epoch' (Wendel, *Calvin*, p. 133). One could also add that Calvin reproduced Luther's teaching on the threefold use of the law (the 'third use' is there explicitly in Luther's later works), and his distinction between spiritual and temporal government (inward, by Christ, in the conscience, and outward by the magistrate), and also that, like Luther, and unlike Zwingli, Calvin would not justify active resistance to the civil power.

22. *Institutes* II.xv.1. For the history of the three-office formula before Calvin, see J. F. Jansen, *Calvin's Doctrine of the Work of Christ* (London: James Clarke, 1956), pp. 23ff.

23. Warfield, *Calvin and Augustine*, pp. 485–86.

24. Regin Prenter, *Spiritus Creator*, trans. J. M. Jensen (Philadelphia: Muhlenberg Press, 1953).

25. *Institutes* II.vii.1.

26. See 'Calvin's Doctrine of the Trinity,' pp. 189ff.

27. Schmidt, *Calvin and the Calvinistic Tradition*, p. 115.

28. H. Quistorp, *Calvin's Doctrine of the Last Things* (London: Lutterworth, 1955), p. 15.

29. Schmidt, *Calvin and the Calvinistic Tradition*.

30. Warfield, op. cit., pp. 491–92.

Notes to Chapter 11

JOHN CALVIN AND THE INERRANCY OF HOLY SCRIPTURE was originally published in *Inerrancy and the Church*, ed. J. Hannah (Chicago: Moody Press, 1984), pp. 143–88. Reprinted by permission.

1. Jack B. Rogers and Donald K. McKim, *The Authority and Interpretation of the Bible: An Historical Approach* (San Francisco: Harper & Row, 1979). A major critical review by John D. Woodbridge ('Biblical Authority: Towards an Evaluation of the Rogers and McKim Proposal') appeared in the *Trinity Journal I* (1980), pp. 165–236. McKim replied in *TSF Bulletin*, April 1981. An expanded critique by Woodbridge, *Biblical Authority: A Critique of the Rogers and McKim Proposal*, has been released by Zondervan (1982).

2. The fact that the Westminster Confession speaks of the 'infallible truth' of Holy Scripture is no doubt a main reason for that: Presbyterians who affirmed infallibility

without inerrancy at the end of the nineteenth century included W. Robertson Smith, T. M. Lindsay, James Denney in Scotland, and C. A. Briggs in the USA. Cf. Rogers and McKim, pp. 380–85 on Lindsay, pp. 348–61 on Briggs.

3. It is noteworthy that the famous essay by A. A. Hodge and B. B. Warfield, 'Inspiration,' first published in the *Presbyterian Review* 2 (1881), pp. 225–60, now reprinted with introduction and appendixes by Roger R. Nicole (Grand Rapids: Baker, 1979), which is often treated as the classic statement of inerrancy, does not use the word, but speaks of infallibility only. It looks as if the free use of the term by critics of the older position, e.g., C.A. Briggs in *Whither?* (New York: Charles Scribner, 1889), was an incentive to the orthodox to embrace and defend it.

4. Cf. J. I. Packer, *Beyond the Battle for the Bible* (Westchester, IL: Cornerstone, 1980), pp. 47–50, for a review of the debate.

5. The Chicago Statement can be found in J. I. Packer, *God Has Spoken* (Downers Grove, IL: InterVarsity Press, 1979), pp. 139–53; and in Carl F. H. Henry, *God, Revelation and Authority,* IV: *God Who Speaks and Shows* (Waco: Word Books, 1979), pp. 211–19. Other relevant ICBI publications are James M. Boice, ed., *The Foundation of Biblical Authority* (Grand Rapids: Zondervan, 1978); Norman L. Geisler, ed., *Inerrancy* (Grand Rapids: Zondervan, 1979); Norman L. Geisler, ed., *Biblical Errancy: An Analysis of Its Philosophical Roots* (Grand Rapids: Zondervan, 1981). See also John W. Montgomery, ed., *God's Inerrant Word* (Minneapolis: Bethany, 1974).

6. *The Works of Rev. John Wesley* (London: Wesleyan Methodist Book Room, n.d.), IX.150; N. Curnock, ed., *The Journal of Rev. John Wesley* (London: C. H. Kelly, n.d.), VI.117, entry for August 24, 1776.

7. Berkouwer's final view (*Holy Scripture,* trans. and ed. Jack B. Rogers [Grand Rapids: Eerdmans, 1975]) is analysed sympathetically by Rogers and McKim, *Authority and Interpretation,* pp. 426–37, and polemically by Henry Krabbendam in Geisler, *Inerrancy,* pp. 413–46.

8. Unshakable confidence in inerrantist exegesis is one of the traits criticized in James Barr's sour but perceptive polemic *Fundamentalism* (London: SCM Press, 1977).

9. See Packer, *God Has Spoken,* pp. 110–14; *Beyond the Battle for the Bible,* pp. 50–61.

10. F. L. Battles and A. M. Hugo, eds. and trans., *Calvin's Commentary on Seneca's De Clementia* (Leiden: E. J. Brill, 1969).

11. T. H. L. Parker, *Calvin's New Testament Commentaries* (London: SCM Press, 1971), p. 59.

12. Ibid., pp. 26–68.

13. John Calvin, *Institutes of the Christian Religion,* trans. F. L. Battles, ed. J. T. McNeill (Philadelphia: Westminster Press, 1960), 'John Calvin to the Reader,' I.4–5; better translated from the 1539, rather than the 1559, wording by T. H. L. Parker, p. 53.

14. Parker, *Calvin's New Testament Commentaries,* pp. 50–54.

15. The commentaries on the Pentateuch, Joshua, Psalms, and Isaiah were written as such; the rest of the Old Testament material is lecture-sermons at a level and in a style similar to the commentaries. The material on 1 Samuel and Job was not included in the Calvin Translation Society's forty-five volumes (reprinted by Eerdmans in 1948). Parker, *Calvin's New Testament Commentaries,* pp. 76–78, doubts the authenticity of Calvin's

reported acknowledgement that he did not understand Revelation and points out that he cited it forty times, quoting from fourteen of its twenty-two chapters.

16. B. B. Warfield, *Calvin and Augustine* (Philadelphia: Presbyterian & Reformed, 1956), pp. 9ff. Calvin's New Testament commentaries have been retranslated under the editorship of D. W. and T. F. Torrance (Edinburgh: Oliver & Boyd and St. Andrew's Press, 1959–72). Older testimonies to Calvin's excellence as a commentator are collected in the Calvin Translation Society's version of the *Commentary on Joshua*, trans. Henry Beveridge (Grand Rapids: Eerdmans, 1948), pp. 376–464.

17. H. Jackson Forstman, *Word and Spirit* (Stanford: Stanford University Press, 1962), ch. 7, pp. 106–23, argues that Calvin would on occasion 'overlook or deny the natural meaning of the inspired text in order to uphold its unity' (p. 123), but the evidence he produces (some of which he seems to misunderstand) fails to prove his point.

18. *Ioannis Calvini Opera quae supersunt Omnia*, ed. N. W. Baum, E. Cunitz, E. Reuss, P. Lobstein, and A. Erichson (Brunswick and Berlin: C. A. Schweiske, 1863–1900). That edition, cited as *CO*, comprises vols. 29–87 of the *Corpus Reformatorum*.

19. Bibliographies: W. Niesel, *Calvin-Bibliographie 1901–59* (München: Chr. Kaiser Verlag, 1961); D. Kempff, *A bibliography of Calviniana 1959–74* (Leiden: E. J. Brill, 1975); T. H. L. Parker, 'A Bibliography and Survey of the British Study of Calvin, 1900–40,' *Evangelical Quarterly* 18 (1946), pp. 123–31; J. T. McNeill, 'Fifty Years of Calvin Study (1918–68),' in Williston Walker, *John Calvin: The Organizer of Reformed Protestantism 1509–64* (New York: Schocken Books, 1969), pp. xvii–lxxvii; E. A. Dowey, 'Studies in Calvin and Calvinism since 1948,' *Church History* 24 (1955), pp. 360–67; 'Studies in Calvin and Calvinism since 1955,' *Church History* 29 (1960), pp. 187–204; J. N. Tylenda, 'Calvin Bibliography pp. 1960–1970,' *Calvin Theological Journal* 6 (1971), pp. 156–93; Peter De Klerk, Calvin bibliographies for each year, 1972–78, *Calvin Theological Journal* 7 (1972), pp. 221–50; 9 (1974), pp. 38–73, 210–40; 10 (1975), pp. 175–207; 11 (1976), pp. 199–243; 12 (1977), pp. 164–87; 13 (1978), pp. 166–94. On Calvin's view of Scripture, the most useful bibliography is that of Richard Stauffer, *Dieu, la creation et la providence dans la predication de Calvin* (Berne: Peter Lang, 1978), p. 72, n. 1.

20. Cf. Basil Hall, 'The Calvin Legend,' in G. E. Duffield, ed., *John Calvin* (Abingdon: Sutton Courtenay Press, 1966), pp. 1–15; J. I. Packer, 'Calvin the Theologian,' this volume ch. 10.

21. Rogers and McKim, *Authority and Interpretation*, pp. 93–98, summarize that well, drawing on an unpublished paper by the late F. L. Battles.

22. H. J. Kraus, *Interpretation* 31 (1977), pp. 14ff., 'For his training in Hebrew Calvin was primarily indebted to Conrad Pellicanus's book *De Modo Legendi et Intelligendi Hebraea*, which appeared in 1503 ... the Reformer used such exegetical works as those of David Kimchi, Abraham ibn Ezra, and Raschi ... there is scarcely a Reformed exegete of the sixteenth century who did not have a good knowledge of Hebrew.'

23. Cf. Packer, *God Has Spoken*, p. 152. 'He never changed his mind on any doctrinal issue. The only alteration in his published views that has been demonstrated to date is that whereas in *Psychopannychia* [Calvin's first theological work, 1534] and the 1536 *Institutio* he ascribed the apocryphal book of Baruch to Baruch, he later concluded it to be pseudonymous.' That statement should have read: '... he considered the apocryphal

book of Baruch canonical, he later concluded it was not so.' For details on Baruch, cf. Warfield, *Calvin and Augustine,* p. 55, n. 19.

24. 'Institutes' as a rendering of Calvin's word *Institutio* goes back to the translation by John Allen (1813), superseding the excellent Elizabethan version by Thomas Norton (1561; last printed 1762), which was titled *The Institution of Christian Religion. Institutio* means 'instruction.'

25. Cf. the excellent 'Introduction' by F. L. Battles to his translation of the *Institutes,* I.xxix–lxxi.

26. 'Theological' is Barth's word for exegesis that focuses on the witness-content of Scripture as proclamation of the living God. More recently, Brevard S. Childs has spoken of 'canonical' exegesis in the same sense.

27. Cf. Packer, *God Has Spoken,* p. 157.

28. Cf. n. 13 above. Calvin announced in the preface to the second and each subsequent edition of the *Institutes*: 'If I shall hereafter publish any commentaries on Scripture, I shall always condense them and keep them short, for I shall have no need to undertake lengthy discussions on doctrines . . . By this method the godly reader will be spared great trouble and boredom, provided he approaches the commentaries forearmed with a knowledge of the present work as his necessary tool.'

29. Rogers and McKim, *Authority and Interpretation,* pp. 92ff. and notes; *Institutes,* trans. Battles, 1.6 and n. 8.

30. Probably against the 'Libertines,' Quintin Thieffry and Antoine Poequet and their followers, rather than against Anabaptists, as has often been supposed. Calvin distinguished between Libertines and Anabaptists. See *Institutes,* trans. Battles, 1.93 and n. 1; W. Balke, *Calvin and the Anabaptist Radicals* (Grand Rapids: Eerdmans, 1981), pp. 10, 98–99, 330.

31. Parker, *God Has Spoken,* p. 57. J. K. S. Reid, *The Authority of Scripture* (London: Methuen, and New York: Harper, 1957), pp. 54ff., lists authorities on both sides. Emile Doumergue's discussion is in *Jean Calvin: Les hommes et les choses de son temps,* 7 vols. (Lausanne: G. Bridel, 1897–1927), 4:70–82. The problem is discussed from different standpoints by E. A. Dowey, *The Knowledge of God in Calvin's Theology* (New York: Columbia University Press, 1952), pp. 99–105; John Murray, *Calvin on Scripture and Divine Sovereignty* (Philadelphia: Presbyterian & Reformed, 1960), pp. 11–31, especially pp. 20–27; Reid, *The Authority of Scripture,* pp. 43–45; R. E. Davies, *The Problem of Authority in the Continental Reformers* (London: Epworth Press, 1946), pp. 113–16. The attempt to find Calvin acknowledging factual errors in Scripture goes back into the nineteenth century, cf. Warfield, *Calvin and Augustine,* p. 65, n. 46.

32. See *Institutes* I.xvi–xviii.

33. Therefore, Calvin vigorously (and successfully) opposed the admission of Sebastion Castellio to the Geneva pastorate, for Castellio regarded the Song of Solomon as a secular love poem and not canonical Scripture. See Warfield, *Calvin and Augustine,* pp. 52ff., and notes 70 and 71 below.

34. *CO,* 54:286, from the twenty-fourth sermon on 2 Timothy.

35. Commentary on 2 Pet. 1:20, cf. Stauffer, *Dieu, la creation et la providence,* p. 64.

36. Cf. R. C. Prust, 'Was Calvin a Biblical Literalist?' *Scottish Journal of Theology* 20 (1967), pp. 321ff.

37. B. A. Gerrish, 'Biblical Authority and the Continental Reformation,' *Scottish Journal of Theology* 10 (1957), pp. 353ff.

38. O. Ritschl, *Dogmengeschichte des Protestantismus* (Göttingen: Vandenhoeck und Ruprecht, 1908), 1:59, is one authoritative scholar who took the term that way.

39. So, when Davies, *Problem of Authority*, p. 114, writes, 'We are forced to conclude, with Seeberg, Bauke, Warfield and Binns, that Calvin committed himself to a completely verbal and mechanical theory of inspiration,' the proper comments are verbal—yes; mechanical—no; theory—confession would be a better word; Warfield—a challenger, not an exponent, of the idea that Calvin's view of inspiration was mechanical; see n. 43 below.

40. Of Gal. 5:12, 'I wish those who unsettle you would mutilate [castrate] themselves!' Calvin said in a sermon, 'Let us fear this sentence, as if we are hearing heaven's thunder against all those who trouble the church; for it is certainly St. Paul who has spoken, but yet the Holy Spirit guided and governed his tongue' (*CO*, 51:15). Again, in *Institutes* I.v.13, biblical material is introduced by the following series of formulae: 'The Holy Spirit pronounces . . . Paul declares . . . Scripture, to make place for the true and only God, has condemned . . . there remains the firm teaching of Paul . . . the Holy Spirit rejects . . .' It is natural to treat that alternation between human and divine as not merely elegant but also explanatory; Calvin was reminding us that what God says in Scripture, man says; what man teaches in Scripture, God teaches also.

41. See *Institutes* I.v.3; III.xxv, etc.

42. It is observable that in *Institutes* I.vi.2, Calvin pleads ignorance of 'whether God was known to the patriarchs through oracles and visions or put into their minds through men's labour and ministry what they should then hand on to posterity.'

43. Gerrish, "Biblical Authority,' p. 355, n. 2. The Warfield quote is from *Calvin and Augustine*, pp. 63ff.

44. Calvin's commentary on 2 Tim. 3:16.

45. Prust, 'Was Calvin a Biblical Literalist?' pp. 317–26, perceives the importance of *doctrina* as the concept in terms of which the God-givenness of Scripture is most adequately understood, though he does not make the best use of his own insight. His idea that *doctrina*, as Calvin conceived it, is essentially non-propositional, preverbal, and incomprehensible is certainly a mistake.

46. *Institutes* IV.viii.5.

47. Ibid., II.ii.20–22; commentaries on Isa. 25:9; 2 Cor. 3:14–17; 1 Pet. 1:10–11.

48. See the quotation from Calvin's commentary on 2 Tim. 3:16 in the previous paragraph.

49. *Institutes* I.vi.2. Battles translates *continuo progressu doctrina* as 'with a continuing succession of teaching,' meaning apparently that once the oracles were made permanently available in writing, they could be taught to each succeeding generation. But *progressus* always signifies 'advance' in some sense, never 'succession,' and *doctrina* in Calvin, as we have seen, ordinarily means the substance of God's teaching, not teaching as a human activity.

50. Ibid., I.vi passim.

51. Ibid., IV.viii.6.

52. Ibid., I.vi.3.

53. Ibid., I.vi.1.

54. Ibid., I.vi.2.

55. Ibid., III.xxi.3. 'Whatever, then, is set down in Scripture, let us labour to learn; for it would be an insult to the Holy Spirit, if we should think that he has taught anything which it is irrelevant for us to know' (commentary on Rom. 15:4).

56. Commentary on Isa. 30:1.

57. Commentary on John 16:13.

58. Commentary on 2 Pet. 3:16.

59. In his commentary on Zech. 1:21, Calvin explained that we should learn to depend on the ministers of the Word to open to us the meaning of Scripture, just as Zechariah had to depend on the angels to interpret to him his visions.

60. Sermon on 1 Tim. 3:8–10 (*CO*, 53:300). Calvin spoke constantly of the Holy Spirit as the giver of spiritual understanding to our sin-darkened minds, cf. Forstman, *Word and Spirit*, pp. 74–79.

61. *Institutes* I.viii.1. As a Renaissance humanist, Calvin took for granted, as the Corinthians had done before him (cf. 1 Cor. 1:17–2:5; 2 Cor. 10:10), that unadorned, unrhetorical expression was always poor style.

62. Commentary on John 3:12.

63. See F. L. Battles, 'God Was Accommodating Himself to Human Capacity,' *Interpretation* 31 (1977), pp. 19–38. Battles quotes Calvin's words in his commentary on 1 Peter 1:20 about the incarnation as marking the acme of divine accommodation: 'In Christ God so to speak makes himself little [*quodammodo parvum facit*] in order to lower himself to our capacity [*ut se ad captum nostrum submittat*].'

64. *Institutes* III.xxi.2.

65. R. S. Wallace, *Calvin's Doctrine of the Word and Sacrament* (Edinburgh: Oliver & Boyd, 1953), p. 99, n. 2.

66. *Institutes* I.vii.4. The later phrase, *testimonium Spiritus Sancti internum* means the same, but Calvin did not seem actually to use that set of words.

67. Ibid., I.vii.4,5.

68. Ibid., I.vii.5.

69. Ibid., I.vii.2, 'As to their question, How can we be assured that it [Scripture] has come from God, if we do not have recourse to the church's decision?—it is like asking, Whence shall we learn to tell light from darkness, white from black, sweet from bitter? Scripture actually [*ultro*] displays as clear evidence [*sensum*] its truth as white and black things do of their colour, or sweet and bitter things do of their taste.'

70. Ibid., I.vii.

71. For discussion of the relation between historical attestation in, to, and by the church and the Spirit's immediate authenticating witness in making known to us the divine authority of Scripture, see Warfield, *Calvin and Augustine*, pp. 48–57, 90–103; Packer, *God's Inerrant Word*, pp. 110ff.; Davies, *Problem of Authority*, pp. 108ff., 141–6. Calvin's key thoughts here seem to have been

(1) The evidence that the canonical Scriptures are from God is objective in the sense of being intrinsic, public, and to anyone whose mind works properly, unmistakable. 'Though learned and most judicious men should rise up in opposition, and bring all their strength of mind into play in this debate, unless they have become hardened to that point of shamelessness which marks the lost [*ad perditam impudentiam*] they will

have to confess that in Scripture clear signs of God speaking [it] are seen, from which it is evident that its teaching [*doctrinam*] is from heaven' (I.vii.4). The fact that some do not confess that argues a defect in them, not in the evidence.

(2) The interior witness of the Holy Spirit is an enlightening of minds darkened to spiritual realities, a restoring of perceptive powers atrophied by sin, so that the objective evidence that the words and contents of Scripture are being spoken by God is received and responded to. Stauffer, *Dieu, la creation et la providence*, pp. 66–67, catalogues 'Calvin's images for that in his sermons: the Spirit 'pierces [opens] the ears,' 'softens the heart,' 'engraves the doctrine [*la doctrine*] presented by Scripture on our hearts,' 'writes in our hearts the doctrine of salvation,' 'signs and seals God's truth, which Scripture attests, in our hearts,' 'opens the eyes,' and gives a 'spiritual view' of the light that shines from God's word. Warfield was right to say that the Spirit's witness as Calvin saw it 'was directed to making men Christians' and right to characterize it as 'what we in modern times have learned to call "regeneration" considered in its noetic effects,' pp. 102ff.

(3) It is frivolous for any present-day individual to challenge any of the church's historic judgements about canonicity, based as they are on earlier testing and enquiry, and confirmed as they have been by the consensus of many generations of Christians in whose hearts the divine authentication has been a reality. One should rather seek humbly to be better taught by God at the point of one's personal eccentricity. That attitude appears in Calvin's report of the Geneva ministers' exchange with Castellio (see n. 33 above): 'We conjured him first of all, not to permit himself the levity of treating as of no account the constant witness of the universal church; we reminded him that . . . this [book] is one which has never been openly repudiated. We also exhorted him against trusting unreasonably in his own judgment' (*CO*, 11:674–74, cited in Warfield, *Calvin and Augustine*, pp. 52ff.).

72. Had that been Calvin's position, he could never have objected to Castellio on the grounds that he did (see previous note).

73. Cf. Packer, 'Infallible Scripture and the Role of Hermeneutics,' in D. A. Carson and J. D. Woodbridge, eds., *Scripture and Truth* (Grand Rapids: Zondervan, and Leicester: InterVarsity Press, 1983).

74. The phrase is Calvin's, *Institutes* I.12, 'To the King of France.'

75. Ibid., I.ix.3.

76. Commentary on Isa. 11:4.

77. Berkouwer, *Holy Scripture*, p. 137.

78. Kraus, *Interpretation*, pp. 12–18.

79. Ibid., p. 13. That and the next ideal are spelled out in Calvin's letter dedicating his first New Testament commentary, that on Romans, to Simon Grynaeus. Parker discusses the contents of the letter, pp. 26–27, 50–51.

80. Cf. A. C. Thiselton, 'Semantics and New Testament Interpretation,' in I. Howard Marshall, ed., *New Testament Interpretation* (Grand Rapids: Eerdmans, 1977), pp. 75–104; G. B. Caird, *The Language and Imagery of the Bible* (Philadelphia: Westminster Press, 1980).

81. *Institutes* III.xvii.14; cf. IV.xv.18, xvi.23.

82. Cf. Forstman, *Word and Spirit*, pp. 107–109.

83. *Institutes* II.viii.8. Cf. rule 4 for interpreting the Decalogue in the Westminster Assembly's Larger Catechism, answer 99: 'That as, where a duty is commanded, the contrary

sin is forbidden, and, where a sin is forbidden, the contrary duty is commanded: so, where a promise is annexed, the contrary threatening is included; and, where a threatening is annexed, the contrary promise is included.'

84. Ibid., III.v.6.

85. Not a metaphor, *pace* Kraus, *Interpretation*, pp. 16ff.

86. *Institutes* IV.xvii.21.

87. *CO*, 47:125, cited from W. Niesel, *The Theology of Calvin* (London: Lutterworth, 1956), p. 27.

88. Kraus, *Interpretation*, pp. 17ff.

89. Kraus, p. 15, notes how Calvin, in expounding the traditional 'Protoevangelium' (Gen. 3:15), declined to take *seed* as a specific reference to Christ, and declares: 'Calvin always reveals himself as an unusually careful interpreter of the Old Testament when it comes to christological interpretations. On Psalm 72:1 he observes. "We must always be careful not to give the Jews any reason to claim that we split hairs in order to find a reference to Christ in passages not directly related to him"' (*CO*, 59:664).

90. Forstman, *Word and Spirit*, p. 109.

91. Ibid.

92. Translated by William Pringle (Grand Rapids: Eerdmans, 1948); also by A. W. Morrison and T. H. L. Parker (Edinburgh: Saint Andrew's Press, 1972).

93. *Harmony of the Gospels,* trans. A. W. Morrison, 1:xiii.

94. *Institutes* I.viii.1. The whole sentence reads: 'It is wonderful how much confirmation comes from pondering with keener study how well ordered and arranged the economy of the divine wisdom appears there, how consistently heavenly is its doctrine, savouring of nothing earthly; how beautiful is the agreement of all its parts with each other: and the other such qualities which conspire to impart majesty to writings.'

95. Dowey, *The Knowledge of God in Calvin's Theology*, p. 104.

96. Thus, for instance, Calvin commented on Rom. 5:15 as follows: 'Although he [Paul] frequently mentions the difference between Adam and Christ, all his repeated statements . . . are elliptical. Those, it is true, are faults in his language, but in no way do they detract from the majesty of the heavenly wisdom which is delivered to us by the apostle' (*The Epistles of Paul the Apostle to the Romans and Thessalonians*, trans. David and Thomas Torrance [Grand Rapids: Eerdmans, 1960], p. 114). Rogers and McKim thus mislead when, attempting to show that Calvin acknowledged minor errors in Scripture, they echo J. T. McNeill's article 'The Significance of the Word of God for Calvin,' *Church History* 28 (1959), pp. 131–46, and claim that Calvin was 'critical of the "defects of the discourse" of the *original text* as for example at Acts 4:6 and Rom. 5:15 where he speaks with reference to the actual biblical writers themselves—Luke and Paul—not just of the "errors" in the text's transmission by careless copyists' (p. 142, n. 254, referring to McNeill, pp. 144ff. [italics theirs]). The 'defects' are of style only, not substance, and Calvin saw divine wisdom in them, for the comment on Rom. 5:15 continues: 'On the contrary, the singular providence of God has passed on to us these profound mysteries in the garb of a poor style, so that our faith might not depend on the power of human eloquence, but on the efficacy of the Spirit alone.' On Acts 4:6 all that Calvin said was that it is *mirum* (remarkable) that Luke said Annas was high priest when Josephus says that officially Caiaphas, his son-in-law, held that office. Modern commentators suppose that the two

men shared the jurisdiction. Calvin's remark notes an oddity that raises a question of fact, but it does not by any stretch of the imagination detect or allege a 'defect.'

97. Doumergue, *Jean Calvin*, 4:70–82.

98. McNeill, 'The Significance of the Word,' pp. 144ff.

99. Rogers and McKim, *Authority and Interpretation*, pp. 109–14.

100. The following paragraphs are based on what I wrote in *God's Inerrant Word*, pp. 105–107.

101. *Institutes* I.xiv.3.

102. Commentary on Gen. 1:16.

103. Commentary on Gen. 1:14–15. Rogers and McKim, *Authority and Interpretation*, p. 112, having correctly concluded from those words that for Calvin 'Moses' comments on the natural world were . . . an example of accommodated communication from God,' then say: 'There was no reason to suppose that Moses knew any more or thought any differently about the natural order than other people of his time and culture'—as if to say: God's accommodated communication was partly a matter of not letting any of Moses' mistaken notions about the natural order get on paper! But the two extracts from Calvin's Genesis commentary that they quote before and after that remark show that Calvin thought Moses knew what he was doing in deliberately declining to talk about the cosmos technically and above people's heads, which Calvin evidently assumes he could have done.

104. Rogers and McKim, *Authority and Interpretation*, p. 110; McNeill, 'The Significance of the Word,' p. 143.

105. Rogers and McKim, *Authority and Interpretation*, pp. 110ff.

106. *Harmony of the Gospels*, on Matt. 2:6.

107. Rogers and McKim, *Authority and Interpretation*, p. 109.

108. Ibid., p. 99.

109. Murray, *Calvin on Scripture*, p. 31.

110. Rogers and McKim, *Authority and Interpretation*, pp. 109–110. They cite Calvin's reply in his comment on Heb. 2:7 to the complaint that the author uses the phrase 'a little lower than the angels' in a sense different from that in which David in Psalm 8 meant it. Calvin wrote: 'It was not the purpose of the apostle to give an accurate exposition of the words. There is nothing improper if he looks for allusions in the words to embellish the case he is presenting.' But why they should treat Calvin's words here or his recognition (p. 110) that in Rom. 10:6 Paul adapted the words of Deut. 30:12 to make them carry new meaning as acknowledgement of a 'technical error' by a New Testament writer nowhere appears. If one is not trying to quote or expound exactly, what error is involved in the fact that one fails to quote or expound exactly? None, according to Calvin.

111. Ibid., pp. 109–14, especially p. 111.

112. Cf. Berkouwer, *Holy Scripture*, pp. 227ff.

113. Ibid., p. 112.

114. So, for instance, Calvin was not indifferent to the apparent discrepancy between 1 Cor. 10:8, where Paul mentions twenty-three thousand being killed instead of twenty-four thousand, as in Num. 25:9. Rogers and McKim (p. 142, n. 252) quote only his statement that 'it is not unheard of, where it is not intended to make an exact count of individuals, to give an approximate number.' That alone might suggest that Calvin simply brushed the matter aside; in fact, however, he also said in that context: 'But . . . it is easy

to reconcile their statements … Moses gives the upper limit, Paul the lower.' There is no question that Calvin, believing all scriptural statements of fact to be God-taught and therefore true, regarded harmonizing (i.e., demonstration of their truth and credibility, so far as one can do that) as part of the commentator's job.

115. Thus, for instance, to maximize Calvin's Augustinian-Platonist credentials, they assimilate his view of general revelation (a relational reality) to Plato's notion of innate ideas (a constitutional fact about man), and let the witness of the Spirit, which brings faith in Scripture, appear to be opposed to any idea of rational argument as a means whereby the Spirit induces that faith, which was certainly not Calvin's perspective.

Notes to Chapter 12

PREDESTINATION IN CHRISTIAN HISTORY was an address originally published in *Tenth* (Philadelphia: Tenth Presbyterian Church), July 1983, pp. 2–16. Reprinted by permission. Scripture quotations are from the New International Version.

Notes to Chapter 13

JUSTIFICATION IN PROTESTANT THEOLOGY was originally published in *Here We Stand: Justification by Faith Today* (London: Hodder and Stoughton, 1986), pp. 84–103. Reprinted by permission. Thanks are due also to the Presbyterian and Reformed Publishing Company of Philadelphia for permission to reprint some of this material which first appeared under their imprint. Scripture quotations are from the Revised Standard Version.

1. G. C. Berkouwer, *Faith and Justification* (Grand Rapids: Eerdmans, 1954), p. 17.

2. *Works* (reprinted, Edinburgh: Banner of Truth, 1975), I.321.

3. 'The sum of this epistle is to pull down, and pluck up and destroy, all the wisdom and righteousness of the flesh … and to affirm and state and magnify sin.' 'For God wills to save us, not by our own righteousness and wisdom, but by one from without … which comes from heaven. Thus it is by all means necessary to learn this external and foreign righteousness: for which reason our own internal righteousness must be first removed.' So declares Luther, *Works*, J. C. F. Knaske et al. (eds.), (Weimar, 1883–), LVI.157, 158; from the *Lectures on Romans* (1515–16).

4. *Tola haec doctrina ad illud certamen perterrefactae conscientiae referanda est. Nec sine illo certamine intelligi potest. Quare male judicant de ea re homines imperiti et profani* (Augsburg Confession XX).

5. The chapter is entitled: 'That we may be thoroughly convinced of free *(gratuita)* justification, we must lift up our mind to God's judgement-seat *(tribunal)*.'

6. *Works*, W. H. Goold ed. (reprinted, London: Banner of Truth, 1967), V.7, 4.

7. Calvin, *Institutes* III.xi.2.

8. The title of *Institutes* II.xvii is: 'It is right and proper to say that Christ *merited* God's grace and salvation for us.' So Anglican Article 11 affirms: 'We are accounted righteous

before God, only for the *merit* of our Lord and Saviour Jesus Christ, by Faith, and not for our own works or deservings.' And the Holy Communion service of the 1662 Book of Common Prayer complements this statement when it speaks of Christ as having 'made (by his one oblation of himself once offered) a full, perfect and sufficient sacrifice, oblation and *satisfaction* for the sins of the whole world.'

9. *Works,* V.608; from the *Commentary on the Psalms* (1519–21).

10. Ibid., LVI.347. Elsewhere Luther speaks of the Christian as *simul justus et peccator*—simultaneously righteous through Christ and a sinner in himself—and as *semper peccator, semper penitens, semper justus*—always a sinner, always penitent, always righteous [i.e., justified]—(ibid., p. 442).

11. Thus what is satisfied is God's *Law,* not just his *honour,* and the analogy for the transaction shifts from compensation, or damages in a civil suit, to the retributive infliction of penalty in a criminal court.

12. *Galatians,* 1535, from the 1575 English translation, ed. Philip S. Watson (London: James Clarke, 1953), pp. 269–71. Galatians was Luther's favourite epistle, and he was pleased with his commentary on it. When the complete Latin edition of his works was being prepared two years before his death, he said: 'If they took my advice, they'd print only the books containing doctrine, like Galatians' (ibid., p. 5). Gustaf Aulén in chapter 6 of *Christus Victor* (London: SPCK, 1931) was right to stress the dynamism of divine victory in Luther's account of the work of Christ, but wrong to ignore the penal substitution in terms of which that work is basically defined. Christ's victory, according to Luther, consisted precisely in the fact that he effectively purged our sins as our substitute on the cross, so freeing us from Satan's power by overcoming God's curse; if Luther's whole treatment of Gal. 3:13 (pp. 268–82) is read, this becomes very plain.

13. Calvin, *Institutes* II.xvi.5, 7. An excellent book on Calvin's doctrine of the cross is Paul Van Buren, *Christ in Our Place: The Substitutionary Character of Calvin's Doctrine of Reconciliation* (Edinburgh: Oliver and Boyd, 1957). Van Buren notes that 'there is no trace of a substitutionary understanding of the trial before Pilate in either (Peter) Lombard or Aquinas,' the two most standard medieval theologians (ibid., p. 46).

14. *Institutes* II.xv.10.

15. Cf. Westminster Confession XI.ii, 'faith . . . the alone instrument of justification . . . is . . . not alone in the person justified, but is ever accompanied with all other saving graces, and is no dead faith but worketh by love.'

16. 'Justification by Faith: the Reinstatement of the Doctrine Today,' *Evangelical Quarterly,* July 1952, p. 166.

17. Among major Reformed treatments of justification (in English) may be mentioned; Owen, *Works,* op. cit.; Jonathan Edwards, 'Justification by Faith Alone,' *Works,* ed. E. Hickman (reprinted, London: Banner of Truth, 1974), I.622–54; J. Buchanan, *The Doctrine of Justification* (reprinted, London: Banner of Truth, 1961); Berkouwer, *Faith and Justification*; C. Hodge, *Systematic Theology* (London: Nelson, 1874), III.114–212.

18. See the decrees of Trent, Session VI.vii. This doctrine is immediately applied in the unhappy canon 9: 'If any say that the sinner is justified through faith alone, in the sense that nothing else is necessary that co-operates to obtain the grace of justification, and that it is not necessary for the sinner to prepare himself, by means of his own will, let him be anathema.'

19. Cf. the remarkable statement of Session V.v: 'Concupiscence, which the Apostle sometimes calls sin, the holy Council declares that the Catholic Church has never understood to be called sin in the sense that it is truly and properly sin in those born again, but in the sense that it is of sin and inclines to sin. Should anyone be of a contrary opinion, let him be anathema.'

20. Hooker, 'A Learned Discourse of Justification,' *Works* (Oxford: Clarendon Press, 1865), II.606. Note how heavily Hooker's statement underlines Calvin's basic perspective, that our union with Christ is the foundation of the imputing of his righteousness to us. Owen underlines the same point with equal emphasis:

> The foundation of the imputation is union. Hereof there are many grounds and causes . . . but that which we have immediate respect unto, as the foundation of this imputation, is that whereby the Lord Christ and believers do actually *coalesce into one mystical person*. This is by the Holy Spirit inhabiting in him as the head of the church in all fullness, and in all believers according to their measure, whereby they become members of his mystical body. That there is such a union between Christ and believers is the faith of the catholic church and hath been so in all ages. Those who seem in our days to deny it, or question it, either know not what they say, or their minds are influenced by their doctrine who deny the divine persons of the Son and of the Spirit [i.e., the Socinians]. Upon supposition of this union, reason will grant the imputation pleaded for to be reasonable; at least, there is such a peculiar ground for it as is not to be exemplified in any things natural or political among men. (*Works*, V.209)

21. For the generalizations of this section, cf. C. F. Allison, *The Rise of Moralism* (London: SPCK, 1966), passim; Peter Toon, *Justification and Sanctification* (London: Marshall, Morgan and Scott, 1983), pp. 89–102; R. A. Leaver, *The Doctrine of Justification in the Church of England* (Oxford: Latimer House, 1979); R. G. England, *Justification Today: The Roman Catholic and Anglican Debate* (Oxford: Latimer House, 1979); Alister McGrath, *Iustitia Dei: A History of the Christian Doctrine of Justification* (Cambridge: Cambridge University Press, 1986), II.1–121; 'The Emergence of the Anglican Tradition on Justification, 1600–1700' (*Churchman*, 1984, XCVIII.1, 28–43); ibid., 'ARCIC II and Justification' (*Anvil* 1984, I.1.27–42); Philip Edgecumbe Hughes, *Faith and Works: Cranmer and Hooker on Justification* (Wilton, CT: Morehouse-Barlow, 1982).

22. *Works*, Library of Anglo-Catholic Theology (Oxford: J. H. Parker, 1847–49), I.114.

Notes on Chapter 14

THOMAS CRANMER'S CATHOLIC THEOLOGY was originally printed in *Thomas Cranmer*, ed. G. E. Duffield (Oxford: Sutton Courtenay Press, 1963), pp. x–xxxvii. Reprinted by permission.

1. J. Foxe, *Acts and Monuments*, ed. S. R. Cattley (London, 1837–39), VIII.86.

2. It is usually assumed that Cranmer read from his speech as originally drafted and changed the final section extempore, but Jasper Ridley's hypothesis of a 'Protestant'

version fully written out is convincing. See his *Thomas Cranmer* (Oxford: Oxford University Press, 1962), pp. 402–408.

3. Foxe, *Acts and Monuments*, p. 88: *inf.*, p. 337. The wording parodies the original draft, for which see Ridley, *Thomas Cranmer*, pp. 401ff.; Cranmer, *Works*, J. E. Cox ed. (Cambridge: Parker Society, Cambridge University Press, 1844–46), II.566.

4. Though Theodore Maynard does his best, describing Cranmer's last words in St. Mary's as blurted out, unpremeditated, in spur-of-the-moment rage because Cole, the preacher, had not announced his pardon (*Life of Thomas Cranmer*, London: Staples Press, 1956), p. 200.

5. C. H. Smyth, *Cranmer and the Reformation under Edward VI* (Cambridge: Cambridge University Press, 1926), p. 301.

6. *Works*, II.227; G. E. Duffield, ed., *Thomas Cranmer* (Oxford: Sutton Courtenay Press, 1963), p. 32.

7. *Narratives of the Days of the Reformation* (London: Camden Society, 1859), p. 219.

8. *Works*, I.374.

9. *Narratives*, p. 219.

10. *Works*, II.223. There is no reason to doubt the correctness of these details, though there are inaccuracies in Foxe's previous paragraph (Ridley, *Thomas Cranmer*, p. 376). Cranmer's problem of conscience was solved by his making a protestation before being consecrated, to the effect that he did not regard his oath to the Pope as binding him to do anything against the law of God or the king or realm of England, or as inhibiting him from 'the reformation of the Christian religion' in the English church (Latin text, *Works*, II.560). Ridley is no doubt right to see this protestation as an instrument of Henry's policy (pp. 56–57), but he is wrong to belittle its significance as a relief to Cranmer's conscience.

11. *Works*, II.327. In 1543 a Canterbury bricklayer claimed that Cranmer had said that he prayed for the overthrow of papal authority in England seven years before it was cast off (*Letters and Papers* [*Foreign and Domestic*] *of the Reign of Henry VIII*, 1509–47, ed. J. Brewer and J. Gairdner, London: HMSO, 1862–1910, XVIII (ii), 546, p. 303). This, if true—and Cranmer might well have said such a thing in a sermon—takes us back to 1526. For the date usually given, 1525, there seems to be no evidence.

12. *Works*, II.213.

13. The relevant passages from Cranmer's notes on Henry's revision of the *Institution* are in *Works*, II.84ff., 113–14, Duffield, *Thomas Cranmer*, pp. 5–12. The Latin text of Article 4 of 1538 is in *Works*, II.473. The teaching on justification in the *Institution* and Cranmer's notes is usefully analysed by D. B. Knox, *The Doctrine of Faith in the Reign of Henry VIII* (London: James Clarke, 1961), pp. 159–71. How large a part Cranmer played in compiling the Ten Articles of 1536, and how far they teach a distinctively reformed doctrine of justification, are disputed questions: see Knox *Doctrine of Faith*, pp. 152ff., and cf. Ridley, *Thomas Cranmer*, pp. 113–14.

14. *Works*, II.203ff. The fact that the notes are mostly in Cranmer's own hand, not his secretary's, unlike the later commonplace books, suggests an early date.

15. *Works*, II.477 (Latin text). Note the anticipation of Article 25 of the Thirty-nine (26 of the Forty-two of 1553).

16. *Works*, II.218. Ridley reached his new view of the eucharistic presence through reading Ratramnus' ninth-century tract *De Corpore et Sanguine Christi*, printed at Cologne in 1532 and Geneva in 1541 (Ridley, *Works*, Henry Christmas, ed., Cambridge: Parker

Society, Cambridge University Press, 1843, pp. 206, 290). This seems to have been in 1545. The date of Cranmer's change of mind is given as 1546 by Sir John Cheke in his preface to the 1557 (Emden) edition of his Latin translation of Cranmer's *Defence* (*Works,* I.6 [second pagination]).

17. *Works,* II.375.

18. *Works,* II.371–72. Latimer, who was always very much under Cranmer's influence, denied at his trial in 1555 that he had ever held the Lutheran position, 'for I never could see how Luther could defend his opinion without transubstantiation' (*Sermons and Remains,* Cambridge: Parker Society, *Works,* G. E. Corrie, ed., Cambridge: Parker Society, Cambridge University Press, 1845, p. 265). This may well reflect Cranmer's own view.

19. *Works,* I.226 (*Defence,* 1550). 'In that Catechism I teach not, as you do, that the body and blood of Christ is contained in the sacrament, being reserved, but that in the ministration thereof we receive the body and blood of Christ . . . add or understand the word "spiritually" . . .' p. 227 (*Answer,* 1551). Cf. also p. 374.

20. For Cranmer's alterations, see Smyth, *Cranmer and the Reformation,* pp. 51–52, and cf. his whole discussion, pp. 50–59. The crucial pages of eucharistic teaching in the catechism (*A Short Instruction into Christian Religion:* pp. 207–10 of the Oxford, 1829, edition) are printed in *Cranmer's Selected Writings,* ed. Carl S. Meyer (London: SPCK, 1961), pp. 50-51. Meyer (p. 51, n. 1) repeats the mistake of 'divers ignorant persons,' as does Ridley (*Thomas Cranmer,* pp. 281–83). Ridley is sometimes unreliable on theological matters.

21. *Narratives,* p. 219.

22. Duffield, *Thomas Cranmer,* pp. 341–65, prints a catalogue of Cranmer's library, which shows this.

23. *Narratives,* p. 249.

24. *Works,* II.77–78. The source quoted here and in note 26 is Burnet's abridgment of a speech of which the manuscript has not survived. See Duffield, *Thomas Cranmer,* p. 16.

25. *Works,* II.59.

26. *Works,* II.77–78.

27. *Works,* II.1–67.

28. The commonplace books, which have never been published nor, it seems, studied, are described by A. J. Mason, *Thomas Cranmer* (London, Methuen, 1898), pp. 85–88. The first fourteen sections contain the material published as *A Confutation . . .* The list of subjects (written, like most of the entries, in Latin) includes ceremonies, Christian sacrifices, sacraments, 'character,' baptism, the eucharist, *poenitentia* (penance or repentance), satisfaction for sin, marriage, orders, unction, laying on of hands, confirmation, holy water, holy days, invocation of saints, images, relics, the religious life, vows, celibacy, the church, church building and ornaments, prayer, fasting, almsgiving, excommunication, the mass, God's laws, grace and merit, free will, purgatory, the Virgin, conversion, works before grace, faith, and obedience to magistrates.

29. *Works,* II.106 (1xxi).

30. Ibid., II.514. Strype ascribed it to Cranmer: style and content make this likely, though not certain.

31. Ibid., II.563: from the fourth recantation.

32. See ibid., II.23, 29.

33. Ibid., II.59.

34. Ibid., II.121; Duffield, *Thomas Cranmer,* p. 37.

35. The three homilies are printed separately in *Works,* II.128ff. and Meyer, *Cranmer's Selected Writings,* pp. 12ff. They are cited here from Corrie's critical edition of the Homilies: *Certain Sermons . . .* (Cambridge, 1850). Their theological content is conveniently analysed by Knox, *Doctrine of Faith,* pp. 265ff.

36. *Certain Sermons,* p. 25.

37. Ibid., p. 20.

38. Ibid., p. 19.

39. Ibid., p. 22.

40. *Works,* II.93 (xxxii).

41. *Certain Sermons,* pp. 34–35.

42. Ibid., p. 27.

43. Ibid.

44. *Works,* II.93 (xxxi).

45. *Certain Sermons,* p. 34.

46. *Works,* II.181. 'Lee' is lye, an alkaline liquid used for washing.

47. *Works,* I.348.

48. G. Dix, *The Shape of the Liturgy* (London: Dacre Press, 1945), p. 672.

49. *Works,* I.377–78.

50. Article 20 of the Forty-two; it reappeared unchanged as Article 19 of the Thirty-nine. It is derived from the Augsburg Confession (VII).

51. *Works,* II.117 (questions 12–14).

52. See the Letters to A Lasco, Hardenberg, Bucer, Melanchthon, Calvin, in Duffield, *Thomas Cranmer,* pp. 311–23.

53. *Works,* I.6; Duffield, *Thomas Cranmer,* p. 57.

54. *Works,* I.38; Duffield, *Thomas Cranmer,* p. 65.

55. *Works,* I.41; Duffield, *Thomas Cranmer,* p. 70.

56. *Works,* I.38–40; Duffield, *Thomas Cranmer,* pp. 65–71.

57. *Works,* I.25; cf. I.92, 11, 181, 341.

58. Ibid., I.11.

59. Ibid., I.185.

60. Ibid., I.43; Duffield, *Thomas Cranmer,* p. 74.

61. *Works,* I.398, 399.

62. *Works,* I.346; Duffield, *Thomas Cranmer,* p. 217.

63. *Works,* I.351; Duffield, *Thomas Cranmer,* p. 225.

64. *Works,* I.353; Duffield, *Thomas Cranmer,* p. 229.

65. *Works,* I.374.

66. Stephen Neill, *Anglicanism* (Harmondsworth: Penguin, 1958), p. 79.

Notes to Chapter 15

RICHARD BAXTER ON HEAVEN, HOPE, AND HOLINESS was originally published in *Alive to God: Studies in Spirituality Presented to James M. Houston,* J. I. Packer and Loren Wilkinson, eds. (Downers Grove, IL: InterVarsity Press, 1992), pp. 161–75. Scripture quotations are from the New International Version.

1. N. H. Keeble, *Richard Baxter: Puritan Man of Letters* (Oxford: Clarendon Press, 1982), p. 104. Keeble illustrates from A. L. Rowse's *Milton the Puritan* (1977).

2. See, for Baxter's role in Puritanism, Keeble, *Richard Baxter*, J. I. Packer, *A Man for All Ministries: Richard Baxter, 1615–1691* (London: St. Antholin's Lectureship, 1991, reprinted in this volume); also in *Reformation and Revival* 1.1 (1992), pp. 53–74; *A Quest for Godliness: The Puritan Vision of the Christian Life* (Wheaton, IL: Crossway, 1990), pp. 60–65, 302–308; *Among God's Giants* (Eastbourne: Kingsway, 1990), pp. 79–85, 397–405; Hugh Martin, *Puritanism and Richard Baxter* (London: SCM Press, 1954).

3. See, for instance, William Haller, *The Rise of Puritanism* (New York: Columbia University Press, 1938); Perry Miller, *The New England Mind, I: The Seventeenth Century* (Cambridge, MA: Harvard University Press, 1939); M. M. Knappen, *Tudor Puritanism* (Chicago: Chicago University Press, 1939); and Martin, *Puritanism and Richard Baxter*.

4. 'Throughout his life he was subject to a bewildering variety of physical ailments, which he details in the *Reliquiae* and to which he refers in passing in many of his books. In one such passage, written in 1671, he recalled that "since fourteen years of age I have not been a year from suffering, and since twenty two but few dayes, from and since 1646 (which is about twenty five years), I have had but few hours free from pain (though through God's mercy not intolerable)." His memory seems not to have exaggerated his plight, for in a letter of 1650 he remarks that relief from pain comes "perhaps once a month for a few hours unexpected"' (Keeble, *Richard Baxter*, p. 11; referring to *Reliquiae Baxterianae* [1696] I.9–11, 80–83, III.60ff., 173ff., 192, 1987 and citing *A Second Admonition to Mr. Edward Bagshaw* [1671], p. 65).

5. Richard Baxter, *Practical Works*, first printed in four folios (1707); reprinted in four volumes in 1838 and now intermittently available by mail order in four volumes from Ligonier: Soli Deo Gloria, 1990–1991. (Postal address: PO Box 451, Morgan, PA 10564, USA.) This is the edition I shall cite.

6. Baxter, *Poetical Fragments* (1681), pp. 38, 40.

7. Keeble, *Richard Baxter*, p. 6.

8. *Reliquiae Baxterianae*, I.108.

9. 'The Heavenly State cost him severe and daily thoughts and Solemn Contemplations for he set some time apart every day for that weighty work' (Matthew Sylvester, 'Elisha's Cry after Elijah's God,' memorial sermon for Baxter appended to *Reliquiae Baxterianae* [1696], p. 15).

10. F. J. Powicke, *The Reverend Richard Baxter under the Cross* (London: George Allen & Unwin, 1927), p. 97. Powicke mistakenly supposes it was written in 1683, but the 1676 date is proved by Baxter's statement on a letter to Sir Matthew Hale, dated May 5 of that year: 'I am writing my own funeral sermon on Phil. 1:23.' He continues: 'We never live like believers indeed till the thoughts of heaven be sweeter to us than all our peace and hopes on earth, and till we truly believe that it is better to depart and be with Christ than to be here.' The letter, first published in *John Rylands Library Bulletin* 24.1 (1940), pp. 173ff., is printed almost in full in N. H. Keeble and Geoffrey F. Nuttall, *Calendar of the Correspondence of Richard Baxter* (Oxford: Clarendon Press, 1991), 2.186ff.

11. William Bates, 'A Sermon on the Death of Mr. Richard Baxter,' *Works* (Harrisonburg: Sprinkle, 1990), 4.338ff.

12. Sylvester, "Elisha's Cry," p. 14.

13. See, in particular, *The Pilgrim's Regress* (London: Geoffrey Bles, 1933) and *Surprised by Joy* (London: Geoffrey Bles, 1955).

14. N. H. Keeble, *'Loving and Free Converse': Richard Baxter in His Letters* (London: Dr. Williams' Trust, 1991).

15. Baxter, *Practical Works*, III.643.

16. Ibid., p. 1036.

17. Ibid., p. 43.

18. Ibid., p. 756.

19. Ibid., p. 1017.

20. Ibid., p. 979.

21. Ibid., p. 1013.

22. Ibid., p. 1012.

23. Ibid., p. 1016.

24. Ibid., p. 1017.

25. Ibid.

26. Ibid., p. 1023.

27. Ibid.

28. Ibid., p. 1006.

29. Ibid., p. 1025.

30. Ibid., p. 319; see Keeble, *Richard Baxter*, pp. 100–103.

31. Ibid., pp. 21–22.

32. Ibid., p. 43.

33. *Reliquiae Baxterianae*, I.129.

34. Baxter, *Practical Works*, III.991.

35. Ibid., p. 270. When in 1670 Giles Firmin queried in print Baxter's insistence on sustained meditation, arguing that it made for imbalance and 'melancholy' (depression), Baxter came back at him with the following rebuttal:

> 'I find that whatever else I think of, of Christ, of Scripture, of Promises, of Threatenings, of sin, of Grace, &c. if I leave out *Heaven* and make it not the chief point of my Meditation, I leave out the sense of life of all. Thence must I fetch my Light, or I must be in Darkness; Thence must I fetch my Life, or I must be Dead, and my *Motives* or I must be Dull, or not sincere ... My hearing, Reading, and Studies grow to common things, if Heaven be not the principal part; My life groweth toward a common and a carnal life, when I begin to leave out Heaven; Death groweth terrible to my thoughts, and Eternity strange and dreadful to me if I live not in such frequent and serious thoughts of the Heavenly Glory, as may render it familiar and grateful to my soul ... And I find myself unfit to Live or to Die, and that my soul is void of true Consolation ... when I grow a stranger to Heavenly Thoughts, and consequently to Heavenly Affections ... And that as nothing will serve turn instead of Heaven to be my happiness so nothing will serve turn instead of Heaven to ... form my Heart and Life to Holiness. And therefore by experience I counsel all Christians that are able to perform especially ministers, and Learned men, to be much in the serious fore-thoughts of Heaven ...' (*The Duty of Heavenly Meditation Reviewed* [1671], pp. 31ff.).

36. Baxter, *Practical Works*, III.249.

37. Ibid., p. 299.

38. Baxter, *Duty*, p. 19.

39. Baxter, *Practical Works*, III.330: 'at least a quarter of an hour, if not more, is best to Edification . . . I prove it from the Aptitude of the Means to its end' (*Duty*, pp. 16ff.).

40. Baxter, *Practical Works*, III.296.

41. Ibid., p. 306.

42. Ibid.

43. Cited from John Booty's introduction to *John Donne* (Classics of Western Spirituality; New York: Paulist Press, 1990), p. 33.

44. Baxter, *Practical Works*, III.316.

45. Ibid., I.133.

46. Ibid., III.318.

47. Ibid., p. 275.

48. Ibid., p. 293.

Notes to Chapter 16

ARMINIANISMS was originally published in *Through Christ's Word* (Phillipsburg, NJ: Presbyterian and Reformed W. Robert Godfrey Publishing, 1985), Jesse L. Boyd III, pp. 121-48. Reprinted by permission.

1. John Wesley wrote: 'It is the duty of every Arminian preacher, . . . never in public or in private, to use the word *Calvinist* as a term of reproach . . . and it is the duty of every Calvinist preacher . . . never . . . to use the word *Arminian* as a term of reproach' (*Works*, 'from the latest London edition' [New York: Lane and Scott, 1850], V.134). To dispute this proposition would be hard.

2. Cf. my introduction to John Owen, *The Death of Death in the Death of Christ* (London: Banner of Truth, 1959).

3. *The Writings of Arminius*, trans. James Nichols and W. R. Bagnall (Grand Rapids: Baker Book House, 1956), I:iii.

4. John Owen, *Works*, ed. W. Goold (London: Banner of Truth, 1967), X:6.

5. Full title, *The Arminian Magazine: Consisting of Extracts and Original Treatise on Universal Redemption*; changed in 1805 to *The Methodist Magazine*.

6. John Fletcher, *Works* (London, 1814), II:232-34. Proof of Fletcher's statement on Wesley's view of man's fallenness, and of the importance Wesley attached to it, is abundantly supplied in *The Doctrine of Original Sin according to Scripture, Reason and Experience* (1757), his 100,000-word reply to Dr John Taylor (*Works*, V.492-669).

7. When the Nazarene theologian H. Orton Wiley calls synergism, defined as 'the cooperation of divine grace and the human will,' a 'basic truth of the Arminian system,' adding, however, that the ability to cooperate is a gift of grace, not an endowment of nature, he reproduces Wesley's view exactly (Christian Theology [Kansas City: Beacon Hill Press], II:355). Carl Bangs, in his admirable *Arminius: A Study in the Dutch Reformation* (Nashville: Abingdon Press, 1971), p. 342, notes that the English Wesleyan theologian W. B. Pope rejected the word 'synergism' since the Lutheran use of it implied that man could cooperate with God by virtue of natural goodness not wholly corrupted by the Fall (*Christian*

Theology [New York: Phillips and Hunt, 1880], II:77–78, 389–90, III:24–25, 74). In this, Pope was identifying with Wesley's view and guarding it against misunderstanding.

8. For Luther, see his reply to Erasmus, *The Bondage of the Will*, trans. and introduced by J. I. Packer and O. R. Johnston (London: James Clarke, 1957). For Calvin, see *Institutes*, III.xxi–xxiv, and his reply to Pighius, *The Eternal Predestination of God*, trans. J. K. S. Reid (London: James Clarke, 1961). For the Anglican Reformers, see Philip Edgcumbe Hughes, *The Theology of the English Reformers* (London: Hodder and Stoughton, 1965), pp. 68–73, and Article 17 of the Thirty-nine. Note that the motives which prompted the Reformers' strong assertion of sovereign predestination were pastoral and doxological; they wanted to induce humble realism about our natural helplessness in sin, pure faith which totally forsakes self-reliance and self-confidence to trust Christ fully, strong hope that God will hold us fast and finish the good work he has begun in our lives, and heartfelt love to God for his great love to us. This is particularly clear in the two pastoral paragraphs which follow the dogmatic definition of predestination in Article 17, '. . . the godly consideration of Predestination, and our Election in Christ, is full of sweet, pleasant and unspeakable comfort to godly persons, and such as feel in themselves the working of the Spirit of Christ, mortifying the works of the flesh, and their earthly members, and drawing up their mind to high and heavenly things, as well because it doth greatly establish and confirm their faith of eternal Salvation to be enjoyed through Christ, as because it doth fervently kindle their love towards God . . . we must receive God's promises in such wise, as they be generally set forth to us in holy Scripture . . .'

9. Arminius, to which Harmenszoon Latinized his name, was originally the name of a first-century Germanic chief who resisted the Romans.

10. Arminius' lifelong friend, Petrus Bertius, said in his funeral oration for the theologian that Arminius' studies led him first to move from supralapsarianism to infralapsarianism and then settle for a position like that of Melanchthon and Nicholas Hem(m)ingius, Lutheran professor of theology at Copenhagen, and once Melanchthon's student. That position was the conditional predestination of individuals based on a synergistic view of how through grace men have faith. Bangs, who cites this (*Arminius*, pp. 138–39), doubts whether Bezan supralapsarianism was ever Arminius' view, but it would be strange if Bertius, who knew Arminius well and speaks positively on the point, was wrong.

11. Arminius' views were based on his understanding of Romans 7 and 9, on both of which he wrote formal treatises. He argues that the 'wretched man' of Rom. 7:14ff., the man who feels himself 'carnal, sold under sin' while he delights in God's law and loathes his involuntary failures to keep it, cannot be regenerate, and goes on to belabour the alternative view as encouraging low moral standards among Christians by teaching them not to expect grace to free them from sin. He misses the point that any devoted Christian expressing his feelings about the shortcomings of his obedience will naturally find himself using Paul's language, nor does he weigh the theological implications of supposing that an unregenerate person can wholeheartedly ('in my inmost self,' v. 22, RSV) delight in God's law. His view of Rom. 9 rests on the hypothesis that the question Paul answers from verse 6 on is not, 'does the word of God fail if most Jews are rejected?' (answer no, for God's election has regularly passed some Jews by), but 'does the word of God fail if God rejects Jews who seek righteousness by works, not faith?' (answer no, for God has always done this). It must be said at once that, if that is what Paul means, his language

is extraordinarily elliptical and misleading. There is a fuller summary of Arminius' arguments in Bangs, *Arminius*, pp. 186ff.

12. For the Remonstrance, see H. Bettenson, *Documents of the Christian Church* (London: Oxford University Press, 1943), XL:iv; Philip Schaff, *The Creeds of Christendom* (New York: Harper and Bros., 1877) I:516ff. Its fifth point, no less than its first four, reproduced the thinking of Arminius: see Bangs, *Arminius*, pp. 216–19, 348–49. The canons of Dort are in Schaff, *Creeds of Christendom*, III:550ff., also, translated from the Dutch version by Dr Gerrit J. Van der Lugt, in *Liturgy and Psalms* (New York: Board of Education, Reformed Church of America, 1968), and, in a most accurate rendering of the original Latin, by Anthony A. Hoekema, in *Calvin Theological Journal* (November 1968). Dr Hoekema's translation is separately available from Calvin Theological Seminary.

13. A. W. Harrison, *Arminianism* (London: Duckworth, 1937), p. 93.

14. Schaff, *Creeds of Christendom*, I:509. The Remonstrant Brotherhood (*Remonstrantse Broederschap*; the Remonstrant-Reformed Church) still exists. Lambertus Jacobus van Holk, one of its theologians, described it in 1960 as 'the only basically nonconfessional denomination in the Netherlands' (*Man's Faith and Freedom*, ed. Gerald O. McCulloh [Nashville: Abingdon Press, 1963], p. 42).

15. Schaff, *Creeds of Christendom*, I:659.

16. For the Lambeth Articles, see C. Hardwick, *History of the Articles* (London, 1859), ch. 7 and app. V; Schaff, *Creeds of Christendom*, I:658ff., III:523.

17. Hence the oft-repeated *bon mot*: 'What do the Arminians hold?' 'The best bishoprics and deaneries in all England.'

18. See Rosalie L. Colie, *Light and Enlightenment: A Study of the Cambridge Platonists and the Dutch Arminians* (New York: Cambridge University Press, 1957). 'Arminianism was in the beginning the result of the common-sense, humanistic attitude towards religion, metaphysics, physics, and human society, attractive to men of good will in England as in Holland: it gave authority to Mede, Whichcote, More, Cudworth and their fellows; it took much in turn from their philosophic idealism . . . the Arminian and Platonist traditions became inextricably mixed' (p. 144).

19. Cf. Calvin, *Institutes* III, especially xi; Hughes, *Theology of the English Reformers*, ch. 2, pp. 54–75.

20. Decrees of the Council of Trent, VI.vii; cf. V.v; both translated in C. F. Allison, *The Rise of Moralism: The Proclamation of the Gospel from Hooker to Baxter* (London: SPCK, 1966), pp. 213–14. Allison's book assembles much thought-provoking material about the declension from the Reformers' view of justification by faith in seventeenth-century England.

21. Englishmen who upheld the Reformation doctrine in print included Richard Hooker, Bishops George Downame, Lancelot Andrewes, John Davenant, James Ussher, Joseph Hall, Thomas Barlow, John Bramhall, Robert Sanderson, William Nicholson, William Beveridge; John Donne, Thomas Gataker, Anthony Burgess, John Owen, Isaac Barrow, Robert Traill.

22. 'It is entirely by the intervention of Christ's righteousness that we obtain justification before God. This is equivalent to saying that man is not righteous in himself, but that the righteousness of Christ is communicated to him by imputation, while he is strictly deserving of punishment. Thus vanishes the absurd dogma, that man is justified by faith

inasmuch as faith brings him under the influence of the Spirit of God, by whom he is rendered righteous . . . You see that our righteousness is not in us but in Christ, that we possess it only because we are partakers in Christ' (*Institutes* II.xi.23). See also Calvin's discussion of session VI of the Council of Trent, *Tracts and Treaties* (Edinburgh: Calvin Translation Society, 1844–51), III:108ff., especially pp. 114–21.

23. When Johannes Piscator of Herborn urged that only the passive obedience of Christ is imputed to believers, Reformed theologians generally rejected his view. This was at the end of the sixteenth century.

24. The fullest and most exact demonstration of this is R. T. Kendall's monograph, *Calvin and English Calvinism to 1649: The Concept of Faith from William Perkins to the Westminster Assembly* (Oxford: Oxford University Press, 1979).

25. 'To a man who believes, faith is imputed for righteousness through grace, because God has sent forth his Son, Jesus Christ, to be a propitiation, a throne of grace, through faith in his blood' (*The Writings of Arminius*, I:264).

26. Bull, *Harmonia Apostolica* (Library of Anglo-Catholic Theology, Oxford: Parker, 1844), I:58, 57. See Allison, *The Rise of Moralism*, ch. 6, 'The Theology of George Bull,' pp. 118–37.

27. *Redemption Redeemed* (1651) was Goodwin's magnum opus, a six-hundred-page folio which he dedicated to Benjamin Whichcote, the Cambridge Platonist, as vice-chancellor of the University, and to all the college heads and divinity students there. Its title-page is a memorable memorial to the days before dust-jackets and publishers' blurbs.

> Ἀπολύτρωσις Ἀπολύτρωσεως; or Redemption Redeemed. Wherein the Most Glorious Work of the Redemption of the World by Jesus Christ, is by Expressness of Scripture, clearness of Argument, countenance of the best Authority as well Ancient as Modern, Vindicated and Asserted in the Just Latitude and Extent of it, according to the Counsel and most Gracious Intentions of God, against the incroachments of later times made upon it, whereby the unsearchable Riches and Glory of the Grace of God therein, have been, and yet are, much obscured, and hid from the eyes of many. Together with a sober, plain and thorough Discussion of the great Questions relating hereunto, as viz. concerning Election and Reprobation, the Sufficiency, and Efficacy of the Means vouchsafed unto Men by God to repent and Beleeve; concerning the Perseverance of the Saints, and those who do believe; concerning the Nature of God, his manner of Acting, his Intentions, Purposes, Decrees, etc., the Dependency of all Creatures, or second Causes upon Him, as well in their Operations, as simple Existencies, or Beings, etc. The Decision of all these Questions founded upon the good Word of God, interpreted according to the generally-received Doctrine, concerning the Nature and Attributes of God, the manifest Exigency of the Words, Phrases, coherencies. In the respective passages hereof relating to the said Questions, as also (for the most part) according to the Judgment and Sence of the best Expositors, as well Modern, as Ancient. With three Tables annexed for the Readers accommodation.

John Owen, then vice-chancellor of Oxford University, replied in 1654 with a folio of similar length, dedicated to Oliver Cromwell, dealing with the theme of perseverance, which had a title-page of almost equal impressiveness.

> The Doctrine of the Saints Perseverance Explained and Confirmed, or, the certain Permanency of their (1) Acceptation with God and (2) Sanctification from God manifested

and proved from the (1) Eternall Principles (2) Effectual Causes (3) Externall Meanes Thereof. In (1) the Immutability of the Nature Decrees Covenants and Promises of God (2) the blation and Intercession of Jesus Christ (3) the Promises, Exhortations, Threats of the Gospell. Improved in its Genuine Tendency to Obedience and Consolation. And Vindicated in a Full Answer to the Discourse of Mr. John Goodwin against it, in his book Entituled Redemption Redeemed. *With some Digressions Concerning (1) the Immediate effects of the Death of Christ (2) Personall Indwelling of the Spirit (3) Union with Christ (4) the nature of Gospell promises &c. also a preface Manifesting the Judgements of the Antients touching the Truth contended for: with a discourse touching the epistles of Ignatius; the episcopacy in them Asserted; and some Animadversions on Dr. H.H: his Dissertations on that Subject.* ('H. H.' was Henry Hammond.)

28. See Allison, *The Rise of Moralism*, ch. 8, pp. 154–77. Allison does not note the Arminian source of the idea, common to Baxter, Hammond, Thorndike, Jeremy Taylor, and John Goodwin, that faith is itself our righteousness by reason of the new principle of acceptance which God enacted for Jesus' sake. But he is right when he says:

> If we are justified only by a righteousness of our own (made acceptable on account of Christ's sacrifice), and if our own righteousness is in fact directly given to us by God, as Baxter seems to say, then it is difficult to distinguish Baxter's position from that of the Council of Trent. (p. 163)

29. John Owen devotes the last part of his treatise on the Holy Spirit (*Pneumatologia*) to correcting the assumption that the Reformed gospel makes holiness needless. 'The Socinians contend that the doctrine of the satisfaction of Christ doth overthrow the necessity of a holy life; the Papists say these are concerning the imputation of the righteousness of Christ unto our justification; the same charge is laid by others against the doctrine of the gratuitous election of God, the almighty efficacy of his grace in the conversion of sinners, and his faithfulness in the preservation of true believers in their state of grace unto the end' (*Works*, III:566–67). But, says Owen, holiness is necessary by reason of (1) God's nature, (2) God's electing purpose, (3) God's command, (4) the goal of Christ's mission, (5) our need to be cured of the inner disorder sin has brought.

30. For the full story, see Peter Toon, *Hyper-Calvinism* (London: The Olive Tree, 1969), ch. 3. On Crisp, cf. Allison, *The Rise of Moralism*, pp. 171–72. Crisp affirmed justification before faith through Christ's substitutionary death for us, and spoke Lutherishly of Christ becoming by imputation a great sinner. His idea of faith as knowledge of Christ's death for me, the sinner, was Lutherish too. Published with the title *Christ Alone Exalted*, Crisp's sermons celebrate the great grace of Christ to great sinners in his atoning death and present acceptance of the worst of us. Crisp disclaims antinomianism, urging holiness as our grateful response. The worst that can be said of him is that some of his language was tasteless and overstrained. John Gill, a hyper-Calvinist but no antinomian, reprinted the sermons later with notes vindicating Crisp's essential soundness; this edition reached its seventh reprint in 1832.

31. The Unitarian historian Alexander Gordon was a case in point. The Richard Baxter Church in Kidderminster today is a Unitarian meeting house.

32. *Arminianism*, p. 111. Amyraldism is evaluated, under the name 'Post-redemptionism,' in B. B. Warfield, *The Plan of Salvation* (Grand Rapids: Eerdmans, 1975), pp. 90–96.

33. The letter is given in Luke Tyerman, *Life and Times of John Wesley* (New York: Harper, 1872), I:39–40; Harrison, *Arminianism*, pp. 189–90; Martin Schmidt, *John Wesley: A Geological Biography* (London: Epworth Press, 1962), I:87–88.

34. Wesley 'rejects the commonly held view that justification is a double act in which the first part takes place in the present and presupposes faith, whilst the second is at the last day and requires works. But for John Wesley there was only *one* justification . . . received by faith alone, and faith was begotten only through grace' (Schmidt, *John Wesley*, II:43).

35. *Institutes* III.ii.7; cf. n. 24 above.

36. Compare this definition of faith, from the 1744 Conference Minutes: 'First, a sinner is convinced by the Holy Ghost, "Christ loved me and gave himself for me." This is that faith by which he is justified or pardoned the moment he receives it. Immediately the same Spirit bears witness, "Thou art pardoned; thou hast redemption in his blood." And this is saving faith, whereby the love of God is shed abroad in his heart.' Cited from Maximin Piette, *John Wesley in the Evolution of Protestantism* (London: Sheed and Ward, 1938), p. 423.

37. Cited from Harrison, *Arminianism*, p. 191. Wesley also wrote: 'No man ever lived, not John Calvin himself, who asserted either original sin or justification by faith in more strong, more clear and express terms, than Arminius has done. In this respect there is not a hair's breadth difference between Mr. Wesley and Mr. Whitefield' (*Works*, V.133). On original sin, Wesley's statement about Arminius is substantially true (cf. Bangs, *Arminius*, pp. 337ff.), but on justification Wesley, if not disingenuous, was not well informed. In *Thoughts on Christ's Imputed Righteousness* (1762: *Works*, V.100ff.) he declines to speak of the imputed righteousness of Christ as the ground of justification simply because it is not a biblical phrase, taking no notice of the difference between Reformed and Arminian conceptions of how Christ's obedience and man's faith relate in justification; yet he republished at different times Richard Baxter's *Aphorisms of Justification* and John Goodwin's *Treatise on Justification*, in both of which the Arminian conception is opposed to the Reformed in quite a sharp way.

38. *Works*, ed. T. Jackson (London, 1829), VIII:336.

39. The phrase 'horrible decree' is Wesley's tendentious rendering of Calvin's description (*Institutes* III.xxiii.7) of God's decree of election and reprobation as '*horrible*'— *meaning something awesome, making one tremble, but not necessarily something repellent.*

40. Cited from Colin Williams, *John Wesley's Theology Today* (London: Epworth Press, 1960), pp. 61–62. Harrison, *Arminianism*, pp. 204ff., traces the course of the debates which the Minutes provoked.

41. *Arminianism*, p. 206. The 1771 Conference declared: 'as the said [1770] Minutes are not sufficiently guarded in the way they are expressed, we hereby solemnly declare, in the sight of God, that we have no trust or confidence but in the alone merits of our Lord and Saviour Jesus Christ, for Justification or Salvation either in life, death or the day of judgment; and though no one is a real Christian believer, (and consequently can not be saved) who doeth not good works . . . yet our works have no part in meriting or purchasing our salvation from first to last, either in whole or in part.'

42. Ames, *De Conscientia*, IV.iv, q. 4; cited in Latin by William Cunningham, *Historical Theology* (London: Banner of Truth, 1960), II:378.

43. The most impressive major demonstration that the Bible speaks in 'Calvinistic' terms remains that of John Owen in various large-scale works; see in particular *The Death of Death in the Death of Christ* (Latin title, *Sanguis Jesu Salus Electorum,* 'the blood of Jesus is the salvation of the elect'); *Justification by Faith; The Doctrine of the Saints' Perseverance;* Πνευματολογια (on regeneration); *Vindiciae Evangelicae* (*Works,* X, V, XI, III, XII). The classic analyses in English of the differences between the rival conceptions remain Owen's *Display of Arminianism* (*Works,* X) and William Cunningham, *Historical Theology,* ch. XXV, II:371–513.

44. Mildred Bangs Wynkoop, *Foundations of Wesleyan-Arminian Theology* (Kansas City: Beacon Hill Press, 1967), p. 81.

45. Basil Hall, 'Calvin against the Calvinists,' in *John Calvin,* ed. Gervase E. Duffield (Abingdon: Sutton Courtenay Press, and Grand Rapids: Eerdmans, 1966), p. 19.

46. Ibid., p. 25.

Notes to Chapter 17

BRITISH THEOLOGY IN THE FIRST HALF OF THE TWENTIETH CENTURY was originally published as 'British Theology in the Twentieth Century' in *Christian Faith Modern Theology* (New York: Channel Press, 1964), pp. 25–43. Reprinted by permission.

1. Vidler, *Essays in Liberality* (London: SCM Press, 1957), p. 21.

2. Essay in *Foundations,* a volume subtitled 'A Statement of Christian Beliefs in Terms of Modern Thought' (London: Macmillan, 1912).

3. *Christus Veritas* (London: Macmillan, 1924); *Nature, Man, and God* (London: Macmillan, 1934).

4. Introduction to the report, *Doctrine in the Church of England* (London: SPCK, 1938, p. 17).

5. F. A. Iremonger, *William Temple* (London: Oxford University Press, 1948), pp. 537–38.

6. A. M. Ramsey, *From Gore to Temple* (London: Longmans, Green and Co., 1960), p. 148.

7. London: Longmans, Green and Co., 1928.

8. *Christendom* (London: Mowbray, 1959), p. 148.

9. *The Person and Place of Jesus Christ* (London: Hodder and Stoughton, 1909), pp. 222–23.

10. New York, London: Harper, 1928.

11. *The International Critical* and *Westminster Commentaries,* the *Cambridge Bible* and *Century Bible* series, Hastings's series of Bible dictionaries, and so forth.

12. J. W. C. Wand, *Anglicanism in History and Today* (New York, London: Thomas Nelson and Sons, 1961), p. 122.

13. *The Bible under Trial* (London: Marshall Bros., 1907), p. 54.

14. *The Bible in the Age of Science* (London: SCM, and Philadelphia: Westminster, 1961), p. 63.

15. *Inspiration* (London: Longmans Green, 1893).

16. Ramsey, *From Gore to Temple,* p. 40.

17. *Christus Veritas,* ch. VIII.

18. *Some Tendencies in British Theology* (New York: Macmillan; London: SPCK, 1951), pp. 26–27.

19. *From Gore to Temple,* p. 156.

20. Mozley, *Some Tendencies in British Theology,* pp. 78–83.

21. *Letters of Principal James Denney to W. Robertson Nicoll* (London: Hodder and Stoughton, 1920), p. xvi.

22. *Letters of Principal James Denney to His Family and Friends* (London: Hodder and Stoughton, 1921), pp. 154, 153.

23. J. Denney, *The Death of Christ* (London: Hodder and Stoughton, 1902), with supplement, *The Atonement and the Modern Mind* (London: Hodder and Stoughton, 1903); *The Christian Doctrine of Reconciliation* (London: Hodder and Stoughton, 1917); P. T. Forsyth, *The Person and Place of Jesus Christ* (London: Hodder and Stoughton, 1910); *The Cruciality of the Cross* (London: Hodder and Stoughton, 1909); *The Work of Christ* (London: Hodder and Stoughton, 1909), these three forming a trilogy; also, *The Justification of God* (London: Duckworth, 1916).

24. *The Modern Churchman,* October 1921, p. 357.

25. *Anglicanism in History and Today,* p. 126.

26. 1917; English translation, New York: Oxford University Press, 1924.

27. *The Natural and the Supernatural* (Cambridge: Cambridge University Press, 1931).

28. *Belief in God; Belief in Christ; The Holy Spirit and the Church* (London: John Murray, 1921–25).

29. Among the *Lux Mundi* group he was really the least affected by immanentism.

30. Most fully in *The Riddle of the New Testament,* with F. N. Davey (London: Faber, 1931).

31. 'The Christ of the Synoptic Gospels,' in *Essays Catholic and Critical,* ed. E. G. Selwyn (London: SPCK, 1926), pp. 177–78.

32. *Theology,* April 1961, p. 146.

33. *The Doctrine of the Trinity* (New York: Charles Scribner, 1944; and London: James Nisbet, 1943).

Notes to Chapter 18

THE THEOLOGICAL CHALLENGE TO EVANGELICALISM TODAY was originally presented at the Spring Meeting of the Fellowship of Evangelical Churchmen, March 20, 1961. Reprinted by permission.

1. London: SCM, 1957.

2. *Minor Theological Works* (1844), II.215.